RUSSIAN APPROACHES TO

Russian Approaches to International Law

LAURI MÄLKSOO

OXFORD
UNIVERSITY PRESS

OXFORD
UNIVERSITY PRESS

Great Clarendon Street, Oxford, OX2 6DP,
United Kingdom

Oxford University Press is a department of the University of Oxford. It furthers the University's objective of excellence in research, scholarship, and education by publishing worldwide. Oxford is a registered trade mark of Oxford University Press in the UK and in certain other countries

First published 2015
First published in paperback 2017

Published in the United States of America by Oxford University Press
198 Madison Avenue, New York, NY 10016, United States of America

British Library Cataloguing in Publication Data
Data available

Library of Congress Cataloging in Publication Data
Data available

ISBN 978–0–19–872304–2 (Hbk.)
ISBN 978–0–19–880804–6 (Pbk.)

Preface to the Paperback Edition

Since I completed this book slightly more than two years ago, a number of things have happened in the state practice that have confirmed the tendency that I point out in the book: that Russia is taking distance from the Western liberal understanding of international law and developing (or rather, going back to) its own concept of international law based on the idea of Russia as at least partly illiberal great power. Below are short updates concerning recent developments in the state practice and scholarship.

In the context of *jus ad bellum*, Russia's military intervention in Syria, on the side of President al-Assad, reasserted Moscow's long-standing argument that international law belongs first of all to sovereign states and their governments; rebellious groups and foreign powers have to recognize this fact notwithstanding any mass violations of human rights on the government's side.

Important developments have also taken place in the area of European human rights law. On 14 July 2015, the Russian Constitutional Court issued a historic judgment in which it set limits to the implementation of judgments of the European Court of Human Rights in Russia. If a judgment of the European Court of Human Rights is deemed unconstitutional by the Russian Constitutional Court, it would not be implemented in Russia. The judgment demonstrates that Russia has added explicit caveats to its acceptance of the jurisdiction of the European Court of Human Rights.

Today, the picture is also clearer in the context of international criminal law. On 16 November 2016, President Putin withdrew Russia's signature from the Rome Statute founding the International Criminal Court, in response to a report of the ICC's lead prosecutor that characterized the Russian annexation of Crimea as occupation and the military conflict in Ukraine as international armed conflict between Russia and Ukraine.

Finally, when I completed the book in November 2014, it was correct to write that no established Russian legal scholar had publicly pointed out the illegality of Russia's annexation of Crimea under international law. The honor of the profession of independent legal scholars in Russia was saved when Elena A. Lukyanova, a constitutional law professor at Higher School of Economics in Moscow, published on 19 March 2015 an extensive analysis in the newspaper 'Novaya gazeta' in which she concluded that the annexation of Crimea had been illegal.

Lauri Mälksoo,
3 January 2017

Preface

Maxim Gorky (1868–1936) once said that everything that was good in him he owed to books, and I always felt rather sorry for him for that. However, to paraphrase the Russian writer, I owe almost everything that might be good in this study to the fact that in 2009–14, I was the recipient of a Starting Grant from the European Research Council (ERC), the first of its kind in Estonia. The grant enabled me to travel to academic conferences in Russia, other CIS countries and the West, to acquire the necessary and occasionally rare scholarly literature, and to collaborate at Tartu University with a team of researchers including Dr Christoph Schewe, who focused on international economic law in Eurasia, and Dr Irina Nossova, who under my supervision defended her Ph.D. on Russian approaches to the international law of the sea. With the help of the ERC grant I was able to organize the Research Forum of the European Society of International Law in Tallinn in 2011 and in 2014 another conference which addressed the question whether liberal states behaved better in the context of international law. As dramatic as this may sound, the ERC grant truly changed my life.

I am thankful to Russian scholars of international law who invited me to their conferences, answered my questions, and who were willing to debate issues of international law with me. Truth, or a sense of how things are, often appeared to me at meetings of the Russian Association of International Law or in conversations with Russian scholars, in addition to studying their books and other writings. I am particularly thankful to international law scholars at the Diplomatic Academy of the Russian Ministry of Foreign Affairs, St Petersburg State University Faculty of Law, Kazan State University, and Higher School of Economics.

My ERC grant also enabled to spend the actual year of writing this study, 2013–14, as Emile Noël Fellow at NYU School of Law. The fellowship was highly valuable from the standpoint of developing a better sense of comparative international law and for improving my understanding of international economic law, and I would like to express my thanks to Joseph Weiler for the opportunity. While at NYU, I greatly benefited from discussions with Professors Philip Alston, José E. Alvarez, Grainne de Búrca, Jerome A. Cohen, and Benedict Kingsbury as well as from many international law events and discussions that took place at the Law School. In the circle of Emile Noël fellows, I would like to thank Christopher McCrudden, Wojciech Sadurski, and Sivan Shlomo-Agon in particular. I am also thankful to Anthea Roberts (Columbia Law School) who became my main discussion partner in comparative international law and to Peter Holquist (University of Pennsylvania), with whom I could discuss Martens and Hrabar, which was a quite exquisite thing to do in New York City and yet still somehow fitted logically in this metropolis. However, as always, none of these scholars is responsible for any of the views in this study; let's just say that they provided an intellectual environment which greatly inspired my research and writing.

At my home university, in Tartu, I owe particular thanks to Kristjan Haller, Jaan Ginter, Raul Narits, René Värk, and Katre Luhamaa, as well as to Kadri Raav, who skilfully managed administrative matters related to my ERC grant. In 2011, together with colleagues at the political science department, including Piret Ehin and Viatcheslav Morozov, we founded an interdisciplinary centre called CEURUS (Center for EU-Russia Studies) which has already managed to become known internationally. In 2012, CEURUS helped me to found the Martens Summer School on International Law in Pärnu, the birthplace of Martens. I have benefited from conversations with Anatoly Kovler, Sergei Marochkin, Anton Burkov, Angelika Nußberger, Eduard Ivanov, Bill Bowring, Erik Franckx, Vera Rusinova, and Christian Tomuschat, who have all taught at Martens Summer School in Pärnu.

Moreover, together with Marju Luts-Sootak, William B. Simons, and others, we decided to continue with studying Russian approaches to human rights law, and in 2014 were successful in obtaining a grant in the framework of institutional research funding from the Estonian Research Council which is also gratefully acknowledged here. Some segments of the present study, especially on the history of international law scholarship, have also benefited from earlier grants from the Estonian Research Council.

I am grateful to Christopher Goddard for carefully double-checking the accuracy of the English language in my study. At Oxford University Press, my editor Merel Alstein and Emma Endean have been very helpful in bringing this book along.

Moreover, I have been very fortunate in that my sister, Maria Mälksoo, is an international relations scholar. My family jokes that when we visit my sister's home I often end up talking with her about international relations and pillaging her IR books rather than being sociable in a more general sense. Thanks to Maria, the conversation between international law and international relations as academic disciplines has become more like a conversation within the family.

Last but not least, my wife Elizabeth and our son Elias have been my castle throughout this project. With patience and humour, they endured my frequent travels to conferences and my constant curiosity about anything Russian, including film and music, which also started to affect their lives. Their wonderful presence in my life sometimes made it technically harder to focus on this project—and yet I thank them wholeheartedly for being so 'distractive'. It is often presumed that many male musicians are doing what they are doing 'to impress their girl', and although international law may not be as universally recognized an attraction as music, still by analogy, this book is for you, Elizabeth.

20 November 2014,
Tallinn

Contents

List of Abbreviations

AJP/PJA	*Aktuelle juristische Praxis/Pratique juridique actuelle*
ASIL	American Society of International Law
BIT	bilateral investment treaty
CIS	Confederation of Independent States
CoE	Council of Europe
CSTO	*Collective Security Treaty Organization*
CUP	Cambridge University Press
ECHR	European Convention on Human Rights
ECT	*Energy Charter Treaty*
ECtHR	European Court of Human Rights
EJIL	*European Journal of International Law*
ERC	European Research Council
ESIL	European Society of International Law
FSB	Federal Security Service
GATT	General Agreement on Tariffs and Trade
ICC	International Criminal Court
ICJ	International Court of Justice
ICSID	*International Convention for Settlement of Investment Disputes*
ICTY	International Criminal Tribunal for the former Yugoslavia
ILC	International Law Commission
ILJ	*International Law Journal*
IMF	International Monetary Fund
IR	international relations
ITLOS	International Tribunal for the Law of the Sea
LGBT	lesbian, gay, bisexual, transgender
MFA	Ministry of Foreign Affairs
MGIMO	Moscow State University of International Relations
NATO	North Atlantic Treaty Organization
NGO	non-governmental organization
OSCE	Organization for Security and Cooperation in Europe
OUP	Oxford University Press
PACE	Parliamentary Assembly of the Council of Europe
PCA	Partnership and Cooperation Agreement
PCIJ	Permanent Court of International Justice
RCADI	*Recueil des cours de l'Académie de Droit International*
RF	Russian Federation
ROC	Russian Orthodox Church
RSFR	Russian Soviet Federative Republic
R2P	responsibility to protect
TNC	transnational corporation
TWAIL	third world approaches to international law

UN GA	United Nations General Assembly
UN SC	United Nations Security Council
UNCITRAL	United Nations Commission on International Trade Law
UNCLOS	United Nations Convention on the Law of the Sea
WTO	World Trade Organization

1

Introductory Themes

1. Formulation of Research Questions

Recent developments in world politics, especially Russia's annexation of Crimea and covert intervention in Eastern Ukraine in 2014, have revived a question that already has a solid history of its own: how is international law understood and used in Russia? Does the Kremlin share more or less the same concept of international law as the West (although the normative unity of the US and EU countries has also been contested)? Or does the Russian government have its own unique understanding of what the law of nations is for and about? Compared to Soviet thinking about international law, what has changed in the understanding of international law in contemporary Russia?

Throughout most of the post-Soviet period the Kremlin has repeatedly and extensively referred to the importance of 'international law', in both the country's foreign policy and strategy documents and in key foreign policy speeches of President Putin and Foreign Minister Lavrov. If one took documents that strongly emphasized 'international law' such as Russia's Foreign Policy Concept of 12 February 2013 at their face value, one may have been quite shocked and surprised by Russia's violation of Ukrainian sovereignty in 2014. Alternatively, perhaps in the West not enough attention had been paid to what official Russia had meant by 'international law' and what ideas and attitudes lay behind this discourse in Russia. When the post-Soviet Kremlin has referred to the importance of 'international law', what exactly has it referred to?

The present study is based on the premise that in order to understand the main trends in contemporary Russian state practice of international law, it is necessary to take a *longue durée* perspective and turn to the history and theory of international law in the country. I will particularly rely on the ideas of three foundational figures in the discipline of international law in Russia: Fyodor Fyodorovich Martens (1845–1909), Mikhail Aleksandrovich Taube (1869–1961), and Vladimir Emmanuilovich Hrabar (1865–1956) because in my opinion their insights and interpretations enable one to capture the long-term historical perspective that is required to situate Russian approaches to international law today.

Thus, the main question in this study is: what is the *philosophy* of international law in Russia and how has it evolved historically? How have scholars and experts construed international law in Russia? How has the conceptual understanding of international law—the way international law as a phenomenon has been construed—been reflected in post-Soviet Russian state practice?

My analytical starting point in this study is that in foreign relations, ideas and ideology in some sense precede action. Thus, in order to understand Russia's state practice in the context of international law, a deeper understanding is needed of the ideas that have lain behind it. In this regard, internal discourse and debates on international law within the country itself are often more revealing than messages sent to the outside world. Thus, the general approach of this study is to probe inside international law as 'language' and discursive practice, and to examine the mechanisms to see how it has been construed and used in Russia.

I largely share the epistemological premise of the Italian international law scholar Carlo Focarelli, namely that international law is a social construct in the sense that it 'does not exist "in itself", regardless of the knowers and their idiosyncrasies and interests'.[1] This epistemological starting point of my analysis is fundamentally different for example from that expressed in the textbook of the Diplomatic Academy of the Russian MFA, which claims that international law 'develops objectively, independently from the will of people'.[2]

Russia's annexation of Crimea will certainly have a considerable impact on the future discourse of international law, in Russia and beyond. Paraphrasing a nineteenth-century Prussian lawyer who said that three words from the legislator have the capacity to transform whole law libraries into waste paper,[3] we can today assume that the decision of President Putin to invade, occupy, and annex Crimea has the potential to transform the way that international law is construed in Russia, and if so then this will have implications for Europe and the whole global 'atmosphere' of international law. For example, the chairman of the Constitutional Court of the Russian Federation, Valery Dmitrievich Zorkin (b. 1943), after the events in Ukraine has already addressed the 'crisis of international law'.[4] Approximately half a year after the annexation of Crimea, on 24 October 2014, President Putin held a speech at the Valdai International Discussion Club in which he justified the annexation with the right of the Crimean people to self-determination and further claimed: 'I will add that international relations must be based on international law, which itself should rest on moral principles such as justice, equality and truth.'[5] Considering the globally predominant criticism of the Russian annexation of Crimea as illegal, the question already formulated above must be asked again: when President Putin refers to 'international law' and its importance, what exactly does he refer to? What ideas does

[1] C. Focarelli, *International Law as Social Construct. The Struggle for Global Justice* (Oxford: OUP, 2012) 90.

[2] S. A. Egorov (ed.), *Mezhdunarodnoe pravo*, 5th edn (Moscow: Statut, 2014) 18.

[3] J. von Kirchmann, *Die Werthlosigkeit der Jurisprudenz als Wissenschaft. Ein Vortrag, gehalten in der juristischen Gesellschaft zu Berlin*, 3rd edn (Berlin: Springer, 1848).

[4] V. Zorkin, 'Krizis mezhdunarodnoga prava. Sovremennyi kontekst', *Rossiiskaya gazeta*, 20.06.2014, <http://www.rg.ru/2014/06/19/zorkin-poln.html>.

[5] President of Russia, Meeting of the Valdai International Discussion Club, 24 October 2014, <http://eng.kremlin.ru/news/23137>.

he associate with this concept, also considering the fact that in the same month of October President Putin told his Serbian colleague during a state visit that Moscow's negative position on Kosovo's statehood will remain a 'principled one and based on international law'?[6]

A number of intertwined and to some extent open-ended research questions in this study implies that it might be in the interest of the reader that I should give away the central argument already at this early stage. Thus, the main argument of this study is the following: Russia's attitude towards international law reflects its predominant concept of public law and the idea of the relationship between law and power more broadly. Thus, it is necessary to take a thorough look inside the state and the society itself, particularly in the world of its predominant ideas that shape the country's understanding of international law. In Russia's case, the country's historically unique on and off and periodically hostile relationship with Europe and nowadays the West, its historically established tendency of authoritarian government, relative weakness of the rule of law inside the country, and the utmost desire to preserve the territorial integrity of Russia as the world's largest territorial state have decisively shaped post-Soviet Russia's approaches to international law. In its philosophical foundations international law is nowadays understood—and applied—somewhat differently in Russia and the West. Such unique features in the concept of international law are supported by idiosyncrasies in Russia's legal-academic culture and overall with 'civilizational' values in Russia which to some extent differ from Western values both in the popular understanding and in academic discourse. The implications of this state of affairs for international law today and in the future will be further elaborated in the concluding part of this study.

Let us now take a closer look at how this all has come into being.

2. Russia and the Soviet Legacy: A Question of Continuities and Discontinuities

The question whether the Soviets understood international law in the same way as the West was asked by many policy makers and researchers during the Cold War period.[7] This is not the place to go in the details of those debates but a short

[6] Putin, 'Rossia zanimaet printsipial'nuyu pozitsiu po kosovskomu voprosu',*Rossiiskaya gazeta*, 16.10.2014 <http://rg.ru/2014/10/16/poziciya-anons.html>.

[7] See E. A. Korowin, *Das Völkerrecht der Übergangszeit. Grundlagen der völkerrechtlichen Beziehungen der Union der Sowjetrepubliken* (Berlin: Stilke, 1929); T. Taracouzio, *The Soviet Union and Internatonal Law. A Study Based on the Legislation, Treaties and Foreign Relations of the Union of Socialist Soviet Republics* (New York: Macmillan, 1935); J. Y. Calvez, *Droit international et souveraineté en U.S.S.R. L'évolution de l'idéologie juridique soviétique depuis de la Révolution de l'Octobre* (Paris: A. Colin, 1953); I. Lapenna, *Conceptions soviétiques de droit international public* (Paris: A. Pedone, 1954); F. de Hartingh, *Les Conceptions soviétiques du droit de la mer* (Paris: R. Pichon, 1960); J. F. Triska and R. M. Slusser, *The Theory, Law and Policy of Soviet Treaties* (Stanford, CA: Stanford University Press, 1962); B. Meissner, *Sowjetunion und Völkerrecht. Eine bibliographische Dokumentation* (Köln: Verlag Wissenschaft und Politik, 1963); E. McWhinney, *Peaceful Coexistence and Soviet-Western International Law* (Alpen aan den Rijn:

overview will still be necessary. Moreover, perhaps today we already have the necessary time perspective in order to actually understand—and better understand than the phenomenon was understood during the Cold War itself—what Soviet attitudes towards international law were about.

The USSR developed a unique and idiosyncratic concept of public international law which was among other things anti-Western. In particular, the Soviets argued the existence of a distinct 'Soviet' or 'socialist' international law and with the help of this concept set clear limits to the existence of general international law, although to a different degree in different decades.[8] Instead, they claimed a regional international law of their own, on a competing universalistic ideological basis.

By doing so, the Soviets rejected the nineteenth-century idea of 'European' international law (*jus publicum europaeum*) and also challenged Western domination in the 'universal' international law of the twentieth century. They carved out a regional Soviet/Russian normative *Großraum*—regional public order—along the lines already theorized by the conservative German legal scholar Carl Schmitt (1888–1985).[9] This constituted a certain paradox because the Soviets emphatically claimed to be the very opposite force in world history to the Nazis in whose number they *grosso modo* counted Schmitt.[10]

Although Soviet legal theory denied any proximity to Schmitt's ideas, the 'socialist international law' propagated by the USSR was in practice very much a 'concrete regional order' (in Schmitt's terms: *konkrete Ordnung*)[11] that challenged the abstract universal logic of the principles of the UN Charter in its realm. In today's Russia, things have changed to the extent that the conservatives set the

A. W. Sijthoff, 1964); W. E. Butler, *The Law of Soviet Territorial Waters. A Case Study of Maritime Legislation and Practice* (New York: Praeger, 1967); B. Maurach and B. Meissner (eds), *Völkerrecht in Ost und West* (Stuttgart: Kohlhammer, 1967); T. Schweisfurth, *Der internationale Vertrag in der modernen sowjetischen Völkerrechtstheorie* (Köln: Verlag Wissenschaft und Politik, 1968); J. L. Hildebrand, *Soviet International Law. An Exemplar for Optimal Decision Theory Analysis* (Cleveland: Case Western Reserve University, 1968); K. Grzybowsky, *Soviet Public International Law. Doctrines and Diplomatic Practice* (Alpen aan den Rijn: A. W. Sijthoff, 1970); W. E. Butler, *The Soviet Union and the Law of the Sea* (Baltimore: Johns Hopkins Press, 1971); H.-J. Uibopuu, *Die Völkerrechtssubjektivität der Unionsrespubliken der UdSSR* (Berlin: Springer, 1975); T. Schweisfurth, *Sozialistisches Völkerrecht? Darstellung—Analyse—Wertung der sowjetmarxistischen Theorie vom Völkerrecht 'neuen Typs'* (Berlin: Springer, 1979); E. Tomson, *Kriegsbegriff und Kriegsrecht der Sowjetunion* (Berlin: Berlin-Verlag, 1979); W. E. Butler, 'Anglo-American Research on Soviet Approaches to Public International Law', in W. E. Butler (ed.), *International Law in Comparative Perspective* (Alpen aan den Rijn: A. W. Sijthoff, 1980) 169–90; E. Rauch, *Die Sowjetunion und die Entwicklung des Seevölkerrechts* (Berlin: WAV, 1982); W. E. Butler (ed.), *Perestroika and International Law* (Dordrecht: Martinus Nijhoff, 1990).

[8] See e.g. V. I. Kuznetsov, B. R. Tuzmukhamedov (eds), *Mezhdunarodnoe pravo*, 2nd edn (Moscow: Norma, 2007) 34.

[9] C. Schmitt, *Völkerrechtliche Großraumordnung mit Interventionsverbot für raumfremde Mächte. Ein Beitrag zum Reichsbegriff* (Berlin: Rechtsverlag, 1941). See also Schweisfurth, *Sozialistisches Völkerrecht?*, 568.

[10] See on Schmitt as 'Nazi internationalist' in E. T. Usenko, *Ocherki teorii mezhdunarodnoga prava* (Moscow: Norma, 2008) 125.

[11] Schmitt laid out his 'konkretes Ordnungsdenken' in C. Schmitt, *Über die drei Arten rechtswissenschaftlichen Denkens* (Hamburg: Hanseatische Verlagsanstalt, 1934) where he argued that law is a tense interplay of 'is' and 'ought' in which concrete, not abstract, living orders emerge.

ideological tone and references to Schmitt's ideas have become favourable and even fashionable in Russia.[12] The Eurasianist theoretician and propagandist Alexander Gelyevich Dugin (b. 1962) has drawn a world map of future 'greater spaces', giving contemporary relevance to Schmitt's core idea.[13]

Both the practice and theory of the Cold War period manifested major challenges to the idea of the universality of international law. The idea of the universality of international law had become predominant in the West after the nineteenth-century discourse that international law regulated only relations between 'civilized'/Western nations had been abandoned in the early twentieth century. Of course one could critically counter that even after the decline of the European colonial empires the West further controlled the making and discourse of international law, only that now it had become wise to disguise its West-centric foundations behind the veil of universality.[14] In this context, the Soviets in Russia were also the main and historically the first challengers of the already well-anchored Western predominance in international law, 'the vanguard of the East' as Dugin has put it.[15] In this sense, Soviet international legal theory implied a break with Europe and its 'bourgeois' legal tradition in Russia.

The Soviet doctrine of international law was carefully studied in the West from the late 1920s. Even after the disintegration of the USSR, Western legal scholars have continued to analyse and evaluate Soviet contributions to international law.[16] For example, John Quigley has concluded that the Soviets made positive contributions to international law, especially in the social sphere, the legacy of which continues to be of global significance today.[17] Of course another question is to what extent some Western scholars of Soviet law during the Cold War period became affected by the failures of Sovietology and were self-interested in portraying the USSR as a normal and occasionally even a progressive country.[18]

Nevertheless, a certain Soviet intellectual influence in the field of international law can be acknowledged even when one takes a highly critical view of the Soviet

[12] See A. G. Dugin, *Geopolitika postmoderna* (St Petersburg: Amfora, 2007) 7 et seq.; A. Filippov, 'Suverenitet kak politicheskii vybor', in N. Garadzha (ed.), *Suverenitet. Sbornik* (Moscow: 'Evropa', 2006) 173–200; N. I. Grachev, *Proiskhozhdenie suvereniteta. Verkhovnaya vlast' v mirovozzrenii i praktike gosudarstvennogo stroitel'stva traditsionnogo obshetva* (Moscow: Zertsalo-M, 2009) 57, 65, 110, 296.

[13] A. Dugin, *Proyekt Evrazia* (Moscow: Yauza EKSMO, 2004) 171.

[14] See further G. W. Gong, *The Standard of Civilization in International Society* (Oxford: OUP, 1984); M. Koskenniemi, *The Gentle Civilizer of Nations. The Rise and Fall of International Law 1870–1960* (Cambridge: CUP, 2002); A. Anghie, *Imperialism, Sovereignty and the Making of International Law* (Cambridge: CUP, 2004).

[15] A. Dugin, *Proyekt Evrazia* (Moscow: Yauza EKSMO, 2004) 437.

[16] B. Bowring, *Law, Rights and Ideology in Russia. Landmarks in the Destiny of a Great Power* (London: Routledge, 2013); J. Quigley, *Soviet Legal Innovation and the Law of the Western World* (Cambridge: CUP, 2012); M. Head, *Evgeny Pashukanis. A Critical Reappraisal* (New York: Routledge, 2008); C. Miéville, *Between Equal Rights. A Marxist Theory of International Law* (Leiden: Brill, 2004); T. Långström, *Transformation in Russia and International Law* (Leiden: Martinus Nijhoff, 2003); J. Toman, *L'Union soviétique et le droit des conflits armés*, Ph.D. thesis (Geneva, 1997); W. E. Butler, *Russian Law of Treaties* (London: Simmonds & Hill, 1997).

[17] J. Quigley, *Soviet Legal Innovation and the Law of the Western World* (Cambridge: CUP, 2012).

[18] Cf. e.g. R. Pipes, *Vixi. Memoirs of a Non-belonger* (New Haven: Yale University Press, 2003) 127 et seq.

period in the history of Russia, as indeed I do. For example, Marxian interpretations of international law in Western Europe were influenced by elements of Soviet theory and doctrine, in particular the so-called dialectical method.[19]

To really grasp the essence of Soviet concepts of international law was not always an easy task for scholars raised and living in the West who inevitably approached international or constitutional law in the USSR from their own cultural-civilizational perspective. Concerning international law and the USSR, among several challenges of interpretation the main one was that actual life often did not correspond to legal texts as e.g. in the case of the right of peoples to self-determination. Law, in other words, has a different meaning and function in society. For example, Stalin's Constitution of 1936 included human rights such as freedom of conscience (Article 124) and freedom of expression (Article 125a) although in reality these rights were non-existent in the USSR.

Moreover, sometimes on purpose and sometimes unconsciously, the Soviets meant different things by the same words as used in the West. For example, the Soviet constitution of 1977 established that all 15 Soviet republics were 'sovereign' even though all competence in foreign relations, and not only that, belonged to Moscow. Although in terms of peoples' rights, the Soviet proclamation of the right of peoples to self-determination and even 'sovereignty' may have been a step forward compared to the Tsarist period,[20] this was still not the way the notion of 'sovereignty' was understood in the West. What the Bolsheviks eventually seem to have meant, was: peoples formerly part of the Russian Empire could have their sovereignty and self-determination *but only under the guidance of Moscow*. In any case, only in 1991 did Soviet international law scholars start to admit that Soviet republics had not actually been 'sovereign' at all.[21]

The Soviets also understood the political world outright differently, e.g. when the leading Soviet international law scholar Grigory Ivanovich Tunkin (1906–93) wrote that socialist democracy was a 'new, higher form of democracy'.[22] Such a thing, if meant seriously, could only be argued from the perspective of an utterly different thought world. Until today, certain concepts are used differently by some Russian scholars—for example when the textbook of the Diplomatic Academy emphasizes that World War II was won by an 'alliance of democratic forces'.[23] However, to call the USSR a democratic force is at least unusual.

Adda B. Bozeman (1909–94), a US scholar with Baltic German roots, noticed in 1971

[19] See e.g. P. Klein, 'Jean Salmon et l'école de Reims', in *Droit de pouvoir, pouvoir du droit. Mélanges offerts à Jean Salmon* (Brussels: Bruylant, 2007) 19–38 at 19–20.

[20] See E. N. Ros'hin, 'Suverenitet. Osobennosti formirovania poniatia v Rossii', in M. V. Il'in, I. V. Kudryashova (eds), *Suverenitet. Transformatsia ponyatii i praktik* (Moscow: 'MGIMO-Universitet', 2008) 58–91.

[21] See for references in P. P. Kremnev, *Raspad SSSR. Mezhdunarodno-pravovye problemy* (Moscow: Zertsalo-M, 2005) 166–7.

[22] G. I. Tunkin, *Teoria mezhdunarodnoga prava*, original in 1970 (Moscow: Zertsalo-M, 2009) 66.

[23] S. A. Egorov (ed.), *Mezhdunarodnoe pravo*, 5th edn (Moscow: Statut, 2014) 18.

the spurious yet largely uncontested use of the Western vocabulary of law and constitutionalism in the Eurasian region dominated by the Soviet Union where an entirely new syndrome of ideology and system has been relayed from Lenin onward in the legal and political language of the West.[24]

Such creative interpretations revealed something about the USSR's 'flexible' and instrumentalist approach to public law generally.[25] In its legal-political culture, the USSR was a non-European power although it had extensively borrowed from a European political theory: Marxism.

It seems that the flexible approach to key legal categories has not disappeared from post-Soviet Russia either. For example, Dmitry Vitalyevich Trenin (b. 1955), the director of Moscow's Carnegie Centre, has argued that in the de facto constitutional practice of the Russian Federation, little but name has remained of the concept of 'federalism',[26] even though no one formally amended the concept in the Russian Federation's Constitution of 1993. Experts favouring a strong central government in contemporary Russia apparently have no problem with the divergence of the text of the Constitution from the political reality because they worry that genuine federalism would endanger the unity and territorial integrity of the country.[27] At the same time, one side-effect of this state of affairs is that in a poll conducted by Moscow's Levada Centre in November 2013, 60 per cent of Russian respondents thought that their government did not respect the Constitution either partly or at all.[28]

Naturally, one of the reasons for Western interest in Soviet approaches to international law was that the USSR was one of the two superpowers at the time. Therefore, the rationale to learn about the normative thinking of the Soviets was almost of an existential character. William E. Butler (b. 1939) has explained immediate post-World War II US scholarship on Soviet law:

> In this era Soviet legal studies to an appreciable degree were a part of the 'know thyne enemy' syndrome: to comprehend how he lives, to facilitate means of understanding and communication so as to avoid miscalculation, to identify and clarify opposed positions and values.[29]

A side-effect of the direct correlation between Soviet power and Western academic curiosity was that in the 1990s when the USSR had collapsed and the

[24] A. B. Bozeman, *The Future of Law in a Multicultural World* (Princeton: Princeton University Press, 1971) 178–9.

[25] See further on constitutionalism in authoritarian states, also with some examples (and anecdotes) from the USSR, in T. Ginsburg and A. Simpser (eds), *Constitutions in Authoritarian Regimes* (Cambridge: CUP, 2014).

[26] D. Trenin, *Post-Imperium. Evraziiskaya istoria* (Moscow: ROSSPEN, 2012) 90.

[27] See V. M. Shumilov, *Mezhdunarodnoe pravo*, 2nd edn (Moscow: 'Mezhdunarodnye otnoshenia', 2012) 114. See also Y. E. Svechinskaya, *Imperskaya ideologia v rossiiskoi gosudarstvenno-pravovoi mysli* (Moscow: Yurlitinform, 2011) 112; I. A. Ivannikov, *Istoria politiko-pravovoi mysli o forme rossiiskogo gosudarstvo* (Moscow: Yurlitinform, 2012) 234.

[28] See 'Rossiyane o Konstitutsii', Levada Tsentr, 10.12.2013, <http://www.levada.ru/10-12-2013/rossiyane-o-konstitutsii>.

[29] W. E. Butler, 'International Law and the Comparative Method', in W. E. Butler (ed.), *International Law in Comparative Perspective* (Alpen aan den Rijn: Sijthoff, 1980) 25–40 at 31.

importance of the Russian Federation in the international community was at its low, many Western law faculties where Soviet law—or more generally the law of socialist countries in Central and Eastern Europe; what was known as *Ostrecht* in Germany—had previously been carefully studied became less interested in the study of legal thinking and practice in post-Soviet Russia. For example, with John N. Hazard (1909–95) and Ferdinand Feldbrugge (b. 1933), the study of Soviet law at Columbia or Leiden Universities at the time of the Cold War was more prominent than is the study of post-Soviet Russian law and legal thinking at the same prestigious Western universities today. The search engines of leading Western universities' law libraries put out quite solid lists of Soviet treatises on international law but relatively few of post-Soviet Russian academic works on the same subject matter.

Igor Ivanovich Lukashuk (1926–2007), Professor at the Institute of State and Law of the Academy of Sciences in Moscow observed, based on his experience as the Russian ILC member in 1997–2002, that with the collapse of the USSR, the global influence of Russian scholars of international law had fallen sharply.[30] Moreover, Valery Zorkin, Chairman of the Constitutional Court of the Russian Federation and an active public commentator on legal matters of importance for Russia, has diagnosed that legal education in Russia is seriously 'behind world standards'.[31]

So, why would the world have cared about the perception of international law in the new, weakened post-Soviet Russia? With the ideological defeat of Marxism-Leninism, the previous ideological otherness of Soviet thinking had disappeared. If anything, it was now assumed that Russia needed catch-up lessons and rehabilitation programmes in European liberalism; to learn about human rights, democracy, and the rule of law. Exactly as did former Warsaw Pact countries that became members of the EU and NATO like Poland or the Czech Republic.

Decision makers in Western countries and political thinkers in academic institutions no longer worried about post-Soviet Russia as a threat to the West. They presumed that with the proclaimed 'end of history',[32] the Russian Federation would have no other choice but to make Western liberal values also its own. Optimists both in Russia and the West argued that in terms of values and normative outlook at the world order, Russia after the Soviet experiment would simply *return* to Europe where it had belonged since Peter the Great.[33] Even today, the alluring slogan that Europe should reach 'from Lisbon to Vladivostok', or the extended West 'from Vancouver to Vladivostok' has not disappeared. In Russia, the Communists were explained away as an abnormality, a historical impasse, a colossal ideological mistake. Characteristically, Butler gave the English language

[30] I. I. Lukashuk, *Sovremennoe pravo mezhdunarodnykh dogovorov*, Vol. 1 (Moscow: Wolters Kluwer, 2004) 59.

[31] V. D. Zorkin, *Konstitutsionno-pravovoe razvitie Rossii* (Moscow: Norma, 2011) 581.

[32] See F. Fukuyama, *The End of History and the Last Man* (New York: Avon Books, 1992).

[33] See further on this time in A. P. Tsygankov, *Russia's Foreign Policy. Change and Continuity in National Identity*, 3rd edn (Lanham: Rowman & Little, 2013) 57 et seq.

version of a Russian biography of the most prominent Tsarist international lawyer, Fyodor Fyodorovich Martens (1845–1909) the title '*Our* Martens'.[34] Thus, Martens came to symbolize that Russia also belonged to Europe after all, that the two had been inseparable before the Bolsheviks took over. Nowadays, it is symptomatic that most thoughtful Western research on international law in post-Soviet Russia tends to be on Russian approaches to European human rights law.[35]

But Russia did not, politically or ideologically speaking, become like Poland or the Czech Republic. It became a member of the OSCE and the Council of Europe but not of the EU and NATO. Quite soon, efforts to 'Westernize' Russia were confronted by serious backlashes and it became obvious that rather than becoming 'Western', Russia was choosing its own way, also ideologically.

The question remains whether the Soviet Union really went away in everything that people at home or abroad associated it with. The relationship of continuities and discontinuities in Russian approaches to international law after 1991 remains an open question.[36] The Russian Federation claimed to be the state successor of the USSR and thus inherited Soviet treaties[37] but in state practice there have been contradictions and complexities. Probably the biggest transformation has taken place in the economic sphere—when the Bolsheviks nationalized foreign investors without compensation, post-Soviet Russia has again accepted private property and foreign investment.[38] However, what has remained unchanged—and this is a main thread of continuity throughout the Tsarist, Soviet, and post-Soviet periods—is the construction of Russia as *derzhava*, a Great Power and perhaps even a modified version of Empire.

In the context of scholarship of international law, Yevgeny Trofimovich Usenko (1918–2010) suggests not putting an automatic 'equals' sign between 'Soviet' and 'Russian' international law scholarship because Soviet international law scholarship also included representatives of other Soviet republics.[39] Indeed, after the collapse of the USSR leading scholars such as Levan Aleksidze (b. 1926) and Rein Müllerson (b. 1944) continued as Georgian and Estonian scholars. Yet some other Russian authors have drawn exactly this kind of equation between 'Soviet' and 'Russian' doctrines of international law,[40] apparently acknowledging Russia's leading role in the USSR.

[34] V. V. Pustogarov, *Our Martens. F. F. Martens, International Lawyer and Architect of Peace*, ed. and trans. from the Russian by W. E. Butler (The Hague: Kluwer Law International, 2000).

[35] See e.g. B. Bowring, *Law, Rights and Ideology in Russia. Landmarks in the Destiny of a Great Power* (London: Routledge, 2013); A. Nußberger, 'The Reception Process in Russia and Ukraine', in H. Keller and A. Stone Sweet (eds), *A Europe of Rights. The Impact of the ECHR on National Legal Systems* (Oxford: OUP, 2008) 603–74.

[36] See also G. Ginsburgs, *From Soviet to Russian International Law. Studies in Continuity and Change* (Leiden: Martinus Nijhoff, 1998).

[37] See e.g. in the context of state immunity in I. O. Khlestova, *Yuridiktsionnyi immunitet gosudarstva* (Moscow: Yurisprudentsia, 2007) 188 et seq.

[38] I. Z. Farkhutdinov, *Mezhdunarodnoe investitsionnoe pravo i protsess* (Moscow: Prospekt, 2013) 111, 246, 332.

[39] E. T. Usenko, *Ocherki teorii mezhdunarodnoga prava* (Moscow: Norma, 2008) 153.

[40] S. V. Bakhin, 'Razmyshlenia o nauchnom nasledii professora R. L. Bobrova (k 100-letiu so dnia rozhdenia)', in *Materialy nauchno-prakticheskoi konferentsii 'Mezhdunarodnoe pravo: vchera,*

In the context of the Russian government's approaches to international law, the question of continuities and discontinuities goes back to the revolutionary year of 1917. Previous research has demonstrated that all ideological difference aside, there was more continuity between Tsarist Russian and Soviet approaches to international law than the ideological differences between the Tsars and the Bolsheviks would have suggested. At least this was the case as far as concerned territorial interests and maintenance of the Empire. Jiři Toman, having examined Soviet and Tsarist approaches to international humanitarian law, concluded:

> When the Bolsheviks came to power in 1917, the change of ideology did not change much in the substance and orientation of Russia; there is continuity in practice and theory before and after 1917, the Soviet and Tsarist regimes.[41]

In the context of the international law of the sea, Butler has demonstrated that at least during the earlier decades of Soviet rule, Moscow relied heavily on Tsarist legislation and practices as far as concerns the regime of territorial waters.[42] In some ways that matter in the context of international law, Russia remained Russia even during the Soviet period.

Moreover, not everything considered Soviet disappeared overnight after 1991—since some of it had been an interpretation of Russian interests anyway.[43] Marxism-Leninism as an ideology withered away but in Putin's Russia we have witnessed the come-back of arguments on historical, cultural, and civilizational distinctiveness in debates about international law, Russia's hostile relationship with the West, and scepticism about the course of globalization.

The leading post-Soviet theoretician of international law, the 'Tunkin of the post-Soviet era', Stanislav Valentinovich Chernichenko (b. 1935) from the Diplomatic Academy of the Russian MFA emphasizes:

> International law is a product of the interaction of different civilizations.... Civilizational stereotypes of behavior may be preserved and often are preserved even when predominant social groups change.... The content of international law, its social nature inevitably includes civilizational components.[44]

It is striking that in their academic works scholars like Chernichenko but also for example Nikolai Ivanovich Grachev, who has studied and advocates the Byzantine concept of imperial sovereignty, continue referring to classics of Marxism and

segodnia, zavtra', 8–9 oktyabria 2010.g. K 100-letiu so dnia rozhdenia professora Romana L'vovicha Bobrova (St Petersburg: 'Rossiya Neva', 2011) 28–40 at 29.

41 Toman, *L'Union soviétique et le droit des conflits armés*, 736.

42 W. E. Butler, *The Soviet Union and the Law of the Sea* (Baltimore: Johns Hopkins Press, 1971) 198. See G. Gidel, *Le Droit international public de la mer*, Vol. *3* (Paris: Recueil Sirey, 1934) 114.

43 See also H. J. Berman, *Justice in the U.S.S.R. An Interpretation of Soviet Law* (Cambridge, MA: Harvard University Press, 1963) 171.

44 S. V. Chernichenko, *Ocherki po filosofii i mezhdunarodnomu pravu* (Moscow: 'Nauchnaya kniga', 2009) 676–7.

Leninism.[45] Thus, different periods of Russian intellectual history come together in one, though surely idiosyncratic, edifice.

After the collapse of the USSR, perceptive scholars in the West have noticed that Russia continues to have a distinct approach to international law. The Israeli scholar and diplomat Shabtai Rosenne (1917–2010) suggested that Russia had all along kept its own tradition of international law:

> Public international law in its historical evolution is essentially the product of European Christian civilization, and for the greater part of Western civilization at that. (A Byzantine strain has always existed, being chiefly expounded by the Russian internationalists. But it is only since the emergence of the Soviet Union, now the Russian Federation and the Commonwealth of Independent States, as a major power that this Russian element, with a strong admixture of Communist doctrine and the methodology of Marxist dialectics, has itself become a major factor in the composition of modern international law.)[46]

Now, almost 25 years after the disintegration of the USSR, post-Soviet Russia is assertively back in the international community. Due in particular to Russia's possession of the world's largest share of natural resources and the potential opening of the Northern Sea Route in the Arctic Ocean,[47] Russia's importance and bargaining power in international relations are unlikely to decline to the extent that some in the West predicted in the 1990s. In 2014, the annexation of Crimea and the covert intervention in Eastern Ukraine demonstrated that Russia has outright revisionist ambitions in its foreign policy. Although in terms of its economic structure Russia resembles rather the global 'South' than the 'North',[48] few would any longer dare to refer to the country as Upper Volta with rockets but rather see in it an energy superpower.

Of course, today's Russian Federation is not as powerful as was the USSR, the other superpower during the Cold War. However, today's Russia seems powerful and for sure assertive enough to make the recent argument of Anu Bradford and Eric Posner that contemporary international law is mainly shaped by three powerful actors—the US, the EU, and China[49]—at best premature. In fact, there are reasons to think that Russia's ideological energy to shape international law and challenge Western normative projects continues to be higher than China's.

[45] Chernichenko, ibid.; N. I. Grachev, *Proiskhozhdenie suvereniteta. Verkhovnaya vlast' v mirovozzrenii i praktike gosudarstvennogo stroitel'stva traditsionnogo obshestva* (Moscow: Zertsalo-M, 2009) 11.

[46] S. Rosenne, 'The Influence of Judaism on the Development of International Law: An Assessment', in M. W. Janis, C. Evans (eds), *Religion and International Law* (Leiden: Martinus Nijhoff, 2004) 63–94 at 63.

[47] See W. E. Butler, *Northeast Arctic Passage* (Alpen aan den Rijn: A. W. Sijthoff, 1978).

[48] See e.g. G. M. Vel'iaminov, *Mehdunarodnoe ekonomicheskoe pravo i protsess* (Moscow: Wolters Kluwer, 2004) 33.

[49] A. Bradford, E. Posner, 'Universal Exceptionalism in International Law', 52 *Harvard ILJ* 2011, 3–54.

3. Russia and the West: Is International Law Different in Different Places?

A study of contemporary Russian approaches to international law requires meaningful points of comparison. As I argued, in the context of international law and legal theory, it makes sense to compare the Russian Federation to its predecessor, the USSR, and thus a temporal comparison of the evolution of international law in Russia between the twentieth and early twenty-first centuries.

It is equally illuminating to compare Russia in the international law context to other significant countries and regions, especially the main countries in the West but also China. In this context, we immediately touch upon a fundamental question for international law, namely, in what sense and to what extent is international law 'universal'. For example, David Kennedy, a critical international law scholar from the US, has argued that 'international law is different in different places'.[50] Carlo Focarelli has noticed 'the countless variations in a law that is deemed to be "common" to all peoples'.[51]

At the same time, it is surprising how relatively little Western international lawyers have tried to analytically penetrate this phenomenon, to combine international legal studies with a kind of normative anthropology interested in regional 'Others'. Quite to the point, Carl Landauer has observed that 'international lawyers avoid, even in their celebrations of regions and regionalism, engaging the specific'.[52]

Nevertheless, in both West and East a recent new wave of scholarship and increasing methodological awareness of comparative international law has sprung up.[53] Interestingly, the concept of comparative international law as such was arguably first introduced and propagated precisely in the context of the study of Soviet approaches to international law.[54] Recently, a call for more studies in comparative international law has been made by Martti Koskenniemi[55] whose influence on the development of international legal scholarship has been profound. For example, as an ILC member, Koskenniemi was responsible for completing a study on fragmentation of international law.[56]

[50] D. Kennedy, 'The Disciplines of International Law and Policy', 12 *Leiden JIL* 2008, 9 at 17.

[51] C. Focarelli, *International Law as Social Construct. The Struggle for Global Justice* (Oxford: OUP, 2012) 130.

[52] C. Landauer, 'Regionalisms, Geography, and the International Legal Imagination', 11 *Chicago JIL* 2010–11, 571.

[53] See A. Roberts, *Is International Law International?* (Oxford: OUP, forthcoming); A. Roberts, P. Stephan, P.-H. Verdier, M. Versteeg (eds), *Comparative International Law* (Oxford: OUP, forthcoming); O. V. Butkevich, *U istokov mezhdunarodnogo prava* (St Petersburg: Izdatel'stvo R. Aslanova 'Yuridicheskii tsentr Press', 2008) 122 et seq.

[54] W. E. Butler (ed.), *International Law in Comparative Perspective* (Alphen aan den Rijn: Sijthoff, 1980).

[55] M. Koskenniemi, 'The Case for Comparative International Law', 20 *Finnish Yearbook of International Law* 2009, 1–8.

[56] M. Koskenniemi, *Report of the Study Group of the ILC, 'Fragmentation of International Law. Difficulties arising from the Diversification and Expansion of International Law'*, 13 April 2006, <http://untreaty.un.org/ilc/documentation/english/a_cn4_l682.pdf>. For discussion in Russia on

While much recent academic discussion has focused on the functional fragmentation of international law (i.e. between subfields such as e.g. international human rights law and international trade law), and the ILC study also focused on this phenomenon, regional or country-specific fragmentation of international law has actually been around for much longer historically.

In an influential study challenging the previous Eurocentrism of the historiography of international law, Onuma Yasuaki from Tokyo (now Meiji) University has argued that international law became (truly) 'international' law only in the twentieth century.[57] Before that, what used to be called 'international' law was in reality 'European international law' whereas other regional normative orders were Eurocentrically not taken into account as manifestations of regional 'international law'. According to Onuma, beside the Westphalian legal order in early modern Europe, other regional normative orders existed such as the Sinocentric tribute system in East Asia and the normative system of *siyar* in Muslim countries.[58]

In other words, while non-European regions may not have had international law in its European version, this does not automatically mean that they had nothing in terms of normative order or even their own versions of 'international law'. While Onuma's interpretation may in turn be challenged (should a regional normative system be called 'international law' even if it did not understand itself exactly in such terms?) in principle it persuasively portrays the regional-civilizational roots of international law in the past. Altogether, regional origins in international law are not sufficiently taken into account in the context of contemporary international law, which is presumed to be universal notwithstanding obvious elements of regionalism.

In his response to Koskenniemi's call for more studies in comparative international law, Ignacio Rasilla del Moral points out that the concept of 'comparative international law' has not yet become fully mainstreamed in scholarship.[59] Here too is the point where the history of regionalism in international law and challenges to comparative international law as research agenda meet. Koskenniemi has pointed out what might be the main ideological obstacle facing comparative international law as a research agenda:

> The reasons for this may be easy to understand. To emphasize local, regional or national approaches to international law might seem to undermine the internationalist spirit of the profession which, as David Kennedy noted many years ago, is so characteristic to it.... The view that there is a single, universal international law with a homogeneous history and an institutional-political project emerges from a profoundly Eurocentric view of the world.[60]

the fragmentation of international law, see e.g. the roundtable in 3 *Rossiiskii iuridicheskii zhurnal* 2013, 8–71.

[57] Y. Onuma, *A Transcivilizational Perspective on International Law* (Leiden: Martinus Nijhoff, 2010) 266 et seq, and 'When was the Law of International Society Born? An Inquiry of the History of International Law from an Intercivilizational Perspective', 2 *Journal of the History of International Law* 2000, 1–66.

[58] Ibid, 2000 and 2010.

[59] I. de la Rasilla del Moral, 'The Case for Comparative International Law in Question—A Response to Martti Koskenniemi's The Case for Comparative International Law', 23 *Finnish Yearbook of International Law* 2012 (forthcoming).

[60] Koskenniemi, 'The Case for Comparative International Law', 3–4.

While I agree that the claim of universality of international law is essentially Eurocentric, it also constitutes a certain paradox because the previous view in the eighteenth to nineteenth centuries, namely that international law *was not* universal, was also Eurocentric, indeed arguably even more so. In the era of colonialism, European and US writers had no problems whatsoever in emphasizing the non-universality of international law.

For example, consider a passage in the work of the US lawyer Henry Wheaton (1785–1848):

> Is there a uniform law of nations? There certainly is not the same one for all the nations and states of the world. The public law, with slight exceptions, has always been, and still is, limited to the civilized and Christian people of Europe or to those of European origin.... Montesquieu, in his *Esprit des Lois*, says, that 'every nation has a law of nations—even the Iroquois, who eat their prisoners, have one. They send and receive ambassadors; they know the laws of war and peace; the evil is that their law of nations is not founded upon true principles.'[61]

European international law scholars also held that international law was not universal.[62]

Retrospectively it seems that the position emphasizing the specialness of European civilization in international law subsided with the decline of colonialism. And paradoxically, Europeans, formerly the flag bearers of the non-universality of international law became the flag bearers of its universality. However, for the sake of fairness, it must be pointed out that in earlier times, universal (Christian) ideas were characteristic of some European natural law scholarship as well—although Grewe points out that the doctrine of the early Spanish school of international law was first of all applicable to Christians, not to everyone.[63]

European scholars have come up with creative rhetorical arguments to support the universality of international law. Gamal M. Badr, a US-based researcher on Islamic concepts of international law has shared with his readers the following illustrative anecdote:

> ... in Geneva I directed a seminar on international law: one of the speakers was Judge Roberto Ago of the International Court of Justice. In arguing against the commonly held view that the origins of international law are European and Christian, Ago made a lapidary statement: 'Law has no religion'.[64]

For international lawyers interested in the history of the discipline, this is fascinating because whole generations of European international lawyers before Ago (1907–95) had asserted that international law *did* have a religion/civilization.

[61] H. Wheaton, *Elements of International Law*, 6th edn (Boston: Little, Brown & Co., 1855), 16–17. Reference to Montesquieu, book 1, chapter 3.

[62] See e.g. R. P. Ward, *An Enquiry into the Foundation and History of the Law of Nations in Europe from the Time of the Greeks and Romans to the Age of Grotius* (London: Strahan and Woodfall, 1795) xiii–xv.

[63] See W. Grewe, *Die Epochen der Völkerrechtsgeschichte* (Baden-Baden: Nomos, 1984) 176.

[64] G. M. Badr, 'A Survey of Islamic International Law', in M. W. Janis, C. Evans (eds), *Religion and International Law* (Leiden: Martinus Nijhoff, 2004) 95–101 at 100.

Today's scholars have also quite convincingly demonstrated how international law reflects its European/Christian cultural and religious origins.[65] However, during the reign of legal positivism, intellectual attempts to link international law with religion, culture, and regionalism, at least outside Europe and the extended West, were eyed with 'methodological' suspicion in European scholarship.

The idea of the universality of international law has made it harder to highlight differences in the reception of international law within its realm of application. For example, in the 1880s, Otto Eichelmann (1854–1943) of imperial Russia's Kiev University, influenced by Hegel's vision of international law as external constitutional law (*äußeres Staatsrecht*),[66] coined the concept of 'Russian international law', meaning by this the application of international law specifically by imperial Russia.[67] Writing during the Soviet period, Vladimir Emmanuilovich Hrabar (1865–1956) discussed whether 'the strange combination of words "Russian international law"' in Eichelmann's study would appear 'ridiculous' or still make some sense.[68] Yet another conservative Hegelian among Tsarist Russian international law scholars, Ewald Karlovich Simson, also held the view that essentially all international law was 'national'.[69]

Nevertheless, comparative international law as an approach has de facto been around for a while already. Beside the multiple Western studies concerning the USSR and international law referred to at the beginning of this study, the Soviet and US approaches to international law were compared in the US and Germany during the Cold War.[70] In 1985 the Soviets themselves published a Russian translation of the 1922 work of the American lawyer Hyde, 'International Law Chiefly as Interpreted and Applied by the United States',[71] obviously with a comparative international law purpose in mind. Furthermore, during the Mussolini period, some Italian scholars referred to the Italian conception of international law[72] while the concept of international law in Nazi Germany has retrospectively been examined by legal scholars in comparative terms.[73]

[65] See e.g. U. Khaliq, 'The International Court of Justice and its Use of Islam. Between a Rock and a Hard Place?', 2 *Oxford Journal of Law and Religion* 2013, 98–118 at 116.

[66] In Russian legal thought during the imperial period, the concept found reception in N. A. Bezobrazov, *Issledovanie nachala vneshnego gosudarstvennogo prava* (St Petersburg, 1838).

[67] O. O. Eichelmann, *Khrestomatia russkogo mezhdunarodnoga prava* (Kiev: Univ. Tip., 1887–9) 2 vols.

[68] V. E. Grabar, *The History of International Law in Russia, 1647–1917* (Oxford: Clarendon Press, 1990) 513.

[69] E. K. Simson, *Sistema mezhdunarodnoga prava*, Vol. 1 (St Petersburg, 1900) 13–14.

[70] W. Friedmann, *The Changing Structure of International Law* (New York: Columbia University Press, 1964); M. A. Kaplan, N. de Katzenbach, G. Tunkin, *Modernes Völkerrecht. Form oder Mittel der Aussenpolitik* (Berlin: Berlin Verlag, 1965); L. Henkin, *How Nations Behave*, 2nd edn (New York: Praeger, 1979).

[71] C. C. Hyde, *Mezhdunarodnoe pravo, ego ponimanie i primenenie Soedinennymi Shtatami* (Moscow: 'Mezhdunarodnye otnoshenia', 1985).

[72] A. P. Sereni, *The Italian Conception of International Law* (New York: Columbia University Press, 1943).

[73] M. Schmöckel, *Die Großraumtheorie. Ein Beitrag zur Geschichte der Völkerrechtswissenschaft im Dritten Reich, insbesondere der Kriegszeit* (Berlin: Duncker & Humblot, 1994).

Another interesting comparative case is the US, where the history of international law has been studied from the viewpoint of the history of ideas, in particular the ideas of American isolationism and exceptionalism.[74] Criticisms of US exceptionalism and US violations of international law have been widespread in Europe and European academia, especially in the context of the 2003 Iraq war and the US-led war on terror.[75]

In a similar way, Russia is an obvious candidate for a study in comparative international law. William E. Butler along with Ukrainian scholars has recently published a collective monograph on the history of international law and holds the view that 'Russian and Ukrainian experiences' form an indispensable part of comparative approaches to international law.[76]

International law scholars who are used to thinking in terms of the universality of international law might nevertheless ask: what is the ultimate point of comparing how different countries practise or scholars in different countries theorize about international law? Sure, one country's constitutional tradition construes international law in a monist and another's in a dualist way, one country ratified a certain UN treaty and another did not, and scholars in different countries might have culturally different angles to approaching international law—but is this what international law is *about*? Isn't the basic idea of international law still that in its foundations, this law is one and the same for all nations—if not for any other reason than because otherwise it would effectively cease to exist? In the West, such questions would be particularly acute in the field of international human rights law—a sub-field of international law—where the belief in the universality of human rights, or in the ideological necessity to argue in favour of such a thing, has been predominant in politics and scholarship.[77]

The claim that international law is (or must be) universal has been quite popular in Russia as well. However, often those who claim universality want international law to be understood and accepted in *their* way. In Russia, the perceived danger to the universality of international law has been US unilateralism and hegemonic aspirations. For example, in a recent Russian textbook on international law, Ruben Amayakovich Kalamkaryan (b. 1947) and Yuri Ivanovich Migachev claim:

> Contemporary international law, being a complete system of law, exercises its regulatory impact on the universal level and in a single regime of mandatory behavior for all

[74] M. W. Janis, *The American Tradition of International Law. Great Expectations 1789–1914* (Oxford: OUP, 2004); *America and the Law of Nations 1776–1939* (Oxford: OUP, 2010); N. Taylor Saito, *Meeting the Enemy. American Exceptionalism and International Law* (New York: NYU Press, 2010).

[75] See further P. Sands, *Lawless World. Making and Breaking Global Rules* (London: Penguin Books, 2006); J. Habermas, 'Does the Constitutionalization of International Law Still Have a Chance?' in *The Divided West* (London: Polity Press, 2006) 115 et seq. See also G. Verdirame, '"The Divided West": International Lawyers in Europe and America', 18 *EJIL* 2007, 553–80.

[76] W. E. Butler in A. I. Dmitriev, W. E. Butler (eds), *Istoria mezhdunarodnoga prava* (Odessa: Feniks, 2013) 52.

[77] See e.g. A. Cassese, 'A Plea for a Global Community Grounded in a Core of Human Rights', in A. Cassese (ed.), *Realizing Utopia. The Future of International Law* (Oxford: OUP, 2012) 136–143 at 136.

countries of the world. Correspondingly, this excludes any kind of possibility of 'particular' (special) international law depending on the racial or religious belonging of various nations. In this sense it is not acceptable to speak, for example, of Islamic, African, or European international law.[78]

Vladlen Stepanovich Vereshtshetin (1932), a former judge at the ICJ, singles out certain 'foreign theories' (the views of US scholar Michael Glennon on the use of military force, the New Haven school, and Onuma's civilizational approach) as constituting threats to the 'universality of international law'.[79]

However, taking an intellectually honest look at regionalist or national approaches to international law is not the same as ideologically promoting them. It just means acknowledging at the outset in a pluralist—or realist—way that there may not be just one universal way of understanding and applying international law. Whether international law in its foundations is the same everywhere is a great question and premise, but whether this is the case in reality—the empirical evidence still needs to be examined in further detail. It is also possible that while scholars and diplomats generally refer to international law as 'universal' for reasons of disciplinary ideology, on the ground that it is subject to differing interpretations and regional or country-specific fragmentation. Ironically, the European understanding of international law is already seen outside Europe as a particularistic and parochial variation on the general theme.[80]

In any case, researchers of international law face the dilemma whether to believe in what they have been told—or in what they can actually see. We have been told by our predecessors to believe in the universality of international law but at the same time one can discover and experience much diversity and regional fragmentation on the ground.[81] This, however, is not to deny the fact that during the Cold War, too, a realist stream existed in Western scholarship of international law which distinguished between the mere international law of coexistence and the evolving international law of cooperation which was possible only with shared values and was not necessarily universal.[82]

For the purposes of this study, I proceed from the hypothesis that the claim about the universality of international law is often of a normative, rhetorical, and political character, rather than fully accurate in the empirical sense. It remains possible that when two world leaders from different regions and civilizations meet and refer in their conversations and debates to 'international law', they have historically and culturally different concepts and associations in mind regarding

[78] R. Kalamkaryan, Y. Migachev (eds), *Mezhdunarodnoe pravo. Uchebnik*, 2nd edn (Moscow: EKSMO, 2006) 336.

[79] V. S. Vereshtshetin, 'O nekotorykh kontseptsiakh v sovremennoi doktrine mezhdunarodnoga publichnoga prava', in V. S. Bakhin (ed.), *Mezhdunarodnye otnoshenia i pravo: vzglyad v XXI vek* (St Petersburg: St Petersburg State University Publishing House, 2009) 43–51.

[80] See A. Bradford, E. Posner, 'Universal Exceptionalism in International Law', 52 *Harvard ILJ* 2011.

[81] See also S. Prakash Sinha, *Legal Polycentricity and International Law* (Durham: Carolina Academic Press, 1996).

[82] See W. Friedmann, *The Changing Structure of International Law* (New York: Columbia University Press, 1964) 364–80.

what international law *implies*. It is fully possible that something similarly 'civilizational' was going on between two politicians when President Bush in June 2006 allegedly said to the visiting Prime Minister of Denmark about his impressions of Russia's President Putin: 'He's not well-informed. It's like arguing with an eighth grader with his facts wrong.'[83]

Altogether, we do not know enough about *why* international law is different in different places; what are the driving forces of regional fragmentation and nationally specific understandings of international law. Realism, the oldest theory of international relations, insists that notwithstanding their sometimes high-minded rhetoric, international law is merely an instrumental tool in the hands of powerful states. However, my starting point for this study differs in one aspect from the mainstream realist thought which tends to treat all Great Powers as functionally alike in the context of international law.[84] My hypothesis is that because of their different history, culture, and 'civilization', different Great Powers tend to perceive and use international law differently, and even if they violate it, they may violate it differently or for different reasons.

Since the theory according to which international law only belonged to civilized nations was morally defeated and ideologically abandoned, the discipline of international law in the West has been reluctant to recognize civilizational-cultural factors and differences that continue to shape the understanding of international law both within and outside the West. However, presuming universality and sameness in contexts where it does not exist may lead to naive diagnoses of the legal-political situation and, consequently, bad policies regarding international law and institutions.

The evolution of the discipline of international law in Russia can be understood in its historic dialogue with the West and Europe in particular. The historical expansion of *droit public d'Europe* in the early modern age was objectively Eurocentric. The leading European powers brought the world together in the early Modern era, through explorations, conquest, and colonialism, and exported to or forced their concept of international law on other, non-European nations.[85] Russia too first encountered international law as a 'non-European' nation, and needed to claim that it was, or was willing to become, 'European' after all.

But Europe and the West have also evolved historically, just as Russia has. In terms of international legal theory in contemporary Europe and the US, there are liberal, conservative, critical, neo-Marxist, and other schools of thought, which often disagree with each other about the nature of international law generally and about the interpretation of its incidents and cases concretely. Continental

[83] See P. Baker, '3 Presidents and a Riddle Named Putin', *New York Times* 23.03.2014, <http://www.nytimes.com/2014/03/24/world/europe/3-presidents-and-a-riddle-named-putin.html?_r=0#/#time315_8525>.

[84] See e.g. E. A. Posner, *The Perils of Global Legalism* (Chicago: University of Chicago Press, 2009) 97.

[85] See C. Schmitt, *Der Nomos der Erde im Völkerrecht des jus publicum europaeum* (Köln: Greven Verlag, 1950).

European and US approaches to international law can also be distinguished, at least in some aspects.

From today's West, I keep particularly in mind the US as a point of comparison for the Russian Federation because it is a more unitary and in this sense a less ambiguous foreign relations actor than are the EU countries currently. In matters of security and geopolitics, it is the US, the main power in NATO, to which the contemporary Kremlin and Russian scholars of international law continue to compare Russia, not necessarily the 'post-modern' and foreign policy-wise fragmented EU.[86]

As a foretaste of this state of affairs, I reproduce here an argument in a Russian textbook of international law:

> Since the US even refused to sign the Rome Statute and continues taking all measures in order to exclude even the possibility of applying the Rome Statute to the personnel of US military forces, for Russia there is no point in ratifying this international treaty.[87]

Indeed, Russia and the US may have certain similarities as Great Powers. Interestingly, Alexis de Tocqueville (1805–59) predicted that the US and Russia, although in his eyes diametrically different countries in their foundations and mentality, one based on freedom and the other on servitude, were each destined to dominate half the world,[88] something that indeed happened during the Cold War. But the US and post-Soviet Russia may also be connected in a more recent sense; consider for example the assumption that President Putin 'learned and copied' from President George W. Bush in terms of putting national interest above international law.[89]

Notwithstanding all the talk about the divided West, which has to some extent subsided with the Obama administration, the US and most EU countries also share a set of common assumptions about international law. In terms of the big picture and underlying philosophy of international law, I see Western thinking about international law as liberal and cosmopolitan in its foundations, with an emphasis on international protection of human rights, democratic accountability of governments and economic integration in the framework of globalization. Of course, one needs to be somewhat cautious here and not overstretch the Kantian turn in Western states' approaches to international law, especially in the case of the US. Nevertheless, philosophically, state sovereignty has become less important than the perspective of the individual and the rights of the individual in Western approaches to international law. The approaches of global and 'humanity's' law have become more

[86] See e.g. D. Kochenov, F. Amtenbink (eds), *The European Union's Shaping of the International Legal Order* (Cambridge: CUP, 2014).

[87] G. M. Melkov, *Mezhdunarodnoe pravo* (Moscow: RIOR, 2009) 648–9.

[88] A. de Tocqueville, *Democracy in America*, ed. J. P. Meyer, trans. G. Lawrence, Vol. 1, part 2 (New York: Harper, 1969), 412–13. Originally published in 1835–40.

[89] See e.g. V. Zastrow, 'Intermezzo. Der Westen und Russland', *Frankfurter Allgemeine Zeitung*, 14.09.2014, <http://www.faz.net/aktuell/politik/ausland/europa/25-jahre-nach-dem-mauerfall-will-russland-eine-weltmacht-werden-13151867.html>.

prominent[90] although this ideological direction existed in the US even during the time of the Cold War.

A representative example of this discourse is how José E. Alvarez from the NYU School of Law explains developments in international law governing foreign investment:

> The investment regime, like other contemporary international regimes, is unquestionably an agent of non-State empowerment. Public international lawyers have generally applauded this as yet another strike against the 'S' word (namely sovereignty).[91]

One should add that in Europe, the unique supranational integration experience of the EU has also significantly contributed to letting go of state sovereignty, for centuries the highest ordering principle of international law in Europe.[92] What is important is that such conceptual tectonic shifts have a real life impact in the construction of concrete situations in international law—from humanitarian intervention (or more recently, the responsibility to protect) to regional integration. The big question is to what extent the ideological movement of leaving state sovereignty behind has reached the world beyond the West, including Russia.

Furthermore, beyond the West, China is an increasingly important global actor and there is a growing interest in the West in Chinese approaches to international law. The post-Cold War Western intellectual fascination with China's approach to law and foreign affairs recalls the Western preoccupation with Soviet law and Soviet approaches to international law during the Cold War.

China is an interesting case when the West and Russia are compared in the context of international law. Over a century ago, Fyodor Fyodorovich Martens argued that Russia constituted a unique bridge between Europe and Asia, and made the point that Russia was in a better position to understand China than West European colonial powers did.[93] On the other hand, Western historians have approached both Russia and China as the two major non-Western countries and studied the reception of Western ideas there.[94] In the context of the history of international law, China encountered Tsarist Russia for most practical purposes as a Western/European nation.

Today, Russia and China are two leading members in the Shanghai Cooperation Organization and students of geopolitical thinking might argue that China, like Russia,[95] continues to be a primarily continental (land) Empire and thus different

[90] For a philosophical justification of this approach, see J. Rawls, *The Law of Peoples* (Cambridge, MA: Harvard University Press, 1999).

[91] J. E. Alvarez, *The Public International Law Regime Governing International Investment* (Leiden: Brill, 2011) 412. See further, and more critically, in J. E. Alvarez, 'State Sovereignty is Not Withering Away: A Few Lessons for the Future', in Cassese, *Realizing Utopia*, 26–37.

[92] See further A.-M. Slaughter, W. Burke-White, 'The Future of International Law is Domestic (or, the European Way of Law)', 47 *Harvard International Law Journal* 2006, 327–52.

[93] F. F. Martens, *Le Conflit entre la Russie et la Chine. Ses origines, son développement et sa portée universalle: étude politique* (Bruxelles: C. Muquardt, 1880).

[94] D. W. Treadgold, *The West in Russia and China. Religious and Secular Thought in Modern Times*, Vol. 1 *Russia 1472–1917* and Vol. 2 *China 1582–1949* (Cambridge: CUP, 1973).

[95] See A. Dugin, *Proekt Evraziya* (Moscow: Eksmo Yauza, 2004) 58, 91, 228, 271, 368; D. Lieven. *Empire: The Russian Empire and Its Rivals* (Yale: Nota Bene, 2002) 224 et seq.; H.

from the maritime, liberal West. Being aware of the main trajectory of Chinese approaches to international law in the context of this study is relevant because notwithstanding its embeddedness in European history, Moscow today has more in common with Beijing than with the Western liberal-cosmopolitan approach to issues such as state sovereignty and human rights.

During the twentieth century, the Chinese borrowed extensively from Soviet Russian theory and criticism of bourgeois international law. In turn, today's Russian analysts seem to be more and more interested in learning from the Chinese how to keep the country together and in Confucian teachings of how to balance human rights with human duties and maintain societal harmony in times of change.[96]

However, for the sake of fairness, it must be said that an alternative view exists which puts Europe and the US on different ideological sides of international law, and equates the US approach with that of China.[97]

4. Outline of Study and Discussion of Methods

In this study I will examine three different problem areas in Russia's relationship with international law: how international law has historically been construed in Russia, how it is theorized and understood in today's Russia, and, thirdly, in the light of the above, how ideas about international law have shaped state practice of post-Soviet Russia.

It is a quite ambitious project to attempt to connect these three sub-areas—history, contemporary legal theory, and recent state practice—in one monograph on international law. It is possible to write monographs on each of these sub-areas of international legal research. However, my deep conviction is that the three sub-areas are interconnected and only when analysed together will they enable us to arrive at a holistic understanding of Russian approaches to international law in the past and in the present. At the same time, constraints connected with this approach dictate that the study is not meant as a detailed 'encyclopedia' of all important aspects of Russian and international law but rather as a conceptual interpretation.

The same caveat applies to the comparative method already raised and discussed. Making comparisons everywhere would explode the scope of the study. Thus, comparisons with other countries in this study are not a goal in themselves. They come into play only to the extent that this may facilitate an understanding of the Russian tradition of international law. I can only hope that other scholars writing further studies in comparative international law will be interested in

Münkler, *Imperien. Die Logik der Weltherrschaft—vom Alten Rom bis zu den Vereinigten Staaten* (Berlin: Rowohlt, 2005) 81.

[96] See I. A. Ivannikov, *Istoria politiko-pravovoi mysli o forme rossiiskogo gosudarstvo* (Moscow: Yurlitinform, 2012), 235; Y. Tavrovskii, 'Ideologia imperatorov i gensekov', 5.12.2012 *Nezavisimaya Gazeta*, <http://www.ng.ru/ideas/2012-12-05/5_ideology.html?insidedoc>.

[97] See S. Hopgood, *The Endtimes of Human Rights* (Ithaca, NY: Cornell University Press, 2013) 4.

taking some of my discoveries, 'translations', and arguments further in the context of their own research projects.

I have already emphasized that at its core, this project takes the constructivist approach to international law.[98] In my understanding, history and culture are among the main sources that make international law different in different places. My understanding is that countries in some ways inherit their concept of international law from the past and this notion is connected to their self-image of who they are and want to become. Thus, it is worthwhile studying this historical evolution of identity from the perspective of international law. My approach is to go, in the words of the semiotician Yuri Mikhailovich Lotman (1922–93), 'inside the thinking worlds' in the context of Russia.[99]

Methodologically and in terms of some of the substantive conclusions on *jus ad bellum*, my project has similar traits to a recent excellent monograph written by Roy Allison.[100] However, Allison approaches the subject matter of international law from the point of view of international relations theories whereas I approach it as an academic lawyer who is open to insights from international relations theories, history, and philosophy. Moreover, Allison's study focuses primarily on international law as a discursive process among the power elites whereas my main focus belongs to the ideas and scholarship behind the discourse of the power elite. Allison's study focuses mainly on the post-Soviet period and covers only *jus ad bellum* whereas I attempt to give to Russia's international law discourse a historical depth and go beyond *jus ad bellum*.

In terms of the history of the subject matter, another recent constructivist international relations monograph on Russia is by Andrei P. Tsygankov.[101] However, Tsygankov's study, although dealing with normative questions, ultimately has little to do with international law.

What distinguishes my academic legal approach from constructivist international relations theory perspectives is that while I share the analytical starting point that international law as language is 'construed', I nevertheless subscribe to the view that law is an autonomous field different from moral and other similar discourses. Not everything is relative in the discourse of international law; it is not so that everything goes. Certain arguments simply do not make sense in the discourse of international law—because they are badly reasoned, not founded on established facts, contradict other arguments of the same actor, and so on. The reader will notice this difference in the last part of the study where I also come to judging post-Soviet Russia[102] based on international law.

[98] On the constructivist approach, see also C. Reus-Smit, 'The Politics of International Law', in C. Reus-Smit (ed.), *The Politics of International Law* (Cambridge: CUP, 2004) 14–44 at 21 et seq.

[99] Y. M. Lotman, *Vnutri myslyashikh mirov. Chelovek—tekst—semiosfera—istoria* (Moscow: 'Yazyki russkoi kul'tury', 1996).

[100] R. Allison, *Russia, the West, and Military Intervention* (Oxford: OUP, 2013).

[101] A. Tsygankov, *Russia and the West from Alexander to Putin* (Cambridge: CUP, 2012).

[102] Cf. negatively about this phenomenon e.g. in Yu. V. Emel'ianov, *Evropa sudit Rossiu* (Moscow: Veche, 2007).

Notwithstanding its constructivist foundations, the philosophical starting point in this study is also influenced by the realist school of thought among international relations theories. Russia as the territorially largest country in the world—and historically for sure, an Empire—and its tumultuous history of conquests and Great Power politics invites acceptance of certain realist assumptions about international law as at least relevant. One realist assumption that I share is that the role of international law has traditionally much to do with the regulation of territorial sovereignty—what land belongs to which sovereign. Some Soviet international law scholars, e.g. in 1945, Fyodor Ivanovich Kozhevnikov (1893–1998) even considered territory to be *the* object of international legal relationships.[103]

The disintegration of the USSR and the loss of the Soviet Empire may have reintroduced a realist outlook on the outside world in Russia. To replace Karl Marx returned Niccolò Machiavelli. Perhaps it was an unintended metaphor when Grigory Ivanovich Tunkin (1906–93), visiting Paris, wrote in May 1993 in one of the last entries in his diary:

> Of course, in our situation in Russia no one even begins to understand. Indeed, we ourselves do not understand it well.... To my surprise, the Bon Marché was open. I went in and purchased Machiavelli, *Le Prince*.[104]

Machiavellian traits have not been alien to the Kremlin's understanding of the outside world. For example, Deputy Prime Minister Dmitry Olegovich Rogozin (b. 1963) who is currently responsible for the development of military industries in the Russian Federation, in 2013 characterized Russia's geopolitical environment as a 'predatory forest'.[105] In international law scholarship, some international law professors in Russia have continued to maintain that the balance of power is a necessary precondition for the functioning of international law.[106] Irina Anatol'evna Umnova (b. 1961) from the Russian Academy of Jurisprudence in Moscow argues that NATO's 'expansion to Eastern Europe' (rather than 'enlargement' as it is called in NATO's member states) has destroyed the balance of power.[107]

As far as international law goes, in this study I am interested in international law in action as much as law in books. One needs to distinguish the rhetoric and the actual sources of behaviour of states in their *politique juridique éxterieure*.[108] It is of course also important to study for example Russia's 1995 Federal Law 'On International Treaties of the Russian Federation'[109] or Russia's foreign investment regulation from the point of view of legal positivism[110] but this method alone does

[103] Referred to in A. N. Vylegzhanin (ed.), *Mezhdunarodnoe pravo* (Moscow: Yurait, 2009) 36.

[104] W. E. Butler, V. G. Tunkin (eds), *The Tunkin Diary and Lectures* (The Hague: Eleven publishing, 2012) 138.

[105] T. Bekbulatova, 'My zhivem v khishnem lesu', *Kommersant* 08.06.2013, <http://www.kommersant.ru/doc/2207919>.

[106] See e.g. E. T. Usenko, *Ocherki teorii mezhdunarodnoga prava* (Moscow: Norma, 2008) 67; S. A. Egorov (ed.), *Mezhdunarodnoe pravo*, 5th edn (Moscow: Statut, 2014) 20–1.

[107] I. A. Umnova, *Pravo mira. Kurs lektsii* (Moscow: Eksmo, 2011) 225.

[108] See further G. de Lacharrière, *La Politique juridique extérieure* (Paris: IFRI Economica, 1983).

[109] State Duma, 15.07.1995, No 101-FZ.

[110] See e.g. W. E. Butler, *Russian Foreign Relations and Investment Law* (Oxford: OUP, 2006); *The Law of Treaties in Russia and the Commonwealth of Independent States* (Cambridge: CUP, 2002).

not really open up the country's actual state practice with international treaties or regulation of foreign investment.

Here is where some Western scholarship on Soviet approaches to international law has to some extent failed because it has taken Soviet declarations about international law too easily at their face value. The official rhetoric about international law can also have deceptive qualities when the purpose may be to mislead the other or to trump him with his own weapon.

It is an interesting question when and to what extent scholars and other commentators on international law are aware of such differences between the official rhetoric and the actual reality on the ground. For example, the international law scholar Nugaeva from Kazan State University writes that in eighteenth-century Europe, 'in the political sphere, international legal regulation remained a fiction'.[111] A similar point in the context of international law of the early nineteenth century was made by Lukashuk.[112] Of course, one then inevitably wonders, what was the function of international law at all if it remained fiction in the 'political' sphere?

The Harvard historian Richard Pipes (b. 1923) wrote that some of his fellow-historians had challenged his contention that the Muscovite variant of absolutism differed fundamentally from the absolutism of early Modern Europe.[113] Pipes challenged his critics on methodological grounds:

> I found that the analogies drawn by some scholars between the two types of monarchical rule rested on a formalistic interpretation of juridical documents, with minimal attention to living reality... If a future historian were to apply such formalistic methodology to Stalin's regime, he might well conclude that it did not significantly differ from those of the contemporary West since it too had a constitution, a parliament and guarantees of human rights.[114]

That law in books and law in practice might be somewhat different things has been considered a particularly relevant insight in the context of Russian law[115] where the difference between formal legal norms and the way things have actually been done in practice has arguably been more marked than in the West (although a certain difference between the text of the law and how it is lived out in practice remains a general characteristic of the law anywhere).

Moreover, sticking to legality as a guiding principle does not in itself reveal what the qualitative content of the law is that is upheld and propagated. That *Recht* could actually be *Unrecht* is sometimes hard to understand in the liberal West because there is the extremely powerful notion that law, in principle, is something positive, and the ideal of it in democracies is associated with justice.

[111] N. G. Nugaeva, in R. Valeev, G. Kurdyukov (eds), *Mezhdunarodnoe pravo. Obshaya chast'* (Moscow: Statut, 2011) 110.

[112] I. I. Lukashuk, *Pravo mezhdunarodnoi otvetstvennosti* (Moscow: Wolters Kluwer, 2004) 37.

[113] R. Pipes, *Russia under the Old Regime*, 2nd edn (London: Penguin Books, 1993) xx.

[114] Pipes, ibid., xx.

[115] J. Henderson, *The Constitution of the Russian Federation. A Contextual Analysis* (Oxford: Hart Publishing, 2011) 8.

However, consider what Harold J. Berman (1918–2007), one of the leading US experts of Soviet law, said on Solzhenitsyn's experience of the Soviet GULAG:

> … the arbitrariness of the system was expressed above all in its legalism. Everything was done in the name of the law—some article of the Code, some regulation of the Ministry or of the Chief Administration or of the Director, some rule of the camps that had to be obeyed.… The forms of law were utilized, but in a completely perverse way.[116]

Finally, this research project seeks to be relevant also for readers who are not legal scholars or even trained to be lawyers but who have an interest in Russia generally or a more philosophical and political interest in the past and future of international law. In particular, I am hoping to reach out to practitioners who in one way or another deal with the Russian government on an international or domestic level.

When Anne-Marie Slaughter (b. 1958), with a strong background in academia, was working at the US State Department, she mentioned in a speech at the annual meeting of the ASIL that she had been counting these few times when no one 'mentioned the word "academic" in the sense of "irrelevant"' at meetings of the US State Department which she attended as director of the Policy Planning Department.[117] Interestingly, similar points were made by Soviet and Russian scholars and practitioners of international law. For example, Lukashuk observed that 'lawyers pay relatively little attention to events based on which political advisers construct their normative view of the world'.[118] Unfortunately, this has also been my experience. For example, I was surprised by the fact that the Georgia–Russia war was very little discussed at the ESIL annual conference in 2008, as was the Russia–Ukraine war at the ESIL annual conference of 2014. There are no good reasons why international law scholarship should not take into account actual political events in the world. The scholarship of international law must also be useful to practitioners; it should not become a parallel world of abstract theorizing.

5. The Objectivity Question and the Estonian School of International Law

Before turning to the analysis itself, one more thing needs to be clarified. That is, I have sometimes been asked by friends and colleagues whether I as an Estonian scholar can 'objectively' study Russian approaches to international law. Estonia, a small country, was part of Russia, a big country, for two centuries

[116] H. J. Berman, 'The Weightier Matters of the Law', in R. Berman (ed.), *Solzhenitsyn at Harvard. The Address, Twelve Early Responses, and Six Later Reflections* (Washington, DC: Ethics and Public Policy Center, 1980) 99–113 at 100.

[117] See also N. Christof, 'Professors, We Need You!', *NY Times* 15.02.2014, <http://www.nytimes.com/2014/02/16/opinion/sunday/kristof-professors-we-need-you.html>.

[118] I. I. Lukashuk, *Sovremennoe pravo mezhdunarodnykh dogovorov*, Vol. 1 (Moscow: Wolters Kluwer, 2004) 57, 62.

(1710–1918) and then again, de facto at least, part of the USSR for almost 50 years (1940/1944–1991). Can an Estonian scholar be objective towards Russia in these circumstances?

This question begs for a somewhat lengthier answer because it is an important one considering the themes that I will raise and the arguments that I will make. The same question also happens to have a number of layers the opening of which will serve as an introduction to the substantive study itself.

As a starting point, I could also respond that researchers from core Western countries where geopolitical circumstances have been more stable and history altogether more benevolent tend to forget to ask the same objectivity question in the context of their own research projects, i.e. reflect on how their own situatedness might influence their own scholarly viewpoint. In an ideal world, each academic study of international law could start with the author's self-reflection on their own preconceptions and possible biases. Yet this is usually not the case.

Koskenniemi has put it quite well:

> When one inhabits the centre, one feels no need to mark out one's place. One is 'there' and everybody knows it. In the periphery, things look different.[119]

However, from the point of view of comparative international law, to be located at the periphery (of the centre) seems actually to have a certain advantage because this may be a more suitable place to get 'under the skin' of the Other.[120] At the border, one does not have to visit one's object of study but just can (or must) live alongside it.

On the other hand, it is true that country-specific narratives of international law have usually been told from within the country itself,[121] often with the accompanying hagiographic purpose in mind to promote the country's prestige or defend its honour internationally. In this sense, my Estonian starting position for this research on Russian approaches to international law is indeed somewhat untypical.

Supposing that as an Estonian I would inevitably be in some ways biased towards Russia then *what* would my Estonian bias be like? The answer is far from obvious. In 1918, the Republic of Estonia became one of the successor states of imperial Russia. While it is true that the USSR de facto liquidated the Republic of Estonia in 1940 and kept the Estonian SSR as part of a wider union until 1991, the historical relationships of dependence and domination within the Russian Empire were more complex than might seem to be the case at first glance.

[119] Koskenniemi, 'The Case for Comparative International Law', 1.

[120] For a semiotic analysis of the crucial role of the 'border' in cultural exchanges between 'semiospheres', see Y. M. Lotman, *Semiosfera* (St Petersburg: Iskusstvo, 2000) 257–67. For the English translation of this work, see Y. M. Lotman, *Universe of the Mind. A Semiotic Theory of Culture, with a foreword by U. Eco* (London: Tauris, 1990).

[121] See C. Landauer, 'Regionalism, Geography, and the International Legal Imagination', 11 *Chicago JIL* 2010–11, 557–95; referring to Alvarez and Latin America, Elias and Africa, Singh and India.

In international law, during the Tsarist period scholars and diplomats originating from Estonia and/or educated at the University of Dorpat (Tartu) were among the most prominent in pre-World War I Russian diplomatic practice and international legal academia.[122] They were imperial Russia's own most genuine Europeans.

The USSR may have illegally annexed Estonia in 1940–91 but in the eighteenth and nineteenth centuries the Baltic Germans in a certain sense had 'colonized' imperial Russia's ministries and other key positions in St Petersburg. Men (they *were* all men at that time) from the Baltic provinces had stood at the roots of international legal and diplomatic activity in the Russian Empire since Peter the Great conquered the Baltic provinces from Sweden.[123] Moreover, Ignatii Ioakinfovich Ivanovskii (1807–86), the international law teacher of the foremost Tsarist Russian international law scholar, Martens, had been educated at the Professorial Institute at the University of Tartu (Dorpat). One enduring legacy symbolizing this history is the bust (sculpture) of Nikolay Ivanovich Pirogov (1810–81) near the university's main building in Tartu. Pirogov was a medical student and later professor at Tartu but is known to international lawyers in Russia as the director of the Russian equivalent of the Red Cross Society (*Khrestovozdvizhenska*) at the time of the Crimean War (1853–6).[124]

Another answer to the question whether Estonian scholars can legitimately study Russian approaches to international law, is that they have been doing this for a while already.

Comparative law and the study of Russian law through the Baltic German/European perspective acquired a marked dynamic in Estonia in the early nineteenthth century.[125] The foundation had already been laid in the late seventeenth century when Swedish scholars at the Protestant university of Dorpat (Tartu) discussed the works of Grotius and Pufendorf, natural law and rights.[126]

In the context of public international law, translating Russia to Western Europe and vice versa has been something that what we could retrospectively call the Estonian School of International Law has been trying to do since the 1880s.[127]

[122] See e.g. K. Grzybowski, *Soviet Public International Law* (Leiden: Sijthoff, 1970) 3.

[123] See V. Illyashevitch, *Pribaltiitsy na rossiiskoi diplomaticheskoi sluzhbe* (Tallinn: Tarbeinfo, 2005).

[124] See e.g. R. Valeev, G. Kurdyukov (eds), *Mezdhunarodnoe pravo. Osobennaya chast'* (Moscow: Statut, 2010) 146; Y. M. Kolosov (eds), *Mezhdunarodnoe pravo* (Moscow: 'Mezdhunarodnye otnoshenia', 2005) 450.

[125] See e.g. J. P. G. Ewers, *Vom Ursprunge des russischen Staats. Ein Versuch, die Geschichte desselben aus den Quellen zu erforschen* (Riga: J. G. Hartmann's Buchhandlung, 1808) and *Das älteste Recht der Russen in seiner geschichtlichen Entwickelung* (Dorpat: A. Sticinsky, 1826). Further, see e.g. E. G. von Bröcker (ed.), *Jahrbuch für Rechtsgelehrte in Russland*, 2 vols (Riga: Häcker, 1822 and 1824); F. Witte, *Ein Blick auf die geschichtliche Entwickelung des älteren russischen Erbrechts, bis zum Gesetzbuche des Zaren Alexei Michailowitch (1649)* (Dorpat: Schünemann's Witwe, 1848); B. Utin, *Über die Ehrenverletzung nach russischem Recht seit dem 17. Jahrhundert* (Dorpat: Laakmann, 1857) and J. Engelmann, *Das Staatsrecht des Kaiserthums Rußland* (Freiburg: J.C.B. Mohr, 1889).

[126] See further G. v. Rauch, *Die Universität Dorpat und das Aufdringen der frühen Aufklärung in Livland. 1690–1710* (Essen: Essener Verlagsanstalt, 1943).

[127] See, further, L. Mälksoo, 'The Science of International Law and the Concept of Politics. The Arguments and Lives of the International Law Professors at the University of Dorpat//Yur'ev/Tartu 1855–1985', 76 *British Year Book of International Law* 2005 (Oxford: OUP, 2006) 383–501.

These practices seem to have originated from the fact that Estonia, a region/country with a Finno-Ugric majority, has for centuries been a frontier/borderland between the Germanic West and Slavic Russia. It turns out that history and geography often shape intellectuals in frontier regions into comparativists.

In cultural-religious terms, the Baltic civil service tradition in the Russian Empire and the study of Russia—an Orthodox Christian country—at Tartu has been a primarily Protestant tradition. Thus, from the beginning certain cultural-political tensions have been built into this translational activity since Russia is a predominantly Orthodox country.

Fyodor Fyodorovich Martens (1845–1909) who was born in Pernau (Pärnu) in Estonia developed the European international legal tradition in Russian public discourse and at the same time actively made international legal arguments in the name of Tsarist Russia. He was a border-goer and while he made great efforts to defend Russia abroad, his diaries reveal that his own personal attitude towards the reality of the Russian Empire and the MFA remained critical.[128]

His international law colleague at Tartu, Carl Bergbohm (1849–1927) translated Martens's textbook on international law into German, thus facilitating reception of Martens's ideas in Western Europe. Translations of Martens's textbook contributed to the perception in the West that imperial Russia had finally arrived in the tradition of European international law not as a passive consumer but as an active discussant and intellectual contributor. Vladimir Hrabar (1865–1956) in turn translated into Russian the international law textbook of the leading German jurist Franz von Liszt (1851–1919).[129]

Another St Petersburg professor and disciple of Martens was Baron Michael von Taube (1869–1961) whose family's roots and summer estate were in North-Eastern Estonia and who, as we will see in the next part of the study, significantly contributed to the understanding of the history of international law in Russia.

Baltic German emigrants from Estonia also contributed significantly to the study of Soviet approaches to international and public law in Germany and the West. Baron Axel Freytag von Loringhoven (1878–1942), Walter Meder (1904–86), and Boris Meissner (1915–2003), all formerly students and/or professors at Dorpat (Tartu), founded and developed the discipline of *Ostrecht* in pre- and post-World War II Germany, as did Reinhart Maurach (1902–76).

Timothy A. Taracouzio (1896–1958) founded research of Soviet approaches to international law in the US during the interwar period.[130] Taracouzio had fought in the Russian White Army against the Bolsheviks and came to the US as a

[128] See for further references in L. Mälksoo, 'F. F. Martens and His Time. When Russia Was an Integral Part of the European Tradition of International Law', 25 *EJIL* 2014, No 3 811–29.

[129] F. von Liszt, *Mezhdunarodnoe pravo v sistematicheskom izlozhenii*, trans. V. E. Hrabar (Yur'ev: Mattiesen, 1909).

[130] See T. A. Taracouzio, *The Soviet Union and International Law* (New York: Macmillan, 1935); W. E. Butler, 'Anglo-American Research on Soviet Approaches to Public International Law', in W. E. Butler (ed.), *International Law in Comparative Perspective* (Alpen aan den Rijn: Sijthoff, 1980) 169–90 at 170.

refugee at the age of 26 without knowing English. In Harvard University records, his home residence was given as 'Narva, Estonia'.[131]

Henn-Jüri Uibopuu (1929–2012) became a refugee at the end of World War II and later a leading specialist of *Ostrecht* in Austria. Rein Müllerson (b. 1944), the Estonian scholar who has worked at leading universities in Moscow and London and currently works at Tallinn University, introduced liberal Western ideas to Soviet international law scholarship during the perestroika period (and advised Gorbachev on international legal matters), and later on, occasionally defended Putin's Russia from being unjustly criticized in the West, including in Estonia. Müllerson's academic work has also remained a steady reference point in contemporary Russian literature on international law.[132]

All these Baltic German and Estonian scholars of international law have been quite different from each other and in terms of their political leanings often came to opposite conclusions. To simplify somewhat, some of them wanted to integrate Russia with the West and advocated Russia as a European country whereas others, especially during the Soviet period, emphasized Soviet Russia's civilizational otherness in the West and even wanted to erect a fence around the country, which they perceived as a threat to the Occident.

The problem had already started in Martens's time—his Baltic German colleagues considered him too pro-Russian.[133] Martens himself called his translator Bergbohm his 'personal enemy'[134] and, when his disciple Taube got the job of representing Russia at the London naval conference in 1907 instead of him, was sarcastic in his diary about the success of 'little Taube'.[135] While Martens publicly spoke *for* imperial Russia, the *Ostrecht* scholars in Germany were highly critical of the Soviet government in Russia and were warning the West of the USSR because of its otherness. Grigory Ivanovich Tunkin wrote in his diary on 7 July 1982 when visiting the Max Planck Institute at Heidelberg:

> I spoke for 20 minutes; put emphasis on the fact that we had created an integral theory of international law. Thereby a blow with regard to reactionary Sovietologists, of which the main one is Meissner. He was present.[136]

Nevertheless, most of these Baltic scholars have been genuine intercultural translators. Thanks to them, the West's knowledge of Russian and Soviet international legal thinking has historically been much more intimate and complex than that of China's, for instance.

[131] See *Harvard University Catalogue* (Cambridge, MA: Harvard University, 1927) 209.

[132] See e.g. Shumilov, *Mezhdunarodnoe pravo*, 49 and I. Z. Farkhutdinov, *Mezhdunarodnoe investitsionnoe pravo* (Moscow: Prospekt, 2013) 23.

[133] See e.g. C. Schirren, *Zur Geschichte des Nordischen Krieges* (Kiel: Walter G. Mühlau, 1913) 125–206. (Review of Vols 5–7 of the treaty collection edited by Martens; concerning Russia's treaties with Prussia and pointing out that commentaries written by Martens were biased in favour of Russian Tsars and diplomats).

[134] G. S. Starodubtsev, *Mezhdunarodno-pravovaya nauka Rossiiskoi emigratsii* (Moscow: Kniga i biznes, 2000) 21 (referring to a private letter of Martens).

[135] Martens's diary.

[136] See Butler, Tunkin, *The Tunkin Diary and Lectures*, 106.

Today, when Estonia is no longer part of Russia, the responsibility—and opportunity—for tackling these issues of translation and interpretation is not necessarily smaller than it historically used to be. Russia's strained normative relationship with Europe continues to be a question of significant practical relevance and consequences. Since the loss of the Baltic republics (as well as, at least formally, Ukraine, Belarus, and Moldova) pushed Russia further away from the West and closer to Asia,[137] there may not always be enough intercultural interpreters left at home in Russia.

One may add that Russian legal scholars themselves have recently been quite active in studying not only EU law but also, from the Soviet period onwards, European and Western approaches to international law. Often, they do not follow blindly but comment critically on what European scholars have argued not just about international law but also EU law.[138] Altogether, it is normal that neighbours are interested in neighbours, and that this interest extends to critical legal analysis.

In addition, I should say on a more personal note that my own interest in Russian approaches to international law has undoubtedly been influenced by my Estonian background. In 1991, I was 16 years old when the independence of the Republic of Estonia was restored. I had learned Russian as my first foreign language in a Soviet Estonian school where study was otherwise all in the Estonian language, which is a Finno-Ugric, not a Slavic, language.

My first encounter with (post-)Soviet approaches to international law may have been when my criminal law seminar teacher at Tartu University authoritatively declared, around 1994, that there was no (or: could not be) 'such a thing as *international* criminal law'.[139] Subsequently, I have been fortunate to study international law in various other countries as well: Germany, the US, and Japan. From 2006 onward, research projects and grants have enabled me to attend international law and human rights conferences in Russia and other CIS countries. Following the Estonian proverb 'one's own eye is king', I have been curious to discover Russian university life and its academic international law scene.

In my doctoral dissertation, which I defended in Berlin in 2002,[140] I analysed (and ultimately, supported) the claim of state continuity of the Republics of

[137] See e.g. K. S. Gadzhiev, *Geopoliticheskie gorizonty Rossii. Kontury novogo miroporyadka* (Moscow: Ekonomika, 2007) 557.

[138] See e.g. A. A. Moiseev, *Suverenitet gosudarstva v mezhdunarodnom prave* (Moscow: Vostok Zapad, 2009) in which part 3 is devoted to a study of the phenomenon of supranationalism in the EU.

[139] This was the predominant position in Soviet doctrine—see e.g. L. N. Galenskaya, 'O poniatii mezhdunarodnoga ugolovnoga prava', *Sovetskii ezhegodnik mezhdunarodnoga prava* 1969 (Moscow: Academy of Sciences of the USSR, 1970) 247. References to this position 'only 20 years old' can also be found in: A. V. Naumov et al. (eds), *Mezhdunarodnoe ugolovnoe pravo* (Moscow: Yurait, 2013) 15; E. T. Usenko, G. G. Shinkaretskaya, *Mezhdunarodnoe pravo* (Moscow: Yurist, 2005) 454; N. I. Kostenko, *Mezhdunarodnoe ugolovnoe pravo. Sovremennye teoreticheskie problemy* (Moscow: Yurlitinform, 2004) 47.

[140] L. Mälksoo, *Illegal Annexation and State Continuity: The Case of the Incorporation of the Baltic States by the USSR* (Leiden: Martinus Nijhoff, 2003). The Estonian and Russian translations were published in 2005 by Tartu University Press.

Estonia, Latvia, and Lithuania and developed the thesis that the Soviet period in the Baltic States must be legally qualified as illegal occupation and annexation.

Research for my Ph.D. thesis gave me insights into Soviet and post-Soviet Russian theory and practice related to state succession and continuity, which is complicated because Moscow has picked and chosen for itself both elements of state continuity and succession.[141] However, after completing my dissertation, I continued to stumble at further Russian official and scholarly perspectives on the legal status of the Baltic States during the Soviet period.[142] It struck me that what international law meant in the Baltic historical context was understood differently in post-Soviet Russia and the Baltic republics. It was not so much about who had a better argument; it was almost that culturally, these were two different languages about international law, its history and territorial entitlement. Each side of the argument also projected to this debate something about the protagonists.

In this context, the debate over whether Soviet rule in the Baltics had been an illegal annexation started to look like a *dialogue de sourds*. With most Western nations recognizing the Baltic state continuity thesis and post-Soviet Russia rejecting it, international law was literally different in different places.

Some Russian historians and international law scholars acknowledge the illegality of the Soviet occupation of the Baltic States in 1940.[143] Nevertheless, probably the majority view in Russia still follows the governmental view and sees the Baltic States in 1991 as a usual case of secession, like the rest of the Soviet republics.[144] Quite characteristically, MGIMO history professor Andrey Borisovich Zubov, who in his works has written about the Soviet 'occupation' of the Baltic States, was fired in March 2014 because of his criticism of Putin's annexation of Crimea.[145] (In this context, one can see how different substantive positions may be interconnected.) Instead, Russian international law scholars, along with the Kremlin, criticize the Republics of Estonia and Latvia for not having granted automatic citizenship rights to all Russian speakers who (were) settled in these countries during the Soviet period, the precise legal qualification of which continues to be contested by Moscow.[146]

[141] See further G. V. Ignatenko, O. I. Tiunov (eds), *Mezhdunarodnoe pravo* (Moscow: Norma, 2013) 102–3; P. P. Kremnev, *Raspad SSSR. Mezhdunarodno-pravovye problemy* (Moscow: Zertsalo-M, 2005) 242.

[142] See e.g. S. V. Chernichenko, *Teoria mezhdunarodnoga prava*, Vol. 2 (Moscow: NIMP, 1999) 72 et seq.

[143] G. M. Melkov et al. (eds), *Mezhdunarodnoe pravo* (Moscow: RIOR, 2009) 81. ('The USSR committed aggression against the Baltic States'); K. A. Bekyashev (ed.), *Mezhdunarodnoe publichnoe pravo*, 2nd edn (Moscow: Prospekt, 2003) 582 ('The USSR violated its treaty obligations towards the Baltic states'); I. Get'man-Pavlova, *Mezhdunarodnoe pravo*, 2nd edn (Moscow: Yurait, 2013) 345. See also A. B. Zubov (ed.), *Istoria Rossii. XX vek: 1939-2007* (Moscow: Astrel' AST, 2009) 16 et seq.

[144] See e.g. Usenko, Shinkaretskaya, *Mezhdunarodnoe pravo*, 119; A. N. Vylegzhanin (ed.), *Mezhdunarodnoe ekonomicheskoe pravo* (Moscow: 'Knorus', 2012) 227; Shumilov, *Mezhdunarodnoe pravo*, 89.

[145] See E. Vlasenko, 'Andrei Zubov: menya uvolili na prikazu sverkhu', *Grani*, <http://grani.ru/Society/Law/m.227066.html>.

[146] See, for many, I. A. Umnova, *Pravo mira: kurs lektsii* (Moscow: Eksmo, 2011) 123.

In retrospect, I see the Baltic state continuity thesis with broader historical layers and connotations. For example, one should be aware that Russia's own continuity claims over the Baltic lands also go quite far back in history. Both Ivan the Terrible (1530–84) and Peter the Great (1672–1725) when trying to conquer the Baltic provinces (Tsar Peter finally succeeded) put forward the argument that according to ancient Russian chronicles (*letopisi*) of the eleventh century these territories had belonged to or at least paid tribute to Princes of ancient Rus'. These historical claims were never corroborated by Western sources.

The debate about the continuity of the Baltic States and the illegality of the Soviet annexation (or its denial) has not been just about these states as such. It seems that the debate has also been about the *limes* between Western Europe and Russia as greater spaces; about which civilizational standard prevails.

Subsequently, I have also had some practical experience with Russian state practice in international law, in the context of the Estonian-Russian border treaty negotiations. Because of the contested World War II history, this treaty became the ultimate political treaty between the two countries, particularly in aspects that concern the Baltic state continuity doctrine and the fate of the Tartu Peace Treaty of 1920 which Moscow insists has become defunct. In 2005 when the two countries signed but failed to ratify the border treaty, I advised the Estonian Parliament (*Riigikogu*). In February 2014 when the border treaty was signed in a slightly revised version, I advised the Estonian MFA.

With this background, my interest in Russian approaches to international law, and in 'getting Russia right', over the last decade has not been merely abstract and academic. However, I prefer to think that the modest practical involvement that I have had for example with Estonian-Russian border treaties rather strengthens than weakens my position as an academic researcher on Russian approaches to international law. These experiences have sharpened my eyes as to how the creation of international law is often a dialogical process that does not necessarily take place in international courts, and how the party with more power tends to turn international law to the direction that is in its interest.

Estonia's failure to fully restore its pre-World War II treaty rights with post-Soviet Russia influenced my further thinking and partly gave birth to the idea of digging further into Russian understandings of international law. In legal terms, Moscow never gave a convincing answer to the question what happened to the pre-World War II treaties between the USSR and Estonia; why exactly in Moscow's view had they become void?

Realist international relations scholars would probably just conclude that historically and structurally there is nothing new in this asymmetric 'dialogue' between Moscow and the Baltic States. Russia was a major power and Estonia a small nation in the way of Athens and Melos in the narrative of the Greek writer Thucydides (460–395 BC), and by the nature of things there could be no genuine reciprocity between them. Russian scholars proudly emphasize that Moscow had a crucial role in the formation of new international law in 1945[147] so they could

[147] S. A. Egorov (ed.), *Mezhdunarodnoe pravo*, 5th edn (Moscow: Statut, 2014) 19.

not have been so 'wrong' after all in World War II. The Baltic States just happened to become 'collateral damage' of the Yalta order which was created in Eastern Europe in the interests of the USSR.

However, my question has been whether there was still more in the story. For example, were there also culturally and historically different ideas of what a treaty implied or involved? When occupying the Baltic States in 1940, Stalin's USSR violated a number of very strong regional and bilateral treaties.

Adda B. Bozeman once characterized the centrality of contract in Western civilization:

> What makes a contract a unique expression of the European time sense is the theory of confidence that it encloses: confidence not only of the ability of men to preempt and order time that lies ahead of them by means of promises to do or refrain from doing something, but confidence also in the binding nature of obligations assumed in the past.[148]

In Baltic-Russian treaty relations, that confidence had historically simply not been there and it probably still is not, at least not yet.

The semiotician Yuri Mikhailovich Lotman (1922–93) argued that Russian culture (or the culture of late medieval Muscovy) was not contractual but instead was based on explicitly non-contractual values.[149] According to Lotman, in Muscovy cheating foreigners was historically considered normal and even the right thing to do whereas cheating someone from amongst one's own people was considered a great sin. Contract in the domestic context was, metaphysically speaking, not even required.[150] The same point has been made by the historian Richard Pipes, who came to the conclusion that feudalism in Western Europe and Muscovy developed in different ways and since Muscovy did not have the system of vassalage it also lacked the tradition of reciprocity and contract.[151] During the Ukraine crisis of 2014, the words attributed to Chancellor Otto von Bismarck (1815–98), formerly also Prussia's Ambassador to St Petersburg and otherwise a big advocate of the German-Russian geopolitical alliance, were often referred to in Western social media—namely that treaties with Russia were not worth the paper they had been written on.

Insur Zabirovich Farkhutdinov (b. 1956), an international law scholar from Moscow's Institute of State and Law of the Russian Academy of Sciences, has argued:

> All national systems recognize the principle *pacta sunt servanda* as such but they recognize it differently. It is insufficient to know generally whether *pacta sunt servanda* is recognized, one must know how it is actually applied and with what consequences.[152]

The presumption (or prejudice?) that treaties were inevitably different with Moscow than for instance with other European nations was widespread in the

[148] A. B. Bozeman, *The Future of Law in a Multicultural World* (Princeton: Princeton University Press, 1971) xvi.

[149] Y. M. Lotman, *Semiosfera* (St Petersburg: Iskusstvo, 2000) 384.

[150] Lotman, ibid.

[151] Pipes, *Russia under the Old Regime*, 51–2.

[152] I. Z. Farkhutdinov, *Mezhdunarodnoe investitsionnoe pravo i protsess* (Moscow: Prospekt, 2013) 389.

West at the time of the Cold War. The emigrant Estonian international law scholar Artur Taska (1912–94) wrote that for the Soviets, treaties with other nations did not mean the same thing as for Western states but were a form of 'political literature'.[153] Another Estonian legal scholar, Jüri Saar (b. 1956) has recently even argued that the civilizational foundations of Russia's legal culture are actually more similar to Islamic countries than to the West.[154]

One US author, apparently thoroughly exasperated by the Soviet 'Other', even nailed down US-Soviet differences to the following formula:

> While cheating is fully justified in Marxism-Leninism... its roots are to be found in the Russian tradition, where deception is as natural a national characteristic as is freedom in the United States.[155]

Such essentialist opinions were not an isolated phenomenon during the Cold War. Already in his famous Long Telegram sent in 1946 from the US Embassy in Moscow to Washington, DC, George F. Kennan (1904–2005) had postulated about the Soviets:

> The very disrespect of Russians for objective truth—indeed, their disbelief in its existence—leads them to view all stated facts as instruments for furtherance of one ulterior purpose or another.... the vast fund of objective fact about human society is not, as with us, the measure against which outlook is constantly being tested and re-formed, but a grab bag from which individual items are selected arbitrarily and tendentiously to bolster an outlook already preconceived.[156]

In contrast, many Soviet international law scholars regularly insisted that it was the US that had an inherent proclivity to violate international law and behave in an imperialistic way. In the post-Soviet period too, Russian experts have found differences between Russia and the US in the culture of international negotiations, arguing that the negotiating style of the US has been 'trade', and the style of Russia a 'search for love':

> Americans are a trading nation, they are used to trading, including in foreign policy. Americans behave in negotiations like businessmen but we [i.e. the Russians] like lovers on a date—we demand honesty, count on reciprocity, want to be loved. They do not understand this and want a more precise and clear formulation of our demands.[157]

If 'love' was a precondition for successful treaties with Russia then it was no wonder that Baltic post-Soviet treaties with Moscow did not work out too smoothly.

[153] A. Taska, 'Enesemääramisõigusest rahvusmõrvani.—Nõukogude Liidu sõnad ja teod Eesti Vabariigi ja rahva suhtes', 2 *Looming* 1989, 235–46.

[154] J. Saar, *XXI sajandi väljakutse: tsivilisatsioonid, kultuurid, väärtused* (Tallinn: Hea raamat, 2014) 188 et seq.

[155] J. D. Douglass, Jr, *Why the Soviets Violate Arms Control Treaties* (Washington, DC: Pergamon-Brassey's, 1988) 62.

[156] 'Telegram, The Charge in the Soviet Union (Kennan) to the Secretary of State', Moscow, 22 February 1946, <http://www2.gwu.edu/~nsarchiv/coldwar/documents/episode-1/kennan.htm>.

[157] See S. Markov, 'Predislovie', in V. Krashennikova, *Amerika-Rossia. Kholodnaya voina kul'tur: kak amerikanskie tsennosti prelomlyayut videnie Rossii* (Moscow: Evropa, 2007) 13.

However, from the point of view of smaller neighbouring nations like Estonia, the official Russia seldom realized the imperialist traits of its extensive desire 'to be loved'.

The idea that Russia is right and the US wrong has been popular in Russian culture in the post-Soviet period as well. For example in the 1990s cult movie, *Brat 2*, the Russian hero-underdog travels to the US and confronts a wealthy but mean American businessman in the culminating scene with the following 'metaphorical' questions:

> So tell me, American, what makes up power? Is it in money? . . . So you have a lot of money and what? I think that power is in being right. Who is right, is stronger. So you cheated someone, took the money, did you become stronger? No, you didn't. Because you are not right.[158]

International law is a language for settling who is right, and all major cultures and power centres want, if possible, to be right. Thus, they tend to construe their international law accordingly.

Now, in order to get a deeper sense of the issues at stake, let us turn more closely to the history of international law and its scholarship in Russia. When Ronald Dworkin suggested taking *rights* seriously,[159] let us now take *Russia*—and especially its internal discourse of international law—seriously.

[158] See the movie *Brat 2*, <https://www.youtube.com/watch?v=K9TRaGNnjEU>, from 1:52:50 (translation into English is mine).

[159] R. Dworkin, *Taking Rights Seriously* (Cambridge, MA: Harvard University Press, 1978).

2

The History of International Legal Scholarship in Russia

1. Introduction

The optimists of the perestroika period and the early 1990s were hopeful that after the demise of Communist ideology, Russia would 'return to Europe', including normatively. In some way, this also meant going back to the time before 1917—because Tsarist Russia had been part of Europe in a way that the USSR no longer was. Thus, contemporary international law scholars in Russia have developed an intense interest in the pre-Bolshevik Russian tradition of international law (and legal thought generally).[1] Sergey Vladimirovich Bakhin (b. 1954), international law professor at St Petersburg State University, now calls this period the 'golden age' of Russian international law scholarship.[2] But what was Russia's pre-1917 international law tradition like? In what ways was Russia historically part of the international legal tradition of Europe?

In principle, one can also approach history from the perspective of the discipline of international relations and its theory, as for example Andrei P. Tsygankov of San Francisco State University has recently done, explaining the history of Russia's behaviour in the international community through the concept of 'honour'.[3] However, while a sense of honour can be an important motivating force in international relations, it is even more elusive and less objective than is international law, which critical legal scholars have characterized as 'indeterminate'. It seems possible to justify almost anything with the concept of 'honour' since national leaders can have an overblown sense of honour and their populations can be manipulated into believing incredible things which in turn can hurt their sense of honour. In my opinion international law, notwithstanding its imperfections, is in practice not so elastic.

[1] See e.g. A. S. Tumanova, R. V. Kiselev, *Prava cheloveka v pravovoi mysli i zakonotvorchestve Rossiiskoi imperii vtoroi poloviny XIX-nachala XX veka* (Moscow: NIU VShE, 2011); A. V. Kornev, A. B. Borisov, *Pravovaya mysl' v dorevolutsionnoi Rossii* (Moscow: EKSMO, 2005); A. Ya. Kapustin (ed.), *Mezhdunarodnoe pravo* (Moscow: Gardariki, 2008) 45.

[2] S. V. Bakhin, 'Paradoksy professora Martensa', *Rossiiskii ezhegodnik mezhdunarodnoga prava* 2009 (St Petersburg: 'Rossia-Neva', 2010) 35–53 at 37.

[3] A. P. Tsygankov, *Russia and the West from Alexander to Putin. Honor in International Relations* (Cambridge: CUP, 2012).

When looking at Russia's role in the history of international law, it must be borne in mind that the content and normative direction of international law has not stood still throughout recent centuries. The principle of inter-temporal law suggests that we ought not to project today's norms of international law on past events. For example, waging aggressive wars was prohibited only with the Kellogg-Briand Pact in 1928 and the UN Charter in 1945. Previously, so-called classical international law essentially recognized *droit de conquête*, although balance of power considerations in Europe restricted its random execution.

Thus, when Prussia, Austria and Russia divided the Kingdom of Poland amongst each other at the end of the eighteenth century, they did not necessarily *violate* international law at the time but *made* it. The eighteenth-century divisions of Poland were meticulously laid down in the treaties that Fyodor Fyodorovich Martens carefully published and commented on in his treaty collection, and that read like amendments to the cadastral register.[4]

Similarly, human rights were included in international law only after World War II (minor precursors initiated during the League of Nations era aside). Writing in the 1870s, the conservative international law scholar and theoretician of legal positivism Carl Bergbohm could not imagine that human rights would ever become part of positive international law.[5]

The history of international law is a classic example of how complicated it can be to keep international law as an 'objective' phenomenon apart from its theory. In international law, history telling tends to be influenced by the underlying political philosophy and scientific method. Writing the history of international law is itself a form of international law scholarship. In historical scholarship, choices have to be made regarding which facts and ideas to focus on or how to interpret connections between them. The author's worldview and interests start to play a role here.

Moreover, in order to learn what international law has been like, one needs to have a theoretical concept of what counts as international law—whether for example the phenomenon of treaty making is enough for the existence of international law or whether one also needs beside treaties as such an articulated theory of international law or something that has been called consciousness of international law. Chernichenko may be right when he presumes that Ramses II when concluding his famous treaty with the Hittite king in 1259 BC 'did not perceive it in the way as we perceive international treaties today'.[6]

In Russia's case things are further complicated because the history of the country is long and complex enough so that a number of ideological constructions bridge the obvious discontinuities. For example, to what extent was medieval Muscovy a successor of the Mongol-Tatar state and to what extent the successor of

[4] See e.g. F. Martens, *Sobranie traktatov i konventsii zaklyuchennykh Rossieyu s inostrannymi derzhavami*, Vol. 2 (St Petersburg: A. Böhnke, 1875) 305–58. Convention concluded in St Petersburg on the definite partition of Poland.

[5] C. Bergbohm, *Staatsverträge und Gesetze als Quellen des Völkerrechts* (Dorpat: Mattiesen, 1877) 8.

[6] S. V. Chernichenko, *Ocherki po filosofii i mezhdunarodnomu pravu* (Moscow: 'Nauchnaya kniga', 2009) 661.

Kievan Rus'? While throughout recent centuries the Russian Empire constantly expanded, in the twentieth century it shrank twice—in 1917/18 and again in 1991. From Kievan Rus' to the post-Soviet Russian Federation a number of significant discontinuities in Russia's history have occurred and the interpretation of different periods and epochal moments in the history of Russia has always been politically charged. Thus, the initial answer to the question what the history of international law and international legal theory has been like in Russia, is: much depends on who has looked at it.

A related question is why any researcher wants to examine the history of international law. For positivist scholars of the twentieth century, one reason has simply been to take a record and, if possible, 'make it all count'. Vladimir Emmanuilovich Hrabar[7] (1865–1956), in his history of international law scholarship of the Tsarist period, has done exactly this. The result is an encyclopedic volume of more than 700 pages that is impressive and intimidating at the same time. Detailed studies of diplomatic history and the evolution of international law have turned out equally voluminous, e.g. Toman's historical study of the Soviet and Tsarist Russian approaches to the laws of war[8] or Grzybowski's and Schweisfurth's studies on the evolution of the Soviet theory of international law.[9]

In the context of this part of the monograph, my main interest is how international law has been historically construed in Russia. The goal is not to offer a new comprehensive history of international law or its scholarship in Russia. Rather, the main question is what has been the historical discourse of international law, what have been the main battles and key issues.

Because of the emphasis on the history of international legal discourse in Russia, in this part of the study I use mostly the narrative method of letting previous scholars speak and argue with each other. My particular attention belongs to the role of international law in Russia's complex relationship with Europe, and the question whether Russia had the same 'civilization' as Europe or a different one. By letting some Russian international law scholars speak and leaving others out, I have of course been selective and discriminatory. The interested reader can find an encyclopedic presentation of almost all earlier Russian authors in the works of Hrabar and Levin.

One criterion for choosing the authors that I have chosen for this narrative has been that during the last decade, the works of Martens, Hrabar, and Kozhevnikov have been reprinted in Moscow in the prestigious series called 'The Russian Juridical Legacy', as have been the memoirs of Baron Taube by another

[7] V. E. Grabar, *The History of International Law in Russia, 1647–1917*, trans. and ed. W. E. Butler (Oxford: Clarendon Press, 1990). In the English translation, Butler has used the Russian transcription of the name 'Hrabar', i.e. 'Grabar'. Cf. that in the Russian transcription, the name of the international law scholar Henkin becomes 'Genkin' as in I. I. Lukashuk, *Mezhdunarodnoe pravo. Obshaya chast'* (Moscow: Beck, 2001) 271. However, Hrabar's articles in Western languages were all authored under the name of 'Hrabar' both before and after 1917. I will therefore stick to the version of 'Hrabar'.

[8] J. Toman, *L'Union soviétique et le droit des conflits armés*, Ph.D. thesis (Geneva, 1997).

[9] See chapter 1, n. 6.

publisher. Portraits of Martens and Hrabar, along with that of Kamarovskii, are even printed on the cover of a recent Russian monograph on dispute resolution in international law.[10] MGIMO-University where Kozhevnikov taught has dedicated a conference and a related publication to his anniversary.[11] I conclude from these facts that these international law scholars and their works continue to mean something for contemporary Russian international law scholars. Frequent references in contemporary Russian legal scholarship to these same authors also seem to prove this.[12]

The research that for instance Taube and Hrabar carried out on Russia and the history and scholarship of international law, although published many decades ago, is fundamental. Moreover, since it concerns earlier epochs, it also does not age in the same way as dogmatically oriented research on international law. To give just one example, the recent history of international law published in Ukraine relies heavily on Hrabar's account of the history of international law scholarship in Russia.[13]

As a starting point, I follow the insight much discussed in historical and political scholarship that Russia as a country and its intellectuals have historically had to figure out how to relate to the country's powerful significant Other which was initially Europe and then, since the twentieth century, the West more generally and in particular the US.[14] Was Russia an Eastern part of Europe, a world of its own, or perhaps a world directly antagonistic to Europe in the context of international law?

2. 1869: Danilevsky and the Declaration that Russia is not Europe

Accounts of Russian nineteenth-century academic approaches to international law usually start with Fyodor Fyodorovich Martens (1845–1909). However, in order to understand Martens, we should first understand the normative debates that had shaped Russian discourse on Europe and the world at the time when Martens published his seminal texts.

For students of Russia's history of ideas, it is a well-known fact that two competing Russian schools of thought, the Westernizing school and the Slavophile/

[10] A. H. Abashidze, A. M. Solntsev, K. V. Ageichenko, *Mirnoe razreshenie mezhdunarodnykh sporov. Sovremennye problemy* (Moscow: Rossiiskyi universitet druzhby narodov, 2011).

[11] A. N. Vylegzhanin et al. (eds), *Rossiya i mezhdunarodnoe pravo. Materialy mezhdunarodnoi konferentsii, posvyashennoi 100–letiyu F. I. Kozhevnikova (Moskva, 15.10.2004.g.)* (Moscow: 'MG IMO-Universitet', 2006).

[12] See e.g. A. Ya. Kapustin, *Mezhdunarodnoe pravo* (Moscow: Gardariki, 2008) 45 and 61 (on Taube) and simultaneously at 65 on Kozhevnikov; G. M. Melkov (ed.), *Mezhdunarodnoe pravo* (Moscow: RIOR, 2009) 68–9 (on Taube and Hrabar).

[13] A. I. Dmitriev, W. E. Butler (eds), *Istoria mezhdunarodnoga prava* (Odessa: Feniks, 2013).

[14] I. B. Neumann, *Russia and the Idea of Europe. A Study in Identity and International Relations* (London: Routledge, 1996).

pan-Slavist/Eurasian school put forward their different visions of civilization and accordingly, Russia's identity and its role in the world. The foundational critical Russian text concerning civilizations and Russia's relationship to Europe is the polemical study by Nikolay Yakovlevich Danilevsky (1822–85), entitled 'Russia and Europe'[15] and written in the aftermath of Russia's defeat in the Crimean war (1853–6).

Danilevsky's study was initially published in 1869 in a newspaper and then as a separate book in 1871. It enjoyed huge success in imperial Russia,[16] in particular during the mid-1870s when the issue of the Balkans became particularly contested in European politics.[17] When Danilevsky's book was reprinted in post-Soviet Russia, in 1995, it again immediately became a best-seller.[18] Today's Russian studies of civilizations treat Danilevsky on a par with Spengler and Toynbee, the leading Western theoreticians and historians of civilizations.[19]

Why Danilevsky's book is relevant in the context of the history of international legal theory in Russia is because in a number of ways the Tsarist Russian School of international law was anti-Danilevsky, pro-European, and, we might today also say, Eurocentric. International law scholars such as Martens and Taube directly responded to and related to the polemical ideas that Danilevsky and other Slavophiles had expressed. It is true that in his book Danilevsky did not speak the language of international law per se; yet in his discussions he included references to legally relevant ideas such as balance of power which had been recognized as a concept of international law in the 1713 Peace Treaty of Utrecht[20] and made normative judgments on the history of wars and conflicts in Europe.

In his narrative, Danilevsky occasionally used arguments of international law *stricto sensu* as well—pointing out that the West European nations did not want to recognize Russia's treaty rights, wished to reserve the right to humanitarian intervention in favour of religious minorities only to themselves but not to Russia, and so on.[21]

Danilevsky lamented that Europe did not consider Russia and the rest of the Slavic world as its own but rather saw in it its natural enemy.[22] Danilevsky came to the conclusion that Europe and Russia were two distinct and mutually hostile 'historical-cultural types', civilizations. 'Europe' was synonymous with Germanic-Romanic civilization[23] and in this sense Russia did not belong to it.[24] Danilevsky sarcastically criticized the Russian Westernizers who were

[15] N. Ya. Danilevsky, *Rossia i Evropa. Vzgljad na kul'turnye i politicheskie otnoshenia Slavjanskogo mira k Germano-Romanskomu*, 5th edn (St Petersburg: Panteleevs, 1895; first print in 1869), <http://www.runivers.ru/bookreader/book10067/#page/51/mode/1up>.

[16] Y. E. Svechinskaya, *Imperskaya ideologia v rossiiskoi gosudarstvenno-pravovoi mysli* (Moscow: Yurlitinform, 2011) 77.

[17] I. Neumann, *Russia and the Idea of Europe* (1996) 55.

[18] D. Trenin, *Post-Imperium. Evraziiskaya istoria* (Moscow: ROSSPEN, 2012) 151.

[19] See e.g. M. V. Gorbachev, *Tsivilizatsionnaya metodologia v politicheskoi komparativistike* (Saratov: Saratovskaya Gosudarstvennaya Akademia Prava, 2011) 43 et seq.

[20] See W. Grewe, *Epochen der Völkerrechtsgeschichte* (Baden-Baden: Nomos, 1984) 328.

[21] Danilevsky, ibid, 12 et seq.

[22] Danilevsky, ibid., 50.

[23] Ibid., 59.

[24] Ibid., 60.

still fighting for Russia's full adoption and cultural acceptance by Europe.[25] In reality, argued Danilevsky, European civilization was one-sided as were all other civilizations; it could not claim to be universal.[26] It was only an illusion that the Germanic-Romanic historical-cultural type had achieved universality in its evolution, as for instance adoption of the French Declaration of the Rights of Man and of the Citizen seems to have claimed.[27]

In this context, Danilevsky criticized his contemporary Russian élites:

> Thus, if possible we declare more loudly that our region is European, European, European; that progress is dearer to us than life; that stagnation is more loathsome than death; that there is no redemption beyond progressive, European, universal civilization; that beyond it there can be no civilization because there is no progress.[28]

Danilevsky pointed out that there were other noteworthy ancient civilizations beyond Europe, in particular China.[29] He held languages and ethnicity to be crucial for the formation of cultural-historic types.[30] His main idea was that Slavs by necessity had to form a distinct civilization, separate from Germanic-Romanic Europe.[31] If, however, Slavs would not follow this historic call, warned Danilevsky, they would have no significance and would be turned into 'ethnographic material' in the hands of other civilizations, particularly the Germanic-Romanic one.[32]

Danilevsky argued that artificial efforts at Europeanization in Russia by Peter the Great and his successors had not made the Russian people European and only generated such characteristics as nihilism and indifference.[33] Danilevsky criticized Europe for being characterized by aggressiveness and easy readiness to use violence.[34] In fact, Danilevsky maintained that Europe had acquired religious tolerance only after religion was no longer considered a priority in its secularized societies.[35]

Russia, according to Danilevsky, was different from Europe. For example, party politics and division of the Russian people based on party interests were organically alien to the Russian people.[36] He was particularly critical of the new tendency to separate the Church from the state in European countries[37] and further criticized the 'English' concept of the purpose of the state: to secure to the members of society the inviolability of personality and property rights.[38] Instead, Danilevsky held that in Russia it was not the personal interests of individuals but national interests as a whole the formed the *raison d'être* of statehood.[39]

However, Danilevsky was critical of the fact that, since Peter the Great, Russia was caught by the disease of trying to be more European than it actually was or ever could be:

> [We] see domestic and foreign relations and questions of Russian life from a foreign, European perspective and through their glasses.... In consequence, what should appear to us as rays of the brightest light looks like complete darkness, and vice versa.[40]

[25] Ibid., 69. [26] Ibid., 71. [27] Ibid., 120. [28] Ibid., 72.
[29] Ibid., 75. [30] Ibid., 130. [31] Ibid., 130. [32] Ibid., 131.
[33] Ibid., 132. [34] Ibid., 191. [35] Ibid., 196. [36] Ibid., 208–9.
[37] Ibid., 223–8. [38] Ibid., 236. [39] Ibid., 237. [40] Ibid., 288.

Summing up his points, Danilevsky held that (Western) Europe was organically hostile to Russia and a battle between the two civilizations was to become inevitable in the future.[41]

Danilevsky's nineteenth-century polemical discourse was a heavily idiosyncratic one and yet it formed part of a backdrop against which Russian discourse on international law established itself in the 1860s and 1870s.

3. 1882: Martens, Founder of the European School in Russia's International Law

In the years following publication of Danilevsky's anti-European polemics, more and more scholarly works on international law were published in imperial Russia. Unlike Danilevsky, the Russian school of international law during the late Tsarist period was pro-European and demonstrated considerable Westernizing zeal. This also had something to do with the fact that a number of leading representatives of this school were part of the Russianized Baltic German elite of the capital St Petersburg (e.g. Martens, Taube) or otherwise came from the Western borderlands of the Russian Empire (e.g. Hrabar, who was born in Vienna and whose family's roots were in Galicia).

For these scholars and practitioners of international law, Danilevsky's Slavophile claim that Russia and Europe were two antagonistic opposites was a cultural-historical nightmare that questioned the Europeanizing work that had been conducted in St Petersburg since Peter the Great. In fact, since Danilevsky had been critical of Russia's Westernizing aristocracy, *inter alia* referring to the overrepresented Baltic German segment, his ideas existentially challenged the very role and status of personalities such as Martens and Taube in Russia, raising the uncomfortable question as to whose interests they had been representing. At the end of the nineteenth century, Martens lamented in his diary that life had become much harder for non-native Russian professionals in St Petersburg.[42] According to Baron Taube, the popular mood in the Russian Empire turned particularly hostile against individuals with Germanic names and roots during World War I.[43]

Friedrich von aka Fyodor Fyodorovich Martens (1845–1909) was a famous Professor of International Law at St Petersburg Imperial University, and simultaneously an influential counsellor at the Russian Ministry of Foreign Affairs. Martens published the first comprehensive Russian textbook of international law in 1882. Martens's work is a vivid illustration of how the history and theory of international law have gone hand in hand.

[41] Ibid., 483.

[42] For specific references, see L. Mälksoo, 'F. F. Martens and His Time. When Russia Was an Integral Part of the European Tradition of International Law', 25 *EJIL* 2014.

[43] M. A. Taube, *'Zarnitsy'. Vospominania o tragicheskoi sud'be predrevolyutsionnoi Rossii (1900–1917)* (Moscow: ROSSPEN, 2007) 206 et seq.

In the foreword to his textbook, which was soon to be translated into a number of other languages, both in Europe and elsewhere, Martens portrayed himself as a kind of Russian Hugo Grotius—not the father as such of international law (since international law had already been talked about for centuries in Europe) but its main intellectual importer to the Russian Empire. Martens carefully staged his appearance as a 'shot in the dark' in Russia's intellectual history, to borrow from Herzen's characterization of Chaadaev's early nineteenth-century public criticism of circumstances in Russia.[44] Martens complained that although Russia as a Great Power had since Peter the Great been an active and influential member in the European community of nations, international law scholarship was only with difficulty getting rooted in Russian soil.[45]

Personally speaking, Russian literature on international law does not even exist and even until our own times there is no single systematic introduction to this science that would have been presented by a Russian scholar.[46]

Martens further downplayed the importance of previous Russian writers on international law such as Kachenovsky, Stoyanov, and Kapustin, calling the Russian literature on international law 'very poor'.[47] Indeed, if Martens's tacit criterion was successful reception of Russian scholarly contributions in the field of international law in Western Europe, he was essentially right since the works of previous Russian scholars had hardly become known there.

Typically of the Westernizing civilizational project in Tsarist Russia, Martens highlighted the importance of Russia's historical treaty relations with the main nations of Western Europe. Peter the Great and Catherine the Great, the Tsars and Empresses who had opened Russia to Europe and made it part of the European Concert, were good whereas Muscovy's isolationist period in the sixteenth and early seventeenth centuries was not.[48] The main historical source of Russia's evils had been the Mongol-Tatar yoke (1230s–1480) which had alienated Russia from the rest of Europe.

Martens's history of international law is noteworthy for what it emphasizes but also for what it leaves out. Throughout his career, Martens published a 15-volume annotated collection of Russia's historic treaties with the West European Great Powers—Austria, Germany (Prussia), England, and France.[49] These were the European powers that in terms of prestige counted most for imperial Russia and relations with which demonstrated in what distinguished company Russia had belonged since the late seventeenth century.

According to Martens, contemporary international law had started with the Peace of Westphalia in 1648. However, Martens did not mention that for example in 1522 Muscovy had suggested to the ambassador of the Turkish Sultan who

[44] See further I. Berlin, *Russian Thinkers* (London: Penguin Books, 1994).

[45] F. F. Martens, *Sovremennoe mezhdunarodnoe pravo tsivilizovannykh narodov*, Vol. 1 (Moscow: Yuridischeskii Kolledzh MGU, 1996) 7.

[46] Ibid., 7. [47] Ibid., 139. [48] Ibid., 82–8.

[49] F. Martens (ed.), *Sobranie traktatov i konventsii, zakljuchennykh Rossieyu s inostrannymi derzhavami* (St Petersburg: A. Böhnke, 1874–1909).

had arrived in Moscow that both parties should conclude a treaty.[50] Moreover, Muscovy had had treaty relations with the Shah of Persia.[51] Martens also had little to say on the Treaty of Nerchinsk that Russia had concluded with China in 1689.[52] For the sake of fairness, it must be added that a collection of Russia's treaties with Turkey, Persia, China, and Japan had already been published earlier by another Russian scholar.[53]

Nevertheless, Russia's treaty relations with China before Tsar Peter's Grand Embassy to Europe (1697–8) fitted badly in Martens's normative scheme, namely that international law only belonged to civilized/Christian nations. Martens made particular efforts to leave the Ottoman Empire out of the European Concert, even after the Treaty of Paris of 1856 that had been a defeat for Russia and as a consequence of which the Ottoman Empire was officially accepted in the European community of states. If uncivilized and semi-civilized countries had concluded treaties with each other all along, then why would they have needed (European) civilization in order to access international law? If international law had been around all along then it was surely not for 'objective' reasons that Russia since Peter the Great had to make such an effort to become 'European'.

The other neglect in Martens's narrative was the treaties that Kievan Rus' had concluded with Byzantium in 875, 907, 911, 944, and 971.[54] Presumably discussion of their place and importance was left out because having gained Christianity from Byzantium one could have also emphasized Russia's separation from Latin Europe during the Middle Ages. The European narrative at that time emphasized the Peace Treaties of Westphalia (1648) as the hour of birth of modern international law. Emphasizing treaties concluded in the tenth century in Eastern Europe would have contradicted this conceptual framework.

Martens concluded his pleadings:

> It follows that the necessary condition for the progress of international communication is the adoption and development by states of all the main elements of European civilization and culture. The level of participation of each nation in international communication always corresponds to the level of its Enlightenment and civicness.[55]

And here is more specifically how Martens made the link between Russia's history and the development of international law:

[50] Grabar, *The History of International Law in Russia*, 5.

[51] Grabar, ibid., 10. See further N. I. Veselovskii (ed.), *Pamiatniki diplomaticheskikh i torgovykh snoshenii Moskovskoi Rusi s Persiei*, 3 vols (St Petersburg: Iablonskii i Perott, 1890–8).

[52] Nevertheless, the Foreign Ministry published a treaty collection on China without the name of Martens attached to it: *Sbornik dogovorov Rossii s Kitaem, 1689–1881 g.* (St Petersburg: Izdatel'stvo MID, 1889). See further on Chinese relations with European powers in H. Scheu, *Das Völkerrecht in den Beziehungen Chinas zu den europäischen Seemächten und zu Russland. Ein Beitrag zur Geschichte des Völkerrechts* (Frankfurt a. M.: difo-druck schmacht, 1971).

[53] T. Iuzefovich, *Dogovory Rossii s Vostokom, politicheskie i torgovye* (St Peterburg: Tip. O. I. Bakst, 1869).

[54] For a contemporary discussion of these treaties, see K. S. Rodionov, 'Iz istorii ektraditsii v Rossii', *Rossiiskii ezhegodnik mezhdunarodnoga prava* 2012 (St Petersburg: 'Rossiya-Neva', 2013) 108–33.

[55] Martens, *Sovremennoe mezhdunarodnoe pravo tsivilizovannykh narodov*, 157.

[Before Peter the Great opened Russia to Europe] the foreign relations of Russia were factual; based on its cultural conditions, the social and political edifice of Muscovy made impossible permanent and legal relations with European nations, based on equality and reciprocity.... The more the Russian government and people strengthen the wish to be truly participant in international communication, the more they try to use the historical experience and fruits of the work of European nations.... [The Russian people] became aware of its deficiencies, stagnation, lack of education, it is raising its self-consciousness and trying to achieve the level of civic life and culture where other more enlightened nations stand.[56]

Thus, Martens accepted the view that in terms of historical evolution and the past of international law, Russia had been a disciple of Western Europe.

Some sources published by Martens confirmed the historical validity of this perspective. Thus, when English and Dutch merchants arrived in the Moscow of Ivan the Terrible in the sixteenth century and when Queen Elizabeth and her envoys had their interactions and correspondence with Tsar Ivan, it was also a clash of normative worlds.[57] In 1583, English envoy Jeremy Bowes, discussing the treaty of alliance desired by Muscovy, raised the 'spirit of Christianity, international law and good faith'.[58] We also know that Tsar Ivan criticized Queen Elizabeth for having to share her power with 'merchants' at home in London and therefore not being an equal sovereign to Ivan himself.[59] According to Pipes (referring to the Pope's envoy Possevino), Ivan the Terrible considered only the Turkish sultan as equal to himself—because his power, as opposed to European monarchs, was absolute.[60]

Martens's historical narrative followed from his theory of international law. When international law belonged to 'civilized' states only, it was important to have an idea what civilization meant. Martens linked the notion of 'civilization' to liberal ideas and in particular human rights. He recommended his readers to look carefully inside the given state in order to understand how it behaved and operated in the context of international law:

Only by knowing the internal life of a country and its state set-up may one understand the principles and rules by which it is animated in relations with other nations.[61]

In the foreword to his textbook, Martens formulated what he saw as general law in the evolution of international law and relations. It is worth referring here to the whole lengthy passage in Martens's textbook:

The level of development of social interests and inner construction of the state determines the level of its participation in international life. In fact, the study of the history of international relations generally and of Russia's participation in particular has led us to the unwavering conviction that the inner life and order of a state have a decisive impact

[56] Ibid., 158.

[57] R. Pipes, *Russia under the Old Regime*, 2nd edn (London: Penguin Books, 1993) 71.

[58] Martens, *Sobranie traktatov* ..., Vol. 9 (St Petersburg, 1892) xxxvii.

[59] Martens, *Sobranie traktatov* ..., Vol. 9, xxiii.

[60] Pipes, *Russia under the Old Regime*, 77.

[61] Pipes, ibid., 27.

on its international relations and politics.... The more governments become aware of their duties towards their subjects, the more they relate with respect to their rights and legal interests, the more stable is the domestic state order and the better is secured the peaceful and law-abiding course of international life.... we came to the conclusion that if in a country the human being as such is recognized as a source of civil and political rights, then international life also presents a higher level of development of order and law. In contrast, in a country where the human does not enjoy any rights, where he is right-less and subjugated, international relations may not develop or be established on solid foundations.[62]

That governments ought to respect the human rights of their citizens is a quintessential idea of liberal political philosophy. In this context Martens also referred to the treatise by English philosopher John Stuart Mill (1806–73) *On Liberty*.[63] It did not hurt that Mill had held the view that non-civilized nations did not have rights under international law.[64]

However, one of the main puzzles in Martens's normative claim was whether at the time of publication of his textbook, in 1882, Tsarist Russia itself corresponded to the criteria laid down by Martens for 'European civilized states'. To the extent that human rights were brought into play, this may not have been the case. In 1881, Tsar Alexander II (1818–81) had been killed by socialist-revolutionary terrorists and in reaction to that with the edicts of 14 August 1881 his son Alexander III (1845–94) established in Russia an arbitrary police state which was considerably more restrictive than in Europe's other autocracies at the time.[65] In 1884, the works of Mill to which Martens positively referred in his textbook were banned from public libraries in Russia.[66] A gap was evident between the practices of the Tsarist government and the aspirations of the liberal Westernizing intelligentsia in Russia. Thus, the strong normative claim made by Martens on what being a civilized state meant could also be understood as liberal criticism of repressive circumstances in Tsarist Russia.

The basic messages of Danilevsky and Martens could not have been more different. For Danilevsky, Europe was bad for Russia whereas for Martens it was a cultural ideal. With his landmark textbook, Martens did not just introduce the 'European' discourse of international law in Russia but also used international law as an ideological tool, as a 'gentle civilizer' for Russia.[67] The point by Martens as to which nation was civilized and which uncivilized in the context of international law, was not merely directed against Russia's geopolitical adversaries such as the Ottoman Empire or Japan but was also a message sent to the Russian people.

To Russia's West European partners, the Westernizer Martens said that Russia was historically Europe's junior partner, its disciple. Considering the fact that Martens was not ethnic Russian, the whole idea had something of a quasi-colonial

[62] Martens, *Sovremennoe mezhdunarodnoe pravo tsivilizovannykh narodov*, 8–9.
[63] Ibid., 145. [64] Grewe, *Epochen der Völkerrechtsgeschichte*, 531, 643.
[65] Pipes, *Russia under the Old Regime*, 305 et seq.
[66] I. B. Neumann, *Russia and the Idea of Europe* (London: Routledge, 1996) 61.
[67] M. Koskenniemi, *The Gentle Civilizer of Nations* (Cambridge: CUP, 2001).

ambience vis-à-vis Russia. In any case, the main idea sounded even more authentic in the French translation:

> [le peuple russe] apprend à connaître ses defauts, le retard où il se trouve en comparaison des autres peuples et son ignorance; il en est frappé et il aspire à atteindre au degré de civilisation des peuples plus éclairés.[68]

However, in colonial state practice in Asia and Caucasus, Tsarist officials and ideologues could successfully use the claim that Russia itself was conducting a European/Christian *mission civilisatrice*.[69] The argument of higher and lower civilizations worked both ways.

4. 1926: Taube, Successor to Martens and International Legal Historian of Europeanism in Russia

Martens died in 1909 and thus did not survive until the Russian Revolution of 1917 brought Tsar Nicholas II down and the Bolshevik revolutionaries to power. However, during the last decade of his life, Martens repeatedly expressed the premonition in his diary that things were going downhill for imperial Russia.[70] His successor as the chair of international law at St Petersburg Imperial University, Baron Mikhail Aleksandrovich (Michael von) Taube (1869–1961), ended up in European exile along with most other international law scholars of the Tsarist era.[71] In the case of most Tsarist scholars of international law, the break of 1917 in Russia was literally physical because they were forced to emigrate when the Bolsheviks came to power.

In exile, Baron Taube further dedicated himself [72] to the study of history of international law in Russia and Byzantium, as if to conduct deeper historical excavations and better to understand the perspective on what had happened in Russia in 1917, and what the historical root causes of the Bolshevik revolution might have been.

In some ways, Taube complemented his teacher's sketchy Eurocentric interpretation of the history of international law and Russia's role in it with his own more elaborate version. Namely, Taube argued that during the Middle Ages Catholic Western Europe and Orthodox Eastern Europe had represented two separate 'historical types of international law'.[73] The epoch of the East European/Russian type

[68] F. De Martens, *Traité de droit international, traduit par A. Léo, Tome 1* (Paris: Librairie A. Maresco Ainé, 1883) 272.

[69] D. Lieven, *Empire. The Russian Empire and Its Rivals* (Yale: Nota Bene, 2000) 218–19 (referring to the memoirs of Count von der Pahlen, who led the conquest of parts of Central Asia).

[70] For specific references, see Mälksoo, 'F. F. Martens and His Time'.

[71] See G. Starodubtsev, *Mezhdunarodno-pravovaya nauka rossiiskoi emigratsii (1918–1939)* (Moscow: Kniga i biznes, 2000).

[72] See M. A. Taube, *Istoria zarozhdenia sovremennogo mezhdunarodnoga prava (Srednie veka)*, Vol. 1 (St Petersburg: I. I. Schmidt, 1894) and Vol. 2 (Kharkov: Zil'berberg, 1899).

[73] Baron M. de Taube, 'Études sur le développement historique du droit international dans l'Europe Orientale', 1926 *RCADI*, 345–533 at 349.

of international law had ended around the late seventeenth century, i.e. with Peter the Great.[74] This historical view emphasizing regionalism fits well in the contemporary narrative of Onuma and others regarding the history of international law.

Thus, Russia's history in the context of international law was no longer in complete darkness before Peter the Great as Martens had suggested. According to Taube, what was crucial for the understanding of the history of Russia in international law was that Kievan Rus' had received Orthodox Christianity from Byzantium in 988. International law in Byzantium had its specific features. In particular, Byzantium was the birthplace of humanitarian intervention in favour of Christians[75] living under Muslim rule. At the same time, Taube argued that the Western just war doctrine remained unknown in Byzantium because Caesaro-Papism determined that all wars were considered legitimate if they benefited the Basileus.[76] In this sense, Byzantium's just war doctrine was specific and self-serving.

Taube held that medieval Russia had itself been a confederation of nations, i.e. ancient Rus' was not a monolithic state but consisted of a group of essentially independent states.[77] Departing from the official pro-Muscovy history writing of the Tsarist period, Taube now argued that the relations between Kiev, Vladimir, Moscow, Chernihov, Galicia, Smolensk, Polotsk, Tver, and Ryazan had been relations of regional international law.[78] Differently from Martens, Taube also paid due attention to the four Russian-Byzantine treaties of 907, 911, 944, and 971 which had been concluded following the model of 'barbarian' Northern merchants arriving in Constantinople.[79]

The bottom line for Taube was that before the Mongol-Tatar invasion in the thirteenth century, ancient Russia belonged to the European (Christian) family of nations.[80] Due to Byzantine influence, international law in Russian lands may have been different in some ways, but these differences did not appear too significant at that time. Taube argued that the split of the Christian Churches in 1054 along Orthodox and Catholic lines did not make much difference on the ground in Russia. This attitude changed when the Germanic crusaders started with their military campaigns at Russia's Western borders in the thirteenth century.[81] Although in Taube's interpretation, medieval Russia had had its own concept of international law, in his construct Russia ended up being somewhat more brutal and less developed than its Western counterparts, especially as far as the laws of war were concerned.[82]

Taube was quite passionate about proving the European-ness of Russia before the Mongol-Tatar invasion in the thirteenth century. The fact that Kievan Rus' had been a European state turned the Slavophile claim of Russia's genuine civilizational difference from Europe into a historical nonsense:

[74] Ibid., 350. [75] Ibid., 361. [76] Ibid., 366–7.

[77] See, however, the warning of Grewe not to treat medieval political units as 'states' in the sense of the Modern Era in Grewe, *Epochen der Völkerrechtsgeschichte*, 57.

[78] Taube, 'Études', 404–5. [79] Ibid., 405. [80] Ibid., 414–21.

[81] Ibid., 437–8. [82] Ibid., 425.

Such are the numerous facts of juridical, religious and political order, evidently not pleasant to old 'Russian Slavophiles', modern 'Eurasianists' and some Orthodox militants of our days.[83]

Taube held that the West had itself some fault in Russia's growing hostility to Europe since the thirteenth century because the campaigns of the Germanic crusaders coincided time-wise with the Mongol invasion and Russia was attacked simultaneously from East and West (and the Prince of Novgorod, Alexander Nevsky, actually allied himself with the Golden Horde in facing attacks by the Teutonic knights).

Yet Taube was also quick to point out that the Germanic invasion to the stretched borders of Russian lands also brought to Eastern Europe 'precious elements of civilization and progress':

One needs to distinguish between the subjective sentiments of people who suffer from foreign invasion and the historian's objective point of view.[84]

The latter was of course something that Taube in his own view possessed. He concluded that from the point of view of 'historic ways of human progress' such a foreign conquest as the German *Drang nach Osten* in the early thirteenth century actually served a good cause because it brought along higher civilization to this new borderland of Europe.[85]

Whereas Martens, politically constrained due to his position in the imperial capital St Petersburg, had been relatively reserved in condemning isolationist Muscovy before Peter the Great, Taube, writing in exile, no longer held back the negative tones. He ridiculed the fifteenth-century doctrine of Moscow as the third Rome—again 'so dear to Slavophiles and pan-Slavists of the 19th century as well as modern Eurasianists of the Russian emigration'.[86] At the same time, Taube further developed the central thesis of Martens, namely that domestic conditions decisively influenced the country's international behaviour:

The old confederation of Russian principalities and republics, with more or less internationalist tendencies, was absorbed in a new Empire with Moscow as political center, in a unitary and despotic state, oriental in foundations, half-way Tatar, half-way Byzantine, with Orthodox mysticism and arrogant and aggressive nationalism. It is evident that these profound changes in the political structure of Eastern Europe . . . did not remain without influence in the domain of international law and the results could only be negative.[87]

In Taube's account, Muscovy in the fifteenth and sixteenth centuries was the historical-empirical proof that was underdeveloped in the narrative of Martens about the decisive impact of the domestic order on international relations and the country's attitude towards international law. Taube lamented that Muscovy in the sixteenth century had transformed into a unitary military state, was semi-barbarian, and almost unknown in Europe while believing itself to be the leader of 'true' Christian civilization.[88] Possevino, the Pope's envoy in the last

[83] Ibid., 438. Against Slavophile interpretations of history, see also 416.
[84] Ibid., 455. [85] Ibid. [86] Ibid., 473. [87] Ibid., 473.
[88] Ibid., 473.

years of the rule of Ivan IV, had written: 'These people think that the whole world is subordinated to their sovereign and that all people are but his slaves.'[89] Taube concluded that in particular in the sixteenth century there was an arrogant and aggressive spirit in the politics of the Tsars vis-à-vis Europe.[90]

According to Taube, the main cultural-historical reason for Muscovy's alienation from *respublica Christiana* was 'the profound Asianisation of all Russia during the 250 years of Tatar domination'.[91] Again, there was a direct link between the internal situation and external behaviour in a country:

> 'Tatarisation of the sovereign power' made the country despotic in the interior and anti-international in its international relations.[92]

Taube pointed out that, paradoxically, the Tatarization of Russia continued even after the Mongol-Tatar yoke ended in 1480 because Tsar Ivan the Terrible conquered the Khanates of Kazan and Astrakhan so that many Tatar noble families were integrated into the court life of Muscovy over the sixteenth and seventeenth centuries.[93] One result according to Taube was that in the sixteenth century, notwithstanding some diplomatic activity, Russia remained outside the civilized community of *respublica Christiana* of Europe that had been established even during the Middle Ages. For example, Muscovy was not present in the diplomatic registries of European sovereigns at the end of the Middle Ages.[94]

Taube's conclusion was that in the conditions described above, it was impossible to speak of a juridical or moral community between Russia and Western Europe in the sixteenth century: 'There was no more "international law" in such an atmosphere.'[95] In Muscovy, there was no respect for the idea of the equality of different nations. Things started to improve slowly only in the seventeenth century and particularly with Peter the Great when just 'one international law' emerged for Russia, as well as for the other members of the European community of states.[96]

In another lecture that Baron Taube gave as guest speaker at Kiel University Faculty of Law in 1927, he further argued that the war and revolution of 1917 had thrown the Russian people back to the Muscovite period of its history.[97] He argued that Soviet Russia was ruled by an oppressive regime and remained outside Europe.[98] So why had this all happened? With a dose of retrospective self-criticism regarding his own aristocratic class in pre-revolutionary St Petersburg, Taube admitted that the pro-European elites of Russia had been too separated from the country's uneducated people:[99]

> There were 'two Russias'—the pro-European upper class and the enormous half-Asiatic Slavic-Finnish-Tatar mass of the people that was unfortunately also very barbarian.[100]

[89] Ibid., 479. [90] Ibid., 473–4. [91] Ibid., 481. [92] Ibid., 482.
[93] Ibid., 482. [94] Ibid., 486. [95] Ibid., 487. [96] Ibid., 492.
[97] M. Freiherr von Taube, *Russland und Westeuropa. (Russlands historische Sonderentwicklung in der europäischen Völkergemeinschaft)* (Berlin: Stilke, 1928) 44.
[98] Ibid., 3. [99] Ibid., 45. [100] Ibid., 46.

Reflecting on this in 1927, Taube argued that there still remained three main differences between Western Europe and Russia, related to constitutional, private, and canonical law.

Firstly, Taube was critical of the fact that the Russian people were thoroughly apolitical and apathetic towards the most important questions of constitutional law such as the form of government.[101] Throughout their history the Russian people had experienced the government not as 'theirs' and not being there for their interests but as something 'alien'.[102] On top of that, there was 'an unbelievable lack of legal consciousness, a childish ignorance of its elementary public duties and rights'.[103]

The second difference between Russia and Western Europe according to Taube was that in the context of private law, Europe owed its strong notion of property rights to the decisive influence of Roman law; 'what belongs to me and what to you'.[104] However, this had not been the dynamic in Russia so that the Russian peasant uprisings and recently the revolution of 1917 had been nourished by the primitive desire to redistribute property and to take away from the rich.[105] Thirdly and finally, unlike Catholic and Protestant lands, Russia had borrowed from Byzantium the Caesaro-Papist model of religious power being fully dependent on the secular authority, which led to autocracy in political life.[106] Essentially, Baron Taube listed up what other authors have called the Oriental patterns in Russia's historical evolution.[107]

At the end of his 1927 Kiel lecture, Baron Taube expressed the hope that Russia would return, 'with Germany's help, to its European history'.[108]

Although written almost 90 years ago, Baron Taube's analysis sounds quite contemporary. When one reads the literature that is critical of the rule of law, democracy and property rights in contemporary Russia, one can encounter the same examples and arguments as explanations for challenges to the rule of law in Russia. Similar, too, is the suggestion that Germany should play a special role in Russia's development and 'Europeanization', and that the two would have a special relationship, even notwithstanding the two World Wars. One remembers the cordial correspondence between 'Nicky and Willy' before World War I broke out or the words of Nicholas I on his deathbed, directed to the Prussian monarch: 'Dites a Fritz de rester toujours le même pour la Russie et de ne pas oublier les paroles de Papa!'[109]

This demonstrates that history can be a very persistent thing and certain concepts in peoples' lives cannot be explained away too easily.

[101] Ibid., 47. [102] Ibid., 48. [103] Ibid., 50. [104] Ibid., 51.
[105] Ibid., 52. [106] Ibid., 56.

[107] D. W. Treadgold, *The West in Russia and China*, Vol. 1: *Russia 1472–1917* (Cambridge: CUP, 1973) at xxii argues that the Oriental patterns as opposed to Western ones meant political and social monism, weak property rights, arbitrariness, and lack of emphasis on the individual. See also Pipes, *Russia under the Old Regime*, 267.

[108] Taube, *Russland und Westeruropa*, 63.

[109] Martens, *Sobranie traktatov . . .*, Vol. 8 (St Petersburg, 1888) vii.

5. 1947 and the Russian Nativist Response: Kozhevnikov's History of *The Russian State and International Law*

Based on dialectical logic, the Eurocentric interpretation of Russia's role in the history of international law was likely to trigger the opposite: Russian nationalist, nativist, and Eurasianist responses. This happened by the end of World War II when Fyodor Ivanovich Kozhevnikov (1903–98) published his two monographs, *The Russian State and International Law* and *The Soviet State and International Law*. Kozhevnikov's monograph *The Russian State and International Law* was reprinted in Moscow in 2006 and in his foreword Lev Nikitovich Shestakov (1937–2009) from Moscow State University referred to the ongoing debate between the Westernizers and the Slavophiles/Eurasianists in post-Soviet Russia:

> A negative assessment of Russia's contribution to world civilization has persisted until our own times. By the way, our own liberals particularly excel in painting the history of our state in dark colours. Their pessimistic voice about the need for Russia to join world civilization has nothing to justify it.[110]

Shestakov's foreword to Kozhevnikov's book of 2006 also illustrates how representatives of the late Soviet generation in international legal scholarship saw the role of international legal studies:

> This work [by Kozhevnikov] enables the generation now entering conscious life to learn about and love this history of the Fatherland by the example of its attitude to international law, to be proud of what Russia has done for the development of international law. Based on indisputable facts [the book] demonstrates Russia's struggle for progressive development of international law and is indispensable for training specialist civil servants.[111]

Kozhevnikov was not just any scholar but a high-ranking figure in the Soviet international law elite. Besides working as an international law professor at Moscow State University and later at the newly founded MGIMO University, Kozhevnikov was a member of the ILC in 1952–3 and a judge at the ICJ in 1953–61.

Whereas for Martens and Taube Russia had historically tried to join (the rest of) Europe and to catch up following the Europeanizing project of Peter the Great, for Kozhevnikov Russia had played a leading role in the history of international law independently of Western Europe and sometimes against Western Europe:

> The advanced nations of the world have a crucial creative influence on the development of the main concepts and institutions of contemporary international law. Amongst these nations and states a noticeable place belongs to the Russian people, to the Russian state.... In this respect it should be pointed out that the Russian state started to respect the norms of international law because it itself recognized the need for stable and normal international relations, but not because it blindly imitated other European nations.... In

[110] L. N. Shestakov, 'Vstupitel'noe slovo', in F. I. Kozhevnikov, *Russkoe gosudarstvo i mezhdunarodnoe pravo* (do XX veka) (Moscow: Zertsalo, 2006) v–viii at vi.

[111] Ibid., vi–vii.

formulating certain concepts in international law, Russia was even ahead of European nations...[112]

Finally, this was a declaration of independence in the context of Russia's historical encounter with European international law. Kozhevnikov argued that Russia's history had been unique in the global context because Russia had gone its own way.[113] Kozhevnikov went through the history of Russia in the context of international law and, unlike Taube, concluded that in the tenth century treaties between Kievan Rus' and Byzantium, Rus' was not only a fully equal party but even the predominant party of the two.[114]

Whereas Taube particularly criticized the Mongol-Tatar yoke and the resulting 'Asianization' of Russia, Kozhevnikov characterized more negatively the Germanic invasion of Russia's North-Western borders in the thirteenth century.[115] Kozhevnikov's account was Muscovy-centric in the sense that when Taube spoke of a confederation of independent states in medieval Russia—Novgorod, Pskov, and others—for Kozhevnikov it had been just one Russia all along that waited to be reunited which was the historic mission that the Principality of Moscow successfully completed.

Whereas Taube had little patience with the customs and practices of Muscovy before Tsar Peter I, Kozhevnikov emphasized the positive role that the events of this period had played in the consolidation of Muscovy's power. No matter that Ivan the Terrible randomly killed thousands of his own subjects during the *oprichnina* if he was successful at territorial expansion, e.g. conquering the Khanates of Kazan and Astrakhan.

Moreover, Kozhevnikov argued that when Ivan the Terrible started the Livonian war in 1558, it was 'just, not aggressive' because Russia simply reclaimed the Baltic lands that Kozhevnikov insisted had 'belonged to it' already before the thirteenth century.[116] Again, Western historians had used to challenge this claim as historically inaccurate.[117] Kozhevnikov concluded that the active participation of the Russian state in the international legal life of nations before the eighteenth century was beyond doubt.[118]

Kozhevnikov's approach to Russia's role in the history of international law was influenced by Russian Messianic ideas. He recalls the words of Dostoevsky in 1880 in his speech in honour of the poet Pushkin, that after Peter I, Russia 'had served Europe maybe more than it had served itself'.[119] Similarly to Danilevsky, Kozhevnikov argued that during the eighteenth and nineteenth centuries Russia had selflessly served the interests of the balance of power in Europe.[120] Kozhevnikov held that Tsarism had its progressive side when for example in the

[112] F. I. Kozhevnikov, *Russkoe gosudarstvo i mezhdunarodnoe pravo (do XX veka)* (Moscow: Zertsalo, 2006) 7–8.

[113] Kozhevnikov, ibid., 18. [114] Ibid., 22–3.

[115] Ibid., 25. See similarly E. T. Usenko, *Ocherki teorii mezhdunarodnoga prava* (Moscow: Norma, 2008) 60.

[116] Kozhevnikov, *Russkoe gosudarstvo i mezhdunarodnoe pravo*, 29, 36.

[117] See e.g. Pipes, *Russia under the Old Regime*, 65, 79.

[118] Kozhevnikov, *Russkoe gosudarstvo i mezhdunarodnoe pravo*, 34.

[119] Kozhevnikov, ibid., 44. [120] Ibid., 48–55.

Balkans, Russia acted during the nineteenth century as liberator of Slavic peoples from Ottoman oppression.[121]

Kozhevnikov presents the idiosyncratic nature of Muscovy's statehood before Peter I with pride and *inter alia* applauds the fifteenth-century doctrine of Moscow as the 'third Rome'.[122] Unlike the Europeanists in Russia such as Baron Taube, Kozhevnikov claims that Russia historically played a particular role in the development of sanctity of treaties and the doctrine of *pacta sunt servanda*.[123] In contrast, the US historian Pipes tells the story how Muscovy was selective about and skilfully manipulated its treaties with other appanage princes in Russia.[124]

Finally, Kozhevnikov makes it clear that his main conceptual disagreement was with Taube and that Russia had not historically needed Europe to recognize and learn about international law:

> This concept of Taube is evidence of the fact that he did not appreciate the role of the Russian state in the sphere of international legal relations and mirrors the negative influence of the German school on certain representatives of historical scholarship in Russia. It deserves to be mentioned that generally foreigners and especially Germans, for understandable reasons, over-exaggerated the so-called 'backwardness' and 'lack of education' of the Russian people in the past.[125]

Although Kozhevnikov's study did not dedicate much space to the history of international law scholarship, he vehemently rejected the view that Russian writers on international law had been simple 'students' of Western European scholars.[126] In particular, Kozhevnikov rejected the claim that noteworthy international law scholarship in Russia had effectively started only with Martens.[127] To this effect, Kozhevnikov particularly emphasized the talent of Kachenovsky[128] and Nezabitovskii among Tsarist Russian international law scholars.[129]

Altogether, Kozhevnikov came to the conclusion that Russian scholarship of international law had historically been 'more progressive' on many occasions than scholarship in Western Europe.[130]

The thesis of the particular progressiveness of Russian international law scholarship remained a dogma for the coming decades in the USSR. In his history of international law scholarship in Tsarist Russia published in 1982, David Bentsionovich Levin (1907–90) repeatedly came to the conclusion that Russian scholarship during the Tsarist period had as a rule of thumb been 'more progressive' than its West European counterpart.[131] The historical comparison with Europe has not disappeared from today's Russian scholarship either—e.g. the recent international law textbook edited by Melkov comes to the conclusion that

[121] Ibid., 72–7. [122] Ibid., 85. [123] Ibid., 90.

[124] Pipes, *Russia under the Old Regime*, 88.

[125] Kozhevnikov, *Russkoe gosudarstvo i mezhdunarodnoe pravo*, 121. [126] Ibid., 122.

[127] Ibid., 127. [128] Ibid., 128. [129] Ibid., 143. [130] Ibid., 122, 132.

[131] D. B. Levin, *Nauka mezhdunarodnogo prava v Rossii v kontse XIX i nachale XX v. Obshie voprosy teorii mezhdunarodnogo prava* (Moscow: Nauka, 1982) 9–10, 78, 86, 159, 193.

by 'progressiveness, depth of analysis, precision of formulations, laconic style and literary form', the pre-1917 Russian scholarship of international law 'often surpassed' the 'world standard'.[132] In contrast, the Kazan University textbook of Valeyev and Kurdyukov is more modest and states that theory in Russia at that time was simply on a 'high level'[133] while Lukashuk concludes that it was on a 'general European level'.[134]

Kozhevnikov also asked the question what at the end of the day could have explained such a distinct and extraordinary role as Russia's in the history of international law. He started with Marxist explanations, briefly looking for possible economic factors but ultimately gave its due primarily to 'subjective factors' such as the 'unusual might of the spiritual forces of the Russian people'.[135] In any case, one practical result was that Russian diplomacy had been 'morally superior to the diplomacy of other nations'.[136]

Where did Kozhevnikov's defence of Russia's nativism originate from? Considering the time of his writing and the generally anti-religious attitude of Stalin's USSR, one interesting aspect in Kozhevnikov's work was that he, following a turn in Stalin's own attitude, emphasized the positive role of the Russian Orthodox Church during World War II.[137]

Thus, it is possible that Messianic arguments about Russia and international law have at least some of their roots in political interpretations of Orthodox Christianity and the emphasis on differences compared to Western Christianity. These are not necessarily deep theological differences but primarily historical, political, and cultural differences—the attitude that Russia is special and different from the West. Writing on the other side of the Iron Curtain, the exiled philosopher of religion and Russian thought Nikolai Berdyaev (1874–1948) also made the point that in their basic mentality and outlook on the world Russian Communists (such as Kozhevnikov in our context) borrowed extensively from, and unconsciously even gave a heretical interpretation of, Russian Orthodox Messianism.[138]

Undoubtedly, Kozhevnikov's monograph was written under the overwhelming emotional influence of World War II which had caused unprecedented human suffering and material damage in Russia and elsewhere in the USSR. In a sometimes caricature-like contrast from previous Eurocentric approaches to the history of international law in St Petersburg, Kozhevnikov in Moscow expressed the 'Eurasianist' idea of Russia's civilizational distinctiveness and in particular its moral superiority to Germanic Europe.

[132] Melkov, *Mezhdunarodnoe pravo*, 65.

[133] R. M. Valeyev, G. I. Kurdyukov (eds), *Mezhdunarodnoe pravo. Obshaya chast'* (Moscow: Statut, 2011) 61.

[134] I. I. Lukashuk, *Pravo mezhdunarodnoi otvetstvennosti* (Moscow: Wolters Kluwer, 2004) 43.

[135] Kozhevnikov, *Russkoe gosudarstvo i mezhdunarodnoe pravo*, 276.

[136] Ibid., 300.

[137] See F. I. Kozhevnikov, *Sovetskoe gosudarstvo i mezhdunarodnoe pravo. 1917–1947 gg. (Opyt istoriko-pravovoga issledovania)* (Moscow: Yuridicheskoe izdatel'stvo, 1948), particularly the discussion of World War II.

[138] See N. Berdyaev, *The Russian Idea* (New York: Macmillan, 1948); N. Berdyaev, *The Origin of Russian Communism* (Ann Arbor: University of Michigan Press, 1962) 140–50.

6. 1958 and Hrabar: The Europeanist Archivist of International Law Scholarship in Russia

Moving closer in time, the third significant European analysis of Russian historical approaches to international law was by Vladimir Emmanuilovich Hrabar (1865–1956) whose encyclopedic study of the history of international law scholarship in Russia was published posthumously in Moscow in 1958. The book is known in the West through its annotated English translation published by Butler in 1990. Whereas Martens, Taube, and Kozhevnikov primarily analysed the history of international law itself and discussed Russia's role in it, Hrabar's main focus was directed to the history of international law scholarship in Russia.

In his work, Hrabar presented all conceivable traces, including the obscure and the marginal, of the discourse of international law in Russia during the seventeenth to early twentieth centuries. Presumably, the exhaustive approach of 'making it all count' was meant to prove that for Russian diplomats and scholars, talking the language of international law was widespread in Russia so that in this sense Russia was just another European country. At the same time, Hrabar's quantitative approach rather reinforces the notion that the Russians were latecomers in European international law scholarship and historically occupied a somewhat peripheral role in it.

Moreover, the fact that everything in Hrabar's history focuses on Russia and on Russian translations from the West and that qualitative comparisons with scholarship in Western Europe are missing inevitably reaffirms the impression that Russia had intellectually been a world apart from Western Europe, a country *sui generis*. This impression is sometimes strengthened by some materials discussed—for example the fact that the treaty collection edited by Martens covered only Russia's treaties with other European nations whereas earlier, West European treaty collections had not been nationally limited in the same way.[139]

Although Hrabar's book was published only posthumously during the Khruschev thaw era, he must still have felt constrained when writing it—at least more constrained than Baron Taube was in his Paris exile and when delivering his Hague lectures. In 1929 and 1930, Hrabar had been criticized in discussions at Moscow State University as non-Marxist;[140] a characterization that some years later could have lethal consequences. The hardline Marxists-Leninists in Soviet Russia may have asked why examine such a topic as Hrabar did in the first place because what useful lessons could good Communists draw from the works of reactionary bourgeois authors of the Tsarist period?

As if securing his position, Hrabar's preface to his book starts with a reference to Kozhevnikov's treatise on Russia's role in the history of international law.[141]

[139] Grabar, *The History of International Law in Russia*, 511.

[140] Y. Ya. Baskin, D. I. Fel'dman, *Istoria mezhdunarodnoga prava* (Moscow: Mezhdunarodnye otnoshenia, 1990) 172.

[141] F. I. Kozhevnikov, *Russkoe gosudarstvo i mezhdunarodnoe pravo* (Moscow: Iurizdat, 1947).

Inevitably, Hrabar's monograph was in dialogue with the work of Kozhevnikov who was higher up in the international law hierarchy at Moscow State University and in the USSR. Certain elements in Hrabar's narrative are directly borrowed from Kozhevnikov and do not make much sense in Hrabar's own account. For example, Hrabar mechanically repeats Kozhevnikov's point that it was the Swedish King Erik XIV (1533–77) who had not recognized Ivan the Terrible as equal,[142] not vice versa as Taube had argued as the historical record seems to indicate.

Hrabar started his treatise by pointing out that Russia had been a latecomer in European international law scholarship:

> The modern science of international law arose in Western Europe among states that originated in the ruins of the Roman Empire and to a significant extent with the aid of Roman law. It was already at least four centuries old when it emerged among us [towards the end of the fifteenth century].[143]

In this way, the theme of Russia's peripheral position in the history of international law scholarship in Europe was laid out. Already Kachenovsky had written in the mid-nineteenth century that 'scholarship of international law came from the West'.[144]

Hrabar's account of the early uses of international legal ideas in the Muscovy and Russia of the sixteenth to eighteenth centuries is quite relevant in our context because it demonstrates how opinions about international law grew initially out of Russian state practice and of the political necessity to make arguments in Europe in favour of one's ruler. Thus, the first vague references to 'international law and diplomacy' were made in Muscovy's Ambassadorial Department (*Posol'skii prikaz*) in the sixteenth to seventeenth centuries[145] and Hrabar emphasized that '[t]he secretaries of this department—Muscovite diplomats—were our earliest spokesmen of international legal views.'[146]

Additionally, some foreign clergymen and scholars had been trying to give advice to the Tsars of Muscovy, such as Maksim Grek (*c.*1480–1556) and the Croat Iurii K. Krizhanich (1618–83); however, both were punished severely by the Tsars for ending up on the wrong sides in the religious-political debates of their time.[147] This was notwithstanding the fact that Krizhanich had agitated the Tsar to take up unification of the Slavs and defended Muscovite autocracy, contrasting it with the state system of Poland, which in his view was incorrectly believed to offer a guarantee of freedom to its subjects.[148] Krizhanich also explained to the Tsar that Muscovy was equal to the West:

> [t]he Roman Empire was never the mightiest of all kingdoms, and in dignity was not a higher kingdom nor a more significant kingdom since there is no higher tsarist dignity

[142] Grabar, *The History of International Law in Russia*, 6. [143] Ibid., 3.

[144] Reference from: E. V. Safronova, *Mezhdunarodnoe publichnoe pravo. Teoreticheskie problemy* (Moscow: RIOR, 2013) 45.

[145] Grabar, *The History of International Law in Russia*, 26.

[146] Ibid., 5. [147] Ibid., 18–26.

[148] Ibid., 20 (referring to the 'Political Thoughts' of Krizhanich).

in the world.... Rus' was never subordinated to the Kingdom of Rome and never had Roman nationality.... the Russian kingdom was equally high and glorious and the same in power as the Roman...the Roman Emperors had no more dignity or might than had the radiant Tsars of Rus'.[149]

In his authoritative treatise on Orthodox Christianity, Timothy Ware (Bishop Kallistos of Diokleia) makes the following historical point that may have political relevance even today:

> Now so long as the Pope claimed absolute power only in the west, Byzantium raised no objections. The Byzantines did not mind if the western Church was centralized, so long as the Papacy did not interfere in the east. The Pope, however, believed his immediate power of jurisdiction to extend to the east as well as to the west; and as soon as he tried to enforce this claim within the eastern Patriarchates, trouble was bound to arise. The Greeks assigned to the Pope a primacy of honour, but not the universal supremacy which he regarded as his due.[150]

By replacing the name of Rome with the US in this discourse, the result is pretty much the political essence of international relations (and law) discourse in Russia in our time as well, especially regarding equal rights in the context of the UN SC and US 'hegemonic aspirations'. However, returning now to Hrabar's account of Krizhanich, it is thus interesting that the first foreign scholar who introduced to Russian literature the notion of *ius gentium*[151] was simultaneously a defender of Muscovy's autocracy and its full parity with the West.

Moving on with Hrabar's account, he further explains about the rule of Peter the Great:

> Justification of Peter's activities—of his internal and foreign policy—was also part of the duties of Petrine diplomats. Peter, as no other sovereign, understood the full significance of the power of literary propaganda.[152]

Thus, the Russian resident in London, Veselovskii, in 1719 submitted a *Memorial* which argued that England's recent alliance with Sweden was concluded in violation of the Treaty of Mutual Assistance concluded between England and Russia in 1715.[153] Similar to Veselovskii's work was Petr Pavolovich Shafirov's (1669–1739) treatise written in justification of Russia's Great Nordic War undertaken against Sweden (1700–21). Here Hrabar makes another interesting stretch in his argument for although he points out that Shafirov was 'the most eminent Petrine diplomat', he distinguishes the work of Shafirov from that of Veselovskii:

> The principal distinction between this work and those considered above consists in the fact that it is not of an official nature.... The author, concealed under the letters P. Sh., emphasized by his initials that he wrote not as an official, but as a patriot, a 'son of the

[149] Ibid., quoting Krizhanich, 23.
[150] T. Ware, *The Orthodox Church* (London: Penguin Books, 1997) 49.
[151] Grabar, *The History of International Law in Russia*, 32.
[152] Ibid., 72.
[153] Ibid.

fatherland'. We have here, therefore, the first original literary work of international law not of an official character.[154]

It is curious that Hrabar tried in this context to prove that Shafirov's work had been 'not of an official character' when it so evidently was. One of the most outstanding diplomats serving Peter, Shafirov even managed to save Peter's army when it was surrounded by the Turks in 1711.[155]

In any case, it becomes evident that historically international legal arguments emerged in Russia, as perhaps they might anywhere, from practical need—from the need to make arguments in favour of state interests. One contemporary Russian author has put it that works at that period had a 'political and polemical character'.[156] Apparently, the need for this kind of literature is perennial and the genre is still blossoming in Russia. For example, in 2014, hardly was the ink on domestic acts of Russia's annexation of Crimea dry when at least one Russian lawyer produced a pamphlet on 'historical-legal grounds' stating why Crimea 'forever' belonged to Russia.[157]

Beyond the points made by Hrabar, rereading Shafirov's treatise is a worthwhile exercise.[158] Shafirov's pleadings in the early eighteenth century were also interesting for another reason than mentioned by Hrabar, namely that it was the first international legal treatise in Russia. Shafirov's pleadings demonstrated how domestic discourse on international law in Russia differed in some nuances from what was presented to the outside world. In the foreword to the Russian version of Shafirov's pleadings, he referred to himself as a 'slave' (*rab*) of Peter the Great.[159] These parts were omitted in the English and German translations because this kind of language would have raised eyebrows in Europe and thus been propagandistically counterproductive.

Yet this detail appropriately reflected what the actual relationship between the Tsar and his subjects was thought to be in Muscovy—including the nobility making international legal arguments.[160] However, these differences had been one of the very reasons why Muscovy had not been seen as part of the *respublica Christiana*. In his *Six livres de la république*, Jean Bodin (1530–96), who is known as the first major theoretician of the concept of 'sovereignty', had listed Muscovy along with the Ottoman Empire as a 'lordly monarchy under which the sovereign was full master of the bodies and goods of his subjects'.[161] In the same treatise, Bodin had insisted that the people of Europe would not endure such a regime.[162]

154 Ibid., 76.

155 Pipes, *Russia under the Old Regime*, at 120.

156 N. G. Nugaeva, in R. M. Valeev, G. I. Kurdyukov (eds), *Mezhdunarodnoe pravo. Obshaya chast'* (Moscow: Statut, 2011) at 110.

157 S. Baburin, *Krym naveki s Rossiyei. Istoriko-pravovoe obosnovanie vossoedinenia respubliki Krym i goroda Sevastopol s Rossiiakoi Federatsiei* (Moscow: Knizhnyi mir, 2014).

158 See P. P. Shafirov, *Rassuzhdenie, kakie zakonnye prichiny Petr I, tsar i povelitel' vserossiiskii, k nachatiu voiny protiv Karla XII, korolya shvedskogo, v 1700 godu imel* (A Discourse Concerning the Just Causes of the War between Sweden and Russia: 1700–21) (Moscow: Zertsalo-M, 2008).

159 P. S. (P. Shafirov), *A Discourse concerning the Just Causes of the War between Sweden and Russia: 1700–1721; with an introduction by W. E. Butler* (Dobbs Ferry: Oceana Publications, 1973) 8, 10.

160 Pipes, *Russia under the Old Regime*, 137–8.

161 Ibid., 65.

162 Ibid.

Indeed, Shafirov complained about Russia being unknown and being treated 'like India or Persia' by Western Europe.[163] In this sense, in the context of international law Shafirov's thesis directly reflected Peter the Great's claim that at least from his time onwards, Russia was a European country. However, the omission of 'slaves' in the Western versions of Shafirov's work suggested that Peter was requiring Russia to be presented as more 'European' than it continued to be in domestic life. A certain double-speak emerged.

Peter the Great himself is recorded to have said. 'We need Europe for a few decades, and then we must turn our back on it.'[164] While Peter the Great may have liked the idea of state sovereignty as an absolute right, he may not have liked aspects that he witnessed inside West European sovereign states, namely that the ruler's once absolute power had started to erode.

Although in matters of state and religion, Peter called himself 'Russia's Pufendorf',[165] he remained ambivalent about European domestic law, which had started to restrict the monarch's power. Once in London when he was near a court and wanted to know who the distinguished men wearing wigs were, he received the answer 'lawyers' and reportedly responded (joked?): 'I have but two in my whole dominions and I believe I shall hang one of them the moment I get home.'[166]

The actual effect of Hrabar's interpretation of the nature of Shafirov's work was that it enabled the beginnings of international law scholarship in Russia to be placed some 150 years back in the past. This diminished the impression that the main literary events in Russia's international law discourse during the earlier part of the St Petersburg period were translations of Pufendorf, Wicquefort,[167] and Nettelbladt[168] as well as the European international law textbooks of Klüber and K. F. von Martens.[169] The tradition of translating prominent West European works on international law continued until the late nineteenth century when translations of textbooks by Bluntschli (1876), Heffter (1880), Rivier (1893), and von Liszt (1902) were published in Russia.[170]

Translation activity in the eighteenth century, in Hrabar's narrative, demonstrates that the Russian Empire functioned in a top-down way—Peter and Catherine themselves decided what to translate and intervened personally in

[163] Shafirov, in *A Discourse*... (ed. by W. E. Butler), 2 (of the reprint of the Russian version of the treaties).

[164] Pipes, *Russia under the Old Regime*, 113.

[165] D. W. Treadgold, *The West in Russia and China. Religious and Secular Thought in Modern Times*, Vol. 1: *Russia 1472–1917* (Cambridge: CUP, 1973) 89.

[166] J. Quigley, *Soviet Legal Innovation and the Law of the Western World* (Cambridge: CUP, 2012) 60.

[167] Pufendorf's *De Officio hominis et civis* appeared in 1726, abridged; Wicquefort, *The Embassador and his Functions*, 1716. See Grabar, *The History of International Law in Russia*, 40.

[168] D. Nettelbladt, *Systema elementare universae iurisprudentiae naturalis* (1770; original 1749). See Grabar, *The History of International Law in Russia*, 132.

[169] J. L. Klüber, *Noveishee evropeiskoe mezhdunarodnoe pravo*, trans. from French (Moscow: August Semen, 1828); K. F. von Martens, *Diplomatiia, ili rukovodstvo k poznaniiu vneshnikh gosudarstvennykh snoshenii dlia posviashaiushikh sebia diplomaticheskoi sluzhbe Barona K. Martensa* (Moscow: Selivanovskii, 1828).

[170] Grabar, *The History of International Law in Russia*, 461.

translations of European treatises on international law.[171] The main works of Grotius were also translated under Peter the Great but for some reason were never made accessible to the public. The impact of European ideas was such that in the early nineteenth century the academic personnel at Russian universities teaching natural law (which international law was considered at that time to belong to) were mostly imports from Germany.[172] Their academic freedom was almost constantly threatened because Tsarist government officials and censors, proceeding from the idea of unlimited autocracy, kept discovering subversive and revolutionary ideas in their lectures and writings.[173]

Another effect of Hrabar's account was to diminish the importance and exclusivity in Russia of the St Petersburg school of international law and in particular Martens and Baron Taube. Kozhevnikov had already been quite resolute in his 1947 book: although Martens was a great figure, international law scholarship in Russia did not 'start' with him, whatever Martens had claimed himself. Thus, when Hrabar listed in the preface of his work 'the best-known representatives of the Russian science of international law', Martens was no longer even *primus inter pares* among Nezabitovskii, Kachenovskii, Kamarovskii, and Aleksandrenko.[174]

Yes, Martens had achieved admirably much, Hrabar admitted, and his fame had even eclipsed that of his earlier namesake in Germany. Nevertheless, Hrabar maintained:

> He achieved this status not only because of his gifts, but by hard work. Without the brilliance of Kachenovskii or the penetration of Nezabitovskii, he gave Russian science of international law a breadth which his more talented predecessors had not succeeded in doing. His motto ran: 'Labour conquers all.'[175]

This characterization came quite close to character assassination because a major scholar who would be pleased to be remembered by posterity as hardworking but mediocre in terms of raw talent has possibly not yet seen the light of day. Yet paradoxically, the account given by Hrabar himself undermines this comparison unfavourable to Martens.

Hrabar recounts how Dmitri Ivanovich Kachenovskii (1827–72), who was professor of international law at Kharkov University, never finalized the publication of his international law course. Hrabar initially characterizes him as an 'armchair scholar' who at the age of 30 years went on a European tour and upon his return to Russia 'while remaining a professor [became] more of a political figure than a scholar; and in his later years...sought consolation in art, his ardour for politics having declined.'[176] Hrabar's suggestion that Kachenovskii's ideas influenced creation of the Institut de Droit International in 1873[177] is interesting but would need further verification with Western sources before the claim can be accepted as such. At least, Koskenniemi in his account of the birth of the Institut and the 'men of 1873' does not refer to Kachenovskii at all.[178]

[171] Ibid., 125. [172] Ibid., 232–46. [173] Ibid., 281–2.
[174] Ibid., preface, lii. [175] Ibid., 387. [176] Ibid., 405. [177] Ibid., 405.
[178] Koskenniemi, *The Gentle Civilizer of Nations*.

Furthermore, Vassili Andreyevich Nezabitovskii (1824–83) was a law professor in Kiev about whom his Russian biographer, to whom Hrabar refers, wrote the following:

> [Nezabitovskii] accepted the chair of all-nations law as the only available vacancy, though his heart really being in the science of Russian law, he had always treated international law with some skepticism. . . . He always thought more than he wrote . . . he hated publication and published only what was essential: a doctoral dissertation, academic addresses, faculty reports . . .[179]

Since Martens in contrast definitely did not 'hate publication' and, moreover, his publications counted for something in the rest of the world as well, it seems that Hrabar's criticism of Martens during the late 1950s was motivated by political factors, i.e. totalitarian and illiberal constraints in the USSR. It was directly from Kozhevnikov that Hrabar copied praise for Kachenovskii and Nezabitovskii at the expense of Martens.[180]

For the same reason, Hrabar also delivers a critique of Taube's work on the history of international law and Russia during the Middle Ages, laconically labelling it 'scientifically rather weak'.[181] Note that this sudden (and unsubstantiated) characterization came from a scholar who demonstrated extraordinary intellectual generosity towards various obscure and marginal figures in Russia's intellectual history who had only in passing had anything to do with the field of international law.

It becomes evident how ideologically charged have the history of international law and its scholarship been in Russia—Hrabar's brief characterization of Taube's work as 'scientifically rather weak' mainly covered an ideological disagreement about Russia's role in the history of international law. The history of international law was highly political subject matter.

Why then does it make sense still to call Hrabar a further European voice in Russia and not place him along with Kozhevnikov in the company of Russian nativists? Because Hrabar's European approach becomes evident precisely when compared to the work of Kozhevnikov, in both its substance and its style. In his *opus magnus*, Hrabar commented on the doctrines of the Slavophiles:

> The Slavophiles stood for pan-Slavic unification under the aegis of Russian autocracy, and their doctrines became more and more reactionary.[182]

Hrabar held a similar attitude towards pan-Slavists before the Bolsheviks came to power. For example, in his March 1917 foreword to the Russian translation of the international law textbook by F. von Liszt, Hrabar said goodbye to imperial

179 Ibid., 416.

180 This is not to say that they were not important scholars as well. References to their works can still be found in contemporary Russian scholarship of international law, e.g. R. A. Kalamkaryan, Yu. I. Migachev, *Mezhdunarodnoe pravo*, 2nd edn (Moscow: EKSMO, 2006) 518 (on Nezabitovsky's theory of state territory).

181 Grabar, *The History of International Law in Russia*, 471.

182 Ibid., 458.

Russia's Slavophile dreams of conquering Constantinople as the birthplace of Orthodoxy.[183]

However, one point where Hrabar's substantive disagreement with Martens and Taube was real was that Hrabar believed that earlier forms of international law had existed in antiquity. According to Hrabar, Martens (and Taube) had proceeded 'from a priori opinions about the introverted nature of states in the ancient world—opinions having no basis in historical fact ...'[184] The impact of this view, as expressed by Martens and Taube, was so strong that almost all Russian textbooks of international law at that time shared it. Here is where Hrabar departed from the classic Eurocentrism that could be associated with the claim that there was no international law (or 'proper' international law) before 1648.

One of the lasting impressions that Hrabar's encyclopedic narrative leaves is the extent to which international law scholarship in Tsarist Russia borrowed from Western Europe and was generally under the influence of European ideas and individuals. Throughout the Tsarist period of St Petersburg, from the early eighteenth century to 1917, many international law voices in Russia were not ethnic Russians and the German or Germanized Baltic influence was particularly significant. One Russian scholar has recently even put it that 'the attitude of Russian scholars to this subject remained sceptical'.[185]

This demonstrates how 'European' imperial Russia indeed was at that time or how European the Tsars wanted it to be or become. However, the question remains whether the Tsarist Russia in love with Europe and European ideas was the 'genuine Russia' or a Protestant quasi-colonial construct of Russia as a 'European civilized nation'. Perhaps Kozhevnikov was a more democratic representative of Russia than Martens or Taube.

7. More Recent Views on the History of International Law in Russia and Ukraine

Further engagements with the history of international law and its scholarship in Russia have been variations on the main themes developed by Martens, Taube, Kozhevnikov, and Hrabar.

Of interest is the work of two Russian international law scholars on the history of international law, David Isaakovich Fel'dman (1922–94) and Yuri Yakovlevich Baskin (1921–2006),[186] partly because it was published during the perestroika era and reflects the unique spirit of those transformative years in the USSR. For example, the study includes a condemnation of the impact on international law of the foreign policy of the 'Stalinist clique', including the secret protocols to the Nazi-Soviet Pact of 1939.[187] This condemnation mainly reflected what had just

[183] V. Hrabar, 'Foreword', in F. v. Liszt, *Mezhdunarodnoe pravo v sistematicheskom izlozhenii*, 4th Russian edn (Yur'ev: K. Mattiesen, 1917) v.

[184] Ibid., 471.

[185] Valeev, Kurdyukov, *Mezhdunarodnoe pravo. Obshaya chast'*, 59.

[186] Baskin, Fel'dman, *Istoria mezhdunarodnoga prava*.

[187] Ibid., 159.

happened in Soviet politics because the secret protocols had been denounced by the Congress of People's Deputies of the USSR in December 1989.

Also of interest in Fel'dman and Baskin's work are references to specific and internationally less known studies on Muscovy's historical relations with its smaller neighbours. Whereas Kozhevnikov had greeted any Russian territorial expansion in the history of international law as 'progressive', Fel'dman and Baskin referred to a historical study by Levan Aleksidze, professor of international law at Tbilisi State University.[188]

Aleksidze had examined Muscovy's treaty relations with Kakheti (today's Georgia) in 1587–9, and discussed the nature and meaning of references to Kakheti's vassal nature in this and similar Muscovy treaties in the sixteenth century. The 1589 Book of Pledge signed with Muscovy's Tsar Feodor I included the notion of 'serf' (*kholop*) vis-à-vis Kakheti's King Alexander II (1527–1605) and yet Aleksidze had argued that the treaty had merely been an alliance of religious patronage, not the usual vassal treaty such as what Muscovy had concluded with the Muslim khanates at its borders.[189] Whatever the merits of the particular claim, such 'native' or even nationalist (other than Russian) voices had earlier not been discussed in Soviet scholarship of international law. The reference also raised the possibility that Tsarist Russia entertained unequal relationships when making new territorial acquisitions at the cost of smaller neighbours.

Baskin and Fel'dman's study also includes an interesting new opening which was the high evaluation of the Peace Treaties of Westphalia in 1648 which, as the authors argued, had after all been 'important' for Muscovy as well.[190] Although Muscovy itself was not a party to the Peace Treaties of Westphalia which made peace between the Catholic and Protestant powers and recognized in Europe the existing de facto established system of sovereign nation states, a reference to Russia had indeed been made in the treaties on behalf of the King of Sweden.[191]

However, historians of international law have not yet been able to clearly interpret this detail concerning Muscovy's inclusion; the issue of Muscovy's relationship with the Peace of Westphalia would need new archival work, in particular in Sweden. It is possible that by speaking in the name of Muscovy as well, Sweden as one of the winners of the new European order in 1648 was trying to further increase its political weight. Recently, Russian scholars have started to support the idea that the Peace of Westphalia was important for Muscovy too because for the first time in its history Russia was recognized 'in the capacity of a generally recognized participant in international communication'[192] or even because 'Orthodox Russia signed the Treaty of Osnabrück together with Sweden'.[193]

[188] L. Aleksizde, 'Vzaimootnoshenia Gruzii i Rossiei v XVI–XVIII vv', in *Trudy Tbiliskogo universiteta*, Vol. 94 (1963) 55. Referred to in Baskin, Fel'dman, *Istoria mezhdunarodnoga prava*, 76.

[189] Baskin, Fel'dman, *Istoria mezhdunarodnoga prava*, 76.

[190] Ibid., 97.

[191] Treaty of Peace between Sweden and the Empire (24 October 1648) (1648) 1 CTS 198, art. 17, para. 11 '*ex parte* serenissimae reginae regnique Sueciae omnes eius foederati ... rex Poloniae, rex et regnum Lusitaniae, magnus dux Muscoviae'.

[192] See Valeev, Kurdyuko, *Mezhdunarodnoe pravo. Obshaya chast'*, 104.

[193] E. T. Usenko, *Ocherki teorii mezhdunarodnoga prava* (Moscow: Norma, 2008) 68.

As already explained, the predominant Russian concept of the history of international law of the Tsarist period was Eurocentric in the sense of having a 'Romano-Germanic' bias. For instance, in 1894 Taube wrote that the Slavs had been unable to 'play any kind of direct role in the process of the emergence of the system of international law which was formed in the West, inside the Romano-Germanic family of nations'.[194]

In contrast, Soviet doctrine of international law made the point that the history of international law had not started around 1648 but whenever states had emerged in history and before Europe was even born, i.e. already some millennia BC.[195] It seems that this point was not just driven by interpretations of Marxist-Leninist philosophy but also constituted an attempt to detach the history of modern international law from its claimed origins in the history of the 'Germanic-Romanic world' of Western Europe; to make the history of international law more palatable to non-Western regions, including Russia.

In any case, it is interesting to see that in contemporary Russian scholarship the seemingly apolitical and highly academic debate on whether international law started in the 4th millennium BC or around 1648 seems to have political undercurrents as well. Scholars who stick to the view that 'international law emerged when states emerged; when class society emerged'[196] seem to combine this view with other nativist idiosyncrasies—for instance, the international law textbook by Melkov discusses in detail the history of international law scholarship...but only in Russia.[197] E. T. Usenko explains how the conceptual change—that international law was born in Europe in the early modern era instead of the 4th millennium BC somewhere in ancient Mesopotamia—was undertaken in Russia precisely in the course of perestroika.[198] Ideologically, the move also meant a step towards 'Europe' but also going back to some pre-1917 historical concepts in European-Russian scholarship, to the intellectual world of Martens and Taube.

The recent history of international law published by Ukrainian scholars and W. E. Butler[199] again makes the Peace Treaties of Westphalia central to the history of international law and is even dedicated to the 365th anniversary of the Peace of Westphalia. This can be understood as a symbolic turn back to a more Eurocentric historical approach. Of course, Kiev with its Mohyla Academy was already a Europeanizing force in Russian history in the seventeenth century. In this book, A. I. Dmitriev and his Ukrainian co-authors make the point that 1648 marks a watershed in the history of international law—according to the authors, before this landmark date, we can speak of 'regional' international law whereas only in 1648 was 'universal' international law born.[200]

[194] M. Taube, *Istoria zarozhdenia sovremennoga mezhdunarodnoga prava (srednie veka)*, Vol. 1 (St Petersburg: I. I. Schmidt, 1894) 362.

[195] See Usenko, *Ocherki teorii mezhdunarodnoga prava*, 48–61.

[196] Melkov, *Mezhdunarodnoe pravo*, 48.

[197] Ibid., 65–72.

[198] Y. T. Usenko, G. G. Shinkaretskaya (eds), *Mezhdunarodnoe pravo* (Moscow: Yurist, 2005) 18–21.

[199] Dmitriev, Butler, *Istoria mezhdunarodnoga prava*.

[200] Dmitriev, ibid., 67 et seq.

However, this interpretation is too centred on Eastern Europe. Indeed, Russia (and Ukraine, which by that time had been annexed to it) joined the European state system around the end of the seventeenth century (although in Martens's and Taube's understanding not yet in 1648) but the same is not true of East Asian and Muslim lands, not to speak of Africa.[201] In the work edited by A.I. Dmitriev, W. E. Butler also postulates that one reason why the traditional view that sees in medieval Rus' little evidence of international law is a result of the fact that in Russian historiography relations between the principalities of Rus' were seen as 'local' and not as an 'international' matter.[202]

In this sense, Taube's approach to medieval legal history in Russia has made a scholarly comeback. The idea that during the Middle Ages there may have been regional concept of international law in Byzantium, Rus', and even Muscovy, has found some support in recent Russian scholarship as well.[203]

Yet the most extensive scholarly account on the question, by Olga Butkevich, also from Kyiv, criticizes Eurocentric readings of the history of international law and argues that international law was already born in Antiquity.[204]

8. Nussbaum and Grewe: Russia in Western Narratives of the History of International Law

So far we have looked exclusively at Russian authors but Russia's role in the history of international law has been discussed in the West as well, at least in fragments. At the height of the Cold War, Western discussion of Russia's role in the history of international law of course followed Taube's and not Kozhevnikov's approach. Historically, German scholars have demonstrated a particular interest in the study of the history of international law. During the Cold War two noteworthy interpretations of Russia's role in the history of international law also stemmed from the pens of German historians of international law.

Arthur Nussbaum (1877–1964) was a German Jewish refugee who had previously worked at Berlin University and published his history of international law in the US as a professor at Columbia University. In his discussion of international law during the Middle Ages, Nussbaum relied heavily on Taube's account as far as Russia was concerned.[205] Moreover, Nussbaum supported Bergbohm's (as opposed to Martens's) interpretation of such a historical landmark in international law of

[201] See again the work of Onuma.

[202] W. E. Butler, 'Teoretiko-metodologischeskie osnovy issledovania istorii mezhdunarodnoga prava', in A. I. Dmitriev, *Istoria mezhdunarodnoga prava*, 7–69 at 46.

[203] Melkov, *Mezhdunarodnoe pravo*, 54; Valeev, Kurdyukov, *Mezhdunarodnoe pravo. Obshaya chast'*, 58.

[204] O. V. Butkevich, *U istokov mezhdunarodnogo prava* (St Petersburg: Izdatel'stvo R. Aslanova 'Yuridicheskii tsentr Press', 2008) 113 et seq. Cf D. Bederman, *International Law in Antiquity* (Cambridge: CUP, 2007).

[205] A. Nussbaum, *A Concise History of the Law of Nations* (New York: Macmillan, 1954) 49–51.

the eighteenth century as Armed Neutrality as proclaimed by Russian Empress Catherine II in 1780.

Bergbohm had argued that although Catherine II became known (and advertised herself) as the initiator of the 1780 Declaration, in reality the Empress had borrowed the idea from the Danish Minister Count Bernstorff.[206] The objective consequence of this historic interpretation—whether true or false—was again that Russia's contribution to international law, already relatively meagre in European eyes, was further diminished, and that something of significance was 'expropriated' from the legacy claimed by the Russians.

Altogether, Nussbaum's opinion of the tradition of international Russia was devastating:

> In Russia, spiritual divergence from the West greatly affected the conception of law. Law (in contradiction, e.g., to religion) meant less to a Russian than to a Westerner.... With regard to international law, the situation was particularly unfavorable. Russia had not participated in the religious and philosophical movement in which the law of nations originated. Instead, Byzantine tradition prevailed in the Russian views on foreign relations. In the eighteenth century and later there was a gradual approximation to Western ideas, accelerated in the closing decades of Czardom. But on the whole, learning in matters of international law was on a low level and was remote from the Russian mind.... The situation changed, however, in 1882 when Fedor Fedorovich (Frederic) Martens published his two volumes *International Law of Civilized Nations*.[207]

Nevertheless, for Nussbaum, Martens too represented a different tradition from the Western one because 'legal argument served him rather as a means of rendering his pleas for Russian claims or defenses more impressive or more palatable'.[208] If so then substantively not much had changed in Russia since Shafirov's arguments.

Another account was by Wilhelm Grewe (1911–2000) who, however, even more than Taube emphasized the division and differences between the Western and Eastern branches of Christianity during the Middle Ages:

> The result of this religious-cultural antagonism was that the Greek-Byzantine circle was excluded from the closer Christian international legal community of the West.[209]

Only with Peter the Great did Russia become a European Great Power.[210] Yet interestingly in our context, Grewe also makes the case that the period of so-called classical international law in Europe was not entirely uniform and was in fact subject to different cultural-political impulses from various European powers. Grewe argues that the continental absolutist monarchies in Eastern and Central Europe—Russia, Austria, and Prussia—during various decades of the nineteenth century developed a somewhat different concept of international law from the parliamentary maritime states of the West, particularly England but at least partly also France.[211]

[206] Ibid., 133. [207] Ibid., 248. [208] Ibid., 249.
[209] Grewe, *Epochen der Völkerrechtsgeschichte*, 79. [210] Ibid., 328.
[211] Ibid., 373, 508–9, 572.

Tsarist Russia was the leader of the anti-liberal camp in Europe, with the Holy Alliance of 1815,[212] the suppression of the uprising in Poland in 1830–1, and its much-criticized role as 'gendarme of Europe' in suppressing the revolutions of 1848. Western-Tsarist conflict (and Western anti-Russian rhetoric) reached its peak at the time of the Crimean War (1853–6).

Grewe interprets nineteenth-century international law in Europe as a competition between democratic liberal ideas and conservative legitimist ones. For example, the European recognition of Latin American states was a defeat of the principles of the Russian-led Holy Alliance.[213] Certain phenomena in nineteenth-century international law—such as the renaissance of arbitration—were primarily influenced by the legal thinking of the British.[214] While at the end of the nineteenth century Tsar Nicholas II (1868–1918) had made similar advances, Russia was not central in the evolution of the institute of arbitration.[215] Only with its first elected parliament in 1906 did imperial Russia domestically take a step towards nascent elements of constitutionalism and parliamentary democracy.[216] However, this development was again interrupted in 1917.

Reading Grewe also reveals that it is not so that liberal Britain in everything had a friendlier approach to international law than authoritarian Russia. For example in the late nineteenth century the British quite systematically opposed codification of the law of war which the last Russian Tsars advocated.[217] Grewe also held the view that the questionable practice of establishing spheres of influence in Afghanistan and elsewhere was primarily a British initiative during that period.

Perhaps the most interesting case concerning Russia in the history of international law that Grewe discusses was about Tsarist Russia's relationship to foreign treaties and the principle of *pacta sunt servanda*. The case had already been discussed in nineteenth-century international law scholarship[218] and its details were the following. In 1856 the Crimean War was ended by the Treaty of Paris, which prohibited Russia from maintaining its Black Sea fleet and declared the Black Sea neutral. However, when the Franco-German war broke out in 1870, Russia issued a circular declaring itself no longer bound by references to the Black Sea in the Treaty of Paris.[219] Since other participants of the Treaty of Paris protested, a common conference of the treaty partners was held in which it was declared that:

> It is an essential principle of the law of nations that no power can liberate itself from the engagements of the treaty, nor modify the stipulations thereof, unless with the consent of the contracting powers by means of an amicable arrangement.[220]

212 Ibid., 505. 213 Ibid.,585. 214 Ibid., 571. 215 Ibid., 615.
216 Ibid., 569. 217 Ibid., 636.
218 See e.g. W. E. Hall, *A Treatise on International Law*, 3rd edn (Oxford: Clarendon Press 1890) 353–6.
219 Ibid., 354. 220 Ibid., 356.

Grewe interprets this statement by the major European powers as a milestone in the development of the understanding of *clausula rebus sic stantibus*, namely that exceptions to the underlying principle of international law, *pacta sunt servanda*, must be construed narrowly.[221] However, the common declaration solving the issue was a peculiar one because although in it Russia agreed to the common statement as a valid legal principle, in terms of *Realpolitik* it got to keep the advances it had made around the Black Sea. In the spirit of legal positivism, the British international law scholar W. E. Hall concluded: 'But the concessions made were dictated by political considerations, with which international law has nothing to do.'[222]

Grewe also held that the international law ideology of the French Revolution which Russia as the leading conservative power on the European continent had vigorously rejected made a renaissance in 1919, in the post-World War I international legal order and the League of Nations.[223] This was at the same time as Soviet Russia detached itself from the European state and value system.

One of the main conclusions of Grewe's analysis is that in nineteenth-century international law, Russia as a conservative autocracy was not the only one with a conservative *politique juridique extérieure*. At least during some decades in the nineteenth century, the monarchies of Russia, Austria, and Prussia built an anti-liberal coalition in Europe and advanced their own normative views on the international order.

A study by the US historian Martin Malia reconfirms the validity of some of the points made by Grewe. According to Malia, around 1830 a 'liberal civilization' was born in Western Europe.[224] After suppression of the revolutions of 1848, autocratic Russia was verbally assaulted as an outcast Empire by West European public opinion.[225] Especially during the Crimean War (1853–6) the Western view that Russia was non-European (due to its illiberal autocracy) grew in intensity.[226] In contrast, Russian scholars have argued that, ideology-wise, an attempt was made to create a 'neo-Byzantian' civilization in Russia after Nicolas I came to power in 1825.[227]

Yet ultimately, before the outbreak of World War I, it was precisely the autocratic East European Empire, Russia, that had become the main ally of the liberal West European nations, England and France, against the conservative Empires of Central Europe, Germany, and Austria-Hungary. Security alliances in Europe were thus shaped by *Realpolitik* and strategic thinking rather than ideological considerations based on the liberal-autocratic divide.

[221] Grewe, *Epochen der Völkerrechtsgeschichte*, 605.

[222] Hall, *A Treatise on International Law*, 356.

[223] Grewe, *Epochen der Völkerrechtsgeschichte*, 498.

[224] M. Malia, *Russia under Western Eyes. From the Bronze Horseman to the Lenin Mausoleum* (Cambridge, MA: Belknam Press, 1999) 94.

[225] Ibid., 150–1. [226] Ibid., 151–8.

[227] A. Yanov, *Patriotizm i natsionalizm v Rossii 1825–1921*, 2nd edn (Moscow: Akademkniga, 2002) 62 et seq.

9. The Question of Tsarist Russia's Contribution to International Humanitarian Law

A main source of pride in Russian scholarly discourse on international law regarding the Tsarist period and international law continues to be Russian initiative and leadership during the 1860s–1890s to internationally codify the laws of war.[228] Russian diplomacy played a leading role at the adoption of the Saint Petersburg Declaration of 1868, the Brussels Declaration of 1874 and during the Hague Peace Conference of 1899. In contrast, liberal Britain at the time was quite reserved about and even partly hostile to the idea of codifying the international laws of war.

Exemplary of this discourse, Igor I. Lukashuk has written:

> Russia played an important role in the emergence of humanitarian norms. This is first of all explained by a concern to make the soldier's life easier. A huge Army remained the basis of the military might of Russia. Concern for its soldiers increased its might.[229]

However, recently the Israeli international law scholars Eyal Benvenisti and Amichai Cohen have offered a less idealistic account of the nineteenth-century international codification efforts in the realm of the laws of war.[230] In particular they explain codification efforts during and after the 1870s with problems that European Empires faced with their conscript armies. According to Benvenisti and Cohen, rather than being animated primarily by idealist motives, the promoters of codification of the laws of war wanted to solve the principal-agent problem of domestic governance; to control their own forces in the first place. Paradoxically, the two scholars claim that successful codification of the laws of war in 1899 enabled rather than prevented the amassing of huge armies in Europe before World War I. And indeed, on the eve of World War I, imperial Russia had the largest conscript army in the world.

It follows that Russia also promoted codification of the laws of war for reasons of realism, not just for high-minded humanism or pacifism. Indeed, the Russian soldier before and during World War I was conscripted from the same 'people's mass'—as Baron Taube would have put it—that did not excel in education or literacy. For Russian imperial administrators, the international law of war may also have been a means of controlling one's own Army.

Nevertheless, Russia's late nineteenth-century codification initiatives in the field of international humanitarian law, whatever their inner reasons and mechanisms,

[228] V. S. Ivanenko (ed.), *100–letiye initsiativy Rossii. Ot Pervoi konferentsii mira 1899 g. k Tret'ei konferentsii mira 1999.g. Sbornik materialov* (St Petersburg: St Petersburg State University, 1999); V. A. Batyr', *Mezhdunarodnoe gumanitarnoe pravo*, 2nd edn (Moscow: Iustitsinform, 2011) 3; A. Ya. Kapustin, *Mezhdunarodnoe pravo* (Moscow: Gardariki, 2008) 55; Melkov, *Mezhdunarodnoe pravo*, 50, 59–60, 153; Safronova, *Mezhdunarodnoe publichnoe pravo. Teoreticheskie problemy*, 33.

[229] Lukashuk, *Mezhdunarodnoe pravo. Osobennaya chast'*, 265.

[230] E. Benvenisti, A. Cohen, 'War is Governance: Explaining the Logic of the Laws of War from a Principal-Agent Perspective', 112 *Michigan Law Review* 2013, 1363–416.

objectively contributed to codification of the laws of war, which was a positive development in the field.

10. Conclusions from History: International Law in Russia as an Encounter with Europe and the West

Previous analysis of works on international law written by Shafirov, Martens, Taube, Hrabar, and Kozhevnikov demonstrates that historically, international law has been a thoroughly 'civilizational' affair in Russia. For Russia, the political dilemma has been enormous: whether to construe itself as part of Europe or as an independent civilization and even hostile to ('Romano-Germanic') Europe. These decisions have significantly shaped Russian attitudes towards international law and its European version in the early modern era, *ius publicum europaeum*.

By an enormous act of will of Tsar Peter the Great, Russia became a participant in *ius publicum europaeum* in around 1700. However, Russia's relationship with the West in the context of European international law had features of the relationship between the centre (the West) and semi-periphery (Russia).[231] In the eighteenth and early nineteenth centuries, this encompassed both intellectual culture as well as the economy of Russia.[232] It was often perceived that the Europeanizing project was imposed on the Russian people from above. Eurasianist writers emphasizing Russia's distinctness from the West even call the Tsarist period in the eighteenth to early twentieth centuries the 'Roman-Germanic yoke',[233] challenging the historical narrative of Westernizers that there was a 'Mongol-Tatar yoke' in Russia's history.

Before Peter the Great, Russia stood apart from the West European *respublica Christiana*. This was partly due to differences between Eastern and Western Christianity and the Messianic interpretation that Moscow had become the Third Rome and the inheritor of Byzantium.

Russia also distanced itself from 'bourgeois' Europe after the Bolshevik revolution in 1917. It is noteworthy that Taube saw civilizational aspects in Russia's Bolshevik revolution of 1917. According to Taube, 'the European element' was literally thrown out of Bolshevik Russia and in civilizational terms Russia returned to its pre-Petrine Muscovite period. Stalin was the reincarnation of Ivan the Terrible, the archetypical Oriental despot that built his world on power and conquest rather than treaties and international law.

This part of the study on purpose did not go into the details of the Soviet concept of international law because there are already excellent detailed Western

[231] See further on the periphery and centre aspect in L. Mälksoo, 'Russia-Europe', in B. Fassbender, A. Peters (eds), *The Oxford Handbook of the History of International Law* (Oxford: OUP, 2012) 764–86.

[232] See further on the economic aspects of this historic centre-periphery relationship in B. Yu. Kagarlitski, *Periferiinaya imperia. Rossia i mirosistema* (Moscow: Librokom, 2011).

[233] A. Dugin, *Proekt Evraziya* (Moscow: Eksmo Yauza 2004) 33 et seq.

studies on this subject, e.g. by Schweisfurth and Grzybowsky. However, the historical discussion here raises the possibility that there was more to Soviet idiosyncratic approaches to international law than the application of Marxism-Leninism. There was a Russian 'civilizational' element to Soviet approaches to international law and Russia's determination to distance itself from the West after having been a disciple of a 'more enlightened' (Martens) Europe for 200 years. It is fascinating to see that when Taube pointed out that Byzantium held that it could by definition only wage just wars, the same was essentially argued in the context of Marxism-Leninism regarding socialist countries.[234]

During the Soviet period, F. F. Martens continued to be remembered as one of the founders of international law scholarship in Russia but the liberal part of his programme entirely failed in his Russian context. After the Bolsheviks came to power in 1917, Russia became a major illiberal power for the whole Soviet period. Martens and his disciples from St Petersburg's European school were unable to bridge the ideological gulf that had already emerged between Russia and liberal Western Europe in the course of the nineteenth century.

1917 also meant another major turn for Russia: while initially, in the 1920s and 1930s, Soviet Russia isolated itself from the West or was isolated by the West, after World War II it became the main propagandist and flag bearer of the anti-colonial and anti-Western camp in the context of international law. In contrast, before 1917 imperial Russia was a major participant in and benefactor of the European discourse that international law was the cultural achievement of European civilized nations, and only them. The enduring legacy depicting this era are the paintings of Vasily Vasilyevich Vereshchagin (1842–1904) in Moscow's Tretyakov Gallery, portraying the Russian Army's advances in Central Asia in an 'Orientalist' fashion.

As a consequence, in post-Soviet Russian public discourse there are two quite different ways of talking about the concept of 'civilization' and 'civilized states' in the context of international law. Writers who want to distance themselves from the West can refer to the concept of 'civilized states' sarcastically, implying that this has primarily been a West European supremacist, not a Russian historical idea in the context of international law and relations.[235] Representatives of this school may celebrate Martens as a Russian who 'made it' in the global/Western discourse of international law but they are not willing to acknowledge the colonial European side in the historical legacy of Martens and Russia.

Alternatively, one can refer to 'civilized states' positively, as still an unachieved (Western-influenced) cultural ideal towards which Russia should aspire and from which it should learn from or go back to.[236] If some behaviour or phenomenon is not right, it is still said that it is 'uncivilized'.

[234] Cf I. A. Umnova, *Pravo mira: kurs lektsii* (Moscow: Eksmo, 2011) 183.

[235] Melkov, *Mezhdunarodnoe pravo*, 186.

[236] See e.g. Marochkin in Valeev, Kurdyukov, *Mezhdunarodnoe pravo*, 53 ('pursuit of the construction of a civilized rule of law state'); V. Zorkin, *Rossia i Konstitutsia v XXI veke*, 2nd edn (Moscow: Norma, 2008) 16 (European countries and the US as a 'so-called civilized community') at 411 ('In the entire civilized world, the position of judge is the height of the legal career'); Lukashuk, *Mezhdunarodnoe pravo. Obshaya chast'*, 280 (human rights as the 'main general principle

Thus, the concept of 'civilization' remains relevant in the Russian normative discourse—for example, President Putin in his Valdai Club speech in October 2014, emphasized the importance of 'civilized dialogue' and asked rhetorically what was the 'civilized way of solving problems' between Russia and the West.[237]

One avenue that has not yet been fully explored by scholars is the connection between the reception of international law and the state of domestic law in Russia—or anywhere outside Europe/the West. *Ius publicum europaeum* also emerged from certain domestic conceptions of both public law and contract and it is unlikely that, in countries where similar concepts of domestic law remained underdeveloped, international law was perceived and applied exactly in the same way as in Western Europe. In the context of the history of law in Russia, Baron Taube has so far been the only one who raised the issue of the relevance of legal nihilism in Russian applications of international law.

Either way, during the period when Russia was officially wedded to European international law, this law was not 'universal' and excluded non-European/non-Christian nations. By a curious twist of history, both Turkey in 1856 and Japan in 1905 successfully gained access to the European-created system of international law, each following imperial Russia's military defeats (although Japan had already opened this door after the 1894–1895 Sino-Japanese War). There had already been plans to include the Ottomon Empire in the European state system in 1815 but they did not materialize, largely thanks to objections from Russian Tsar Alexander I.[238] Even in 1882, the international law scholar Martens ideologically objected to the idea of extending international law to the Ottoman Empire.[239]

If we ought to pin down Russia's history and interaction with international law to one single central theme that would capture most preoccupations, it would probably be the concept of 'territory' and the phenomenon of territorial acquisitions. Possibly in response to its cold climate and semi-peripheral status in the world economy, the Russian Empire became the global leader in territorial acquisitions. Here is an area where Western historical research on Russia can come to help explain conditions for Russia's historical attitudes towards international law as well. In particular, I am referring to the classic historical study of Richard Pipes, *Russia under the Old Regime*.

Pipes points out the amazing fact that between the middle of the sixteenth century and the end of the seventeenth, Muscovy acquired an area equivalent to the territory of modern Holland *every year for a consecutive 150 years*.[240] After Peter the Great integrated Russia with the European community of nations and its system of international law in the early eighteenth century, the territorial conquests of imperial Russia slowed down somewhat but still continued. During

of the law of civilized nations'); I. Z. Farkhutdinov, *Mezhdunarodnoe investitsionnoe pravo i protsess* (Moscow: Prospekt, 2013) at 111 ('private property as the foundation of any civilized economics').

[237] President of Russia, Meeting of the Valdai International Discussion Club, 24 October 2014, <http://eng.kremlin.ru/news/23137>.

[238] A. Bozeman, *The Future of Law in a Multicultural World* (Princeton: Princeton University Press, 1971) 50.

[239] Martens, *Sovremennoe mezhdunarodnoe pravo tsivilizovannykh narodov*, Vol. 1, 143–4.

[240] Pipes, *Russia under the Old Regime*, 83.

World War I, Russia and England concluded a secret treaty that in the case of common victory attributed Constantinople to the Russian Empire. Apparently, classical international law was a singularly useful tool because it facilitated territorial conquest or at least was unable to limit it beyond the concept of the balance of power.

In Russian historiography, there has always been a tendency to see these territorial conquests as 'normal', necessary, and progressive. Pipes, who wrote during the Cold War era, made ironic comments about Soviet historians who justified all Russia's conquests as 'national tasks':

> ...it is difficult to accept the proposition that Russia needed a powerful modern army in order to realize alleged 'national tasks': recovery from the Poles of the lands which had once been part of the Kievan state, and access to warm-water ports. It is a matter of historical record that realization of both these 'tasks' in the course of the eighteenth century did nothing to assuage Russia's appetite for land.... Since it is always possible to justify new conquests on the ground that they are required to protect the old—the classic justification for all imperialisms—explanations of this kind can be safely discounted: the logical sequence of such reasoning is mastery of the globe, for only at that point can any state be said to be fully protected from external threats to its possessions.[241]

However, the same logic of justification has not disappeared from Russian international law scholarship—for example, Pavel Nikolaevich Biryukov (b. 1966) from Voronezh State University writes in his textbook of international law that in the eighteenth century, 'Russia solved the Turkish and Swedish problems...using contradictions among Western states.'[242]

Thus, the picture that emerges in Pipes's analysis is less rosy about Russia's benevolent role in the historical development of international law as it is a popular position in the country's scholarship:

> Having been eminently successful in acquiring power through the accumulation of real estate, [the country's sovereigns] tended to identify political power through the accumulation of real estate, they tended to identify political power with the growth of territory, and the growth of territory with absolute, domainial authority. The idea of an international state system with its corollary, balance of power, formulated in the west in the seventeenth century, remained foreign to their way of thinking. So did the idea of reciprocal relations between state and society.[243]

According to Pipes, one consequence of treating sovereign territory as the ruler's private possession was that, compared to Western Europe, civil and human rights remained historically underdeveloped in Russia.[244] Moreover, mainly due to the organization of landownership, collective values (*sobornost'*) remained culturally predominant in Russia as opposed to individualist and rights-oriented values in the West.[245]

[241] Ibid., 118.
[242] P. N. Biryukov, *Mezhdunarodnoe pravo*, 5th edn (Moscow: Yurait, 2011) 51.
[243] Pipes, *Russia under the Old Regime*, 84.
[244] Ibid., 51–2, 105, 111, 137–8.
[245] Ibid., 267.

Of course the Russian Eurasianists and nativists would counter such critical interpretations of Russian history in the context of international law by saying that most Western historians are negatively biased regarding Russia.[246] The argument would a fortiori be held against Baltic researchers. However, unless one is willing to focus on concrete facts and arguments rather than use the disqualifying *argumentum ad hominem*, it is impossible to reach any common ground about the historical role of the Russian state in international law and relations.

Altogether, Russia's history in the context of international law is not only history. One of the main questions of Russia's history—is she part of Europe or not—continues to play a decisive role in today's arguments and interpretations. A number of 'Slavophile' normative claims already made by Danilevsky continue to be popular in public discourse in contemporary Russia—e.g. that the West hypocritically measures Russia with 'double standards'[247] or that the West is 'aggressive' by nature.[248]

Today's Russia has inherited more from the past than is immediately visible to the eye. For example, historically in Russia (as well as in China) moralistic normative language has dominated over the legalistic,[249] referring to ideas of justice and fairness rather than legal rights *stricto sensu*. In the context of human rights, Olesya Zakharova from Irkutsk State University points out that today too Russian public discourse is focused on moral language in contrast to the more legalistic language of the West.[250] Finally, and not surprisingly, the Russian search for 'true' Europe continues also in the normative realm. Reacting to the conflict in (and over) Ukraine and the critical reactions of the West towards Moscow's actions, the publicist Yegor Kholmogorov concludes: 'Let's be frank: both our government and the majority of our society want to Europe. However, not to Europe of Merkel and Hollande but to Europe of Bismarck and Alexander III.'[251]

[246] A. Dugin, *Projekt Evraziya* (Moscow: Yauza EKSMO, 2004) 5 et seq.

[247] Danilevsky, *Rossia i Evropa*, 19, 51. See on Western or NATO's 'double standards' in Melkov, *Mezhdunarodnoe pravo*, 325, 685; G. V. Ignatenko, O. I. Tiunov (eds), *Mezhdunarodnoe pravo* (Moscow: Norma, 2013) 66 (referring to NATO); A. I. Filimonova (ed.), *Dvoinye standarty v zashite pravcheloveka. Kazus professor Sheshelya* (Moscow: 'Fond istoricheskoi perspektivy', 2009); G. M. Vel'iaminov, *Mezhdunarodnoe ekonomicheskoe pravo i protsess* (Moscow: Wolters Kluwer 2004) 32, 145; V. M. Shumilov, *Mezhdunarodnoe pravo*, 2nd edn (Moscow: 'Mezhdunarodnye otnoshenia', 2012) 102, 104, 193.

[248] In analysing the 2013 December anti-government protests in Ukraine, the writer and politician Eduard Limonov came to the conclusion that the 'aggressive nature of the West has not changed'. See E. Limonov, 'Bitva za Ukrainu', *Izvestia*, 28.11.2013, <http://izvestia.ru/news/561521>. Discussing the history of international law, E. V. Safronova refers to the 'aggressive nature' of Germanic tribes in medieval Europe, in *Mezhdunarodnoe publichnoe pravo. Teoreticheskie problemy*, 30.

[249] See e.g. Ko Kwan Sik, 'The Establishment of Diplomatic Relations and the Scope of Diplomatic Immunity. The Dutch Experience with China', in J. A. Cohen (ed.), *China's Practice of International Law. Some Case Studies* (Cambridge, MA: Harvard University Press, 1972), 57–85 at 85.

[250] O. Zakharova, 'Na raznykh yazykakh. Evropa apelliruet k pravovym tsennostiam, Rossia—k moral'no-nravstevennym', 25.03.2013 *Nezavisimaya gazeta*, <http://www.ng.ru/ideas/2013-03-25/9_values.html>.

[251] Y. Kholmogorov, 'Organizatsia pobezhdennykh natsii', *Izvestia*, 27.10.2014. <http://izvestia.ru/news/578574>.

In the following, we should examine what the collapse of the USSR and Russia's declared 'return to Europe' meant for international legal thinking in the country. Obviously, Marxism-Leninism withered away—but what thinking came instead and how does the state of international legal theory still reflect previous historical discussions and arguments?

3

Theory of International Law in Contemporary Russia

'Ideological and class struggle may not lie at the foundation of peaceful international relations.'[1]

'It would be erroneous to think that with the end of the Cold War the ideological struggle also ended.'[2]

'To the contrary, humanitarian sciences, including international law, are the arena of the harshest ideological struggle. More than that, lately the ideological component of international law has increased, not decreased. . . .'[3]

In this part of the study, we shall leave the history of international legal scholarship behind and move to the theoretical construction of international law in contemporary Russia. How is international law understood, theorized and construed in the country's expert circles? Is the way international law is seen and theorized different from or similar to previous Soviet or, on the other hand, today's Western approaches? In this chapter, I will expose how the predominant philosophy of international law and relations in contemporary Russia shapes the understanding of concrete issues in international law.

1. The Debatable Nexus between Legal Scholarship and State Practice of International Law in Russia

To start with, it is worth contemplating what the role of international law scholarship in Russia has been. In fact, one could ask: what has it been anywhere?

[1] K. A. Bekyashev (ed.), *Mezhdunarodnoe publichnoe pravo* (Moscow: Prospekt, 2003) 352.

[2] Y. M. Kolosov, E. S. Krivchikova (eds), *Mezhdunarodnoe pravo*, 2nd edn (Moscow: 'Mezhdnarodnye otnoshenia', 2005) 561. I. I. Lukashuk in *Mezhdunarodnoe pravo. Obshaya chast'* (Moscow: Beck, 2001) at 47, writes in the same vein: 'Theory of international law remains an important field of ideological struggle.'

[3] S. V. Bakhin, 'Razmyshleniya o nauchnom nasledii professora R.L. Bobrova (k 100–letiu dnya rozhdenia), in *Materialy nauchno-prakticheski konferentsii 'Mezhdunarodnoe pravo: vchera, segodnya, zavtra', 8–9 oktyabrya 2010.g. K 100–letiyu so dnya rozhdenia professora Romana L'vovicha Bobrova* (St Petersburg: 'Rossiya-Neva', 2011), 28–40 at 35.

Concerning Tsarist Russia, Hrabar already offered historical insights into how the discipline of international law historically kicked off; how it emerged when Russia (re)joined Europe in around 1700.

Hrabar also delicately revealed the impact of Russia's authoritarianism on the evolution of the discipline of international law. Jiři Toman, who analysed Soviet and Tsarist approaches to international humanitarian law, starts with the—by then—almost axiomatic observation that international legal scholarship had historically not been 'free' in Russia.[4]

During the Soviet period, Western international law experts assumed that state views and scholarly doctrine in the USSR were more or less identical, and that Soviet scholarship merely explained and legitimized Moscow's official views—in fact, that this was its *raison d'être*.[5] The suggestion that such a state of affairs was always the case in Russia and that legal scholars there had not been free echoes strongly in Western discussions of Tsarist era international lawyers such as Martens.[6]

In retrospect, it appears that at least in international law scholarship there was more scholarly freedom in late Tsarist Russia than in the USSR. A recent monograph on the history of international law published in Ukraine cites the example that while the Tsarist government had a conservative approach toward the extradition of criminals (claiming extradition also for political crimes but for liberals too many activities qualified as crimes at that time), some Russian international law scholars held more progressive views, supporting the exception of political crimes to extradition.[7] During almost all of the Soviet period such a gap between the government's and scholarly views would have been unimaginable. Again, Pipes was correct when he observed that 'the Communists... deprived Russian culture of that freedom of expression which it had managed to win for itself under the imperial regime'.[8]

Of course, minor disagreements and factions existed even in Soviet international law scholarship.[9] However, after the controversial Evgenyi Bronislavovich Pashukanis (1891–1937) was 'liquidated' by Stalin's regime[10] any such differences were better hidden from the outside world. In any case, there was indeed a strong connection between the Soviet foreign policy programme and the concepts that Soviet international law scholarship promoted.

[4] J. Toman, *L'Union soviétique et le droit des conflits armés* (Ph.D., Geneva, 1997) 7.

[5] T. Schweisfurth, *Sozialistisches Völkerrecht? Darstellung—Analyse—Wertung der sowjetmarxistischen Theorie vom Völkerrecht 'neuen Typs'* (Berlin: Springer, 1979) 39, 556 et seq.

[6] See A. Nussbaum, 'Frederic de Martens. Representative Tsarist Writer on International Law', 22 *Nordisk Tidsskrift International Ret og Jus Gentium* 1952, 51–66.

[7] A. I. Dmitriev, W. E. Butler (eds), *Istoria mezhdunarodnoga prava* (Odessa: Feniks, 2013) 290.

[8] R. Pipes, *Russia under the Old Regime*, 2nd edn (London: Penguin Books, 1993) 280.

[9] For example, in 1964, Tunkin entrusted to his diary that Kozhevnikov, Korovin, and Blishtshenko opposed him in the Soviet Association of International Law. See W. E. Butler, V. G. Tunkin (eds), *The Tunkin Diary and Lectures* (The Hague: Eleven International Publishing, 2012) 26.

[10] See further J. N. Hazard, 'Cleansing Soviet International Law of Anti-Marxist Theories', 32 *AJIL* 1938, 244–52.

A random but quite characteristic example is what Anatoly Nikolayevich Talalaev (1928–2001) wrote about Soviet treaty practice, apparently without irony:

> The USSR always impeccably fulfils its treaty and other international obligations and demands precisely the same also from other states. [11]

The best way to understand the difference between the Soviet scholarly approach and US approaches at the time is to compare the statement made by Talalaev for example with works by US international law scholars Wolfgang Friedmann (1907–72) or Louis Henkin (1917–2010) in which criticism of Soviet violations of international law goes along with discussion of US violations, even though both authors ultimately concluded that all negative counter-examples aside, the 'free world' had a tendency to behave in a more law-abiding way than the totalitarian USSR.[12] However, during the Cold War US scholarly discourse on international law also included more radical and critical Left voices such as Richard A. Falk (b. 1930), who has challenged a number of US practices in international law.[13] The bottom line is that such a discourse has been possible in the US—while it has not, for most of modern history, been possible in Russia.

In post-Soviet Russian scholarship, the previous practice of never admitting to any of the country's violations of international law shows some signs of modification. For example, the textbook of international law edited by Melkov, after listing US Cold war-era aggression such as against Nicaragua and Grenada, admits that the USSR committed aggression against Finland in 1939 and Afghanistan in 1979.[14]

Soviet scholarship had a geopolitical trait that was sometimes hidden behind high-minded rhetoric. In the West scholars pondered what exactly the Soviet concept of 'peaceful coexistence' meant[15] since the Soviets insisted that of all principles of international law, this was the most central during the Cold War period.[16] However, here is how Grigory I. Tunkin from Moscow State University saw it in his diary on 18 September 1967:

> The day before yesterday the XXII Session of the General Assembly opened. The [Romanian] Minister of Foreign Affairs, Manescu, was elected President of the Assembly. For the first time a representative of a socialist country had become the President of the General Assembly. The situation which had existed did not correspond very much to the principle of peaceful coexistence.[17]

[11] A. N. Talalaev, *Pravo mezhdunarodnykh dogovorov*, 2 vols (Moscow: Garant, 2011) 4; reprint of a work initially published in the 1980s.

[12] L. Henkin, *How Nations Behave*, 2nd edn (New York: Praeger, 1979) 113–14; W. Friedmann, *The Changing Structure of International Law* (New York: Columbia University Press, 1964) 268.

[13] R. A. Falk (ed.), *The Vietnam War and International Law* (Princeton: Princeton University Press, 1970).

[14] G. M. Melkov (ed.), *Mezhdunarodnoe pravo* (Moscow: RIOR, 2009) 84, 621.

[15] See e.g. B. Ramundo, *Peaceful Coexistence: International Law in the Building of Communism* (Baltimore: Johns Hopkins Press, 1967).

[16] See R. M. Valeev, G. I. Kurdykov (eds) *Mezhdunarodnoe pravo. Obshaya chast'* (Moscow: Statut, 2011) 50.

[17] Butler, Tunkin, *The Tunkin Diary and Lectures*, 42.

Thus, international legal theory (such as the concept of 'peaceful coexistence') in practice served quite a realist purpose and was meant to support the balance of power, including concessions from the historically over-powerful West.[18]

At the same time, as Igor I. Lukashuk has pointed out, the Russian Ministry of Foreign Affairs and leaders of legal academia in Russia may have been more separated from each other during the overly ideological Soviet period than they are nowadays.[19] While Russia's 1993 Foreign Policy Concept was apparently exclusively written by Ministry officials, from 2000 onwards Russia's leading scholars of international law and relations have been asked to contribute to subsequent editions of the Foreign Policy Concept.[20] Lukashuk further argues that effective state policy needs a scientific basis and that in international law the interrelationship between theory and practice is particularly tense.[21] Moreover, Lukashuk has held that from the perspective of Russian doctrine of international law, this law remained an 'instrument' of foreign policy.[22]

In any case, after the most recent Concept of the Foreign Policy of the Russian Federation was adopted on 12 February 2013, Oleg Nikolaevich Khlestov (b. 1923), Professor of International Law at the Diplomatic Academy in Moscow and long-time director of the international treaty department at the Ministry of Foreign Affairs of the USSR, and also the head of the Soviet delegation at the Vienna conference on the law of international treaties in 1969, published an article on the Russian doctrine of international law in which he claims:

> International legal doctrine is closely connected with the foreign policy doctrine of the state, its foreign policy, and usually reflects the goals and tasks that the latter pursues in the international arena.... Depending on the character of the foreign policy of the state, the doctrine gives bigger or smaller importance to certain or other norms of international law.[23]

According to Khlestov, Western states have massively violated international law in Libya and Syria and now Russia needs to do more to defend international law, partly because 'contemporary international law' (i.e. of the UN Charter) 'corresponds to the national interests of Russia'.[24] In this context, Khlestov calls on Russian international law doctrine to further be 'progressive' and have a positive impact on the foreign and domestic policies of the Russian Federation.[25] Khlestov also emphasizes the continuity between Soviet and post-Soviet Russian international legal doctrines and concludes:

> The Russian doctrine of international law is progressive. In many ways, it corresponds to the official positions of our country.[26]

[18] For a similar understanding, see C. Osakwe, *The Participation of the Soviet Union in Universal International Organizations. A Political and Legal Analysis of Soviet Strategies and Aspirations inside ILO, UNESCO and WHO* (Leiden: A.W. Sijthoff, 1972) 35 et seq.

[19] I. I. Lukashuk, *Sovremennoe pravo mezhdunarodnykh dogovorov*, Vol. 1 (Moscow: Wolters Kluwer, 2004) 24.

[20] Ibid., 36. [21] Ibid., 44–5.

[22] Lukashuk, *Mezhdunarodnoe pravo. Obshaya chast'*, 41.

[23] O. N. Khlestov, 'Rossiiskaya doktrina mezhdunarodnoga prava', 3 *Evraziiskii juridicheskii zhurnal* (58) 2013, 19–22 at 19.

[24] Ibid., 20–1. [25] Ibid., 21. [26] Ibid., 22.

At the annual meeting of the Russian Association of International Law in Moscow in June 2013, a resolution along the lines suggested by Khlestov's article and speech on the Russian doctrine of international law was adopted by the plenary of the Association.[27] The Association had earlier adopted resolutions taking a clear stance on 'political' issues as well, e.g. in 2006 condemning certain activities of the ICTY.[28]

In March 2014 during the Crimea crisis, Khlestov was the first Russian international law scholar who publicly argued that Russia's intervention in Crimea corresponded to international law, and moreover, that the West was not in a position to criticize Moscow because it had itself violated international law in Kosovo, Iraq, and elsewhere.[29]

Looking at the approach advocated by Khlestov, not so much has changed since the Soviet period or perhaps not from Shafirov who made his arguments as a self-proclaimed 'slave' of Peter the Great. Some leading international lawyers of the older generation in Russia see it as their vocation to support the Kremlin with all the weight of the 'science' of international law. In the Russian language, the discipline of international law is indeed called a 'science' (*nauka*) in the same way as are astronomy or chemistry, which in the eyes of a layman might add to it some additional authority and certainty.

Making the government the holder of the truth is the opposite of the approach that for example the critical US international law scholar David Kennedy has suggested international lawyers as experts should take: speaking truth to power.[30] However, maybe this is exactly the intended point since Russian international law scholars and diplomats such as Khlestov now see global power—to which Russia must tell the 'multilateral truth'—as being situated in and abused by the US.

Khlestov's approach has a following among some younger scholars as well—for example, Vladimir Mikhailovich Shumilov (b. 1954), international law professor at the All-Russian Academy of Foreign Trade of the Ministry of Economic Development of the Russian Federation, argues that the Russian doctrine of international law 'creatively and by taking the initiative uses international legal instruments in the reorganization of the world order and securing the interests of Russia and post-Soviet states'.[31] Moreover, Shumilov maintains that state interests and international law are 'notions that are closely connected with each other'.[32]

[27] See L. V. Korbut, 'Analiticheskii obzor raboty 56–go Ezhegodnogo Sobrania Rossiiskoi Assotsiatsii mezhdunarodnoga prava 26–28 iunya 2013.g', in *Rossiiskyi ezhegodnik mezhdunarodnoga prava 2013* (St Petersburg: 'Rossiya-Neva', 2014) 409.

[28] See A. B. Mezyaev, *Pravo obvinyaemogo v mezhdunarodnom ugolovnom prave* (Kazan: 'TISBI', 2010) 65.

[29] See interview with Prof Khlestov, <https://www.youtube.com/watch?v=ovVJqGtEBG8&list=UUAYiTNgrhlJ0yQXdhW7ZVLg>.

[30] D. Kennedy, *The Dark Sides of Virtue. Reassessing International Humanitarianism* (Princeton: Princeton University Press, 2004) 345.

[31] V. M. Shumilov, *Mezhdunarodnoe pravo*, 2nd edn (Moscow: 'Mezhdunarodnye otnoshenia', 2012) 15.

[32] Ibid., 26.

Nevertheless, the attitude propagated by Khlestov is no longer necessarily characteristic of all international law experts in post-Soviet Russia. Compared to the Soviet period, the level of academic freedom has grown and space to disagree and to be less servile to government positions has grown among scholars. Not all international law scholars may want to support the government's line in such an obvious way as Khlestov has suggested. For example, the textbook by Irina Viktorovna Get'man-Pavlova of Moscow's Higher School of Economics praises the 'Western democracies' for having included human rights in the body of international law, advocates closer Russian integration with NATO and criticizes the discourse of Russian political leaders on a number of occasions (e.g. its blocking attitude to the Kosovo crisis in 1999, its overreaction to the Markin case in the ECtHR in 2010).[33] In a common article, two younger attorneys implicitly raise doubts about the legality of Russia's annexation of Crimea and remind the government that international law should apply to all states, i.e. including Russia.[34]

In this light, Khlestov's call to arms regarding the Russian doctrine of international law could also be interpreted as an attempt to make things the way they used to be, and to knock on the patriotic consciousness of the upcoming generation of Russian international law scholars.

At the same time, since Putin's Russia is increasingly seen as an autocracy and the freedom of NGOs as well as academia has recently been restricted, it would be naive to presume that no political constraints exist for international law scholarship in Russia.

Moreover, the arrival of more academic freedom in Russia compared to the Soviet period does not necessarily mean that international law scholars will inevitably be more liberal than the government. Sometimes the opposite is the case and Russian scholars of international law criticize their government for *not* having been tough and principled enough in protecting Russia's interests, especially vis-à-vis the US and the West.

For example, Gennady Mikhailovich Melkov (b. 1932) insists in his textbook of international law that the Russian State Duma should not ratify the 1990 USSR–US (Shevardnadze–Baker) agreement on maritime delimitation in the Bering Sea because the agreement was not favourable to Russia.[35] Moreover, he criticizes the Energy Charter Treaty of 1994 (an investment protection treaty between West and East European countries), that Russia signed but did not ratify, for not being in Russia's interests.[36] Finally, Melkov criticizes the fact that representatives of the Russian government participated in drafting the 1994 San Remo Manual on International Law applicable to Armed Conflicts at Sea although its stipulations are 'clearly detrimental to

[33] I. Get'man-Pavlova, *Mezhdunarodnoe pravo*, 2nd edn (Moscow: Yurait, 2013) 56, 136, 274, 301.

[34] M. Davletbaev, M. Isayeva, 'Arkhaichnyi iazyk rossiiskoi diplomatii', *Vedomosti*, 13.08.2014, <http://www.vedomosti.ru/opinion/news/32059251/arhaichnyj-yazyk-rossijskoj-diplomatii>.

[35] Melkov, *Mezhdunarodnoe pravo*, 189.

[36] Ibid., 367.

Russia' in the context of neutrality rules and concerning the types of prohibited torpedoes.[37]

Not only scholars comment on governmental activities but people in the government can be active publicists while in public office. In contemporary Russia, the most noteworthy example is Valery Zorkin, Chairman of the Constitutional Court of the Russian Federation, who while being the country's top judge also acts as its chief legal ideologue. Zorkin regularly publishes articles in *Rossiiskaya gazeta* on legal-political matters and even writes reaction papers to the work of legal scholars.[38]

It is striking that Judge Zorkin is polemically very active and often passes sharp judgments. Yet at the same time he has lamented that critical constitutional law scholarship lacks teeth in Russia; that Russian constitutional law scholarship has not been sufficiently up to the task of offering 'serious analyses' of the judgments of the Constitutional Court of the RF[39] and in this sense, scholars have failed to fulfil the role of 'expressing the views of Russian society'.[40]

However, bearing in mind the history of authoritarianism in Russia, how likely do public law scholars look forward to hearing it in public from the Chairman of the Constitutional Court in person that their ideas are 'wrong'? Maybe it would be more benevolent for the development of critical legal scholarship in Russia if the Chairman of the Constitutional Court himself exercised more polemical restraint, and let the judgments of the Court speak for themselves? In any case, in summer 2014 the Constitutional Court already had to decide on a citizen's complaint in this regard but came to the conclusion that the Court's Chairman had the right to enlighten the citizens of Russia with his articles.[41]

It seems that governments are particularly prone to turn to academic international lawyers in times of major foreign policy crises. For example, the governments of the Russian Federation, Germany, and France stood firmly against the US-led intervention in Iraq in March 2003. Presidents Putin and Chirac as well as Chancellor Schröder met in April 2003 at St Petersburg State University Faculty of Law where Putin as well as Dmitry Anatolyevich Medvedev had been students and where Chancellor Schröder was about to receive his honorary doctorate. Resembling a nineteenth-century gathering of European continental Emperors worried about balance of power issues, the three top leaders of their countries discussed matters of international law together with a selected group of international law scholars.

[37] Ibid., 617.

[38] See e.g. V. D. Zorkin, *Konstitutsionno-pravovoe razvitie Rossii* (Moscow: Norma, 2011); *Konstitutsia i prava cheloveka v XXI veke. K 15–letiu Konstitutsii Rossiiskoi Federatsii i 60–letiu Vseobshei deklaratsii prav cheloveka* (Moscow: Norma, 2008); *Rossia i Konstitutsia v XXI veke*, 2nd edn (Moscow: Norma, 2008).

[39] Zorkin, *Konstitutsionno-pravovoe razvitie*, 887.

[40] Ibid., 688.

[41] A. Kornya, 'Konstitutsionnyi sud ne nashel politiki v stat'yakh svoego predsedatelya', *Kommersant*, 04.08.2014, <http://www.vedomosti.ru/politics/news/30942521/politprosvet-ot- zorkina>.

In his opening statement, President Putin encouraged the scholars who had gathered at the symposium:

> Now as never before it is important to rely on the opinion of the expert community—lawyers, political scientists, specialists in different fields of international relations... We, of course, will impatiently wait for the results of your work, fresh ideas, suggestions.[42]

Whatever the agendas and motives, it is not every day that international law scholars get this kind of attention from Presidents in office.

Even in old democracies with an established tradition of free speech, it is questionable whether state practice and international law scholarship are so separated from each other as the academic self-image sometimes suggests. Often, accomplished experts in the field of international law combine careers as scholars and diplomats, state representatives, governmental advisers, judges, participants in international codification efforts, and so on. Carlo Focarelli is quite explicit in this regard when he observes that 'most lawyers tend to align with their government's view and to make a case for its action'.[43] Thus, it is fair to point out that it is not a specific Russian phenomenon.

In countries of the continental European tradition—and Europeanizing Tsarist Russia borrowed historically particularly from Prussia's model—law professors at state universities have anyway been appointed by the government, making them something like a specific type of civil servants in the eyes of domestic law.

It must be borne in mind that scholars in the West have globally certain comparative advantages to start with—they benefit from the dominant position of English (and to a lesser extent, French) in the global discourse of international law, and from the fact that almost all important institutions of international law are situated in the West.

In this sense, the role of academic international lawyers may differ in the global centre from in the peripheries or semi-peripheries; individual awards are brought home by different academic strategies. Scholars in the West do not *need* to talk about international law like Khlestov.

As an illustration of this still hegemonic position of the West, José E. Alvarez writes in the context of international investment law about the perception that:

> ...the existing arbitration world is essentially too cozy and consists of a small number of repeat players dominated by prominent legal academics in Europe and the United States, along with a handful of law firms in London, Paris, New York and Washington, DC ...[44]

[42] V. S. Ivanenko (ed.), *The International Scientifically Practical Conference 'The World, Safety (sic) and International Law: A Sight in the Future', St Petersburg, 12 April 2003* (St Petersburg: St Petersburg University Publishing House, 2004).

[43] C. Focarelli, *International Law as Social Construct. The Struggle for Global Justice* (Oxford: Oxford University Press, 2012) 135.

[44] J. E. Alvarez, *The Public International Law Regime Governing International Investment* (Leiden: Brill, 2011) 404. See also 427.

Perhaps then those legal academicians outside the West, who cannot break into this 'inner circle', are even more likely to actively support their home governments.

Of course, there are also other ways in which international law scholars and government interact. In Russia, lawyers among the politicians have learned about international law from Russian scholars. Professor Ludmila Nikiforovna Galenskaya (b. 1932) from St Petersburg State University has already received two beautiful *Festschrifts* by her international law colleagues showcasing the best of Russian international law scholarship.[45]

Sergei Vladimirovich Bakhin from the same university honours Galenskaya with the following praise:

> Her students work not only in leading scientific centers; there are even more those who work as practicing lawyers, in judicial bodies but also in the organs of state power.[46]

Most expert readers of these lines in Russia would know that one of Professor Galenskaya's students in Leningrad was Vladimir Vladimirovich Putin who graduated from Leningrad State University in 1975, submitting a thesis on 'The Most Favoured Nation Trading Principle in International Law'.

Historically, the paths of international legal scholars and future political leaders have crossed too. Taking law exams as an extern at St Petersburg Imperial University, Vladimir Ulyanov/Lenin (1870–1924) gave his international law exam to Martens although admittedly this brief encounter did not turn the young Ulyanov into a liberal.

Wilhelm Grewe has suggested that in the history of international law, the study of state practice and legal doctrine should go hand in hand because the two cannot be meaningfully separated.[47] Therefore, to sum up on this point, while it is important to distinguish between state practice/positions and scholarly doctrine and not to assume that scholars would automatically speak as 'state agents', we can nevertheless treat governmental and scholarly discourses on international law as interconnected. We may treat these two aspects together as different sides of international legal discourse in a particular country.

It is particularly insightful to discover disagreements between parts of the expert community and the government, and to reveal competition among experts in terms of whose strategic view on international law will be taken up by the government. Such debates spotlight significant political and philosophical dilemmas facing the country.

[45] S. V. Bakhin (ed.), *Public and Private International Law. Problems and Prospects: Liber Amicorum in Honour of Ludmila N. Galenskaya* (St Petersburg: Publishing House of St Petersburg State University, 2007); S. V. Bakhin (ed.), *International Relations and Law. A Look into the XXI Century: Materials of Conference in Honour of Professor Ludmila N. Galenskaya* (St Petersburg: Publishing House of St Petersburg State University, 2009).

[46] S. V. Bakhin, 'Predislovie', in Bakhin, *Public and Private International Law*, 13.

[47] W. Grewe, *Epochen der Völkerrechtsgeschichte* (Baden-Baden: Nomos, 1984) 21.

2. Post-Soviet Russian Scholarship of International Law: Some Basic Facts

To continue, some historical and sociological facts about international law scholarship in post-Soviet Russia should be mentioned. After the collapse of the USSR in 1991, the Soviet Association of International Law, which had been established in 1957 at the initiative of Grigory Ivanovich Tunkin, was named the Russian Association of International Law.[48] The Association's main periodical publication—the *Soviet Yearbook of International Law*, now the *Russian Yearbook of International Law*—is published in Russian and its editor is currently Lyudmila N. Galenskaya.

Other main periodicals in the field of international law are the *Moscow Journal of International Law* (formerly *Soviet Journal of International Law*),[49] the *Russian Law Journal* (*Rossiiskii yuridicheskii zhurnal*),[50] and the *Eurasian Law Journal* (*Evraziiskii juridicheskii zhurnal*).[51] The latter is an interesting phenomenon because it seems to promote a clear political agenda for Eurasian integration in the CIS countries and beyond. However, the quality of its content seems to vary too much. Perhaps the most Western-style international law journal is the relatively new *Mezhdunarodnoe pravosudie* (International Justice)[52] which *inter alia* focuses on international court practice, detailed analysis of which is otherwise often neglected in Russian scholarship. Less regularly published is the *Kazan Journal of International Law*.

Although in Russia there are no university rankings that explicitly focus on international law, it can be said that the leading academic institutions in the field of international law are the Diplomatic Academy of the Russian MFA, the MGIMO University of the Russian MFA, and the Faculties of Law of Moscow State University, St Petersburg State University, and Kazan State University. The other academic institutions where Russia's leading international law scholars work are the Kutafin State Law University, the Peoples' Friendship University, the Institute of State and Law of the Russian Academy of Sciences, the Higher School of Economics (all in Moscow), the Urals Law Academy in Yekaterinburg, Voronezh State University, Tyumen State University, Immanuel Kant University in Kaliningrad, and the Far Eastern Federal University in Vladivostok.

In the following, I will examine the theory and doctrine of international law mostly in Russian textbooks and monographs of international law, less so in scholarly articles—for the simple reason that covering journal articles as well would explode the scope of the study. Nevertheless, I believe that what is discussed as

[48] For the Association's membership directory, see S. V. Bakhin (ed.) *Rossiiskaya Assotsiatsia Mezhdunarodnoga Prava 1957–2007. Biograficheskii slovar'* (St Petersburg: Publishing House of St Petersburg State University, 2007). Throughout this study, I have taken the birth (and, if applicable, death) dates of Soviet and Russian scholars from this directory.

[49] See <http://www.mjil.ru/index_eng.htm>.

[50] <http://www.ruzh.org/>.

[51] See <http://www.eurasialaw.ru/>.

[52] See <http://ilpp.ru/journal/mp/>.

most important can be detected from a reading of monographs and textbooks since book-length studies continue to reflect the utmost intellectual effort in international law scholarship. Those who wish to go even deeper into specific issues can further consult the bibliography of scholarly articles as well. [53]

3. The Distinction between 'Native' and 'Western' in Russian Scholarship of International Law

One thing that can at the outset be observed about international law scholars in contemporary Russia is that the scholarly community continues to be linguistically and network-wise relatively distinct and separated from international law scholars in the West. Any look at the geographic distribution of speakers at annual conferences of the American Society of International Law, European Society of International Law, or even the Russian Association of International Law will prove this point.

Russian-speaking scholars of international law form a separate epistemological community that is tied together by a common language, history, and geographical space in the former USSR. The 'self-contained' nature of international law scholarship in Russia has roots in the Soviet period when the government with its isolationist attitudes created a parallel world to the West. This had repercussions, including in the world of science and scholarship.

Russian international law scholars are often first of all *Russian* international law scholars. Almost all contemporary Russian academic works on international law distinguish between 'native' (or: domestic, local, national, homegrown, indigenous) scholarship (*otechestvennaya doktrina; nauka; literatura*) and 'foreign' or 'Western' scholarship[54] in much the same way as academic Soviet works differentiated between 'socialist' and 'bourgeois' (or 'Western') authors.[55] Moreover, Russian scholars often prefer to discuss the views of other 'native' rather than foreign authors, and sometimes explicitly say that they do so.[56]

[53] See L. N. Galenskaya, G. I. Kurdyukov, S.V. Bakhin (eds), *Mezhdunarodnoe pravo: Bibliographia. 1991–2005* (St Petersburg: 'Rossiya-Neva', 2010).

[54] See e.g. R. Kalamkaryan, Y. Migachev, *Mezhdunarodnoe pravo*, 2nd edn (Moscow: EKSMO, 2006) 15, 18, 25, 39, 62–4, 87, 131, 154–5; A. Kovalev, S. Chernichenko, *Mezhdunarodnoe pravo*, 3rd edn (Moscow: Prospekt, 2008) 26–31, 187, 214, 236–40; G. Ignatenko, O. Tiunov, *Mezhdunarodnoe pravo*, 6th edn (Moscow: Norma, 2013), 83; A. Kapustin, *Mezhdunarodnoe pravo* (Moscow: Gardariki, 2008) 39; Valeev, Kurdyukov, *Mezhdunarodnoe pravo. Obshaya chast'*, 15, 156, 373; Melkov, *Mezhdunarodnoe pravo*, 45; A. A. Moiseev, *Suverenitet gosudarstva v mezhdunarodnom prave* (Moscow: Vostok Zapad, 2009) 22, 37, 240, 297, 343; A. V. Naumov, A. G. Kibal'nik, V. N. Orlov, P. V. Volosyuk (eds), *Mezhdunarodnoe ugolovnoe pravo* (Moscow: Yurait, 2013) 38; G. M. Vel'iaminov, *Mezhdunarodnoe ekonomicheskoe pravo i protsess* (Moscow: Wolters Kluwer, 2004) iv, 37; A. N. Vylegzhanin (ed.), *Mezhdunarodnoe ekonomicheskoe pravo* (Moscow: 'Knorus', 2012) 17, 24, 32; E. T. Usenko, *Ocherki teorii mezhdunarodnoga prava* (Moscow: Norma, 2008) 37, 39, 48, 94, 124.

[55] See e.g. G. I. Tunkin, *Teoria mezhdunarodnoga prava* (Moscow: Zertsalo, 2009), original from 1970; 28, 80, 124.

[56] S. V. Chernichenko, *Teoria mezhdunarodnoga prava*, Vol. 2 (Moscow: NIMP, 1999) 6.

Sometimes, the 'native' doctrine simply becomes *the* doctrine—e.g. when Safronova discusses theoretical problems of international law,[57] the textbook edited by Valeev and Kurdykov discusses the concept of 'international control',[58] or Chebotareva discusses the notion of 'special principles' in international law.[59] Chernichenko's *Theory of International Law*, perhaps the theoretically most ambitious monograph of the Post-Soviet era, almost entirely refers to Soviet and Russian authors in the discipline of international law.[60]

The main message of such a nativist approach seems to be: we, i.e. Russian scholars, will need to settle first of all among ourselves how international law applies in and what it means *for our country*. It seems that by debating theoretical problems of international law, Russian authors are solving not just 'international' riddles but at least as importantly Russian ones as well. The notion of 'native doctrine' also conveniently builds a bridge between Soviet and post-Soviet scholarly works in Russia. Shumilov puts it most explicitly: it is not necessary to copy views represented in foreign schools; instead, it is better to have a critical approach to them.[61]

The distinction between 'native' and 'foreign' scholars is sometimes made even in unexpected junctures when one would prima facie not expect noteworthy differences in doctrine, e.g. when discussing what the principle of good faith means in international law.[62]

Occasionally, however, the distinction between 'foreign' and 'native' scholarship drives home a substantive comparative point—international law in Russia is understood or talked about differently from in the West. For example, Kolosov and Krivchikova argue in their textbook on international law that 'there is no right to intervention contrarily to what some representatives of foreign science of international law maintain, especially no right to "humanitarian intervention" '.[63] Chernichenko points out that Western and native authors have a different understanding of what the domestic affairs of a state include.[64] Georgi Mikhailovich Vel'iaminov (b. 1925) from the Institute of State and Law at the Russian Academy of Sciences and Pavel Nikolaevich Biryukov from Voronezh State University distinguish between 'foreign' and 'Russian' concepts of private international law,[65] and as we will see later, they are indeed somewhat different.

[57] E. V. Safronova, *Mezhdunarodnoe publichnoe pravo. Teoreticheskie problemy* (Moscow: RIOR Infra–M, 2013).

[58] L. Mingazov, in Valeev, Kurdyov, *Mezhdunarodnoe pravo. Obchaya chast'*, 289.

[59] I. A. Chebotareva, 'Ponyatie spetsial'nykh printsipov mezhdunarodnoga prava', in V. S. Bakhin (ed.), *Mezhdunarodnye otnoshenia i pravo: vzglyad v XXI vek* (St Petersburg: St Petersburg State University, 2009) 254–70.

[60] S. V. Chernichenko, *Teoria mezhdunarodnoga prava*, Vol. 1 (Moscow: NIMP, 1999) 12 et seq.

[61] Shumilov, *Mezhdunarodnoe pravo*, 525.

[62] Kalamkaryan, Migachev, *Mezhdunarodnoe pravo*, 87.

[63] Kolosov, Krivchikova, *Mezhdunarodnoe pravo*, 77.

[64] Chernichenko, *Teoria mezhdunarodnoga prava*, Vol. 1, at 182.

[65] Vel'iaminov, *Mezhdunarodnoe ekonomicheskoe pravo i protsess*, 46; P. N. Biryukov, *Mezhdunarodnoe pravo*, 5th edn (Moscow: Yurait, 2011) 28, 31.

One textbook of international law in which the distinction between 'native' and 'Western' is persistent is the textbook of the Diplomatic Academy of the Russian MFA, edited by Kovalev and Chernichenko. The authors conclude that Western doctrine has understood the prohibition of non-intervention in another sovereign's matters narrowly whereas Russia's 'native' doctrine has understood the same prohibition much more broadly.[66]

The Diplomatic Academy's textbook also points out that the establishment of a world government has been propagated by 'Western states' but will for objective reasons not arrive in the foreseeable 25–30 years.[67] Moreover, Western doctrine uses the concept 'international legislation' which is not used in Russian doctrine.[68] On some occasions, Western doctrine is singled out as incorrect, for example in the context of expatriation of nationals.[69] Some differences, however, are mostly linguistic-semantic—for example in Western doctrine, the concept of 'reparations' in the international law of state responsibility has been understood more broadly than in Russia.[70]

Altogether, it seems that the distinction between 'native' and 'foreign' scholarship is more popular among Russian authors who are more sceptical of the West and want to maintain the distance between Russia and the West. Sometimes, Anglo-Saxon doctrine is singled out as a particularly virulent form of Western international legal doctrine—for example when Vladimir Semenovich Kotlyar (b. 1933) concludes that the right to preventive and anticipatory self-defence is claimed only in 'Anglo-Saxon doctrine' but is not recognized elsewhere.[71]

To the extent that they regularly compare Western and 'native' theoretical and doctrinal approaches, Russian scholars systematically engage in comparative international law. In this sense, a number of Russian academic works of international law are far from parochial. It can be said that Russian authors have generally been more interested in Western scholarship of international law than has the West in Russian views on international law. Lukashuk has even observed:

> The monocultural approach is characteristic of the Anglo-American doctrine of international law. The theory and practice of other nations is little used in it.[72]

This is also by and large what Anthea Roberts in her forthcoming study on comparative international law has found regarding international law scholarship in the US.[73] In contrast, for example, the textbook of Valeev and Kurdyukov includes a chapter on international law in different legal systems of the world, including references to Africa and Islamic law.[74] Another example is the textbook by Kolosov

[66] A. A. Kovalev, S. V. Chernichenko, *Mezhdunarodnoe pravo*, 3rd edn (Moscow: Prospekt, 2008) 52.

[67] Ibid., 18.

[68] Ibid., 28. See further on this theme in J. E. Alvarez, *International Organizations as Law-Makers* (Oxford: OUP, 2005).

[69] Kovalev, Chernichenko, *Mezhdunarodnoe pravo*, 192.

[70] Ibid., 240.

[71] V. S. Kotlyar, *Mezhdunarodnoe pravo i sovremennye strategicheskie kontseptsii SShA i NATO*, 2nd edn (Kazan: Tsentr innovatsionnykh tekhnologii, 2008) 374.

[72] Lukashuk, *Mezhdunarodnoe pravo. Obshaya chast'*, 47.

[73] A. Roberts, *Is International Law International?* (Oxford: OUP, forthcoming).

[74] A. B. Mezyaev, in Valeev, Kurdyukov, *Mezhdunarodnoe pravo. Obshaya chast'*, 167–83.

and Krivchikova, which includes a chapter on religion and international law, discussing the interrelationship of the world's main religions and international law.[75]

At the same time, references to Western works in Russian treatises sometimes come with a time lag. For example the textbook edited by Kovalev and Chernichenko uses the Soviet Russian translation of Lassa Oppenheim's (1858–1919) textbook of international law (1948) as a 'Western example' for the claim that international public and private law must be kept conceptually apart.[76] Frequently, the preferred foreign doctrine is conveniently taken from textbooks translated into Russian during the Soviet period: Verdross,[77] Anzilotti,[78] Brownlie,[79] and the Uruguayan lawyer and ICJ President Jiménez de Aréchaga.[80]

In the early Soviet period, Soviet Russian scholars used to make comparisons with views represented in scholarship in the capitalist West. Boris N. Mamlyuk and Ugo Mattei have even argued that Soviet Russian scholars such as Yevgeni Aleksandrovich Korovin (1892–1964) were in some ways pioneers in the academic and political project of comparative international law.[81] Nevertheless, post-Soviet Russian scholars' genuine interest in the West as Russia's powerful historical Other has to their minds not led to a convergence and melding of the Western and Russian schools of international law into one 'global' international law scholarship.

In the West, there has been discussion as to what extent US and European scholarship and international legal worldviews have drifted apart from each other since the end of the Cold War but in the perception of Russian scholarship, *zapad* (the West) usually remains a coherent *zapad* and includes both Western Europe and the US.

In Russian scholarship of international law, one consequence of extensive nativism is the perspective in which the role of Russian scholars in the global world of scholarship seems much bigger than in the West, where the contribution by the Russians has been relatively little noticed during the first two post-Soviet decades. However, Shumilov, after establishing that the Russian school of international law steps up with 'uniform positions' simply concludes that it is 'one of the best in the world'.[82]

For example, the MGIMO textbook on 'European International Law' draws the following balance on scholars who have contributed to the field of international law in Europe:

> Scholars from all European states have made considerable contributions to the development of European international law. Among them one may mention such Russian

[75] Y. E. Karlov, in Kolosov, Krivchikova, *Mezhdunarodnoe pravo*, 572–94.

[76] Kovalev, Chernichenko, *Mezhdunarodnoe pravo*, 92.

[77] A. Verdross, *Mezhdunarodnoe pravo* (Moscow: Inostrannaya literatura, 1959).

[78] D. Anzilotti, *Kurs mezhdunarodnoga prava* (Moscow: Pravovedenie, 1961).

[79] I. Brownlie, *Mezhdunarodnoe pravo (v dvukh knigakh)* (Moscow: 'Progress', 1977).

[80] E. Jimenez de Arechaga, *Sovremennoe mezhdunarodnoe pravo* (Moscow: 'Progress', 1983).

[81] B. N. Mamlyuk, U. Mattei, 'Comparative International Law', 36 *Brooklyn Journal of International Law* 2011, 385–452, at 390 et seq.

[82] Shumilov, *Mezhdunarodnoe pravo*, 106, 525.

scholars as V. E. Hrabar, G. I. Tunkin, S. B. Krylov, V. N. Durdenevskyi, F. I. Kozhevnikov, G. I. Morozov, E. A. Shibaeva, I. I. Lukashuk, N. A. Ushakov, E. A. Korovin, I. P. Blistshenko, D. B. Levin, R. L. Bobrov, L. A. Modzhoryan, Y. Ya. Baskin, D. I. Feldman, S. A. Malinin, V. I. Kuznetsov, G. P. Zhukov, E. T. Usenko, Y. M. Kolosov, E. S. Krivchikova, S. V. Molodtsov, S. V. Chernichenko, A. L. Kolodkin, and many others.

From foreign authors one may mention such scholars as V. M. Koretskyi, L. A. Aleksidze, V. A. Vasilenko, L. Oppenheim, R. Ago, J. Brierly, A. de Luna, M. Lachs, P. Reuter, S. Bastide, G. Scelle, I. Sinclair, I. Brownlie, H. Waldock, J. Fitzmaurice, A. Verdross, and others.[83]

However, the extensive emphasis on 'native' views in Russian scholarship of international law also means that in some ways Russian theoretical perspectives are inward rather than outward looking. In the academic discipline of international relations (IR) theories, two leading IR scholars originating from Russia, Andrey Makaryshev and Viatcheslav Morozov, have warned Western scholars not to over-idealize 'independent' IR theories in non-Western countries like Russia for often such 'native' theories have been convenient ways to escape global academic competition of ideas and arguments.[84] In this sense, languages and 'native' doctrines can also act as protective castles.

Whatever the merits of the political claim that Russian and English should be equal as languages of global political conversation may have been at the time of the Cold War in the UN, this rationale no longer makes sense in international law scholarship taken globally. The volume and wealth of international legal literature in the English language is nowadays many times bigger than the respective literature in any other language including Russian (or even French). Globalization—or, its critics would say, the unification of the world under Anglo-Saxon cultural terms—has progressed further and outstanding representatives of for example German and Japanese scholarship of international law are increasingly publishing their academic works on international law in English. These significant intellectual streams are nowadays all part of the academic ocean that international law scholarship published in English has become.

By keeping a mental distance from Western sources and developments in international law and presuming that there exists a unique self-contained 'native' Russian science of international law, contemporary Russian scholarship may be doing an intellectual disservice to the country's international law students of the next generation. But ultimately, this seems to be a political matter—an issue of autonomy and independence for the Russians. If American scholars can be monocultural, why not Russians?

[83] Yu. A. Reshetov, in Yu. M. Kolosov, E. S. Krivchikova, P. V. Savas'kov (eds), *Evropeiskoe mezhdunarodnoe pravo* (Moscow: 'Mezhdunarodnye otnoshenia', 2005) 21.

[84] A. Makarychev, V. Morozov, 'Is "Non-Western Theory" Possible? The Idea of Multipolarity and the Trap of Epistemological Relativism in Russian IR', 15 *International Studies Review* 2013, 328–50.

In the UN Audiovisual Library of International Law, most of the Russian scholars who have received an invitation to lecture there have decided to give their lectures in Russian (Professors Abashidze, Galenskaya, and Kapustin; Judge Neshataeva).[85] The only exception so far is former judge of the ICJ, Vladlen Stepanovich Vereschchetin (b. 1932) who delivered his lecture in English.

In this way, few international law scholars or students outside the former USSR will be able to learn from these academic presentations. It is interesting to observe that the German and Japanese scholars mentioned all give their lectures on the same UN web platform in English. This, paradoxically, secures them a wider audience globally, unlike most Russian international lawyers in this context. But then, these two countries did not win World War II either.

Of course, a different and more sympathetic view of the phenomenon of nativist pride in Russia would be to think along the lines of the metaphor of German philosopher Martin Heidegger (1889–1976) that language is 'the home of one's existence' and that 'thinkers and poets are the guardians' of this existence.[86]

Guarding is a useful metaphor indeed. The determination to maintain linguistic independence in Russia's historical 'sphere of influence' in the context of international law scholarship may reflect more generally a determination to emphasize the country's mental and geopolitical independence from the West. The idea is that those who are weak will culturally give in to the globalization of international law scholarship whereas the culturally strong—such as Russia—will want to maintain their independence.

It seems that Columbia University law professor Oscar Schachter (1915–2003) was oversimplifying the sociological reality when he metaphorically referred to *the* 'invisible college of international lawyers'.[87] Analysis of Russian scholarship suggests that instead of one huge global college there are several regional colleges, in the plural. It only may appear so that meetings of the ASIL or ESIL, or the Russian Association of International Law or the Asian Society of International Law, represent the 'universality' of the scholarly world of international law. Perhaps members of each of these regional colleges think subjectively that they are more important and universal than they actually are, at least from the perspective of other regional colleges.

[85] See <http://www.un.org/law/avl/>.

[86] 'Die Sprache ist das Haus des Seins. In ihrer Behausung wohnt der Mensch. Die Denkenden und Dichtenden sind die Wächter dieser Behausung. Ihr Wachen ist das Vollbringen der Offenbarkeit des Seins, insofern sie durch ihr Sagen zur Sprache bringen und in der Sprache aufbewahren.' M. Heidegger, 'Brief über den 'Humanismus', in M. Heidegger, *Gesamtausgabe I, Abteilung: Veröffentlichte Schriften 1914–1970, Band 9: Wegmarken* (Frankfurt a. M.: Vittorio Klostermann, 1976) 333.

[87] O. Schachter, 'The Invisible College of International Lawyers', 72 *Northwestern University Law Review* 1977, 217.

4. Extensive Scientism and Theorizing in Russian Scholarship of International Law

Post-Soviet Russia has seen a boom in publishing textbooks on international law. Each major university with an ambitious chair in international law has made an effort to come forward with its own textbook.

Usually, international law textbooks in Russia have collective authorship and some authors have contributed to different textbooks. For example, the textbook edited by Melkov refers to the work of Ludmila Petrovna Anufrieva (b. 1946) in another textbook although Anufrieva contributes to Melkov's textbook itself as well.[88] The practice of collective authorship in textbooks sometimes also leads to inconsistencies. For instance, in the textbook edited by Bekyashev the editor supports the idea of recognizing individuals and transnational corporations (TNCs) as subjects of international law[89] but in the same textbook, Melkov argues that making them subjects of international law would 'contradict the very foundations of the status of legal subjects in public international law.'[90]

Apparently due to market demand in legal education in Russia, international law textbooks have become a major forum for integrating new facts and ideas in scholarship and putting forward the best arguments.

Russian textbooks of public international law tend to be theoretical and philosophical in a scholastic way. Koskenniemi has observed that in pre-World War I Germany, the academic discipline of international law equalled 'philosophy'[91] and one can make a similar association when reading the general parts of most of the early twenty-first century Russian textbooks on international law. The doctrine is based rather on deduction than induction; 'logical' arguments rather than analysis of cases and other empirical material. Perhaps this is one reason why Sergey Yur'evich Marochkin (b. 1956) from Tyumen State University regrets that textbooks in Russia are doing better in terms of their 'general-educational' goals and less in terms of their usefulness for practitioners.[92]

By way of example, let us look at one such textbook, by Kalamkaryan and Migachev.[93] In this textbook, a considerable amount of energy is directed at discussions of definitions and classifications such as what is the correct view on the notion of the 'system' or 'object' of international law;[94] what are the proper categories of 'legal relations',[95] unilateral juridical acts,[96] and so on. Often, such deliberations are based on exercises in formal logic rather than critical analysis

[88] Melkov, *Mezhdunarodnoe pravo*, 41 (referring to the textbook edited by Bekyashev).

[89] K. A. Bekyashev (ed.), *Mezhdunarodnoe publichnoe pravo* (Moscow: Prospekt, 2003) 120.

[90] Ibid., 29.

[91] M. Koskenniemi, *The Gentle Civilizer of Nations. The Rise and Fall of International Law 1870–1960* (Cambridge: CUP, 2001) 179–265.

[92] S.Yu. Marochkin, *Deistvie i realizatsia norm mezhdunarodnoga prava v pravovoi sisteme Rossiiskoi Federatsii* (Moscow: Norma, 2011) 55.

[93] Kalamkaryan, Migachev, *Mezhdunarodnoe pravo*.

[94] Kalamkaryan, Migachev, ibid., 163–8. [95] Ibid., 39–48. [96] Ibid., 54–9.

of the historical practice of international law. Thus, Kalamkaryan and Migachev refer to Shurshalov's theoretical view on custom as 'logical' and praise the 'logical nature' of a theoretical argument made by Lukashuk.[97] Lukashuk himself argues with Chernichenko based on the 'logic' of a certain theoretical position.[98] In turn, Chernichenko argues that dualism is more 'logical' than monism[99] and generally operates based on formal logic, arguing that certain theoretical positions either are or are not 'logical'.[100] Furthermore, Farkhutdinov wants to decide upon the question whether individuals and TNCs have become subjects of international law based on 'objective scientific logic'.[101]

In this sense, international law is presented as *Buchrecht* or *Professorenrecht* and is stylistically quite different from Anglo-Saxon works which emphasize state practice and are generally not extensively theoretical or dogmatic. Theorizing, to the extent it is seen as relevant, is left more for monographs and scholarly papers.

Sometimes, theoretical distinctions seem artificial or even superfluous from the practical point of view. The textbook edited by Usenko and Shinkaretskya makes a distinction between territorial 'debates' and 'pretensions'[102] or the textbook of Valeev and Kurdyukov between the 'international legal system' and the 'system of international law'.[103] In the textbook by Kalamkaryan and Migachev, points are driven home by a specific antiquated philosophical scientism—for example, the authors argue that the distinction occasionally made between legal and political disputes in international relations is 'anti-scientific and erroneous'.[104] The authors proceed from the presumption that international law is not identical with what international courts and tribunals do. For example, they are critical that international tribunals did not always 'correctly' make the distinction between general principles of *law* and general principles of *international* law.[105]

That the scholarship of international law in Russia is theoretically oriented was already part of the identity and a source of pride for Soviet scholars. Tunkin wrote in his diary when lecturing in South Korea during the last year of his life, in 1993:

> I think about the Korean professors. Not strong and from where. Studied in the United States where the science of international law does not shine. Except for English, they do not know other languages. The teaching of international law has only practical, narrowly practical purposes. They understand very little of theory.[106]

[97] Ibid., 33 and 166.

[98] I. I. Lukashuk, *Pravo mezhdunarodnoi otvetstvennosti* (Moscow: Wolters Kluwer, 2004) 308.

[99] S. V. Chernichenko, *Ocherki po filosofii i mezhdunarodnomu pravu* (Moscow: 'Nauchnaya kniga', 2009) 707.

[100] Chernichenko, *Teoria mezhdunarodnoga prava*, Vol. 1, 10, 44, 121, 274, 330.

[101] I. Z. Farkhutdinov, *Mezhdunarodnoe investitsionnoe pravo i protsess* (Moscow: Prospekt, 2013) 57.

[102] E. T. Usenko, G. G. Shinkaretskaya (eds), *Mezhdunarodnoe pravo* (Moscow: Yurist, 2005) 79.

[103] Valeev, Kurdyukov, *Mezhdunarodnoe pravo. Obshaya chast'*, 146–7. The topic of the proper 'system of international law' is generally popular in Russian scholarship, see e.g. E. T. Usenko, *Ocherki teorii mezhdunarodnoga prava* (Moscow: Norma, 2008) 80–121 and Safronova, *Mezhdunarodnoe publichnoe pravo*, 44–62.

[104] Usenko, Shinkaretskaya, *Mezhdunarodnoe pravo*, 73.

[105] Ibid., 175.

[106] Butler, Tunkin, *The Tunkin Diary and Lectures*, 137.

In such self-appraisals as that of Tunkin, the adjective 'theoretical' means of high value, both intellectually and morally. It is as if Tunkin wanted to protest that there was no higher meaning and profoundness in the overly 'practical' Anglo-Saxon scholarship of international law.

However, there is also another, less idealistic explanation for the extensive theorizing in Russian (and Soviet) scholarship of international law. Marochkin has put it that international legal theory and practice in the USSR 'developed in parallel'.[107] This may reflect the historically developed division of labour between law and politics, governmental practice and legal academia in Russia. In totalitarian countries, expressing opinions in public on things that mattered politically has been potentially dangerous for international law scholars whereas 'being philosophical' as such, if it followed the rules established by the government, was tolerated because it mattered less in practice.

Stakes in debates on whether or not international humanitarian law dogmatically includes human rights law, what is the right 'system' of international law,[108] whether the topic of subjects of international law constitutes an independent 'branch' or 'institution' of international law[109] or what are the peculiarities of the technical 'structure' of international legal norms compared to domestic ones,[110] are not too high in state practice. Thus, such pseudo-debates can form a comfortable escape for international law scholars deprived of practical relevance beyond praising their government, for example as critical human rights lawyers of state-investor treaty arbitrators.

Sergey Vladimirovich Bakhin from St Petersburg State University would also like to see more real-life engagement from Russian international law scholarship:

> Sometimes the impression emerges that the science of international law is transforming step by step into a thing in itself, i.e. into a field of strictly theoretical knowledge ...[111]

At the same time, Bakhin's ideal of the proper relevance of international law scholarship seems to be shaped by the Soviet tradition:

> The Soviet science of international law always carried out a frontal attack not only for settling the interests of one's own state but also of those progressive ideas that were at the foundation of the concept of the right to peaceful coexistence, respect for state sovereignty and the interests of the world community. But now, deprived of any ideological foundation, our science very often transmits ideas and concepts that have been elaborated in Western philosophical and legal doctrine. At the same time, there is no critical

[107] Marochkin, *Deistvie i realizatsia ...*, 44.

[108] See e.g. Safronova, *Mezhdunarodnoe publichnoe pravo*, 44–62.

[109] For a discussion on these issues, see e.g. Melkov, *Mezhdunarodnoe pravo*, at 199 and 111 respectively. However, Usenko and Shinkaretskayan, *Mezhdunarodnoe pravo*, conclude that the topic of subjects of international law is the 'institution' of international law, 37.

[110] Chernichenko, *Teoria mezhdunarodnoga prava*, Vol. 1, at 38 et seq.

[111] S. V. Bakhin, 'Razmyshlenia o nauchnom nasledii professora R. L. Bobrova (k 100–letiu so dnia rozhdenia)', in *Materialy nauchno-prakticheskoi konferentsii 'Mezhdunarodnoe pravo: vchera, segodnia, zavtra', 8–9 oktyabria 2010.g K 100–letiu so dnia rozhdenia professora Romana L'vovicha Bobrova* (St Petersburg: 'Rossiya Neva', 2011) 28–40 at 37.

reflection, no linking with the legacy that had accumulated in native legal scholarship and philosophy.[112]

These perplexed words capture well the ideological troubles of countries in (perpetual?) 'transition', and express the worry that Russians may not have a very comfortable place in the world united under the ideology of human rights rather than state sovereignty.

5. Scarcity of Court Practice in Russian Theoretical Works on International Law

A related phenomenon to extensive theorizing in Russian textbooks of international law is that references to court decisions and judgments are few, at least beyond the most well-known judgments of the ICJ and the PCIJ. It seems that a connection exists between the 'scientific'-philosophical way in which international law is approached in Russian textbooks and the relative scarcity of cases in those same textbooks. Lukashuk has diagnosed:

> The legal system of the former USSR did not excel at active interaction with international law. The course of international law in juridical academies was taught mainly as a general-educational (*obsheobrazovatel'nyi*) subject.[113]

Elsewhere, Lukashuk has added that the teaching of international law in the USSR had no 'practical applicability'.[114]

Naturally, there is a distinction between common law and civil law countries as far as court cases and judicial precedents are concerned. In France and Germany too, court cases are much less important in textbooks of international law than in the US or UK. In this sense Russia is not the only civil law country where textbook authors demonstrate less interest in cases of international courts and tribunals or domestic court cases than Anglo-Saxon textbooks do.

Nevertheless, in Russia's case the same impression is even stronger than in textbooks from West European civil law countries because noteworthy Russian court cases on international law are relatively few; at least they have not been referred to in the textbooks. And how could there be many such cases when in Russia the judiciary only very recently became independent from the all-powerful executive, if it ever truly did?

An example of the scarcity of court practice in Russia would be the monograph by Lukashuk himself on the international law of state responsibility and the ILC's 2001 Draft Articles on State Responsibility.[115] It is striking that of all the cases and examples in the history of international law of state responsibility, very few

[112] Ibid., 37. [113] Lukashuk, *Mezhdunarodnoe pravo. Obshaya chast'*, v.

[114] I. I. Lukashuk, 'Foreword', in S. Bakhin (ed.), *Bibliograficheskii slovar' Rossiiskoi Akademii Mezhdunarodnoga Prava 1957–1997* (St Petersburg: Izdatel'stvo yuridicheskogo fakul'teta St Petersburg State University, 2008) 4.

[115] Lukashuk, *Pravo mezhdunarodnoi otvetstvennosti.*

actually involved Russia or the USSR. Lukashuk's main examples are arbitration in the Permanent Court of Arbitration in 1912 between Russia and the Ottoman Empire regarding the failure of the Ottomans to pay back their loans to Russia,[116] and the case when the Soviet sputnik 'Kosmos-954' fell on Canadian territory in 1978 and the Soviets finally agreed to pay an *ex gratia* sum as compensation.[117] Surprisingly, Lukashuk does not deal with Western cases in the interwar period that dealt with Bolshevik expropriations in Russia.

Otherwise, the cases concerning state responsibility mentioned by Lukashuk all concern other states, such as the US and the UK, which creates the impression that Russia as a state has historically kept itself at a safe distance from the practical application of state responsibility in the context of international law. The other major powers such as the US that had more arbitral and court cases in their practice are as a consequence also more vulnerable to criticisms expressed by Lukashuk.[118] But this is an unequal starting point of comparison because obviously such nations also end up violating international law more often than they have had the courage to subject themselves to the jurisdiction of international courts and tribunals.

In contrast, in Russian theological-philosophical fiction literature, Messianic moralistic ideas about human responsibility have stood out, e.g. when in Dostoevsky's 'The Brothers Karamazov' a character declares that everyone is really responsible for all men and for everything. When this idea is translated into the context of international law, one could read in it the beginnings of *jus cogens* and of obligations *erga omnes*. At the same time, the starting point of state responsibility in international law must nevertheless be bilateral and concrete, not abstract and Messianic.

Moreover, state practice as analysed in Russian textbooks on international law usually concerns high politics, conflicts that took place between governments in matters of war and peace and territorial debates.

Quite often, Russian textbooks on international law also resort to extensive descriptions of international treaties and institutions, without much critical analysis. This may be a continuing legacy of nineteenth-century legal positivism which methodologically never seems to have experienced a considerable critical counter-movement in Russia. For example, a recent textbook on investor-state arbitration extensively describes the significance of ICSID and the Energy Charter Treaty in general but has very little to say on Russia's non-ratification of the treaties.[119]

Vladislav Leonidovich Tolstykh from Novosibirsk State University admits that Russian international law scholarship deals mostly with the content of treaties and little with international and foreign cases. As a reason of this phenomenon, he mentions the poor command of English and French in Russia; Russian scholars

[116] Lukashuk, ibid., 165, 177, 183–4, 289. [117] Ibid., 224.

[118] Ibid., 116, 119, 228, 277, 312, 342–74.

[119] A. A. Danelyan, I. Z. Farkhutdinov, *Mezhdunarodnyi investitsionnyi arbitrazh. Uchebnoe posobie* (Moscow: Tsentr gumanitarnykh initsiativ, 2013).

do not take into account more cases and judgments because they cannot if they have not been translated into Russian.[120]

6. The Debate between the Statist and the Pro-Individual Schools

The major difference compared to the Soviet period in contemporary Russia is that nowadays it is in principle allowed to think differently within the framework of the theory of international law although perhaps not about concrete politically contested questions such as whether Russia's annexation of Crimea was illegal. In today's Russian scholarship there is an intense debate ongoing between the statists and pro-human rights scholars about the nature of international law. To dramatize this difference somewhat and give it a human face, I here label these two schools of thought the Stanislav Valentinovich Chernichenko 'statist' school of the Diplomatic Academy of Russian MFA (in Moscow) and the Gennady Vladimirovich Ignatenko 'pro-non state actors' school at the Urals State Juridical Academy in Yekaterinburg.

While the Chernichenko school of thought is strictly Grotian and occasionally even comes across as twenty-first century Hegelianism, the Ignatenko school of thought is more open to Kantian and, in the Russian context also, modern Western influences in international law. The Chernichenko school is essentially positivist (although, paradoxically, Chernichenko himself in a philosophical work recognizes the existence of natural law[121]) whereas the Ignatenko school is influenced by at least some natural law ideas.

The two schools essentially debate the relationship between the principles of state sovereignty, human rights, and national self-determination. That all these notions echo very strongly in the recent political history of Russia can for example be seen from the fact that in 1990, President Yeltsin declared at the first assembly of national deputies of the Russian Federation that from then onwards, the 'first sovereignty in Russia will be the human being' (*sic*).[122] Coincidentally (or not?) for our context, Yeltsin's political base was Yekaterinburg (formerly: Sverdlovsk) in the Urals.

In post-Soviet Russia, Ignatenko tried to take on himself the liberal ideological direction of Martens, and has for example encouraged St Petersburg international law scholars to come out with their own original textbook of international law, criticizing use of the idiosyncratic textbook edited by Melkov as an 'absurd

[120] V. L. Tolstykh, 'Iazyk i mezhdunarodnoe pravo', 2 *Rossiiskii yuridicheskii zhurnal* 2013, 44–62 at 61.

[121] S.V. Chernichenko, *Ocherki po filosofii i mezhdunarodnomu pravu* (Moscow: 'Nauchnaya kniga', 2009) 721, 751.

[122] Quoted in M.V. Il'in, 'Suverenitet: razvitie ponyatinoi kategorii', in M. V. Il'in, I. V. Kudryashova (eds), *Suverenitet. Transformatsia poniatii i praktik* (Moscow: 'MGIMO-Universitet', 2008) 14–42 at 19.

misunderstanding'.[123] Ignatenko's coded call for more human being-focused scholarship, however, is in some ways a misunderstanding itself, because in the same volume the chair of international law at St Petersburg State University, Sergey Vladimirovich Bakhin, although otherwise a great admirer of Martens, takes a clearly statist position on international law:

> Attempts to raise doubts about sovereignty as the foundation of contemporary international law, to include individuals and other non-state actors among the subjects of international law, to promote to the level of legal categories such notions as 'soft law' and the like, all this will lead ultimately to the questioning of international law itself as an actually existing social phenomenon.[124]

The statist school of thought continues to be dominant in the leading universities of the capital city, the Diplomatic Academy and MGIMO, both related to the Russian MFA. International law scholars from these elite universities theorize about the foundations of international law as in-house lawyers of the world's largest state, worrying about state sovereignty and the 'exaggerated role of the individual in international law'.[125] Furthermore, statists are more likely to be nostalgic towards the achievements of the USSR and the Russian Empire and generally more suspicious of the West or Western doctrine of international law.

The liberal-leaning minority in post-Soviet Russian international law scholarship has tried to challenge the statists but with only limited success so far. Why such a conclusion? Firstly, for foreign policy and governmental elites, universities such as the Diplomatic Academy of the Russian MFA, where statists rule, mean so much more than provincial universities where some Russian liberals may be lurking.

Secondly, with President Putin, the theoretical debate between the statist and pro-human rights schools has a clear political winner—the statists. Their views correspond much more to actual realities in Russian state practice, as we will see later, in the last part of this study. The arguments of Ignatenko's school of thought about international law point to the direction that Russia too should become more like the West, even though these scholars usually do not have an uncritical view towards the West either. Ultimately, by discussing the philosophical foundations of international law in reality both schools of thought are also discussing the present and future of Russia. However, the statist school talks about 'is' and the pro-human rights school about 'ought'—an alternative vision of what Russia could have become like—but did not.

In the following, let us look at some concrete examples of how statism comes to play in Russian scholarship of international law. In doing so, we should keep in mind where Russia comes from historically and that the ideology of international

123 G. V. Ignatenko, 'Roman L'vovich Bobrov—uchenyi, myslitel', nastavnik, kollega', in *Materialy nauchno-prakticheskoi konferentsii 'Mezhdunarodnoe pravo: vchera, segodnya, zavtra', 8–9 oktyabrya 2010.g. K 100–letiu so dnya rozhdenia professora Romana L'vovicha Bobrova* (St Petersburg: 'Rossia-Neva', 2011) 5–10 at 10.

124 Bakhin, 'Razmyshlenia o nauchnom nasledii professora R. L. Bobrova', 38.

125 Chernichenko, *Teoria mezhdunarodnoga prava*, Vol. 1, 11.

law in the USSR was entirely statist and illiberal, with no exceptions allowed. Moreover, in the following there is no possibility of covering all theoretically relevant aspects. For example, I will not discuss theoretical issues related to sources of international law in depth. It seems that Soviet resistance to and scepticism about customary international law as a source of international law[126] has by and large faded away in contemporary Russian theory.[127] In this sense, the statism of today's Russian legal theory is milder than its Soviet version—it is accepted that a sovereign does not have to agree to something explicitly each time and in written form in order to be bound by a rule.

7. The Conceptualization of State Sovereignty

Russian legal scholars strongly emphasize state sovereignty as the foundational principle of international law. At the same time, they often give a specific illiberal meaning to the concept of state sovereignty.

There is something nineteenth-century Hegelian about these positions in the sense that they glorify the state as such, an embodiment of the Absolute Idea, often detaching the state from its democratic legitimacy. For example, Chernichenko has repeatedly argued that the drafters of the Constitution of the Russian Federation of 1993 got it wrong from the viewpoint of legal theory: the people of the Russian Federation cannot logically be the 'bearer' (*nositel'*) of sovereignty; the 'bearer' of sovereignty can only be the Russian Federation itself, i.e. the state.[128] In political terms, this interpretation means that Russia's sovereignty does not, and should not depend on whether the country is a democracy or autocracy.

This view seems to identify the idea of popular sovereignty as a dangerous Western, especially US constitutional idea, and vividly exposes how key theoretical questions in international law are linked with the respective constitutional theory.[129] Grachev in his monograph on the historical origins of sovereignty, also emphasizes that in traditionalist thinking, the people cannot be the bearer of sovereignty; only the state itself (if not the ruler) can.[130]

[126] See e.g. G. M. Danilenko, *Law-Making in the International Community* (Leiden: Martinus Nijhoff Publishers, 1993).

[127] See e.g. the overall positive attitude to 'soft law' in the context of international environmental law in R. M. Valeev, *Mezhdunarodnoe ekologicheskoe pravo* (Moscow: Statut, 2012) 70 et seq.

[128] S. V. Chernichenko, 'Vzglyad na opredelennye polozhenia konstitutsii Rossiiskoi Federatsii s mezhdunarodno-pravovykh pozitsii' in *Vestnik Diplomaticheskoi Akademii MID Rossii. Mezhdunarodnoe pravo* (Moscow: Diplomaticheskaya Akademia, 2013) 44–63 at 45. This view is also repeated and supported by Moiseev in *Suverenitet gosudarstva v mezhdunarodnom prave*, 53 and A. L. Bredikhin, *Suverenitet kak politiko-pravovoi fenomen* (Moscow: Infra-M, 2012) 42, 72.

[129] For a comparative analysis on who in the world's constitutions are seen as bearers of sovereignty, see Ya. I. Vaslavskyi, 'Nositeli suvereniteta. Analiz konstitutsionnykh dokumentov', in M. V. Il'in, I. V. Kudryashova (eds), *Suverenitet. Transformatsia ponyatii i praktik* (Moscow: 'MGIMO-Universitet', 2008) 92–102.

[130] N. I. Grachev, *Proiskhozhdenie suvereniteta. Verkhovnaya vlast' v mirovozzrenii i praktike gosudarstvennogo stroitel'stva traditsionnogo obshestva* (Moscow: Zertsalo-M, 2009) 289–94.

Contrast this view with that of Yale international law scholar Michael W. Reisman expressed in 1990: undemocratic governments lack the sovereignty that is a prerequisite to the enjoyment of statehood in the international community.[131] Consider in particular the fact that especially at the time of President Putin Russia has been perceived and criticized in the West as an authoritarian country.

In the context of international law, sovereignty means the right of each state to be a full master in its own house. Whether this is still the case in the post-Cold War era has preoccupied leading Russian legal minds. Quite symbolically, the Chairman of the Constitutional Court of the Russian Federation, Valery Zorkin, has entitled his programmatic article on international law 'An Apology for the Westphalian System'.[132] With this title, the main point is already stated. Zorkin argues that the Westphalian system is currently under attack from two directions: on the one hand, human rights and the right of peoples to self-determination are set against state sovereignty and territorial integrity, and on the other hand, nation states are considered ineffective administrators in conditions of globalization.[133]

Zorkin's article reveals that fear of disintegration of the Russian Federation remains central in the minds of the country's top lawyers. Zorkin explains how the Constitutional Court had to deal with and confront separatist tendencies in Tatarstan, Chechnya, and elsewhere during the 1990s.[134] He particularly criticizes Western theories according to which networks of global governance would replace state sovereignty and the Westphalian system. For example, Zorkin criticizes US international law academic Michael Glennon for his dismissal of the principle of sovereign equality of states, and even compares Glennon's approach to that of the Nazi ideologue Alfred Rosenberg (1893–1946).[135] Zorkin also calls on Russian legal scholars to study and answer the question what 'complete' sovereignty means nowadays.[136]

One elaborate response is given by Professor Alexei Alexandrovich Moiseev (b. 1971) from the Diplomatic Academy of the Russian MFA, a disciple and colleague of Chernichenko. In a monograph dedicated specifically to the question of state sovereignty in the context of international law, Moiseev argues that as a legal category, sovereignty is absolute and indivisible—it cannot be 'limited'.[137]

Moiseev relies particularly on the views of Chernichenko so there is a clear continuity of tradition here. According to Moiseev, from the viewpoint of legal theory, it is wrong to argue that globalization would lead to 'restrictions' of state sovereignty.[138] Moiseev holds that it is just Western propaganda that with globalization, nation states are losing their importance or are even about to disappear.[139]

[131] M. W. Reisman, 'Sovereignty and Human Rights in Contemporary International Law', 84 *AJIL* 1990, 866 at 866.

[132] V. Zorkin, *Rossia i konstitutsia v XXI veke*, 2nd edn (Moscow: Norma, 2008) 379–87 (originally published in the No 3 May–June issue of *Rossia v global'noi politike* in 2004).

[133] Ibid., 380. [134] Ibid., 381. [135] Ibid., 383. [136] Ibid., 385.

[137] Moiseev, *Suverenitet gosudarstva v mezhdunarodnom prave*, 55–87. [138] Ibid., 95.

[139] Ibid., 96.

Moiseev also gives a long list of examples of how the notion of 'sovereignty' has been used in a corrupted and relativized way, both in legal and especially in politological literature.[140]

One consequence of the emphasis on the category of state sovereignty in Russian scholarship of international law is that Russian authors tend to be against Western schools of 'global' law or law of 'humanity',[141] the theory of the constitutionalization of international law[142] and generally the idea that the future of international law might be 'global government'.[143] Little Russian literature enthusiastically embraces the idea that international law has made a giant leap from bilateralism to community interest.[144] From the perspective of many Russian scholars, these are corrupt Western, especially US theories about international law.[145] Although some Russian international law scholars like Shumilov have started to make cautious positive references to them,[146] such views are rejected by others as fundamentally erroneous.[147]

Altogether it appears that Russian international law scholarship at the time of Martens was more 'cosmopolitan' and at least rhetorically more oriented towards integration, if not with the whole world then at least with the West, and less focused on state sovereignty as such than is the case nowadays.[148] Elena Viktorovna Safronova from Belgorod National Research University describes how during the Tsarist period, the theories of Russian scholars Yastchenko and Mikhailovskyi were informed by cosmopolitan values but comments that 'fortunately, their ideas were not widespread in Russia'.[149]

The context of Russian debates on sovereignty reveals that when sovereignty is praised, it is not necessarily sovereignty in the abstract but *Russia*'s sovereignty. Regarding the essence of the sovereignty of Russia as a Great Power and Empire, some authors actually come to conclusions that ideologically question the sovereignty of smaller neighbouring states.

Some theoreticians interested in the concept of sovereignty go beyond international law and have rediscovered the imperial historical context of the notion of sovereignty. In a monograph entitled 'The Origin of Sovereignty', Grachev goes back to the traditionalist concept of sovereignty in the Byzantine Empire which in his view was passed on to the Grand Duchy of Moscow.[150] Based on the example of

140 Ibid., 62.

141 R. G. Teitel, *Humanity's Law* (Oxford: OUP, 2011).

142 See e.g. A. Peters, 'Are we Moving towards Constitutionalization of the World Community?' in A. Cassese (ed.), *Realizing Utopia. The Future of International Law* (Oxford: OUP, 2012) 118–35.

143 J. P. Trachtman, *The Future of International Law: Global Government* (Cambridge: CUP, 2013).

144 See B. Simma, 'From Bilateralism to Community Interest in International Law', 250 *RCADI* 1994, at 217 et seq.; U. Fastenrath et al., *From Bilateralism to Community Interest. Essays in Honor of Judge Bruno Simma* (Oxford: OUP, 2011).

145 Safronova, *Mezhdunarodnoe publichnoe pravo*, 16.

146 V. M. Shumilov, *Mezhdunarodnoe ekonomicheskoe pravo* (Rostov: Feniks, 2003) 35, 88; Shumilov, *Mezhdunarodnoe pravo*, 71.

147 See e.g. Safronova, *Mezhdunarodnoe publichnoe pravo*, 16–19; Vel'iaminov, *Mezhdunarodnoe ekonomicheskoe pravo i protsess*, 40–4; Farkhutdinov, *Mezhdunarodnoe investitsionnoe pravo i protsess*, 63.

148 Cf. the analysis (and references to the textbook by Martens) in Safronova, *Mezhdunarodnoe publichnoe pravo*, 6.

149 Safronova, ibid., 11.

150 Grachev, *Proiskhozhdenie suvereniteta*, 189.

Byzantium, which Grachev evaluates highly positively, he distinguishes Empires and usual states:

> Empire and other state forms have many things in common. An empire is a state in all meanings.... At the same time, it is also something bigger than a state in that it is the state form of a particular civilization.[151]

This is pretty much the Schmittian distinction between 'usual' states, *Staaten* and the Great Powers with a legitimate entitlement to regional dominance, *Reiche*.[152]

According to Grachev, the idea of Empire continues to be an essentially religious idea even in the modern era:

> ... the idea of Empire does not die and continues to be regarded by the majority of its citizens as a goal of the historical process... This gives reasons to regard any Empire as a state that to a greater or lesser extent has a traditional and organic character.[153]

Grachev's views are ideologically influenced by Dugin, who after the Iraq invasion in 2003 argued that the era of state sovereignty was over and the future was either a US-led world government or regional 'greater spaces' with Russia as the Eurasian Empire.[154] Dugin himself puts the whole idea even more bluntly: Russians are by nature an imperial people and their historical geopolitical vocation is to stand against the hegemonial aspirations of the maritime West, nowadays the US.[155] Dugin borrows extensively from Nazi German authors and argues along with Nazi scholars that instead of states, peoples (in terms of ethnic groups) should be recognized as the main subject of international law.[156] In the context of post-Soviet borders, this theory directly challenges the sovereignty and territorial integrity of a number of states with ethnic Russian minorities in the same way as the Nazi concept of peoples as the main subjects of international law challenged the borders of some of Germany's neighbours.

However, such views as Dugin's that potentially challenge the territorial integrity of Russia's neighbours and idealizing the Russian Empire as a state of higher order have so far not been characteristic of Russian literature on international law. At the same time, the idea that Great Powers have a different quality from small nations sometimes finds echoes in Russian international law scholarship as well. Shumilov argues that 'the Russian school of international law' does not see any violations of the principle of sovereign equality of states in the UN SC's P5 veto rights, rights of the signatories to the 1968 Treaty on Non-Proliferation of Nuclear Weapons, or voting rights in the IMF.[157]

Moreover, Lukashuk writes that Russia is a Great Power (*velikaya derzhava*).[158] In a section of his textbook entitled 'Great and Small Powers', Lukashuk refers to

[151] Ibid., 211.
[152] See C. Schmitt, *Völkerrechtliche Großraumordnung mit Interventionsverbot für raumfremde Mächte* (Berlin: Rechtsverlag, 1941).
[153] Grachev, *Proiskhozhdenie suvereniteta*, 217.
[154] A.G. Dugin, *Geopolitika postmoderna* (St Petersburg: Amfora, 2007) 93.
[155] A. Dugin, *Projekt Evraziya* (Moscow: Yauza EKSMO, 2004) 339 et seq.
[156] Ibid., 156–7.
[157] Shumilov, *Mezhdunarodnoe pravo*, 231.
[158] Lukashuk, *Mezhdunarodnoe pravo. Obshaya chast'*, 321.

the 'irresponsibility of small nations' in the context of the UN and argues that '[t]he consolidation of the legal order makes it possible to overcome the psychology of the small state, the egoism of the weak, its irresponsibility.'[159] However, Lukashuk does not specify whether the very *existence* of small states is an expression of their egoism and irresponsibility, or whether they would first have to behave in a certain way in order to display the egoism of the weak.

Of course, scepticism about the explosion of sovereignty at the cost of former Great Powers and the respective fragmentation of main actors in international law can also sometimes be encountered in the realist brand of US scholarship, which means that such views in the Russian literature are not so unique after all.[160]

Chernichenko acknowledges that the world's states are de facto not equal; they are only equal in terms of their sovereignty as a legal category.[161] He adds that stability in international relations depends on the interaction between nations that are powerful in the military and economic sense.[162]

8. Who are Subjects of International Law?

One theoretical question is debated with particular ideological energy in Russian textbooks of international law, namely: who else, besides states and international organizations, can be subjects of international law?[163] The answer given to this question creates a lens revealing how one sees international law as a phenomenon.

The Soviet position was that states were essentially the only true subjects of international law. Initially, Soviet scholars even fought against accepting international organizations as subjects of international law but this view has now completely passed in Russia.[164] However, having accepted international governmental organizations as subjects of international law, the statists among today's international law scholars in Russia have otherwise remained faithful to the previous conceptual position emphasizing the role of states. On the other hand, scholars in the minority who see themselves as progressive and who are in this context Kantian argue that nowadays human beings and increasingly also NGOs and TNCs should be—and have already been—recognized as subjects of international law.

Altogether, the question of subjects has become probably the main test question in Russian scholarship as to which ideological camp each scholar belongs to. It seems that in the Russian context, the debate about subjects of international

[159] Ibid., 323.

[160] See E. A. Posner, *The Perils of Global Legalism* (Chicago: University of Chicago Press, 2009) 81 et seq.

[161] S. V. Chernichenko, *Ocherki po filosofii i mezhdunarodnomu pravu* (Moscow: 'Nauchnaya kniga', 2009) 678, 690.

[162] Ibid., 676.

[163] See also L. Mälksoo, 'International Legal Theory in Russia—A Civilizational Perspective, or: Can Individuals be Subjects of International Law?' in F. Hoffmann, A. Orford (eds), *The Oxford Handbook on the Theory of International Law* (Oxford: OUP, forthcoming in 2015).

[164] A. Ya. Kapustin, 'Kontseptsia mezhdunarodnoi organizatsii. Sovremennye tendentsii i protivorechivye tolkovania', in V. S. Bakhin (ed.), *Mezhdunarodnoe publichnoe i chastnoe pravo. Problemy i perspektivy* (St Petersburg: St Petersburg State University 2007) 85–113 at 97.

law is a proxy debate and that what is at stake is not only the question what is international law but also in what direction the Russian state and Russian society should develop.

As a rule, scholars who support individuals as subjects of international law are more at ease with or even supportive of Russia moving away from its authoritarian and imperial past whereas statists who reject the inclusion of individuals among the subjects of international law seem more to hold on to the idea that the glory of Russia has historically been primarily due to collective and hierarchical societal arrangements. According to this view, too much 'empowered self at the time of individualism'[165] might endanger Russia's greatness and probably even her territorial integrity. In other words, in Russia scholars who support individuals as subjects of international law tend to be Westernizers, while those who reject this are 'nativists' building on the idea that Russia is a unique and non-Western power or even a 'civilization'.[166]

There is no single correct and universal answer to the question whether individuals, NGOs,[167] and TNCs can be subjects of international law. The answer to the question who are subjects of international law has varied historically.[168] The debate about this question is a philosophical one rather than legal *stricto sensu*. As José E. Alvarez points out in his article discussing the question whether corporations should be recognized as subjects of international law, it is also—or primarily—a matter of legal policy.[169]

In the West, the more traditionalist international law scholars have also expressed scepticism about the eagerness of human rights-minded progressives to include the individual among the subjects of international law.[170] They maintain that in its essence and core, international law even in the twenty-first century remains intergovernmental, interstate law. The more 'utopian' progressives, however, want to emphasize 'world law' or cosmopolitan ideals of international law, and to leave states as intermediaries of human beings and their collective (democratic) interests.[171] Alvarez also points out a certain gap between European and US scholars, at least as far as concerns the issue of the legal subjectivity of corporations.[172]

The difference between Western and Russian scholarship is that in the West the view that one way or another international law is inclusive towards individuals

[165] Cf. T. M. Franck, *The Empowered Self. Law and Society in the Age of Individualism* (Oxford: OUP, 1999).

[166] Cf. Safronova, *Mezhdunarodnoe publichnoe pravo*, 79.

[167] See further A.-K. Lindblom, *Non-governmental Organisations in International Law* (Cambridge: CUP, 2005).

[168] See further J. E. Nijman, *The Concept of International Legal Personality. An Inquiry into the History and Theory of International Law* (The Hague: TMC Asser, 2004); K. Parlett, *The Individual in the International Legal System. Continuity and Change in International Law* (Cambridge: CUP, 2011); R. Portmann, *Legal Personality in International Law* (Cambridge: CUP, 2010).

[169] J. E. Alvarez, 'Are Corporations "Subjects" of International Law?', in 9 *Santa Clara JIL* 1 (2011), available at <http://digitalcommons.law.scu.edu/scujil/vol9/iss1/1>.

[170] J. Crawford, *Brownlie's Principles of International Law*, 8th edn (Oxford: OUP, 2012) 121.

[171] A. Cassese, *International Law*, 2nd edn (OUP: Oxford, 2005) 142–50.

[172] Alvarez, 'Are Corporations "Subjects" of International Law?', 8.

and non-state actors has become predominant[173] whereas the Russian debate continues to be dominated by the statist school of thought. The West inclines towards the anthropocentric view of international law whereas the influential majority of experts in Russia hold on to the classical state-centric position.

For the argument that individuals, NGOs, and TNCs have become subjects of international law, we could look at the textbook edited by Ignatenko (1927–2012) and Tiunov (b. 1937).[174] The late Ignatenko refers to the *La Grand* and *Avena* cases in which besides the rights of the respective states, the ICJ recognized certain rights of individuals as protected by international law.[175] Ignatenko presents the question of subjects of international law as a topic in historical evolution—when in the nineteenth century, only 'civilized nations' were recognized as subjects of international law then in the twenty-first century individuals, NGOs, TNCs, and within certain limits units in federal states have also become subjects of international law.[176]

Again, the issue of federal units as subjects of international law as discussed by scholars of the Ural State Juridical Academy is fascinating because Yekaterinburg has sometimes been mentioned by the Russian media as an example of 'federalist'—and during the early 1990s even separatist—tendencies as well as for criticism of Moscow's centralist use of resources drawn from the provinces.[177]

While Ignatenko concedes that both views—that there can or cannot be other subjects of international law besides states and international organizations—have a 'right to exist', he still regards the view that individuals and others can also be subjects of international law as 'more contemporary'.[178]

Other textbooks also support or incline towards the view of Ignatenko and Tiunov's textbook recognizing individuals as subjects of international law.[179] Sergei Yur'evich Marochkin from Tyumen State University writes in a textbook of international law edited by Valeev and Kurdyukov that international law is becoming less 'statist' and supports the inclusion of non-state actors and individuals among the subjects of international law.[180] Another author in the same textbook comes to the conclusion that individuals and TNCs have become subjects of international law.[181] The anthropocentric cause is also supported in scholarly articles dedicated to the same topic.[182]

[173] See e.g. N. Bhuta, 'The Role International Actors Other Than States can Play in the New World Order', in Cassese, *Realizing Utopia*, 61–75.

[174] Ignatenko, Tiunov, *Mezhdunarodnoe pravo.*

[175] Ibid., 32–3.

[176] Ibid., 70–3.

[177] O. Gerasimenko, 'Mestnykh stavit' nel'zya—oni dogovoryatsya i ustroyat respubliku', 02.07.2012 *Kommersant Vlast'*, <http://www.kommersant.ru/doc/1966881>.

[178] Ignatenko, Tiunov, *Mezhdunarodnoe pravo*, 70–1.

[179] K. A. Bekyashev (ed.), *Mezhdunarodnoe publichnoe pravo* (Moscow: Prospekt, 2003) 119–20; V. A. Kartashkin, *Prava cheloveka v mezhdunarodnom i vnutrigosudarstvennom prave* (Moscow: Institut gosudarstva i prava RAN, 1995) 100.

[180] Marochkin in Valeev, Kurdyukov, *Mezhdunarodnoe pravo. Obshaya chast'*, 52, 54.

[181] U. Y. Mammadov, in Valeev, Kurdyukov, *Mezhdunarodnoe pravo. Obshaya chast'*, 325.

[182] T. D. Matveeva, 'Evolyutsia doktriny mezhdunarodnoi pravosub'ektnosti', *Rossiiskiy ezhegodnik mezhdunarodnoga prava* 2012 (St Petersburg: 'Rossiya-Neva', 2013) 27–42 at 33; T. D. Matveeva, 'Chelovek i mezhdunarodnoe pravo (k voprosu o mezhdunarodnoi pravosub'ektnosti individa)', *Rossiiskiy ezhegodnik mezhdunarodnoga prava* 2010 (St Petersburg: 'Rossiya-Neva', 2011) 52–67.

Some textbooks essentially sympathetic to individuals try to create a certain theoretical compromise—for example, the President of the Russian Association of International Law, Anatoly Yakovlevich Kapustin, argues that individuals are subjects of international law but in a 'limited way' because they have been made subjects only by primary subjects, i.e. states.[183] However, Chernichenko insists that international legal subjectivity is such a category that one cannot be 'a little bit' subject of international law; one either is fully or is not at all.[184] Again, 'logic' is made a decisive factor in solving this theoretical problem.

As already pointed out, the majority of international law scholars at the *grandes écoles* in Moscow reject the idea that individuals, NGOs, or TNCs have become subjects of international law. The earlier MGIMO University textbook edited by Kolosov and Krivchikova maintained:

> According to international law, only states may give international legal subjectivity to other entities. If such an objective need were to emerge, the state would give such a capacity to individuals. But there are no international acts based on which one could infer the international legal subjectivity of individuals.[185]

The newer version of the MGIMO University textbook adds that 'some' have reached the conclusion that individuals can have certain characteristics of international legal subjectivity but then continues with the same dismissive passage already quoted above.[186]

The textbook of the Diplomatic Academy asserts clearly which view predominates in 'native doctrine':

> In native doctrine another view is predominant the point of which is that individuals cannot objectively be participants in intergovernmental, interstate relations and, as such, subjects of international law. …[187]

According to Shumilov, the view that individuals cannot be subjects of international law is representative of the 'classical Russian school'.[188]

The authors of the Diplomatic Academy textbook continue with the argument that the increasing protection of human rights in international law does not turn individuals into subjects of international law but only indicates that the parties to the respective treaties, i.e. states, take upon themselves the mutual obligation to secure the access of individuals to international mechanisms through the legal and organizational means at their disposal.[189]

Stanislav Valentinovich Chernichenko from the Diplomatic Academy has been the most prominent defender of and speaker for the view that individuals should not be recognized as subjects of international law.[190] His main argument

[183] A. Ya. Kapustin (ed.), *Mezhdunarodnoe pravo* (Moscow: Gardariki, 2008) 21, 110.

[184] S. V. Chernichenko, *Ocherki po filosofii mezhdunarodnomu pravu* (Moscow: Nauchnaya kniga, 2009) 652.

[185] Kolosov, Krivchikova, *Mezhdunarodnoe pravo*, 107.

[186] A. N. Vylegzhanin (ed.), *Mezhdunarodnoe pravo* (Moscow: Yurait, 2009) 137.

[187] Kovalev, Chernichenko, *Mezhdunarodnoe pravo*, 170.

[188] Shumilov, *Mezhdunarodnoe pravo*, 434. [189] Ibid.

[190] Chernichenko, *Teoria mezhdunarodnoga prava*, Vol. 1, 113 et seq.; 'Eshe raz o mezhdunarodnoi pravosub'ektnosti individov', *Moskovski zhurnal mezhdunarodnoga prava* 2005 No 4, 11–26;

is difficult to argue with since he insists that individuals cannot be subjects of international law for 'objective reasons' and because of the 'objective limits' of international law.[191]

Chernichenko has a number of followers in Russian international law academia.[192] For example, Melkov from the Russian State Trade Economic University counters the argument—which he himself refers to—that the prohibition of piracy in international law among other factors proves the historical focus of this law on the individual. In that case, argues Melkov emotionally, 'prostitutes, keepers of public houses, counterfeiters and other criminals based on international conventions that combat crimes of an international character' would also be subjects of international law 'which, of course, cannot be'.[193]

Melkov dismisses the possibility that the individual could be a subject of international law and concludes:

> Recognition of the individual as a subject of international law would require changing the very nature of this law.... Individuals could hardly use their rights alongside states.[194]

The same position is almost word for word repeated by Lukashuk[195] who also points out that neither the *La Grand* case in the ICJ nor the practice of the ECtHR 'prove' that individuals have nowadays become subjects of international law.[196] Lukashuk is critical of a situation where by mentally including individuals and TNCs in the circle of subjects of international law the West intends to turn international law into 'transnational law', 'world law' or 'global law'.[197] Concepts like Anne-Marie Slaughter's focus on intergovernmental and other networks of global governance are dismissed as 'scholastic in character but not accepted in practice'.[198]

The same arguments as to the impossibility of including individuals as subjects of international law seem to be applied a fortiori to the idea of including NGOs and especially TNCs as subjects of international law, which is dismissed as a 'Western' idea.[199] For example, the authors of the textbook of the Institute of State and Law of the Russian Academy of Sciences write:

> In Western doctrine the opinion is widespread of recognizing the international legal status of TNCs, taking into account their huge economic power. At the same time, such an approach is in principle not acceptable formal-juridically and not realistic practically.[200]

Ocherki po filosofii i mezhdunarodnomu pravu (Moscow: 'Nauchnaya kniga', 2009) 651; 'Vopros o sootnoshenii mezhdunarodnoga i vnutrigosudarstvennogo prava kak pravovykh sistem (razmyshlenia po povodu nekotorykh knig kolleg), in Bakhin, *Mezhdunarodnye otnoshenia i pravo*, 52–89.

[191] Chernichenko, *Teoria mezhdunarodnoga prava*, Vol. 1, 117–21.

[192] See e.g. Shumilov, *Mezhdunarodnoe pravo*, 70.

[193] Melkov, *Mezhdunarodnoe pravo*, 132–3.

[194] Ibid., 135.

[195] Lukashuk, *Mezhdunarodnoe pravo. Obshaya chast'*, 27.

[196] Lukashuk, *Pravo mezhdunarodnoi otvetstvennosti*, 74.

[197] Lukashuk, *Mezhdunarodnoe pravo. Obshaya chast'*, 11.

[198] Ibid., 12.

[199] Kovalev, Chernichenko, *Mezhdunarodnoe pravo*, 170; S. V. Bakhin, 'Pravo integratsionnykh obrazovanii. Voprosy konkurentsii system prava', in Bakhin, *Mezhdunarodnye otnoshenia i pravo*, 90–145 at 96, 103; Shumilov, *Mezhdunarodnoe pravo*, 411.

[200] Usenko, Shinkaretskaya, *Mezhdunarodnoe pravo*, 398.

Safronova refers to UN practice when arguing that TNCs do not have 'independent legal status' based on 'contemporary norms of public international law'.[201] She argues that TNCs are in direct competition with nation states and the 'contemporary financial oligarchy' around TNCs wants to take lucrative 'progressive industries' out of state control.[202] Mikhail Berandze, a younger scholar at the Diplomatic Academy of the Russian MFA, comes to the conclusion that the Western idea of recognizing TNCs as subjects of international law would not correspond to the interests of the Russian Federation.[203]

Altogether the Russian statists have understood well from which ideological directions the main danger comes. For them, the question whether individuals can be subjects of international law is not an innocent theoretical *Glasperlenspiel*. Instead, Chernichenko and his colleagues see well where this all eventually ends up; that the issue is not to somehow include human beings in a legal order dominated by sovereign states but to eventually turn international law into cosmopolitan law where individuals and states change places in the overall hierarchy. For example, Anne Peters, director of Heidelberg's Max Planck Institute, has written:

> The constitutionalist approach offers a new foundation for the view that the ultimate international legal subjects are *individuals*. Constitutionalism postulates that natural persons are the ultimate unit of legal concern. *States* are no ends in themselves, but merely instrumental for the rights and needs of individuals.[204]

This is exactly the opposite of what Chernichenko has written and argued for.

In some ways, there is little that is entirely new in this debate between Russian and Western international law scholars because Soviet scholars such as Tunkin had already vehemently rejected what they called Western blueprints for a 'world state'.[205] In this context, a strong continuity exists between the Chernichenko school of thought and Soviet era views. Chernichenko's own first academic work arguing that individuals could 'in no case whatsoever' be subjects of international law was published in 1974.[206]

To conclude I must agree with Focarelli that international legal personality is a construction which is open to manipulative use to favour 'deserving' actors.[207] Focarelli expresses a thought that clearly contradicts the line of thinking of Chernichenko:

[201] Safronova, *Mezhdunarodnoe publichnoe pravo*, 82. [202] Ibid., 39.

[203] M. R. Berandze, 'K voprosu o pravosub'ektnosti transnatsionalnykh korporatsii v mezhdunarodnom prave', in I. A. Tarkhanov et al. (eds), *Materialy mezhdunarodnoi nauchno-prakticheskoi konferentsii 'Mezhdunarodnyi pravoporyadok v sovremennom mire i rol' Rossii v ego ukreplenii', posvyashennoi 90–letiu professora Fel'dmana Davida Isaakovicha* (Moscow: Statut, 2014) 268–74 at 274.

[204] A. Peters, 'Are We Moving towards Constitutionalization of the World Community?' in Cassese, *Realizing Utopia*, 118–35 at 129.

[205] See e.g. G. I. Tunkin, *Theory of International Law*, trans. W. E. Butler (Cambridge, MA: Harvard University Press, 1974).

[206] S. V. Chernichenko, *Lichnost' i mezhdunarodnoe pravo* (Moscow: 'Mezhdunarodnye otnoshenia', 1974) 149.

[207] Focarelli, *International Law as Social Construct*, 223.

What is to be avoided is the instrumental use of the concept of international personality as the 'logical' premise from which mechanically to draw any sort of legal rights and duties for any purpose.[208]

However, by insisting that individuals cannot 'objectively' be subjects of international law, Chernichenko does exactly that.

Focarelli also suggests a realistic account of what international legal personality of individuals actually means—it is 'more often than not an empowered domestic legal personality which results from international law but is different from international personality.'[209] To the extent that this is true, international law is again 'different in different places' because consequently the individual in some states is more (recognized as) a subject of public law than others. Nevertheless, the predominant school of thought among Russian international law scholars in Moscow has said *n'et* to the question of the individual as a subject of international law.

9. How Close or Distant is International Law to Russia's Legal Order?

Another prominent conceptual debate in Russian scholarship of international law that is closely related to the range of its subjects concerns the place of international law in Russia's legal system. The question of how international and national law relate to each other is a perennial theme and has inspired interesting theoretical and empirical research in the West.[210] The respective legal situation in post-Soviet Russia has already been studied in the West from comparative perspectives.[211]

In Russia, the starting point for this discussion is of course the Constitution of the Russian Federation adopted in 1993. Thus, the issue of the relationship between international and constitutional law received much visibility in the Russian media in December 2013 when the twentieth anniversary of the Russian constitution was celebrated. A number of observers then challenged the international law friendliness of the 1993 Constitution[212] and deputies from the governing United Russia party's *Duma* faction suggested legislative changes which would have established the priority of constitutional law over the ECtHR in particular.[213]

[208] Ibid., 239. [209] Ibid., 239.

[210] See A. Nollkaemper, J. E. Nijman (eds), *New Perspectives on the Divide between National and International Law* (Oxford: OUP, 2007); B. Fassbender, '"Völkerrecht und Landesrecht". Zur Genese und heutigen Bedeutung der Konfrontation zweier Rechtsordnungen', 4 *AJP/PJA* 2014, 437–50.

[211] M. Hussner, *Die Übernahme international Rechts in die russische und deutsche Rechtsordnung* (Stuttgart: ibidem Verlag, 2005); W. Rückert, *Das Völkerrecht in der Rechtsprechung des russischen Verfassungsgerichts* (Berlin: Berliner Wissenschaftsverlag, 2005).

[212] D. Simes, 'Glavenstvo rossiiskoi konstitutsii', *Izvestia* 14.11.2013, <http://izvestia.ru/news/560625>; I. Rodin, 'Vlast' menyaet taktiku v otnoshenii Konstitutsii', *Nezavisimaya Gazeta* 28.11.2013, <http://www.ng.ru/politics/2013–11–28/1_konstitutsia.html>.

[213] E. Teslova, 'Reshenia ESPCh perestanut' byt' obyazatel'nymi dlya rossiiskikh sudov', 24.12.2013 *Izvestia*, <http://izvestia.ru/news/563034>.

Interestingly, there does not seem to be one single official translation of the Constitution of the Russian Federation in English and a number of translations are circulating in cyberspace.[214]

Article 15 para 4 of the Constitution of the Russian Federation stipulates:

> The universally-recognized norms of international law and international treaties and agreements of the Russian Federation shall be a component part of its legal system. If an international treaty or agreement of the Russian Federation fixes other rules than those envisaged by law, the rules of the international agreement shall be applied.

When this constitutional provision was adopted, it was praised by Russian and foreign legal experts as path-breaking in the fragile history of Russia's constitutionalism because for the first time, international law was apparently given priority over domestic law.[215] The previous Soviet constitutions, including the Brezhnev constitution of 1977, contained no similar stipulation specifically regulating the role of international law in the country's legal system.[216]

Article 29 of the 1977 USSR Constitution simply listed the principles that the USSR intended to follow in its foreign policy. These mainly corresponded to the international law principles of the UN GA's 1970 Friendly Relations Declaration. Article 29 *inter alia* referred to the intention to honour obligations stemming from generally recognized principles and norms of international law in good faith. However, Chernichenko points out that contextually the whole concept was built on the policy ground of state aspirations rather than firm constitutional-legal commitments because the respective chapter in the Soviet Constitution was entitled 'Foreign Policy'.[217]

In 1993, key provisions in the new Russian presidentially oriented constitution were apparently copied from the constitution of France adopted in 1958 which also establishes a presidential system of government. In the constitution of France and other West European nations, the emphasis on international law had found constitutional recognition after World War II.

Russia's constitutional provision of 1993 may appear quite straightforward at first glance but in Russian scholarship there is an ongoing debate what exactly these words mean, and what the relationship of Russia's constitutional law to international law is. Moreover, even efforts by the Supreme Court of the Russian Federation to enlighten judges and the legal public and create further acceptance of the norms of international law in legal practice have changed little in the thinking of the conservative faction of Russian theory of international law. On 10 October 2003, the Plenary Session of the Supreme Court of the Russian Federation adopted ruling No 5 entitled 'On Application by Courts of General

[214] Regarding Article 15 para. 4, the translation is linguistically deficient e.g. in <http://www.constitution.ru/en/10003000-02.htm>.

[215] Cf further e.g. A. V. Naumov, A. G. Kibal'nik, V. N. Orlov, P. V. Volosyuk (eds), *Mezhdunarodnoe ugolovnoe pravo* (Moscow: Yurait, 2013) 9.

[216] See, also for further references, S. Yu. Marochkin, *Deistvie i realizatsia norm mezhdunarodnoga prava v pravovoi sisteme Rossiiskoi Federatsii* (Moscow: Norma, 2011) 18, 37.

[217] Chernichenko, in Kovalev, Chernichenko, *Mezhdunarodnoe pravo*, 102.

Jurisdiction of the Commonly Recognized Principles of International Law and the International Treaties of the Russian Federation' which explicitly recognizes the possibility of the direct applicability in Russia of certain norms of international law.[218] The fact that this position of the Supreme Court has not been accepted as the last word in all factions of Russian scholarship reveals *inter alia* the limits of inherent intellectual authority of the judicial branch among some Russian law professors.

In scholarship, the ideological frontlines are basically the same as with the question of the subject status of the individual—the same scholars who are more open to individuals as subjects of international law also tend to embrace international law more intensely in the context of the Russian legal system. At the same time, scholars who reject the subject status of individuals prefer to keep international and domestic law safely apart.

Few Russian scholars argue about this question in terms of whether the Russian Federation is a monist or dualist country. The theory of dualism according to which international law and domestic law are two different legal systems has been so deeply ingrained in Russian (and Soviet) legal theory that 'outing' oneself as monist would probably not be tactically wise for scholars who are more open towards the direct application of international law. Nevertheless, some dualists in Russia criticize and label as 'monists' those scholars who interpret Article 15 para. 4 of the Constitution to mean that there is now primacy of international law.[219]

Concretely, the main practical question under debate is whether norms of international law can sometimes be applied directly and, in this sense, whether Russia recognizes some international law norms as self-executing. Of course, the question how much international law should be applied in domestic courts is not important only in Russia but also continues to generate interesting discussions in the West.[220]

A related question that is discussed in the Russian literature but that I will not look at here in detail is the nature of the hierarchy and interrelationship between the Russian constitution itself and foreign treaties.[221]

As the main statist example, let us see again how the already familiar textbook of the Diplomatic Academy of the Russian MFA edited by Kovalev and Chernichenko deals with the subject matter. The chapter in question is written by Chernichenko himself:

[218] <http://www.supcourt.ru/catalog.php?c=English&c2=Documents&c3=&id=6801>, in particular pp. 3–5.

[219] E. T. Usenko, *Ocherki teorii mezhdunarodnoga prava* (Moscow: Norma, 2008) 153–68.

[220] Y. Shany, 'Should the Implementation of International Rules by Domestic Courts be Bolstered?', in Cassese, *Realizing Utopia*, 200–9; M. Iovane, 'Domestic Courts Should Embrace Sound Interpretative Strategies in the Development of Human Rights-Oriented International Law', in Cassese, *Realizing Utopia*, 607–25; A. Nollkaemper, *National Courts and the International Rule of Law* (Oxford: OUP, 2012).

[221] See e.g. V. S. Ivanenko, 'Mezhdunarodnye dogovory i konstitutsia v pravovoi sisteme Rossii. 'Voina verkhovenstv' ili mirnoe vzaimodeistvie?', in 3 *Pravovedenie* 2010 (290), 135–61.

In native doctrine the type of dualist theory that finds serious support is the one that scholars sometimes suggest calling dialectical or objective dualism. According to this variant of dualist theory international and domestic law are divided by objective boundaries. ... International law is created by participants in interstate relations for the regulation of these relations and because of this objectively cannot regulate domestic relations.... In the international legal literature of the USSR the thought was sometimes expressed that monist theory may be used for interventions in the domestic affairs of states ... [222]

Chernichenko continues that one can also proceed from the position of the 'primacy' of international law when one holds on to dualism. In that case, one should not mean the hierarchical supremacy of international norms over constitutional ones but in the case of a conflict the 'necessity' to amend the domestic law so that it would correspond to the nation's international obligations.

Chernichenko concludes his argument regarding the question of virtues of dualism as opposed to monism:

Dualist theory appears preferable because it is based on objective criteria enabling to see the difference between domestic and international law in the character of relations that are regulated.[223]

At the same time, Chernichenko is aware that 'some native lawyers-internationalists' had concluded based on Article 15 para. 4 of the Constitution that the constitutional stipulation is based on the monist theory according to which international law and domestic law are parts of one and the same integral legal system.[224] However, Chernichenko's bad news for authors who want to bring in monist ideas through the direct applicability of international legal norms is the following:

When one keeps in mind the state's domestic sphere and the regulation of domestic regulations, the expressions 'direct effect' and 'direct applicability' of international treaties are not precise because it is objectively impossible.[225]

Chernichenko also illustrates in his account how Russia's constitutional relationship with international law has grown out of the history of the Soviet period. Chernichenko also recognizes certain flaws in the legal system of the USSR:

The closed-ness of the first Constitutions of the RSFR and the USSR for foreign relations, especially in terms of penetration of international legal principles and norms, was a means of self-preservation of the state. During the longer period when law and legality in the USSR were flouted in all ways, this closed-ness also served as a guarantor for the non-accountability of the state apparatus whose victims would have taken the opportunity to turn to the means of protection provided by international law.[226]

This is a significant aspect—but what guarantees that dualist theory will not be used in a similar blocking way in Russia in the future?

Another author in the same textbook, Sergei Alekseevich Yegorov (b. 1946), Professor at the Diplomatic Academy of the Russian MFA and former judge at the

[222] Kovalev, Chernichenko, *Mezhdunarodnoe pravo*, 80–1. [223] Ibid., 82.
[224] Ibid., 87. [225] Ibid., 88. [226] Chernichenko, ibid., 103.

International Criminal Tribunal for Rwanda, presents a specific example of how, in history, Russia's generally reserved attitude towards international law effectively shaped its practice. The case in point is international humanitarian law[227] and the fact that it took the USSR so long to ratify the Geneva conventions and their additional protocols.[228]

Moreover, Yegorov is critical of the fact that Russia has incorporated crimes against humanity and other crimes under international criminal law in the Russian Criminal Code in an unsatisfactory way.[229] Lukashuk has also criticized the fact that the Russian government has done too little in terms of harmonizing the country's legislation with its international legal commitments in the field of international humanitarian law.[230] According to Bakhtiyar Raisovich Tuzmukhamedov (b. 1955), the whole of international humanitarian law has essentially been squeezed into one Article of the Criminal Code.[231]

Yet Chernichenko's own theoretical account is ultimately not so different from what the Soviet scholars had written on international human rights and domestic law. For example, a booklet printed in Moscow in 1986 that explained to foreign readers, in English, the Soviet concept of human rights started with the following statement:

> There are principles and norms in current international laws relating to human rights. This does not mean that human rights are regulated by international law directly, or that they have ceased to be the internal affair of every state.[232]

It was clear that this theoretical vision went together with a specific understanding of what human rights meant in concrete instances, e.g. that freedom of expression was not guaranteed in the USSR. In the words of the same Soviet booklet published in 1986:

> . . . the Constitution guarantees the exercise of political rights and freedoms in order to carry out the tasks formulated in the preamble: lay the material and technical foundation of communism . . . Accordingly, it is impossible to guarantee the freedom of ideas or opinions that are in opposition to these constitutional aims. . . . Current Soviet legislation contains a number of other restrictions on the freedom of speech, the press and criticism, which are aimed at protecting society against the abuse of these freedoms, if they are used contrary to the interests of Soviet society or the state, to the detriment of state or public security, and the morals of citizens . . .[233]

[227] See generally S. Weill, *The Role of National Courts in Applying International Humanitarian Law* (Oxford: OUP, 2014).

[228] Yegorov, in Kovalev, Chernichenko, *Mezhdunarodnoe pravo*, 815.

[229] Ibid., 816. Yegorov expresses the same criticism in another textbook as well: V. I. Kuznetsov, B. R. Tuzmukhamedov (eds), *Mezhdunarodnoe pravo* (Moscow: Norma, 2007) 868–70 and in 'Vklad Rossii v razvitie mezhdunarodnogo gumanitarnogo prava' in *Vestnik Diplomaticheskoi Akademii MID Rossii. Mezhdunarodnoe pravo* (Moscow: Diplomaticheskaya Akademia, 2013) 69–85 at 78.

[230] Lukashuk, *Mezhdunarodnoe pravo. Osobennaya chast'*, 309–10.

[231] B. Tuzmkukhamedov, 'Kak voevat' po pravilam?', *Nezavisimaya Gazeta* 15.02.2010, <http://www.ng.ru/courier/2010-02-15/11_wars.html>.

[232] V. Kudryavtsev, V. Chkhikvadze, E. Lukasheva (eds), *International Covenants on Human Rights and Soviet Legislation* (Moscow: Novosty Press Agency, 1986) 5.

[233] Ibid., 35.

Thus, this is the historical legacy that forms the backdrop to the current debate about the status of the individual and the role of international law in domestic law in Russia. Essentially, it is the same strong type of dualism that Chernichenko favoured during the late Soviet period and that he continues to defend now:

> In contemporary Western doctrine the predominant majority of authors regard the direct access of individuals to international judicial organs as a process party as one of the main proofs of direct regulation of the situation of the population by international law. In native doctrine, different viewpoints are expressed on this issue. Often it is said that agreements that foresee direct access of individuals to international court organs are extremely rare, untypical and they cannot change the general rule. Sometimes it is highlighted that the international legal subjectivity of individuals has on such occasions a deductive, limited character and should not oppose state sovereignty. Alongside this also exists an opinion based on which these kinds of agreements concerning direct access of individuals to international judicial organs create only mutual rights and obligations for their participants, and cannot objectively turn individuals into subjects of international law ...[234]

In this way, the issue of who are the subjects of international law and how open the country's legal system is towards its obligations under international law become essentially two different sides of the same coin.

Chernichenko's strict 'objective dualism'[235] is defended and developed further by Bogdan Leonidovich Zimnenko (b. 1973), Professor at the Russian Judicial Academy, who argues that national courts may not, 'for objective reasons', apply international law directly.[236] Chernichenko's core argument of 'objective boundaries of international law' runs like a red thread through Zimnenko's work—norms of international law may not, for 'objective reasons' become part of national law;[237] state organs in their relationships with subjects of national law do not have 'objective possibilities' to interpret norms of international law;[238] international law may not, for 'objective reasons', regulate intra-state relations;[239] a collision between international legal norms and domestic norms is 'objectively' impossible because the two are different legal systems.[240]

In Zimnenko's analysis, 'objective boundaries of international law' are not so much explained but taken for granted, as an indisputable dogmatic starting point. This method even leads Zimnenko to the awkward conclusion that the constitutional provision of Article 15 para. 4 should not be interpreted, in order not to reach wrong conclusions, 'word by word'.[241] Zimnenko also concludes that no norm of international law can ever be self-executing—even if such a norm would appear to the interpreter to be self-executing at first glance, in reality it is not because it cannot 'objectively' be, at least from the correct doctrinal point of view.[242]

234 Chernichenko, in Kovalev, Chernichenko, *Mezhdunarodnoe pravo*, 186–7.

235 Chernichenko, *Ocherki po filosofii mezhdunarodnomu pravu*, 648, 650; Chernichenko, *Teoria mezhdunarodnoga prava*, Vol. 2, 339.

236 B. L. Zimnenko, *Mezhdunarodnoe pravo i pravovaya sistema Rossiiskoi Federatsii* (Moscow: Statut, 2010) 40. See also Chernichenko, *Ocherki po filosofii mezhdunarodnomu pravu*, 645, 650.

237 Ibid., 85, 135. 238 Ibid., 115. 239 Ibid., 138–9.

240 Ibid., 231. 241 Ibid., 136. 242 Ibid., 139.

Such positions read more like contemporaries of German international law scholar Heinrich Triepel's (1868–1946) work *Völkerrecht und Landesrecht* (1899)[243] rather than post-Cold War European analyses of the close interaction between international and domestic law. The larger ideological goal of statist scholars in Russia seems to be to keep international law at a safe distance from Russia's own—narrowly construed—legal system. It is an interpretation of state sovereignty. However, it is also a mental departure from the original meaning of Russia's Constitution of 1993.

In the same context, the role of the European Court of Human Rights—Russia is subject to its jurisdiction since 1998—is also strategically downplayed. Authors such as Zimnenko emphasize the limits of the legal authority of the ECtHR rather than the importance of its case law for Russia's judiciary.[244] Because Zimnenko's book is addressed primarily to Russian judges, he also has useful advice for his audience: although the principle of separation of powers exists, judges should remember that international treaties are first of all the business of the executive so if ever judges encounter any questions on interpretation, they 'not only have the right but also the duty' to turn to the executive for help with the question.[245]

The Chernichenko school of thought also extends the interpretation of the relationship between international and constitutional law to EU law which it perceives as an empirical challenge and even threat for its 'objective dualist' theory. Thus, the textbook co-edited by Chernichenko holds the view that in the EU, individuals and companies cannot be subjects of law; only states can.[246] Moreover, the so-called direct effect of EU law is rather an illusion than reality.[247] Because the EU is acknowledged as an international organization rather than something *sui generis* in statist Russian scholarship, it is quite clear that the EU fits only poorly in such 'strictly dualist' theoretical schemes. In addition, Sergei Vladimirovich Bakhin is critical that European legal scholars have had a Eurocentric and quite arrogant image of the centrality and specialness of EU law, even occasionally claiming the priority of European law over general international law.[248] Without further going into the subject matter, this criticism may contain a grain of truth.

Chernichenko and his statist colleagues do not usually offer policy arguments but instead argue in the ritualized limits of formalist logic and positivism, thus keeping open politics away from the theory of international law. However, as an exception in this camp Yevgeni Trofimovich Usenko (1918–2010) also made the policy argument quite clear: dualist theory is in the best interest of the Russian state so that to deny that theory is essentially a form of dangerous anti-statism.[249]

[243] One of the Russian dualists, Usenko, includes an in-depth and highly favourable study of Triepel's book in his argumentation of why dualism prevails. Usenko, *Ocherki teorii mezhdunarodnoga prava*, 122 et seq.

[244] Zimnenko, *Mezhdunarodnoe pravo i pravovaya sistema Rossiiskoi Federatsii*, 214–21. For a similar view, see also Biryukov, *Mezhdunarodnoe pravo*, 502, 510.

[245] Zimnenko, *Mezhdunarodnoe pravo i pravovaya sistema Rossiiskoi Federatsii*, 132.

[246] M. Biryukov, in Kovalev, Chernichenko, *Mezhdunarodnoe pravo*, 698.

[247] Ibid., 700. See also Chernichenko, *Ocherki po filosofii mezhdunarodnomu pravu*, 653.

[248] Bakhin, 'Pravo integratsionnykh obrazovanii', 118, 124–6.

[249] Usenko, *Ocherki teorii mezhdunarodnoga prava*, 153.

Usenko also makes the comparative point that Russia should not become more friendly towards international law as are the US and UK—even though both recognize international law as the 'law of the land', the UK, according to Usenko, regards its Parliament's law as higher than customary international law and in the US a later Act by the Congress would prevail over an international treaty.[250] Usenko connects the influx of monist ideas in Russia with the decline of the USSR—the new 'liberal' interpretations 'were objectively directed against the state sovereignty of the country' whereas their enthusiastic promoters may not even have been themselves always aware that this was the case.[251]

It will be interesting to see how the sovereignist school will further react to ruling No 21 of the plenary session of the Supreme Court of the Russian Federation, adopted on 27 June 2013, 'On Application of the Convention for the Protection of Human Rights and Fundamental Freedoms of 4 November 1950 and Protocols thereto by Courts of General Jurisdiction'[252] which again seeks to be quite open and inclusive towards Strasbourg jurisprudence in the Russian judicial context.[253]

Coming now to the other school of thought advocating more openness towards international law in Russia, then again one of its leaders was Gennady Vladimirovich Ignatenko from Yekaterinburg. Shortly before Ignatenko died, he published a collection of articles that demonstrate the evolution of his views on the question of subjects of international law and the interaction between international and domestic law throughout the last 40 years.[254] During the Soviet period there was no freedom of choice on these theoretical questions and Ignatenko too then supported the general view in the USSR, namely that individuals could not be subjects of international law and that direct applicability of international law in the USSR was not a possibility.[255]

Such a personal archaeology of views by Ignatenko is movingly honest and demonstrates how debate over the nature of international law could emerge in Russia only at the time of perestroika.[256]

Ignatenko recollects how in around 1978 during a heated theoretical debate at the Soviet Association of International Law in Moscow a colleague rhetorically equated the idea of direct applicability of international legal norms in the domestic sphere with 'pouring water to the mill of imperialism'.[257] Ignatenko also regretted that some of his 'very important colleagues' continued to demonstrate a sharply negative attitude towards 'dissidents' in the context of the question of domestic applicability of international legal norms.[258]

[250] Ibid., 158, 165. [251] Ibid., 164.

[252] <http://www.supcourt.ru/catalog.php?c1=English&c2=Documents&c3=&id=9155>.

[253] See further A. Kovler, O. Chernishova, 'The June 2013 Resolution No. 21 of the Russian Supreme Court. A Move Towards Implementation of the Judgments of the European Court of Human Rights', 33 *Human Rights Law Journal* 2013, 263–6.

[254] G. V. Ignatenko, *Mezhdunarodnoe pravo i vnutrigosudarstvennoe pravo. Problemy sopryazhennosti i vzaimodeistvia* (Moscow: Norma, 2012). [255] Ibid., 24.

[256] See also N. D. Zakharova, 'Individ—sub'ekt mezhdunarodnoga prava', 11 *Sovetskoe gosudarstvo i pravo* 1989, 112–18; R. A. Müllerson, in R. A. Müllerson, G. I. Tunkin (eds), *Kurs mezhdunarodnoga prava v 7 tomakh*, Vol. 1 (Moscow: Nauka, 1989) 161.

[257] Ignatenko, *Mezhdunarodnoe pravo i vnutrigosudarstvennoe pravo*, 307.

[258] Ibid., 307.

Ignatenko further lamented that the legal education of judges in Russia has been such that they have not become used to applying international law and moreover, that in their interpretations the Supreme Court and the Constitutional Court of the Russian Federation had taken a rather restricted and quite conservative view towards the applicability of international law in the country's courts.[259] In other words, these high courts did not use all the possibilities that the wording of Article 15 para. 4 of the Russian Constitution of 1993 offered. However, when Ignatenko was writing, on 10 October 2003 the Plenum of the Supreme Court of the Russian Federation (not to be confused the Constitutional Court) had already adopted the ruling 'On Application by Courts of General Jurisdiction of the Commonly Recognized Principles and Norms of International Law and the International Treaties of the Russian Federation'.[260]

Ignatenko's conclusion was that of course direct applicability of international legal norms in Russia's domestic courts had become possible.[261] In the international law textbook that was already published posthumously, Ignatenko was quite sarcastic about the views of the Chernichenko camp, which he considered antiquated:

> These days a sense of anachronism permeates propositions in some contemporary (by year of publication) textbooks that international law is not 'objectively' (?) capable of regulating relations within the state, that its norms 'from the outset are not meant' (?) to regulate such relations. These claims are not supported and cannot be supported by real arguments . . .[262]

Ignatenko's views have been developed further by his disciple, Professor Sergei Yurevich Marochkin (b. 1956) who works at Tyumen State University in Siberia. Just like Ignatenko, Marochkin criticizes the 'objective limits' thesis of the Chernichenko School[263] and suggests that the constitutional term 'legal system' should be interpreted to include international legal norms.[264] Marochkin raises doubts whether some of the federal legislation on international law actually corresponds to the constitutional formulation of 1993[265]—which is a quite courageous statement in the context of Russian legal scholarship, considering its historical limits when to say that the main branches of the government had got it wrong was basically not allowed. Unlike Zimnenko, who argues that collisions between norms of international and domestic law are 'objectively impossible', Marochkin holds the view that such collisions are fully normal.[266]

Marochkin favours direct applicability of international legal norms and in his analysis works out criteria for self-executing norms in the Russian legal context.[267]

[259] Ibid., 358, 368–9.
[260] See <http://www.supcourt.ru/catalog.php?c1=English&c2=Documents&c3=&id=6801.
[261] Ignatenko, *Mezhdunarodnoe pravo i vnutrigosudarstvennoe pravo*, 124.
[262] Ignatenko, in Ignatenko, Tiunov, *Mezhdunarodnoe pravo*, 37.
[263] S. Yu. Marochkin, *Deistvie i realizatsia norm mezhdunarodnoga prava v provovoi sisteme Rossiiskoi Federatsii* (Moscow: Norma, 2011) 47, 77, 115.
[264] Ibid., 61. [265] Ibid., 55. [266] Ibid., 279. [267] Ibid., 50, 83, 238 et seq.

Marochkin points out that it was because of strict dualism and its concept of the necessity of 'transformation' that international law remained distant to the USSR:

> It was no coincidence that a gap existed between native law and the international obligations of the country; many international law norms 'waited their turn' for many years. . . . As a consequence, the law of the country as a whole was 'closed off', not capable of dynamically reacting to international treaties that were newly adopted and entered into force.[268]

Another Russian scholar, Boris Ivanovich Osminin, gives a useful comparative analysis of how other countries have dealt with the question of direct applicability of treaty norms. He points out that the constitutional systems in certain countries (Great Britain, Australia, Canada, Ireland, Malta, Israel as well as the Scandinavian countries Denmark, Sweden, Norway, and Iceland) do not accept and allow self-executing treaty norms.[269] Since these are Western nations and also economically among the most developed, the dilemma between direct applicability is globally not of 'civilization' (coming from the goodness of international law) versus autarchic countries.

Another scholar supporting Russia's openness towards international law, Viatcheslav Viatcheslavovich Gavrilov (b. 1963) at the Far Eastern State University in Vladivostok, has studied the application of international law in dualist Great Britain and points out the extensive court practice on international law there. Gavrilov makes an implicit comparison between Britain and Russia when he rejects the 'negative' appraisal of Lukashuk on court practice in Britain:

> In our view, more negative for the development of international treaty law are situations where a constitutional norm in a declaratory way proclaims treaties to be part of the law of the country whereas even minimal court practice on this question is lacking as indeed is the willingness to develop it.[270]

If such a hypothetical country could have been the USSR then Gavrilov favours the British model to the Soviet one. Gavrilov also argues that a governmental 'quasi- boycott' of international law would not work in the long run because the internationalization of law will not go away but, rather, will increase.[271]

Because of the Soviet legacy, the debate on the possibility of self-executing norms has specific cultural-historic dimensions in Russia where the statists see themselves as defenders of the Russian state's greatness while the 'progressives' essentially want Russia, with the help of international law, to become a more open and modern (and in this sense, inevitably also, more 'Western'), country.

However, they are warned by statists, e.g. by Usenko, that their ideas are, in fact, too Western:

[268] Ibid., 85.

[269] B. I. Osminin, *Zaklyuchenie i implementatsia mezhdunarodnykh dogovorov i vnutrigosudarstvennoe pravo* (Moscow: Infotropic, 2010) 264–5.

[270] V. V. Gavrilov, 'Mesto i rol' mezhdunarodnogo prava v pravovoi sisteme Velikobritanii', in 4 *Pravovedenie* 2008 (279), 209–17 at 213.

[271] Ibid., 217.

> Many theoreticians in the West presume that international law regulates not only interstate relations but also relations between individuals, that in one or another way it determines their rights and duties. Erasing the limits between international and national law and putting the former above the latter, they objectively create possibilities to justify the politics of intervention by some states in the domestic affairs of other sovereign states.[272]

During the Soviet period, the courts only seldom applied international law.[273] It is fascinating that 20 years after adoption of the constitution in 1993, Russian experts of international law are still not sure whether in the actual practice of courts Russia allows direct applicability of international treaty norms. Osminin's study ends with a call (to the legislator?) to finally decide whether and to what extent the direct applicability of self-executing norms in Russian courts is encouraged.[274]

Mark L'vovich Entin (b. 1950) from MGIMO University of the Russian MFA, who does not see any 'Chinese wall' between international and national[275] law, writes aptly:

> The existing Constitution of Russia is based on the supremacy of the norm of international law in the domestic legal order.... But this is only the first step. The second would be to concretize what meaning we give to this principle, with what content it is to be filled. Be it in the judgments of the Constitutional Court or by the plenary of the Supreme Court. The third step would be to apply it in practice logically, clearly and uniformly. At the same time, notwithstanding efforts that have been made, to a large extent neither the second nor the third steps have been undertaken until now ...[276]

In other words, the constitutional opening and emphasis of 1993 regarding international law has so far remained primarily a declared aspiration rather than an everyday legal reality on the ground. The predominant Chernichenko School is at least clear about what they do not want, notwithstanding what the Constitution of 1993 says: exactly the kind of 'moderate monism' that is propagated by Western scholars who take a constitutionalist approach to international law and conceptually send the principle of state sovereignty to the backseat.[277]

Historically, we should keep in mind that in Soviet scholarship of international law, during the Stalin era the infamous Andrey Yanuarevich Vyshinsky (1883–1954) argued explicitly in favour of the supremacy of Soviet law over international law.[278] Should the Vyshinsky approach again make a comeback in Russia, this would have an explosive revanchist geopolitical potential in the region. For example, the point that the USSR was not dissolved 'legally', i.e. following its own

272 Usenko, *Ocherki teorii mezhdunarodnoga prava*, 131.

273 Valeev, Kurdyukov, *Mezhdunarodnoe pravo. Obshaya chast'*, 49.

274 Osminin, *Zaklyuchenie i implementatsia mezhdunarodnykh dogovorov i vnutrigosudarstvennoe pravo*, 283–6.

275 M. L. Entin, 'Vyzovy vremeni i novoe videnie mezhdunarodnoga, nadnatsional'nogo i vnutrigosudarstvennogo prava', in A. G. Lisitsyn-Svetlanov (ed.), *Novye vyzovy i mezhdunarodnoe pravo* (Moscow: Institut gosudarstva i prava RAN, 2010), 27–44 at 42.

276 Ibid., 39–40.

277 See e.g. A. Cassese, 'Towards a Moderate Monism. Could International Rules Eventually Acquire the Force to Invalidate Inconsistent National Laws?', in Cassese, *Realizing Utopia*, 187–99.

278 A. Ya. Vyshinski, *Voprosy mezhdunarodnoga prava i mezhdunarodnoi politiki* (Moscow: Gosiurizdat, 1951).

constitutional provisions, has sometimes been made by Russian international law scholars who are nostalgic about the USSR, its international status, and Moscow's power.[279]

In a monograph on the dissolution of the USSR, Petr Petrovich Kremnev (b. 1954) from Moscow State University discusses the Russian-Ukrainian treaties of the 1990s and questions the constitutionality of some aspects of these treaties under Russian constitutional law.[280] However, according to the Vienna Convention on the Law of the Treaties, these possible constitutional issues in the Russian Federation could not devaluate those treaties in the context of public international law.

In the meantime, the theory of dualism protects Russia's state sovereignty and usefully tolerates discrepancies between international law and Russia's domestic law.[281] The opinion is increasingly expressed that should a stipulation of a treaty contradict the Constitution of the Russian Federation, it should not be applied by Russia, notwithstanding the international law principle *pacta sunt servanda*.[282] Russia's constitution may be monist but conservative scholars continue to interpret the position of international law in Russia in a dualist fashion. Moreover, the more the Russian government has run into conflicts with norms of international law, the more audible has become the voice in the country's politics that demands amendment of the constitutional provision stipulating the priority of international law over domestic law. As the deputy Yevgeny Alekseevich Fedorov (b. 1963) from the governing 'United Russia' fraction argues populistically, currently the priority of 'international law' actually means the priority of 'American law'.[283]

10. Impact of Statism on the Understanding of Concrete Sub-Fields of International Law

We have so far seen that influential Russian scholars construe international law in a statist way that keeps individuals and other non-state actors away from international law while keeping international law at a safe distance from Russia's domestic law. The statist School is not the only one but it is the predominant School—a matter of fact which becomes obvious when one looks at the concrete implications of general philosophy in international legal doctrine. The main aim of this section

[279] Vel'iaminov, *Mezhdunarodnoe ekonomicheskoe pravo i protsess*, 128.

[280] P. P. Kremnev, *Raspad SSSR. Mezhdunarodno-pravovye problemy* (Moscow: Zertsalo-M, 2005) 89.

[281] See e.g. A. Semakov, 'Sootnoshenie mezhdunarodnoga i rossiiskogo prava kasatel'no korennykh narodov', *Gumilev Center*, 20.04.2011, <http://www.gumilev-center.ru/soootnoshenie-mezhdunarodnogo-i-rossijjskogo-prava-kasatelno-korennykh-narodov/>.

[282] I. I. Karandashov, 'Printsip *pacta sunt servanda* i chast' 4 stat'i 15 Konstitutsii Rossiiskoi Federatsii. Predely ikh tolkovania i primenenia v Rossiiskoi Federatsii', *Rossiiskii ezhegodnik mezhdunarodnoga prava* 2012 (St Petersburg: 'Rossiya-Neva', 2013) 174–89.

[283] A. Parfenova, 'Posle reshenia Gaagskogo suda izmenenia v Konstitutsii neobkhodimy', 05.08.2014, *Kommersant*, <http://www.kommersant.ru/doc/2539335>.

is to explore the impact of such theoretical views on the conceptualization of concrete sub-fields of international law in Russian scholarship.

i. International human rights law

How the theoretical question of the range of subjects of international law is solved also creates a certain hierarchy; in matters related to international legal regulation, a 'subject' is obviously higher than a 'non-subject'. That the state is higher and more important than the individual mirrors an ideological continuity in Soviet and mainstream Russian approaches to international law. Shurshalov wrote in 1971 that individuals cannot be subjects of international law because they are 'under the power of the state' and cannot, therefore, act in international relations in their own name.[284]

Similarly, if international law and domestic law interact only a little then in countries with historically weak mechanisms of human rights protection such as Russia, fewer chances will arise for international human rights law to 'break through' to the actual people, to become a tool in the defence of their rights and interests.

In the context of international human rights law, most academic works on international law in Russia treat human rights as one of the ten or so principles of international law and not necessarily as *primus inter pares* in the UN Charter.[285] The focus of the 'main principles of international law', usually reflecting the UN GA's Friendly Relations Declaration of 1970, has been recognized as one of the characteristic features of the Russian doctrine of international law.[286] However, as is well known, most of these principles deal with derivations of state sovereignty rather than human rights. In fact, Biryukov argues that it is not correct to say that the Universal Declaration of Human Rights reflects customary international law.[287]

Moreover, Russian textbooks of international law often *describe* international legal norms and institutions in the area of human rights from a safe distance rather than critically engaging for example ECtHR case law that has already for a while been both extensive and intense regarding the Russian Federation. For such statist writers, individual violations of human rights, while deplorable, are not comparable to all the damage that abuse of Western-inspired human rights discourse could do to Russia as a country. Too much human freedom and rights talk might endanger the territorial integrity of the vast country.

The textbook by Kovalev and Chernichenko introduces protection of human rights with the following comments:

[284] V. M. Shurshalov, *Mezhdunarodnye pravootnoshenia* (Moscow: 'Mezhdunarodnye otnoshenia', 1971) 77.

[285] See further on how the principles of international law are theorized in Safronova, *Mezhdunarodnoe publichnoe pravo*, 105–19.

[286] Shumilov, *Mezhdunarodnoe pravo*, 49–50.

[287] Biryukov, *Mezhdunarodnoe pravo*, 469.

...no references to the necessity to protect human rights may justify attempts to violate such principles as the sovereign equality of states, non-intervention of states in each other's internal affairs, use or threat of force in international relations.... It follows from the sovereignty of the state that the sphere of the mutual relationship with its own population is on one or another level an internal question, realized at the national level.... The field of international cooperation in humanitarian questions (first of all on questions of human rights) must be deideologized and depoliticized. At the level of official international contacts on humanitarian questions it is deemed necessary to exclude polemics of an ideological character and use of the questions under discussion for purely propagandistic goals.[288]

However, when discussing human rights with each other members of the international community have always spoken about human rights in a politicized way,[289] and Russia itself has been no exception.

Seeing similar concerns and building on their view that individuals 'objectively' cannot be subjects of international law, Usenko and Shinkaretskaya write in their textbook:

Abuse of international human rights norms is not permissible. Protection of those rights must be carried out in line with international law.[290]

Once again, protection of human rights is here interpreted as just one of ten or so key principles in international law, as a principle that ultimately must be subordinated to state sovereignty and its related principles.[291]

In another textbook, Melkov emphasizes:

Some Russian and foreign (especially US and UK) lawyer-internationalists...give priority to the principle of respect for human rights and freedoms to the detriment of the principles of sovereign equality of nations, non-intervention in the domestic affairs of states, non-use or threat of force. It is impossible to agree with these authors ...[292]

The textbook of Kuznetsov and Tuzmukhamedov simply starts with the statement that the principle of protection of human rights is one of the most 'difficult and problematic' in international law.[293]

Nevertheless, Vladimir Alekseevich Kartashkin (b. 1934) in the same textbook clearly distances himself from Soviet attitudes towards international human rights law, and criticizes the extreme positivism in the USSR that rejected any idea of the natural law origin of human rights.[294] Kartahskin admits that although the

288 Kovalev, Chernichenko, *Mezhdunarodnoe pravo*, 277–9.

289 See e.g. R. Freedman, *The United Nations Human Rights Council. A Critique and Early Assessment* (London: Routledge, 2013).

290 Usenko, Shinkaretskaya, *Mezhdunarodnoe pravo*, 46.

291 For a general tendency to analyse international law through the lens of its main principles, see e.g. L. N. Galenskaya, 'Kategoria printsipov kak pravovykh regulyatorov mezhdunarodnykh otnoshenii', *Materialy nauchno-prakticheskoi konferentsii 'Mezhdunarodnoe pravo: vchera, segodnya, zavtra', 8–9 oktyabrya 2010.g. K 100–letiu so dnya rozhdenia professora Romana L'vovicha Bobrova* (St Petersburg: 'Rossia-Neva', 2011) 58–79.

292 Melkov, *Mezhdunarodnoe pravo*, 78.

293 Kuznetsov, Tuzmukhamedov, *Mezhdunarodnoe pravo*, 224.

294 V. A. Kartashkin, in Kuznetsvov, Tuzmukhamedov, *Mezhdunarodnoe pravo*, 323.

USSR ratified both UN human rights covenants in 1973, it 'did not observe them in practice'.[295]

However, mildly critical voices like Kartashkin are not necessarily the mainstream in contemporary Russian international law scholarship. The same phenomena can be looked at very differently, depending on the scholar's ideology. For example, in contrast to Kartashkin Oleg Nikolaevich Khlestov observes with pride that the USSR was the first permanent member of the UN SC that 'ratified' the two UN Covenants in 1973.[296]

In monographs and scholarly articles, one may also encounter outright human rights-scepticism. For example, Safronova rejects the idea that protection of human rights should somehow be 'higher' than other central principles of international law, especially state sovereignty:

> Today most horrible international crimes in the world are committed under the pretext of protection of human rights and freedoms. Raising the principle of protection of human rights and freedoms, giving it the status of a 'general' principle, threatens the quality of interconnectedness and complexity of the main principles of international law and will lead to ideas of step by step rejection of the inviolability of a number of principles, especially in favour of recognizing the principle of humanitarian intervention under the pretext of protection of human rights and freedoms.[297]

Similar views are held by Vladimir Semenovich Kotlyar, who criticizes the approach that human rights have become more important than state sovereignty as a dangerous and imperialist Western concept.[298] Kotlyar expresses his support for the fundamental civilizational human rights criticism that Patriarch Kirill of the Russian Orthodox Church has made over the last decade.[299] Vel'iaminov criticizes the West for trying to make human rights the 'paramount' principle in international law, and for using human rights as excuses for interventions and acts of aggression.[300] Shumilov argues that the ideology of human rights in its Western understanding has been turned into an instrument of intervention and expansion.[301]

But of course none of these statist views in Russia are comparable to the radicalism of Dugin who has expressed his negative views on human rights in the following tirade:

[295] Ibid., 327.

[296] O. N. Khlestov, 'OON i aktual'nye problemy zastshity prav cheloveka', in *Vestnik Diplomaticheskoi Akademii MID Rossii. Mezhdunarodnoe pravo* (Moscow: Diplomaticheskaya Akademia, 2013) 15–31 at 23.

[297] Safronova, *Mezhdunarodnoe publichnoe pravo*, 115–16.

[298] V. S. Kotlyar, *Mezhdunarodnoe pravo i sovremennye strategicheskie kontseptsii SShA i NATO*, 2nd edn (2008) 107–17.

[299] Ibid., 20. See also Patriarch Kirill of Moscow, *Freedom and Responsibility. A Search for Harmony—Human Rights and Personal Dignity* (London: Darton, Longman and Todd, 2011).

[300] Vel'iaminov, *Mezhdunarodnoe ekonomicheskoe pravo i protsess*, 29, 31, 102.

[301] Shumilov, *Mezhdunarodnoe pravo*, 228.

We need to forget about this horrible dream that is called 'Western civilization', 'globalization', 'political correctness', 'liberalism', 'human rights'. We need to forget all about this horrible delirium.[302]

However, it must be said that Dugin's radical rejection of human rights has not been echoed positively in Russian international law scholarship. In post-Soviet international law scholarship in Russia, human rights is a subject treated with great interest and sometimes even enthusiasm but it is nevertheless subjugated to the principle of state sovereignty.

ii. Self-determination of peoples

The argument that human rights should not go against state sovereignty also extends to the right of peoples to self-determination. A representative example of how the worry about 'atomization' of state and society into many independent individuals with extensive rights and claims (human rights) is linked with the worry of too much self-determination of smaller peoples is a thought expressed by Igor I. Lukashuk:

As a result atomization occurs in contemporary society, which basically means that everyone is free to secure their elementary personal needs [and also] a tendency to establish small states based on ethnic allegiance. These states try to rid themselves of the burden of responsibility to solve common problems which cannot but have negative consequences, including for those states themselves.[303]

In other words, separatism based on claims to self-determination of peoples is a dangerous idea. On the other hand, in 1882 this was already the view of Martens in the imperial capital St Petersburg when he warned that the principle of self-determination of peoples was 'capable of destroying a lot'.[304]

Further, in his textbook on international law Lukashuk writes:

One should not absolutize the right to self-determination, to tear it off from other principles of international law.[305]

Lukashuk adds that a significant body of authors limits the effect of the principle of self-determination to cases related to colonialism.[306] However, since the USSR never officially acknowledged that the country might have had colonial relationships, it follows that the right of peoples to self-determination was not a Soviet or Russian problem.

The textbook edited by Kuznetsov and Tuzmukhamedov also warns the reader regarding the principle of self-determination:

302 A. G. Dugin, *Geopolitika postmoderna* (St Petersburg: Amfora, 2007) 109.

303 Lukashuk, *Pravo mezhdunarodnoi otvetstvennosti*, 15.

304 F. F. Martens, *Sovremennoe mezhdunarodnoe pravo tsivilizovannykh narodov*, Vol. 1 (Moscow: 'Yuridischeki kolledž MGU', 1996) 121.

305 Lukashuk, *Mezhdunarodnoe pravo. Obshaya chast'*, 280.

306 Ibid., 300.

In recent years the threat of misuse of this principle has emerged and become reality. Political, nationalist, separatist, criminal and other factors are often becoming the motive for use of this principle in a self-seeking way. For many nations a real danger to their territorial integrity is created. For that reason, realization of this principle should not lead to the destruction of existing states.[307]

Moreover, Galina Georgievna Shinkaretskaya of the Institute of State and Law of the Russian Academy of Sciences wrote in 2010 that the right of peoples to self-determination does not give the right to separate from the existing state and should a referendum decide on the question of separation, it is legitimate only when carried out throughout the whole country, not just in the separatist region.[308] Similar views can be encountered in other works.[309] However, this view also carries a certain Soviet nostalgia because if the principle suggested by Shinkaretskaya had been applied in 1991, since Mr Gorbachev also wanted to have it, no Soviet republic could have legally separated from Moscow. At the referendum of 17 March 1991 the majority of citizens in the USSR supported the preservation of the USSR although the republics that predominantly favoured separation from Moscow boycotted the Soviet referendum and organized referendums of their own.

To sum up the Russian discussion, one may refer to the straightforward conclusion and policy guideline in the international law textbook of Shumilov, the bottom line of Russian views on the matter: no nationality in the Russian Federation has the right to separate from the country.[310]

iii. International economic law

How international economic law is theorized provides another context in which questions of the range of subjects of international law as well as international law's interrelationship with domestic law have become practical and relevant. When foreign governments and TNCs make deals and do business with each other, is this 'international law' or not?

Insur Zabirovich Farkhutdinov (b. 1956) from the Institute of State and Law of the Russian Academy of Science and one of Russia's most prolific authors on international investment law discusses the problem of subjects of international law from the very perspective of international economic law and reaches the conclusion that only states are full subjects of international law.[311] Farkhutdinov argues that globalization and the flow of capital over borders in the form of investments can become a challenge for state sovereignty, and yet the principle of economic

[307] V. S. Ivanenko and V. I Kuznetsov, in Kuznetsov, Tuzmukhamedov, *Mezhdunarodnoe pravo*, 215.

[308] G. G. Shinkaretskaya, 'Polozhenie fakticheski sushestvuyushikh rezhimov (nepriznannykh gosudarstv)', in Lisitsyn-Svetlanov, *Novye vyzovy i mezhdunarodnoe pravo*, 158–75 at 168, 172.

[309] Kapustin, *Mezhdunarodnoe pravo*, 105; Kovalev, Chernichenko, *Mezhdunarodnoe pravo*, 58.

[310] Shumilov, *Mezhdunarodnoe pravo*, 437.

[311] I. Z. Farkhutdinov, 'Mezhdunarodnaja pravosubyektnost' v XXI veke: problemy i tendentsii', in Bakhin, *Mezhdunarodnye otnoshenia i pravo*, 198–214 at 209–10.

sovereignty must remain central in international economic law.[312] Companies and individuals are not 'subjects' of international economic law but simply 'participants' in the process of its application.[313]

Lukashuk admits that TNCs have become ever more important subjects of 'international economic relations'[314] but this is distinguishable from being subjects of *international law*. Aleksandr Nikolaevich Vylgezhanin (b. 1953) from MGIMO-University admits that TNCs are important 'players' and 'participants' in international legal relations but does not give a clear answer whether they have become 'subjects' or not.[315]

Sometimes political factors justifying scepticism towards TNCs are also referred to. The textbook by Lukashuk (this chapter is written in co-authorship with Dmitrieva) criticizes the fact that foreign countries, especially the US, have often controlled the activities of TNCs.[316] Aleksei Aleksandrovich Moiseev makes the equation between TNCs and Western economic interests,[317] which is a point that was already widespread in Soviet scholarship.

One consequence of the predominance of the statist position in Russian scholarship is that most of what is theorized as international economic law in the West is treated as a relatively marginal field of international law in Russian scholarship. Compared to Western approaches, most textbooks of international law pay little attention to international economic law. International law is about high politics, not so much about international business. The chapter discussing international economic law is usually hidden somewhere at the end between (and in terms of length 'equal to') the chapters on aviation law, space law, law regulating international criminality, and so on. Ten years after Thomas M. Franck spoke of 'the emerging right to democratic governance' in international law,[318] the Diplomatic Academy textbook of Kovalev and Chernichenko refers to international economic law as only an 'emerging field of international law'.[319]

Moreover, in contemporary Russian theory, international economic law is predominantly labelled as 'private' rather than 'public' international law, thus conceptually belonging to the domestic law of the respective country in the first place.[320] According to Lukashuk, public and private international law must be kept apart as separate fields:

> In the literature the view is expressed on the need to merge international public and private law. Such views have not found recognition.[321]

[312] I. Z. Farkhutdinov, 'Suverenitet gosudarstva i mezhdunarodnoe pravo. Vyzovy globalizatsii', in Lisitsyn-Svetlanov, *Novye vyzovy i mezhdunarodnoe pravo*, 53–66 at 54.

[313] Farkhutdinov, *Mezhdunarodnoe investitsionnoe pravo i protsess*, 56.

[314] Lukashuk, *Mezhdunarodnoe pravo. Osobennaya chast'*, 167.

[315] Vylegzhanin, *Mezhdunarodnoe ekonomicheskoe pravo*, 54–5.

[316] Lukashuk, *Mezhdunarodnoe pravo. Osobennaya chast'*, 163.

[317] Moiseev, *Suverenitet gosudarstva v mezhdunarodnom prave*, 259.

[318] T. M. Franck, 'The Emerging Right to Democratic Governance', 86 *AJIL* 1992, 46–91.

[319] Kovalev, Chernichenko, *Mezhdunarodnoe pravo*, 32.

[320] See e.g. Usenko, Shinkaretskaya, *Mezhdunarodnoe pravo*, 28, 32; Kovalev, Chernichenko, *Mezhdunarodnoe pravo*, 91–2.

[321] Lukashuk, *Mezhdunarodnoe pravo. Obshaya chast'*, 14.

Whenever individuals and TNCs come into play, the view is that this is essentially 'private international law', i.e. regulated by the state itself [322] since it would be 'premature' to recognize TNCs as subjects of international law.[323] Galenskaya emphasizes that 'private international law' is broader than the conflict of laws of the respective country.[324] It follows that the Russian notion of 'private international law' is broader than is common in Anglo-Saxon countries. Part of what is understood as 'international law' in the West is not seen by the majority of Russian scholars as international law proper but as 'private international law', i.e. as a specific part of Russian law.[325] Russian literature has a visual expression for it—'diagonal relationships'[326] which implies that a private actor is not equal to a foreign sovereign, even though they may be parties to a significant deal.

In Western scholarship, the view has gained popularity that in particular in connection with investor-state arbitration, the neat distinction between public and private international law has broken down in international economic law.[327] In academic works of general international law, international economic law is emphasized as one of the main vehicles of globalization, economic cooperation, and development. The scholarly literature on developments in WTO law and investor-state arbitration is booming, and since 2008 there even exists a Society of International Economic Law. However, Farkhutdinov concludes that even if the investor-state contract includes an arbitration clause, it is a (Russian) native contract, not an 'internationalized' contract.[328]

The theoretical problem of distinguishing between public and private international law goes hand in hand with the practical problem of to what extent to recognize the power of TNCs. Thus, Aleksei Aleksandrovich Moiseev, professor of international law at the Diplomatic Academy of the Russian MFA, writes:

> TNC as a subject of domestic law and even a subject of international economic relations continues to remain the subject of private international law but not of public international law.[329]

Translated into more political language, this way of putting it means that TNCs should not expect to become legally equal *under international law* to the Russian state (government) when doing business in Russia.

[322] Cf. Kolosov, Krivchikova, *Mezhdunarodnoe pravo*, 736. [323] Ibid., 108.

[324] L. N. Galenskaya, 'Tendentsia razvitia pravovoga regulirovania mezhdunarodnykh otnohenii v XXI veke', in Bakhin, *Mezhdunarodnye otnoshenia i pravo*, 28–41 at 37.

[325] See further L. P. Anufrieva, *Sootnoshenie mezhdunarodnogo publichnogo i mezhdunarodnogo chastnogo prava (sravnitel'noe issledovanie pravovykh kategorii)* (Moscow: Rossiiskyi gosudarstvennyi torgovo-ekonomicheskii universitet, 2002).

[326] See e.g. Farkhutdinov, *Mezhdunarodnoe investitsionnoe pravo i protsess*, 65.

[327] See e.g. A. Lowenfeld, 'Public Law in the International Arena. Conflict of Laws, International Law, and Some Suggestions for their Interaction', 163 *RCADI* 1979–II (Leiden: Martinus Nijhoff) 311; A.-M. Slaughter, 'International Law in a World of Liberal States', 6 *EJIL* 1995, 503–38 at 516.

[328] Farkhutdinov, *Mezhdunarodnoe investitsionnoe pravo i protsess*, 390.

[329] Moiseev, *Suverenitet gosudarstva v mezhdunarodnom prave*, 261.

To the extent that investors are not recognized as subjects of international investment law, investor-state arbitration remains problematic from the viewpoint of Russian doctrine of international law:

> Subjects of international investment law are 'public persons'—states and international organizations. The circle of investors is wider. Investors are most often private persons, first of all multinational corporations.[330]

Thus, legal protection of investments is classified as 'private international law' in Russian scholarship[331] which downplays the international legal aspect of this protection, i.e. the multilateral and bilateral investment treaties (BITs) that have been concluded by many countries, including some 60 treaties by the late USSR and Russia.[332] Aleksei Stanislavovich Ispolinov (b. 1964) from Moscow State University points out recent signs of a 'legitimacy crisis' in investor-state arbitration in the West as well[333] and Andrei A. Danelyan from the Diplomatic Academy critically observes that in such arbitrations, investors usually end up winning and states losing.[334] The general conclusion tends to be that in investor-state arbitration, private interests are too predominant.[335] Thus, although the field of international investment law has been introduced in post-Soviet scholarship, it is with strong doses of scepticism.

Another issue is that of state immunity in international law[336] and whether Russian approaches have changed since the Soviet era's firm insistence on absolute state immunity, i.e. the claim that no foreign court is ever entitled to accept a claim against the Soviet government. Some scholars indeed also continued to support the Soviet position of absolute immunity in the post-Soviet period.[337] At the same time, in contemporary scholarship in Russia, voices have become more audible arguing that Russia should nowadays reverse the Soviet position and adhere to the doctrine of functional immunity but no longer the absolute immunity of states.[338] In particular the Arbitrazh Procedural Code of 2002 has been interpreted as having made a step in this direction.[339]

330 Kuznetsov, Tuzmukhamedov, *Mezhdunarodnoe pravo*, 731.

331 N. G. Doronina, 'Istoria pravovoga regulirovania investitsii v mezhdunarodnom chastnom prave', in Bakhin, *Mezhdunarodnoe publichnoe i chastnoe pravo*, 272–92.

332 Farkhutdinov, *Mezhdunarodnoe investitsionnoe pravo i protsess*, 140.

333 A. S. Ispolinov, 'Rol' investitsionnykh arbitrazhei v razvitii sovremennogo investitsionnogo prava', in *Vestnik Diplomaticheskoi Akademii MID Rossii. Mezhdunarodnoe pravo* (Moscow: Diplomaticheskaya Akademia, 2013) 180–93 at 193.

334 A. A. Danelyan, 'Mezhdunarodnyi investitsionnyi arbitrazh—institut mezhdunarodnogo investitsionnogo prava', in *Vestnik Diplomaticheskoi Akademii MID Rossii. Mezhdunarodnoe pravo* (Moscow: Diplomaticheskaya Akademia, 2013) 201–21 at 220.

335 O. S. Shaposhnikova, 'Mezhdunarodnyi investitsionnyi arbitrazh. Istoria i aktual'nye problemy', *Rossiiskii ezhegodnik mezhdunarodnoga prava* 2012 (St Petersburg: 'Rossiya-Neva' 2013) 207–19 at 218.

336 See generally X. Yang, *State Immunity in International Law* (Cambridge: CUP, 2012).

337 N. A. Ushakov, *Mezhdunarodnoe pravo* (Moscow, 2000) 98–9.

338 V. M. Shumilov, *Mezhdunarodnoe finansovoe pravo* (Moscow: 'Mezhdunarodnye otnoshenia', 2005) 69; Shumilov, *Mezhdunarodnoe ekonomicheskoe pravo*, 83. Kuznetsov, Tuzmukhamedov, *Mezhdunarodnoe pravo*, 713.

339 Farkhutdinov, *Mezhdunarodnoe investitsionnoe pravo i protsess*, 319.

At the same time, some of the same group of contemporary authors favouring functional over absolute immunity seem to admit that state practice in Russia is not yet clear on this position and legislative practice has started to move away from the doctrine of absolute immunity only recently.[340] Irina Olegovna Khlestova (b. 1948) from the Institute of Legislation and Comparative Legal Studies of the Government of the Russian Federation suggests that Russia needs a new federal act recognizing functional immunity.[341] However, no such legislation has yet been passed. The authors of the textbook edited by Valeev and Kurdykov at Kazan State University favour functional over absolute immunity but admit that Russian legislation seems still to favour absolute immunity.[342]

It is also clear where, philosophically, such doubts about functional immunity of states originate—because states have 'legal protection that is not accessible to individuals or juridical persons'.[343] In other words, with the question of whether state immunity is absolute or functional, one is back to theoretical square one and the question whether legal protection of individuals and companies could at least be comparable to that of states in international economic law.

Statist, anti-Western, and anti-globalist approaches influence the understanding of international economic law in Russia, as can for example be seen in a textbook by one of Russia's leading experts on international economic law, Georgy Mikhailovich Vel'iaminov (b. 1925) from the Diplomatic Academy of the MFA.[344] Vel'iaminov argues that the US wants to strategically contain Russia and for years created obstacles so that Russia would not become a member of the WTO.[345] Moreover, he argues that double standards were used against Russia in the context of the WTO.[346] The ideology of globalism is in many ways the ideology of pan-Americanism.[347] The international law of the UN Charter has come under enormous 'pressure', *inter alia* with the claim that TNCs and individuals should now be recognized as subjects of international law.[348]

Vel'iaminov suggests that Russian authors should resist these subversive Western approaches.[349] Furthermore, he criticizes the 'Western' approach, as expressed by French scholars Dominique Carreau and Patrick Juillard in their textbook on international economic law, which has been translated into Russian,[350] for their attempts to blur the lines between public and private international law and to include agreements between foreign governments and private actors in the realm of international economic law.[351] In the specific context of international economic

340 I. O. Khlestova, *Yurisdiktsionnyi immuniteet gosudarstva* (Moscow: Yurisprudentsia, 2007) 183.
341 Ibid., 200.
342 Valeev, Kurdyukov, *Mezhdunarodnoe pravo. Obshaya chast'*, 430–1.
343 Vylegzhanin, *Mezhdunarodnoe ekonomicheskoe pravo*, 51.
344 Vel'iaminov, *Mezhdunarodnoe ekonomicheskoe pravo i protsess*.
345 Ibid., 20, 129, 314–16. 346 Ibid., 316. 347 Ibid., 22, 32.
348 Ibid., 31. 349 Ibid., 75.
350 See D. Carreau, P. Julliard, *Droit international économique*, 3rd edn (Paris: Dalloz, 2007). Russian version: *Mezhdunarodnoe ekonomicheskoe pravo* (Moscow: 'Mezhdunarodnye otnoshenia', 2002).
351 Vel'iaminov, *Mezhdunarodnoe ekonomicheskoe pravo i protsess*, 39–46, 80–2.

law, Vel'iaminov notes critically that the BITs concluded by the US are predominantly in the interests of the investors.[352]

Comparable views are held by Vladimir Mikhailovich Shumilov (b. 1954), another leading Russian scholar writing on international economic law.[353] Shumilov expresses the already familiar point that the West was egoistic about the European Energy Charter Treaty and, as a consequence, Russian and Western obligations were not balanced.[354] Like Vel'iaminov, Shumilov criticizes the practice of extending national protection regime to BITs, considering it an 'egoistic' US initiative.[355] US attempts to create extraterritorial application for its laws such as the Helms-Burton Act of 1996 are also severely criticized.[356] Shumilov concludes that international investment law works in favour of the West and a just international financial order of the future should take more into account the interests and values of other states, *inter alia* the states of 'other civilization types'.[357]

In another textbook on international economic law Shumilov seems to acknowledge more than Vel'iaminov or anyone else in Russian scholarship that in the sphere of economic regulation, international and domestic law are growing together.[358] Shumilov even sees a new 'global law' emerging in the future that would embrace both international and domestic law.[359] However, Shumilov's strategic analysis of the future of international economic law is as critical of the West as Vel'iaminov's. In particular, Shumilov argues that in the long run Russia's strategic interests may just be too different from states of the 'Western civilization type'.[360]

Shumilov argues that Russia must defend its natural resources from countries like the US.[361] He points out that Russia has a tremendous reservoir of natural resources such as forests, fresh air, and water while at the same time the Russian economy constitutes only 2 per cent of the world's economy. De facto then Russia is an ecological and implicitly also an economic donor to the rest of the world, and as a consequence, Shumilov suggests:

> Such a burden on Russia must be compensated in one or another (economic, financial) form when multilateral problems in ecology and other spheres are solved.[362]

Thus, according to Shumilov, the rest of the world owes Russia in terms of the free use of its vast clean nature.

In his analysis of international economic law, Shumilov repeatedly and critically refers to states of the 'Western civilization type' while at the same time arguing that CIS countries are the civilizational space for Russia.[363] At the same time, he observes that the West wants to prevent a deeper Eurasian integration.[364]

It is interesting to see that notwithstanding Russia's joining the WTO in 2012, in the latest edition of Shumilov's textbook on international economic

[352] Ibid., 362, 364. [353] Shumilov, *Mezhdunarodnoe finansovoe pravo.*
[354] Ibid., 304. [355] Ibid., 308. [356] Ibid., 315. [357] Ibid., 360–1.
[358] Shumilov, *Mezhdunarodnoe ekonomicheskoe pravo*, 15, 55. [359] Ibid., 35, 88.
[360] Ibid., 29. [361] Ibid., 30–3. [362] Ibid., 44.
[363] Ibid, 67–8, 86, 116, 225. In particular, 'competition' is the highest value in the economies of Western civilization type, ibid., 67.
[364] Ibid., 226.

law, anti-Westernism and emphasis on Russia's civilizational otherness have become even more poignant whereas now Shumilov is already speaking of the 'Russian doctrine of international law' in the context of international economic law.[365]

Altogether, these positions and discussions demonstrate that the approach of Russian academic lawyers to international economic law is in a number of ways ideologically closer to third world approaches (TWAIL) rather than to mainstream Western approaches that conceptually embrace and facilitate the phenomenon of economic globalization. Shumilov suggests that the task of Russia together with other non-Western civilizational centres is to carry out 'correctives' in the architecture of international economic law.[366]

It is also interesting to note that the language sceptical of the Western bias in international economic law and institutions has not changed much since Russia's accession to the WTO in 2012. Shumilov thus effectively echoes Dugin's dismissive words that the West is merely a 'market' civilization.[367] If so then the law of the WTO must be nothing more than the international law of 'market civilization'; but the fact remains that Russia too now participates in it. Specialized literature on international economic law in the form of monographs has started to emerge only relatively recently, but it has started to emerge.[368]

iv. Ius ad bellum

In Russian scholarship, issues related to the international legal regulation of military conflicts are probably the central question in international law, and questions such as protection of human rights are often discussed in the light of this question as well.

During the Soviet and the immediate post-Soviet period, Russian scholars took a straightforward conservative view on what Article 2 para. 4 and Articles 42 and 51 of the UN Charter imply. The use of military force is only legal if it is carried out in self-defence against armed attack or when authorized by the SC. At least up until Russia's invasion and annexation of Crimea in March 2014 this position has been the view shared by the majority of international law scholars in Russia.[369]

However, in some aspects post-Soviet Russia's scholarly doctrine on this question has begun to change compared to the straightforward Soviet position. To

[365] V. M. Shumilov, *Mezhdunarodnoe ekonomicheskoe pravo*, 6th edn (Moscow: Yurait, 2014) 32, 219–20.

[366] Ibid., 131.

[367] A. Dugin, *Proekt Evraziya* (Moscow: Yauza EKSMO, 2004) 369, 374.

[368] See R. A. Shepenko, *Vvedenie v pravo VTO. Kurs antidempingovogo regulirovania* (Moscow: Prospekt, 2014); D. S. Boklan, *Mezhdunarodnoe ekologicheskoe pravo i mezhdunarodnye eonomicheskie otnoshenia* (Moscow: Magistr Infra-M, 2014).

[369] See e.g. S. V. Chernichenko, 'Vzglyad na opredelennye polozhenia konstitutsii Rossiiskoi Federatsii s mezhdunarodno-pravovykh pozitsii', in *Vestnik Diplomaticheskoi Akademii MID Rossii. Mezhdunarodnoe pravo* (Moscow: Diplomaticheskaya Akademia, 2013) 44–63 at 63.

start with, there have been some changes in the government's policy documents regarding the use of force, especially in the context of preventive self-defence and protection of nationals abroad. The USSR did not have many nationals permanently living abroad, in neighbouring states, to protect militarily.

However, Russia's Military Doctrine of 2010 already 'legalized' the use of force for securing the interests of Russian citizens outside the territory of the country, 'in accordance with generally recognized principles and norms of international law and international treaties of the Russian Federation'.[370] This was a clear departure from Soviet era positions. Concerning self-defence, the Russian government has started increasingly to borrow from US and NATO post-Cold War doctrines which have made a move towards preventive self-defence. Western doctrines have been studied and criticized in detail by the country's leading international law experts such as Vladimir Semenovich Kotlyar, Professor at the Diplomatic Academy of the Russian MFA.[371]

Almost all Russian textbooks of international law refer to NATO intervention against Yugoslavia (in favour of Kosovo Albanians) in 1999 and the US and UK-led coalition invasion of Iraq in 2003 as examples of illegality, as crimes of aggression.[372] In the same breath, some scholars in Russia and other CIS countries also refer to the military campaign in Afghanistan in 2001 as illegal.[373] However, different authors use these cases with different intensity and sophistication—the record is probably owned by the international law textbook edited by Melkov that in order to drive the point home refers on approximately ten occasions to the cases of Kosovo, Afghanistan, and Iraq as Western aggression.[374] Moreover, Melkov also suggests that in the case of Yugoslavia, legally speaking, (apparently Russian?) 'nuclear weapons could have been used' against NATO aggression.[375]

Shumilov does not have 'illusions' about US power either, considering it the 'world champion' of the use of military force and the American official doctrine of international law being in favour of the priority of force, not international law.[376] For Shumilov, the fact that the US considers its Constitution to be higher than its international legal commitments is the main source of its 'international legal nihilism'.[377]

[370] *Military Strategy of the Russian Federation*, Presidential Decree of 5 February 2010 No 146, point 20.

[371] V. S. Kotlyar, *Mezhdunarodnoe pravo i sovremennye strategicheskie kontseptsii SShA i NATO*, 2nd edn (Kazan: Tsentr innovatsionnykh tekhnologii, 2008).

[372] See e.g. Shumilov, *Mezhdunarodnoe pravo*, 157: Kolosov, Krivchikova, *Mezhdunarodnoe pravo*, 70, 428; K. A. Bekyashev (ed.), *Mezhdunarodnoe publichnoe pravo*, 2nd edn (Moscow: Prospekt, 2003) 221, 353, 595, 615; Kovalev, Chernichenko, *Mezhdunarodnoe pravo*, 241; Vylegzhanin, *Mezhdunarodnoe pravo*, 672. (Arguing that NATO's Kosovo intervention had 'undoubtedly' non-humanitarian motives.); Valeev, Kurdyukov, *Mezhdunarodnoe pravo. Obshaya chast'*, 33; Chernichenko, *Teoria mezhdunarodnoga prava*, Vol. 2, 516.

[373] See e.g. A. F. Douhan, *Printsip nevmeshatel'stva vo vnutrennie dela gosudarstv. Sovremennye tendentsii* (Minsk: 'Pravo i ekonomika', 2009) 244–51.

[374] Melkov, *Mezhdunarodnoe pravo*, 10, 18, 64, 88, 117, 124, 325, 594, 597, 642–3, 678.

[375] Ibid., 88.

[376] Shumilov, *Mezhdunarodnoe pravo*, 189, 198.

[377] Ibid., 111, 135.

Generally, the US and NATO have been depicted as aggressive and systematically violating international law after the end of the Cold War:

> Based on NATO's Strategic Concept of 1999 and the US Strategy of National Security of 2002, NATO is attempting to push aside the UN and the OSCE from the resolution of security issues in Europe. The activities of NATO violate the stipulations of the UN Charter on non-use of force and sovereign equality of states ...[378]
>
> Notwithstanding the clearly expressed *opinio juris* that the intervention of member states of NATO in the domestic affairs of the Federal Republic of Yugoslavia should not be seen as a precedent, the further policies of the US have in many ways been based on treating it as such.[379]

A position critical of the US and NATO's use of military force and favouring a relatively strict prohibition of the use of force has also been predominant in monographs and scholarly articles.[380] Russian scholars who adhere to the view that the use of force must be maximally restricted in international law have even criticized remarks and statements by Russian government members that have been more permissive and open towards the possibility of preventive self-defence.[381]

However, the minority opinion so far has started to welcome and endorse such statements.[382] It is possible that this view will gain more popularity among Russian scholars after the invasion and occupation of Crimea in 2014. By the previous criteria of the main representatives in Russian scholarship on international law, Russia's invasion and annexation of Crimea can only be labelled as 'aggression'. However, virtually no Russian international law scholars have publicly called the annexation of Crimea 'aggression'.

What was not sufficiently noticed in the West is that some Russian international law scholars had made claims regarding Crimea even before the annexation of 2014, calling it a historic Russian land and arguing that Russia could take it back if it wanted to.[383]

The new school that is more open to use of military force argues along the lines that if NATO can violate international law and/or make new rules (or exceptions) for itself, Russia has no choice but to follow its example. Shumilov argues that the US can be forced to multilateral measures only if Russia first copies the US unilateralist 'pattern of behaviour'.[384]

A few Russian experts on international law have also raised doubts whether official Russia should be so conservative about the UN Charter and *jus ad bellum* because in reality, due to the hegemonial behaviour of the US, international law already *is* in deep crisis.[385] Natalia Alekseevna Narotchnitskaya (b.1948), a Russian

378 Biryukov, *Mezhdunarodnoe pravo*, 449.

379 Douhan, *Printsip nevmeshatel'stva vo vnutrennie dela gosudarstv*, 265.

380 V. S. Kotlyar, 'O mezhdunarodno-pravovoi pozitsii Zapada v svyazi s novymi vyzovai i ugrozami', in Lisitsyn-Svetlanov, *Novye vyzovy i mezhdunarodnoe pravo*, 91–9; S. V. Chernichenko, 'O bor'be s terroristami na inostrannoi territorii', in Lisitsyn-Svetlanov, *Novye vyzovy i mezhdunarodnoe pravo*, 99–103.

381 V. S. Kotlyar, *Mezhdunarodnoe pravo i sovremennye strategicheskie kontseptsii SShA i NATO*, 2nd edn (2008) 369–70.

382 Shumilov, *Mezhdunarodnoe pravo*, 199.

383 Ibid., 222, 233.

384 Ibid., 199.

385 Vel'iaminov, *Mezhdunarodnoe ekonomicheskoe pravo i protsess*, 33.

politician, historian, and publicist has argued that the West has systematically undermined 'classical international law and its main foundation—sovereignty'.[386]

In international law scholarship, an example of this emerging school is Yuri Nikolaevich Maleev (b. 1938) from MGIMO University in Moscow. In an article published in 2010, Maleev suggested that instead of strict adherence to the concept of non-use of military force, as has been typical of Soviet and Russian international law scholarship, it now makes sense to accept the fact that 'evidently, in international relations the principle of adequate and proportional use of force is becoming established'.[387]

Maleev argues:

> Today in many ways a new legal model in international relations, new international law, is lined up. As in the previous model, behind it undoubtedly stands power. Just another kind of power.[388]

As a consequence, Maleev argues that the right to self-defence is no longer restricted to responses to concrete armed attacks and in one's own territory.[389] Maleev admits that 'native' scholarship has been very torn about this issue because for decades Russian and Soviet scholars used to argue in favour of strict limitations on the use of military force.[390]

The view that international law as one knew it had already ceased to exist was already expressed in 2003 by realists in political science. For example, Dugin argued in an interview in 2003:

> The American invasion of Iraq is the final stage of the collapse of the world of Yalta.... Continuation of the international system in the 'old spirit' is ruled out. The UN today is incapable of fulfilling the functions foreseen by the UN Charter.[391]

There is also a less emotional and more analytical approach by the likes of Get'man-Pavlova who thinks that by the force of historical events, the international law of the UN era concerning *jus ad bellum* may simply have come to an end in 1999.[392] Get'man-Pavlova suggests that the UN would no longer be able to play such a role as it did from 1945 to 1999.[393]

Of course, realists would argue that this change of views on *jus ad bellum* in Russian international law scholarship is simply due to Russia's changing power, especially vis-à-vis the US. During the Soviet period, Moscow was saturated in terms of territorial conquest and its main worry was how to keep its territorial possessions. After the collapse of the USSR and the emergence of 15 independent states in the former territory of the USSR, Russia's main concern is quite

386 N. Narotchnitskaya, 'Rossiya v novykh geopoliticheskikh real'nostiakh', in: '...*I vremya sobirat' kamni* ... ' *Evraziiskaya integratsia segodnya. 20 let posle raspada SSSR* (Moscow: Fond istoriechskoi perspektivy, 2012) 4 et seq.

387 Y. N. Maleev, 'Primenenie sily v mezhdunarodnyh otnosheniakh v sovremennom ponimanii', in Lisitsyn-Svetlanov, *Novye vyzovy i mezhdunarodnoe pravo*, 75–91 at 76–7.

388 Ibid., 78. 389 Ibid., 84. 390 Ibid., 87.

391 A. G. Dugin, *Geopolitika postmoderna* (St Peterburg: Amfora, 2007) 92.

392 I. Get'man-Pavlova, *Mezhdunarodnoe pravo*, 2nd edn (Moscow: Yurait, 2013) 232.

393 Ibid., 234.

different—how to maintain control over or at least some leverage in the country's historical 'sphere of influence' where, however, sovereignty now belongs to someone else. But attitudes also reflect a growing impatience with the fact that hundreds of thousands of ethnic Russians now live abroad as minorities.

Finally, whatever the discourse of international law scholars, in all major countries realist voices are raised regarding international law and the use of military force. In Russia's case for instance Dugin, who has made the classic realist point: 'Geopolitical laws are merciless. The law belongs only to the stronger, the one capable of proving and defending it.'[394] This attitude has become known in international law literature as well—for instance, based on NATO's Kosovo intervention, Shumilov regrets that 'peace on Earth is still secured by Force, not Law; Interests, not Justice'.[395] Apparently then the same 'merciless geopolitical law' was envisaged to work in Russia's favour in Crimea's case.

v. International criminal law

Throughout the Soviet period, international criminal law was associated in Soviet literature with the seminal role that the USSR played at the Nuremberg trials. However, things have evolved since 1945. What are Russian attitudes to international criminal law in the post-Soviet period?

In the field of international criminal law, the authors of a recent Russian textbook on this specific sub-field of international law express their regret that in Russia no direct applicability of norms of international criminal law is allowed—even in cases when a direct analogue in the Russian Criminal Code is missing or when the specific crime has been transformed from international law into domestic law in a deficient manner.[396] As has already been pointed out, Russian scholars such as Egorov have referred to inconsistencies in the way war crimes and other international crimes have been 'translated' in the Criminal Code.

Doctrinally, statists among Russian theoreticians continue to support the concept of 'state crimes'[397] even though this concept was not included in the 2001 *Draft Articles of State Responsibility*—thanks mostly to the efforts of the representatives of the Anglo-Saxon doctrine, as Chernichenko points out.[398] The Soviet doctrine of international law even supported the concept of subjective 'guilt' of states,[399] which demonstrates to what extent the phenomenon of statehood was personified in the USSR, certainly also based on the experience of World War II. The textbook by Valeev and Kurdyukov is not fully certain of the element of 'guilt' of states but supports the notion of 'international crimes'.[400]

394 A. Dugin, *Proekt Evraziya* (Moscow: Yauza EKSMO, 2004) 426.
395 Shumilov, *Mezhdunarodnoe pravo*, 158.
396 Naumov et al., *Mezhdunarodnoe ugolovnoe pravo*, 52.
397 Chernichenko, *Teoria mezhdunarodnoga prava*, Vol 2, 406 et seq.
398 Kovalev, Chernichenko, *Mezhdunarodnoe pravo*, 239.
399 M. V. Keshner, in Valeev, Kurdykov, *Mezhdunarodnoe pravo. Obshaya chast'*, 462.
400 Ibid., 462.

The most widespread thesis in Russian textbooks and academic works on international criminal law seems to be condemnation of the ICTY as an institution. The main arguments are that the ICTY was established on a legally dubious basis by the UN SC and that it has been politically biased against the Serbs.[401] While somewhat more modest and balanced voices on the ICTY exist,[402] they seem to be in the minority.

In 1999 the Commission on the International Legal Qualification of Events around the Federal Republic of Yugoslavia was established in the Russian Federation and a number of leading international law scholars in Russia became members—Kuznetsov, Chernichenko, Kolosov, Blishchenko, Galenskaya, Abashidze, Bakhin, Laptev, Egorov, Reshetov, Malinin, Kotlyar, and some others.[403] The Commission qualified NATO's bombing of Yugoslavia in 1999 as aggression and qualified a number of NATO military acts as war crimes.[404]

The academic work of one scholar, Aleksandr Borisovich Mezyaev (b. 1971) from Kazan's TISBI University, in particular circles around the theme of the illegitimacy and even 'criminality' of the ICTY.[405] Mezyaev concludes that the UN SC exceeded its authority when establishing the Tribunal, the ICTY does not guarantee basic human and procedural rights, is not an independent court of law, judges are not impartial, and so on.[406] Emotionally, Mezyaev's attitude towards the ICTY is best captured by his argument that Yugoslavia's ex-President Slobodan Milošević had been 'killed' in The Hague.[407]

At the same time, there is no big enthusiasm in the literature to consider that international criminal law could play a certain role in Russia's own historical and political contexts. As in Nuremberg, international criminal law is a good thing—but for others. For example, legal scholar Irina Umnova considers it a 'grave violation of political ethics' that in 2003 and 2009 the Parliamentary Assembly of the Council of Europe passed resolutions encouraging the establishment of an international tribunal for Russian war crimes committed in Chechnya. [408]

Moreover, in Russian scholarship on international criminal law, there is almost no explicit policy-related discussion on whether the Russian Federation should ratify the Rome Statute and become a member of the ICC. On 8 September 2000,

[401] N. I. Kostenko, *Mezhdunarodnoe ugolovnoe pravo. Sovremennye teoreticheskie problemy* (Moscow: Yurlitinform, 2004) 22; Naumov et al., *Mezdhunarodnoe ugolovnoe pravo*, 221–31; Kovalev, Chernichenko, *Mezhdunarodnoe pravo*, 567; Ignatenko, Tiunov, *Mezhdunarodnoe pravo*, 433; I. A. Umnova, *Pravo mira. Kurs lektsii* (Moscow: Eksmo, 2011) 380 et seq.

[402] For example, I. S. Marusin, 'Mezhdunarodnyi ugolovnyi tribunal po byvshei Yugoslavii', in Bakhin, *Mezhdunarodnoe publichnoe i chastnoe pravo*, 262–71.

[403] A. B. Mezyaev, 'Mezhdunarodnyi ugolovnyi tribunal po byvshei Yugoslavii—nezakonnyi, zavisimyi i pristrastnyi sud', in A. I. Filomonova (ed.), *Dvoinye standarty v zashite prav cheloveka. Kazus professor Sheshelya* (Moscow: 'Fond istoricheskoi perspektivy', 2009) 47.

[404] Ibid., 47–8.

[405] A. B. Mezyaev, *Pravo obvinyaemogo v mezhdunarodnom ugolovnom prave* (Kazan: 'TISBI', 2010).

[406] Ibid., 298 et seq.

[407] A. B. Mezyaev, *Ubiistvo Slobodana Milosevica v Gaagskom tribunale. Nekotorye fakty i voprosy mezhdunarodnoga prava*, <http://www.trinitas.ru/rus/doc/0215/003a/02151012.htm>.

[408] Umnova, *Pravo mira*, 397.

Russia signed the Rome Statute but the document has not been officially published or ratified.[409]

A recent textbook by Naumov and his colleagues on international criminal law is laconic on this matter:

> Russian researchers attribute different factors as reasons for this, characterizing different aspects of the problem: constitutional, international legal, criminal law and criminological.[410]

However, the textbook does not specify *what* these problems ('factors') are; why Russia has not ratified the Rome Statute. Nevertheless, the authors of the same textbook point out as a cautionary tale that in August 2008, the government of Georgia filed a complaint at the ICC against Russia's political leadership.[411] More likely, such factors would be even more relevant after the occupation and annexation of Crimea in 2014.

Thus, although Russian literature on the ICC cautiously welcomes the Court as such,[412] it does so from a relatively safe distance. There is no burning desire for Russia to become a member of the ICC. The literature avoids the politically sensitive question whether the Rome Statute should be ratified or rejected by Moscow. Nikolai Ivanovich Kostenko describes how the administration of President George W. Bush in the US worked against the ICC Statute but in international law scholarship there is no open discussion on Russian domestic politics regarding the same matter.[413] Is this because there is only one place in Moscow where such a decision can be made, and elsewhere, including in scholarship, no one wants to get it wrong?

The other silence in Russian academic works on international criminal law concerns the critical history of the Nuremberg trials and the question whether Stalin's USSR may itself have committed crimes of aggression, crimes against humanity, and war crimes during, before, and after World War II.[414] Considering the fact that the Russian government has had to deal with the killing of Polish officers in Katyn in World War II, the question of the *kholodomor* in Ukraine during the 1930s, legal qualification of the Hitler–Stalin Pact of 23 August 1939, and so on, one would imagine that these would be relevant issues for Russia in the context of international criminal law. However, they are hardly mentioned in the respective legal literature. Apparently, this is a Pandora's box that Russians do not want to see opened.

The Nuremberg trials are construed as an entirely positive contribution by the USSR to the development of international criminal law.[415] One particular point

[409] Naumov et al., *Mezdhunarodnoe ugolovnoe pravo*, 414. See also B. Tuzmukhamedov, 'Yuridicheskie spory v Kampale', *Nezavisimaya Gazeta* 07.06.2010, <http://www.ng.ru/dipkurer/2010–06–07/9_kampala.html>.

[410] Naumov et al., *Mezdhunarodnoe ugolovnoe pravo*, 414.

[411] Ibid., 422.

[412] Ibid.; Kostenko, *Mezhdunarodnoe ugolovnoe pravo*, 37.

[413] Kostenko, *Mezhdunarodnoe ugolovnoe pravo*, 34–6.

[414] See further e.g. L. Mälksoo, 'Soviet Genocide? Soviet Mass Deportations in the Baltic States and International Law', 14 *Leiden Journal of International Law* 2001, 757–87.

[415] Naumov et al., *Mezdhunarodnoe ugolovnoe pravo*, 229.

that is popular in Russian literature is that it was the USSR that insisted on putting the Nazis on trial, even when the Western allies were hesitant. The general narrative is that in World War II 'democratic forces', i.e. including the USSR, became united against the Axis powers.[416] At the same time, the more strongly anti-US voices point out that the US committed crimes against humanity when dropping atomic bombs in Hiroshima and Nagasaki.[417]

Moreover, in Russian scholarship, there does not seem to be much awareness of how Stalin's USSR decisively shaped the definition of genocide in 1948,[418] arguing against the inclusion of social or politically defined groups in the Convention's official definition of the 'crime of crimes'. Referring to Lukashuk, Kostenko calls Pol Pot's crimes in Cambodia 'genocide',[419] apparently not being aware that in 1948 the USSR made enormous diplomatic efforts at the UN to avoid qualifying the annihilation of certain social classes of one's own people as 'genocide'. Only younger specialists of international law have started to take the historical biases and complexities of the definition of 'genocide' into account in their discussions of international criminal law.[420]

vi. Disputed territorial issues

As a last concrete example, it can be seen that Russian works on international law, including textbooks, pay quite a lot of attention to specific territorial issues. Territorial issues and the limitation of state borders remain a major intellectual preoccupation.[421] The main topic for the future will certainly be the Arctic. For example, based on a treaty concluded on 9 February 1920, Russia insists on certain extraterritorial rights in Norway's Svalbard archipelago's biggest island Spitzbergen, *inter alia* arguing that it should remain a neutral territory.[422] Moreover, although the 1920 treaty recognizes full sovereignty of Norway over these islands, it also recognizes certain rights of economic use by other countries as well, making it a sovereign state territory with an atypical regime of international usage. Some Russian scholars now argue that an environmental act adopted by the Norwegian parliament in 2001 violates the stipulations of this old treaty.[423]

One of the big debates in Russian literature is—what are the most convincing arguments for Russia to claim more of the Arctic Ocean and its continental shelf for itself. In 2001, the Russian government submitted its claims according to the procedure laid down in the UN Law of the Sea Convention. The majority opinion

416 Kovalev, Chernichenko, *Mezhdunarodnoe pravo*, 15.

417 Shumilov, *Mezhdunarodnoe pravo*, 158.

418 See W. A. Schabas, *Genocide in International Law* (Cambridge: CUP, 2000) 139 et seq.

419 Kostenko, *Mezhdunarodnoe ugolovnoe pravo*, 122.

420 A. Yu. Skuratova, *Mezhdunarodnye prestuplenia. Sovremennye probemy kvalifikatsii* (Moscow: Norma, 2012) 16

421 See e.g. A. N. Vylegzhanin, *Reshenia mezhdunarodnoga suda OON po sporam o razgranichenii morskikh prostranstv* (Moscow: Yuridicheskaya literatuura, 2004).

422 Kapustin, *Mezhdunarodnoe pravo*, 331.

423 Usenko, Shinkaretskaya, *Mezhdunarodnoe pravo*, 91.

in Russian scholarship now supports the government view that Russia's claims in the Arctic must be based on the 1982 Law of the Sea Convention.[424] However, in particular Vylegzhanin from MGIMO-University has criticized this opinion as essentially being too considerate regarding the interests of other nations, as not in Russia's best interest. Vylegzhanin continues to argue that a better position would be to continue presenting Russia's claims based on the Soviet-supported sectorial theory, and essentially divide the Arctic territories and resources among the five adjacent nations.[425]

As Western nations and scholars from Western nations have also formulated their claims and theories regarding the Arctic,[426] the issue of how to apply international law to the race for resources in the Arctic will become even more important in the twenty-first century. Consequently, the study of Russian legal positions on the Arctic will also remain important.[427] Rereading Richard Pipes, one cannot escape the association that in the twenty-first century we are witnessing in the Arctic Ocean the same extensive extension of sovereignty as Muscovy pursued in Siberia in the sixteenth and seventeenth centuries.

11. International Legal Theory in Russia and the Recent Construction of Russia's Civilizational Otherness from the West

It is time to finish discussion of concrete examples in Russian theory and doctrine of international law. It is fair to conclude that contemporary theory and doctrine of international law in Russia have different accents than in the Western mainstream. In a certain sense then, international legal theory is indeed also 'different in different places', once again to use this phrase from David Kennedy. The main questions discussed in international legal theory and doctrine in Russia are of course in themselves no different from what is discussed in the West but frequently the answers to these questions do differ. My own conclusion differs from some earlier accounts which conclude that Russian international law theory differs little from that in the West, nor even did Soviet theory.[428]

The differences are grounded in the *philosophy* of international law, which has much to do with the prevailing philosophy of statehood in the respective country and ultimately with the prevailing values in society. These values and philosophy

[424] Kovalev, S.V. Chernichenko, *Mezhdunarodnoe pravo*, 392–3.

[425] Vylegzhanin, *Mezhdunarodnoe pravo*, 181–209.

[426] See e.g. M. Byers, *Who Owns the Arctic? Understanding Sovereignty Disputes in the North* (Vancouver: Douglas & McIntyre, 2009).

[427] See I. Nossova, *Russia's International Legal Claims in Its Adjacent Seas. The Realm of Sea as Extension of Sovereignty*, Ph.D. thesis, University of Tartu (2013), <http://dspace.utlib.ee/dspace/bitstream/handle/10062/31198/nossova_irina.pdf?sequence=1.

[428] S. Pritzkow, 'Kontinuität und Diskontinuität. Sowjetisches und modernes russisches Völkerrechtsdenken im Vergleich', 6 *Osteuropa Recht* 2008, 397–406 at 406.

have taken hundreds of years to develop and sporadic post-Soviet intellectual and policy efforts to move from a state-centric collectivist worldview to an anthropocentric individualist one have had only limited success so far.

During the Soviet period, statism, anti-human-rightism and other similar features in Russian-language theory of international law were justified by Marxist-Leninist ideology. It is thus fascinating that although Marxism-Leninism has vanished, some of the main statist elements of Soviet international law theory have maintained their positions, even today giving Russian theory of international law its unique accents. Of course, this is not surprising in the sense that the disintegration of the USSR did not, in the context of international law, bring any significant discontinuity of academic personnel in Russia.

The balance point between the principles of state sovereignty and human rights has altogether been found to be in a different place in Russia and the West. Western scholars usually emphasize human rights and the individual in the context of international law while in terms of the hierarchy of principles Russians continue to give priority to the principle of state sovereignty. On the level of predominant ideas in scholarship, many international law scholars in EU countries have become adherents of the political philosophy that emphasizes human rights and makes a distinction between liberal and illiberal states whereas Russia has intellectually remained a sovereignist stronghold, a conservative and illiberal force in international law.

As demonstrated in this part of the study, some more liberal and cosmopolitan theoretical voices exist in Russia as well but overall it is clear that the liberal European tradition of Martens has remained a minority in contemporary Russia—notwithstanding hortatory appraisals that Martens as a foundational figure has generated in post-Soviet Russian scholarship of international law. In the main directions of Moscow's contemporary international legal theory, the nativist Soviet Russian scholar Kozhevnikov would probably feel more at home than the Westernizer Martens.

What, then, is the foundational idea, explaining differences and idiosyncrasies of international legal theory in Russia compared to the Western mainstream in this post-Cold War and post 9/11 era? I would argue that 'civilization', this historically ambiguous and laden concept, continues to be extremely relevant in the context of international legal theory in Russia. Russian scholars who draw a clear difference between the understanding of international law in Russia and the West increasingly claim that Russia must be recognized as a unique 'civilization', not a perennially flawed part of Europe.

The picture that emerges from a number of Russian academic works on international law is of the West, and especially the US, as Russia's *dangerous Other*.[429] Occasionally, the distinction already discussed between 'native' and 'Western' becomes outright anti-Westernism. In such academic works, the West and its

[429] A. Ya. Kapustin, 'Mezhdunarodnoe gumanitarnoe pravo i novye vyzovy', in Lisitsyn-Svetlanov, *Novye vyzovy i mezhdunarodnoe pravo*, 44–53 at 46.

currently most powerful representative, the US,[430] serve as bad examples—partly because the US 'puts itself above the law'.[431]

For example, a recent textbook on international criminal law discusses the 'crimes of the West against Yugoslavia' in 1999 although it also specifies that 'in the first place', these were the crimes of NATO.[432] In such explanations, critique of the West acquires a 'civilizational' dimension.

When relationships between global centres grow tense, civilizational critique of the Other makes its entrance in the discourse of international law. In his monograph on state sovereignty in international law, Aleksei Aleksandrovich Moiseev, Professor of the Diplomatic Academy of the Russian MFA, criticizes the West as the self-proclaimed 'centre of civilization' and characterizes the West in the following way:

> The values of Western society are well known, they are connected with the cult of consumption and acquisition, with the desire to rule nature in order to satisfy one's own interests. The triumph of pragmatism, rationality and 'professionalism' as the highest benefits of society leads to a lowering of the general moral level. In such a construction of the world, the goals of development are subjugated to the mercenary interests of a financial oligarchy that is trying to unify and standardize the human intellect, to transform it into 'productive forces' and the main source of economic growth. The mass media propagate the idea that globalization enriches peoples in terms of culture but in reality the 'globalization of culture' means cultural unification under the influence of the culture of Western civilization.[433]

This negative characterization of Western civilization is in its essence surprisingly similar to Dugin's anti-Western tirades.[434] But sophisticated Russian thinkers in the past such as Aleksandr Zinovyev (1922–2006) have critically associated the West in particular with capitalism and orientation to business.[435]

Professor Shumilov from the All-Russian Academy of Foreign Trade of the Ministry of Economic Development of the Russian Federation has brought the civilizational approach to the mainstream and voices the criticism that international law has been too strongly predominated by the 'Western type of civilization'.[436] He suggests that this state of affairs must come to an end and international law must also start representing the interests of other, non-Western civilizations.[437]

In 2005 Shumilov argued:

[430] A. Kh. Abashidze, 'Kontseptsia "gegemonii" v sovremennom mezhdunarodnom prave', in *Vestnik Diplomaticheskoi Akademii MID Rossii. Mezhdunarodnoe pravo* (Moscow: Diplomaticheskaya Akademia, 2013) 166–79 at 178.

[431] Lukashuk, *Pravo mezhdunarodnoi otvetstvennosti*, 374.

[432] Naumov et al., *Mezhdunarodnoe ugolovnoe pravo*, 221.

[433] Moiseev, *Suverenitet gosudarstva v mezhdunarodnom prave*, 147–8.

[434] A. Dugin, *Proekt Evraziya* (Moscow: Yauza EKSMO, 2004) 115 ('American culture lacks higher purpose'), 220 (the US as 'an artificial civilization of artificial people'), 430 (the West characterized by 'utilitarianism, optimization, pragmatism, individualism, alienation, moral flexibility, plutocracy, etc.').

[435] A. Zinov'ev, *Zapad* (Moscow: Algoritm, 2007) 54 et seq.

[436] Shumilov, *Mezhdunarodnoe pravo*, 41.

[437] Ibid.

The main problem today is to accommodate sovereignty with the need to lower administrative thresholds in conditions where globalization is carried out by the financial-economic rule of a narrow group of countries of the Western type of civilization.[438]

In a recent work too, Shumilov emphasizes that Russia is a unique civilization, 'not "part of Europe" '.[439] His advice is that Russia should never become part of the EU because this would be against the 'geostrategic interests of Russia and its peoples'.[440] Instead, the interaction of Russia and the EU is 'cooperation and antagonism of two civilizational centres and centres of economic power'.[441] This view is quite a departure from other attempts by Russian legal scholars and their European, in particular German, colleagues to construe Russia and the EU as strategic partners and to construe Russia as a member of the wider European family of nations.[442]

Safronova from the Research University in Belgorod also draws a clear distinction between Western and Russian civilizations:

Universal (global) civilization is impossible, as the universal human being is impossible. ... The idea of the possibility of 'universal civilization' is primarily a Western idea and is in direct contradiction with the national mentality and uniqueness of a number of cultures that it threatens with destruction. Values which are most important for European and American (Anglo-Saxon) civilization are much less important for other peoples. Thus, in Orthodox, Islamic, Buddhist and Confucian cultures many Western ideas such as individualism, liberalism, democracy, separation of church from state, etc. find practically no resonance.... There are peoples whose legal culture is characterized by legal nihilism but also those that are characterized by the idealization of law. Unfortunately, the conduct of current legal standardization is based on the values of West European legal culture.[443]

However, Safronova does not specify how cultures which in their order of values prioritize law such as in the West should take into account the ideas and values of those cultures that do so less. Again, there are similarities with Dugin's ideas here for he also emphasizes fundamental historical differences of the Russian legal tradition from Roman law and contemporary concepts of European law.[444]

Other legal scholars, too, call for maintaining and resurrecting Russia's civilizational identity in the context of international relations.[445] This seems to have become the new trendy political slogan in Russia. Moreover, when

[438] Shumilov, *Mezhdunarodnoe finansovoe pravo*, 74. The same passage appears in Shumilov, *Mezhdunarodnoe ekonomicheskoe pravo*, 3rd edn, 86.

[439] Shumilov, *Mezhdunarodnoe ekonomicheskoe pravo*, 6th edn, 131.

[440] Ibid., 130–1.

[441] Shumilov, *Mezhdunarodnoe pravo*, 285.

[442] See D. Rauschning, V. N. Rusinova (eds), *Rossiiskaya Federatsia v Evrope. Pravovye aspekty sotrudnichestva Rossii s evropeiskimi organizatsiami* (Moscow: 'Mezhdunarodnye otnoshenia', 2008); P. A. Kalininchenko, *Evropeiskyi Soyuz. Pravo i otnoshenia s Rossiei* (Moscow: Norma Infra-M, 2012); M. L. Entin, *V poiskakh partnerskikh otnoshenii III. Rossia i Evropeiskii soyuz v 2008–2009 godakh* (Moscow: Zebra E, 2010); M. L. Entin, *V poiskakh partnerskikh otnoshenii. Rossia i Evropeiskii soyuz v 2004–2005 godakh* (St Petersburg: 'Rossiya-Neva', 2006).

[443] Safronova, *Mezhdunarodnoe publichnoe pravo*, 42–3.

[444] A. Dugin, *Proekt Evraziya* (Moscow: Yauza EKSMO, 2004) 238 et seq.

[445] E. L. Sadykova, 'Mezhtsivilizatsionnyi dialog kak institut sistemy mezhdunarodnykh otnoshenii', in *Vestnik Diplomaticheskoi Akademii MID Rossii. Mezhdunarodnoe pravo* (Moscow: Diplomaticheskaya Akademia, 2013) 248–57 at 256.

Shumilov speaks of the 'civilizational space of Russia'[446] this goes further from Russia itself being a 'civilization' different from the West. In fact, this is a claim for a greater space (*Großraum*); a sphere of influence in the countries of 'near abroad'. Yet such claims are not compatible with the international law of the UN Charter, after the former Soviet republics became independent states in 1991.

One of the most active discussants and proponents of Russia's civilizational difference from the West has become Patriarch Kirill I of Moscow, the head of the Russian Orthodox Church, who has offered a systematic criticism of the universalism of human rights thinking in the West.[447] Kirill, like the Chairman of the Constitutional Court, Mr Zorkin, is another person in Russia who is a scholar-thinker and visible power holder at the same time. Quite interestingly, the leading daily newspaper *Nezavisimaya gazeta* measures Patriarch Kirill's popularity among other Russian top politicians monthly.

Unlike individual scholars, Patriarch Kirill can indeed claim that he represents many more people than himself, i.e. the whole ROC. It is fascinating and significant that in his publicist work, Patriarch Kirill has turned to criticism of the Western concept of human rights. The result is a remarkable collection of speeches, writings, and interviews on human rights that reflect Kirill's engagement with—and rejection of—the Western concept of human rights over recent decades.

Patriarch Kirill favours traditionalism of cultures over the idea of universality of human rights[448] and argues that the current 'individualistic' Western concept of human rights has been historically a product of Protestant Christian and Jewish thinking.[449] Patriarch Kirill thus juxtaposes Orthodox Christianity in Russia alongside other more 'traditional' world religions to Western Christianity and liberalism.[450]

In his address to the 10th World Council of the Russian People which on 6 April 2006 adopted the 'Orthodox Declaration of Human Rights. Declaration on Human Rights and Dignity',[451] Kirill argued that Russia is a unique civilization, different from the West.[452] The main spiritual source of Russian civilization is Orthodox Christianity which was historically more preoccupied with spiritual values and less with the material world and 'everyday advantages' (i.e. unlike the West).[453]

Kirill even picks up and repeats Berdyaev's idea that Russian Communism reflected certain civilizational values normatively characteristic of Old Russia:

> Indeed, the forms of social relations that were shaped in twentieth century Russia were to a significant extent secularized variants of values characteristic of the Russian spiritual

446 Shumilov, *Mezhdunarodnoe pravo*, 111, 524.

447 Patriarch Kirill of Moscow, *Freedom and Responsibility. A Search for Harmony—Human Rights and Personal Dignity* (London: Darton, Longman and Todd, 2011).

448 Ibid., 38, 73.

449 Ibid., 6–7, 55–6.

450 Ibid., 34.

451 <http://www.pravoslavieto.com/docs/human_rights/declaration_ru_en.htm>.

452 Kirill, *Freedom and Responsibility*, 4, 58–60.

453 Ibid., 71.

tradition: collectivism was a secularized variant of *sobornost* and the communal idea, a single-state ideology, substituted the spiritual authority of the Church, and so on and so forth.[454]

To the extent that this point is true, the Soviet order must then not have been as 'alien' to Russia as for example the liberal dissident Andrei Dmitrievich Sakharov (1921–89) or the perestroika era anti-Communist leader Boris Nikolayevich Yeltsin claimed. The question of how to interpret the Soviet period in Russia's history again demonstrates the centuries old split between the Westernizers and 'Slavophiles' in Russia.

The lens of civilization and the discussion of how Russia's claimed civilizational differences from the West have influenced the country's practical engagement with the idea of human rights has also become a theme in the scholarly literature on human rights.[455]

The idea that religion is the foundation of civilizations has made its way into Russian international law literature.[456] If Russia ought to be recognized as a separate civilization from the West, the main source of this distinctiveness would indeed be the Orthodox Christianity. The Western and Eastern Churches split in 1054 and the bridging of the Great Schism agreed upon at the Council of Florence in 1439 was not recognized by Muscovy. After Byzantium fell in 1453, the idea of Moscow as the 'third Rome' was born. Ever since, state-centrism and top-down governance have been characteristic of the Russian state in its various incarnations. Historians also claim that institutionally the Russian Orthodox Church never acquired the kind of autonomy and power that the Pope in the West did, not to speak of Protestant Europe where individuals became historically liberated from the supreme authority of the Church.

Carl Schmitt observed that all poignant concepts of modern constitutional theory are secularized theological concepts.[457] However, what he meant specifically was *Catholic*, i.e. Western, Latin theology. Modern international law is a relatively young discipline and tradition compared to Catholic theology; in fact, it emerged together with the rise of Protestantism in Northern Europe. The historical separation of the Western and Eastern Christian Churches may explain certain deeper cultural-historical forces behind the fact that the discourse of international law has its unique features in Russia, compared to the West.

Take the emphasis on 'native' doctrine and sources in Russian scholarship. The semiotician Boris Andreyevich Uspensky (b. 1937) and a colleague of Yuri Mikhailovich Lotman in the Tartu-Moscow semiotics school, has demonstrated how in the pre-Petrine period in Muscovy, the lingua franca of the West at the time, Latin, was considered impure and heretical by Muscovy's Orthodox clergy. Truthful theological literature could only be published in

[454] Ibid., 82.

[455] E. A. Lukasheva, *Chelovek, pravo, tsivilizatsia. Normativno-tsennostnoe izmerenie* (Moscow: Norma, 2009).

[456] Shumilov, *Mezhdunarodnoe pravo*, 24.

[457] C. Schmitt, *Politische Theologie. Vier Kapitel zur Lehre von der Souveränität*, 7th edn (Berlin: Duncker & Humblot, 1996) 43.

the Old Slavonic language.[458] Thus, the form of ideas (language) in many ways shaped and even determined their content (the correct theoretical interpretation). Possibly these historically persistent theological approaches have also paved the way to today's Russian focus on 'native doctrine' in international law scholarship and scepticism of Western anthropocentric ideas about international law as 'global law'.

My purpose at this point is not to assert that Russia *does* represent a different civilization from the West. However, it is significant that an increasing number of scholars and power players in Russia are making the argument that Russia is a unique civilization. I argued at the beginning of this study that international law is a social construct and to the extent that civilizational rhetoric is increasingly popular and relevant in Russia, it does become part of how international law is understood in that country.

It seems to me that because of its historical European/Western bias, the global discourse of international law is not too willing to accept religious and civilizational differences as significant and even essential for the field. Again, we are back with the question of universality and fragmentation of international law. But even the foundational concept of international law, state sovereignty, may have different aspects of sanctity attached to it in different regions and religions of the world.

Harvard political scientist Samuel P. Huntington (1927–2008) explained this phenomenon in quite straightforward terms:

> Universalism is the ideology of the West for confrontations with non-Western cultures. ... The non-Wests see as Western what the West sees as universal.... In the modern world, religion is a central, perhaps *the* central, force that motivates and mobilizes people.[459]

However, the problem with too extensive universalism is that it does not allow the difference of the Other to be seen—or realistically acknowledge the extent to which cultures such as Russian culture construes the West as the hostile Other. As in the Middle Ages, Rome and Byzantium, or later Muscovy, construed Christianity with different accents, they now lend different accents to the discourse of international law. The contemporary international legal theoretical debate on how state sovereignty and human rights relate to each other is led as intensely and ferociously as the medieval Catholic-Orthodox theological debate on *Filioque*.[460] Today, too, Russian legal and normative thinkers feel like responding to Western criticisms on human rights and democracy that—whatever Russia's flaws in human rights and democracy—Russians might be better Christians after all. This, however, is a theme that is very difficult to 'convincingly' argue about because the debate about who is a better Christian is already centuries old in Western and Eastern Europe.

[458] B. Uspenski, 'Kirikulõhe ja XVII sajandi kultuurikonflikt', in *Vene kultuuri jõujooni. Valik artikleid*, trans. from Russian to Estonian by P. Lepik (Tartu: Ilmamaa, 2013) 295–349.

[459] S. P. Huntington, *The Clash of Civilizations and the Remaking of World Order* (New York: Simon & Schuster, 1996) 66.

[460] T. Ware, *The Orthodox Church* (London: Penguin Books, 1997) 211 et seq.

4

Patterns of Post-Soviet Russian State Practice in International Law

Finally, it is time to turn from legal theory to post-Soviet state practice. What scholars think and argue is not yet 'international law' itself; it only gives significant insights into what the issues in international law are. First of all, actual international law plays out in state practice, in the relationship between states. The political leaders are in a position to ignore what international law scholars in their country or abroad speak for and advocate. For example, 'enlightened' scholars may advocate the functional immunity of states in the context of international law but more conservative national officials and judges may still favour the doctrine of absolute immunity in state practice, hoping to save their government from foreign lawsuits. In a similar way, progressive scholars may celebrate constitutional openness to international law and treaties but the men of state, *gosudarstvenniki*, may have a different opinion on this in giving shape to actual state practice. But the other way around too—legislators may ratify the European Convention on Human Rights (ECHR) and thus acknowledge the right to individual petition but conservative scholars may still continue to hold the view that individuals cannot be subjects of international law.

It remains an open question to what extent legal theory influences or is mirrored in state practice. In the final part of this study, I will turn to contemporary Russia's state practice in international law and link it with previously elaborated historical and theoretical materials. At the same time, my ambition here is not to present an exhaustive account of what has happened in the Russian Federation's state practice in international law after the collapse of the USSR. This is not necessary in the framework of the present project. Rather, my plan is to move closer to an understanding of general patterns in post-Soviet Russia's state practice and create an analytical overview rather than an exhaustive description.

On a conceptual level, one may wonder in what ways post-Soviet Russian state practice differs from the US, Chinese, French, or Turkish or any other state practice in international law. One possible key to this question is the international legal consciousness in each country and the idea that this consciousness may be different in different nations.

For example, the international law textbook edited by Kazan scholars Valeev and Kurdykov argues that the effectiveness of international law depends considerably on the 'state of the individual and collective legal consciousness in the given country'.[1] As discussed previously, the same idea was pioneered in Russia by Martens already in the 1880s. Along the same lines, Chernichenko has argued that there is something like an international legal consciousness that is different in each society and that connects ideological, psychological, and emotional views on international law, making international law 'alive'.[2] In this way, international legal consciousness may well be the most genuine link between a country's legal scholarship and state practice.

One aspect of international legal consciousness in a country is the way its key foreign policy decisions are made; how many people are involved with making crucial international law-related decisions and what is their legitimacy. In autocracies, the practice of international law might be crucially influenced by the individual consciousness and psychology, possibly pathological psychology, of the national leader. In the 1990s, Anne-Marie Slaughter and some other US international law scholars argued that democracies and authoritarian regimes have inherently different approaches to international law.[3] This insight is potentially relevant in the context of post-Soviet Russia as well because, for example, over recent years the US-based watchdog organization Freedom House has labelled Russia as 'not free', i.e. an illiberal country.

The government's international legal consciousness is first of all reflected in its official positions concerning policy on international law. We could therefore start with the question how has international law been rhetorically construed at the governmental level in Russia? And further from governmental rhetoric, what has the Kremlin's actual *politique juridique extérieure* been like, again to use the phrase coined by the French international lawyer and former ICJ judge Guy Ladreit de Lacharrière (1919–87)? After clarifying the Russian government's official self-image in the context of international law, we can examine its adequacy and put it in a critical perspective with the help of empirical material, *inter alia* using previous insights gained from the history and theory of international law.

1. The Russian Government's Official Self-Image in the Context of International Law

The post-Soviet Russian government's self-image in the context of international law has been quite extraordinary, coming close to seeing Moscow as the protector of 'international law' as such, the restrainer (in Greek: *katechon*) of the main power that from the Kremlin's perspective has been threatening the multipolar

[1] R. Valeev, G. Kurdyukov (eds), *Mezhdunarodnoe pravo. Obshaya chast'* (Moscow: Statut, 2011) 151.

[2] S. V. Chernichenko, *Ocherki po filosofii i mezhdunarodnomu pravu* (Moscow 'Nauchnaya kniga', 2009) 717, 720.

[3] A.-M. Slaughter, 'International Law in a World of Liberal States', 6 *EJIL* 1995, 503–38. See further R. Buchan, *International Law and the Construction of the Liberal Peace* (Oxford: Hart Publishing, 2013).

world order after the end of the Cold War, i.e. the US. This has entirely followed the Soviet tradition which also, whatever the USSR was undertaking, loudly argued that Moscow was more than covered by international law.

In the post-Soviet and post-9/11 period, Moscow has seen the UN Charter as the foundation of the international legal order and has perceived it as being under systematic attack by a unilateralist and hegemonic US. Occasionally, the governmental discourse of international law in Russia also has Messianic traits, a feature that some philosophers have considered a persistent characteristic in Russia's history of ideas.[4]

Thus, President Putin's speech at the Munich Conference on Security Policy on 12 February 2007 was understood as the Kremlin's battle cry against the US and its unilateralist hegemonic tendencies. In his Munich speech, President Putin touched upon international law as a central theme:

> We are seeing a greater and greater disdain for the basic principles of international law. And independent legal norms are, as a matter of fact, coming increasingly closer to one state's legal system. One state and, of course, first and foremost the United States, has overstepped its national borders in every way.... In international relations we increasingly see the desire to resolve a given question according to issues of so-called political expedience.... no one can feel that international law is like a stone wall that will protect them.... The use of force can only be considered legitimate if the decision is sanctioned by the UN.[5]

In September 2013 during the peak of the Syria crisis, President Putin published an article in the *New York Times* in which he warned that the then intensely discussed US military strike on Syria 'could throw the entire system of international law and order out of balance'. President Putin further declared Moscow's standpoint regarding international law:

> We're not protecting the Syrian government, but international law.... The law is still the law, and we must follow it whether we like it or not. Under current international law, force is permitted only in self-defense or by the decision of the Security Council. Anything else is unacceptable under the United Nations Charter and would constitute an act of aggression.[6]

Moreover, in his annual Presidential Address to the Federal Assembly on 12 December 2013, President Putin insisted that Russians 'will strive to be leaders, defending international law ...'[7]

Furthermore, the Russian Federation is also the country where the importance of 'international law' is specifically and extensively emphasized in the Foreign

[4] See e.g. M. Sarkisyants, *Russland und der Messianismus des Orients* (Tübingen: J. C. B. Mohr, 1955).

[5] See<http://www.washingtonpost.com/wp-dyn/content/article/2007/02/12/AR2007021200555.html>.

[6] V. V. Putin, 'A Plea for Caution from Russia', *NYTimes*, 11.09.2013, http://www.nytimes.com/2013/09/12/opinion/putin-plea-for-caution-from-russia-on-syria.html?hp&_r=0.

[7] 'Presidential Address to the Federal Assembly', 12.12.2013, <http://eng.kremlin.ru/transcripts/6402>.

Policy Concept, National Security Strategy, and other relevant national policy documents. In these official documents, Russia's view on 'international law' is defensive and the image of the post-Cold War US and its allied NATO countries is that of past and potential future violators of international law.

But what attention should one give to official policy documents emphasizing that the government values 'international law' more than anything? One of the post-Soviet doyens of international law experts in Russia, Igor Ivanovich Lukashuk, has argued that Foreign Policy Concepts have a 'largely informative-propagandistic character'.[8] If so, then they also represent governmental advocacy; in these documents, governments are promoting the point that they are good—also vis-à-vis their own population.

Nevertheless, at least in the context of strategic documents of the US and NATO, Vladimir Semenovich Kotlyar from the Diplomatic Academy of the Russian MFA has recommended a careful study of these documents because they might predict the future behaviour of Western countries:

> The study of the strategic concepts of states helps to foresee with a significant degree of probability their application in concrete situations which may occur in the development of international relations.[9]

If the same logic applies then it is also relevant at least to become aware of what has been claimed regarding international law in the Russian Federation's strategic concepts.

Thus, for example, the Concept of the Foreign Policy of the Russian Federation, approved by President Putin on 12 February 2013, emphasizes the 'primacy of international law, including, first of all, the UN Charter'.[10] Specifically, the Foreign Policy Concept postulates:

> Another risk to world peace and stability is presented by attempts to manage crises through unilateral sanctions and other coercive measures, including armed aggression, outside the framework of the UN Security Council. There are instances of blatant neglect of fundamental principles of international law, such as the non-use of force, and of the prerogatives of the UN Security Council when arbitrary interpretation of its resolutions is allowed. Some concepts that are being implemented are aimed at overthrowing legitimate authorities in sovereign states under the pretext of protecting the civilian population. The use of coercive measures and military force bypassing the UN Charter and the UN Security Council is unable to eliminate profound socioeconomic, ethnic and other antagonisms that cause conflicts.[11]

[8] I. I. Lukashuk, *Sovremennoe pravo mezhdunarodnykh dogovorov*, Vol. 1 (Moscow: Wolters Kluwer, 2004) 40.

[9] V. S. Kotlyar, *Mezhdunarodnoe pravo i sovremennye strategicheskie kontseptsii SShA i NATO*, 2nd edn (Kazan: Tsentr innovatsionnykh tekhnologii, 2008) 3.

[10] 'Concept of the Foreign Policy of the Russian Federation', 12.02.2013, <http://www.mid.ru/bdomp/brp_4.nsf/e78a48070f128a7b43256999005bcbb3/76389fec168189ed44257b2e0039b16d!OpenDocument>, at I, 1, c.

[11] Ibid., ii, 15.

As a solution, Russia's Foreign Policy Concept considers the Rule of Law a high priority in international affairs:

Russia consistently advocates strengthening the legal basis of international relations and complies with its international legal obligations in good faith. Maintenance and strengthening of the international rule of law is among its priorities in the international arena. The rule of law is intended to ensure peaceful and fruitful cooperation among states while preserving the balance of their often conflicting interests as well as safeguarding the stability of the global community in general. Russia intends to:

a) support collective efforts to strengthen the legal basis of interstate relations;
b) counter attempts by certain countries or groups of countries to revise the universally recognized norms of international law established in universal documents such as the UN Charter, the 1970 Declaration on Principles of International Law concerning Friendly Relations and Co-operation among States in accordance with the UN Charter, as well as in the Final Act of the Conference on Security and Co-operation in Europe (Helsinki, 1 August 1975). Arbitrary and politically motivated interpretation of fundamental international legal norms and principles such as non-use of force or threat of force, peaceful settlement of international disputes, respect for sovereignty and territorial integrity of states, the right of peoples to self-determination, in favor of certain countries pose a particular danger to international peace, law and order. Likewise, attempts to represent violations of international law as its 'creative' application are dangerous. It is unacceptable that military interventions and other forms of interference from without which undermine the foundations of international law based on the principle of sovereign equality of states, be carried out on the pretext of implementing the concept of 'responsibility to protect';
c) contribute to the codification and progressive development of international law, first of all under the auspices of the UN, help ensure the inclusiveness of international UN treaties and their uniform interpretation and application.[12]

Earlier versions of the Foreign Policy Concept such as the one adopted on 12 July 2008 included similar passages, emphasizing the importance of international law and Russia's intention to protect and promote it globally.

Similar supportive ideas about international law were expressed in Russia's National Security Strategy to 2020 approved by President Medvedev on 12 May 2009. The National Security Strategy states:

In the long term, the Russian Federation will seek to construct international relations based on the principles of international law, and on the institution of reliable and equal security of nation-states. For the defense of its national interests, Russia, while remaining within the boundaries of international law, will implement a rational and pragmatic foreign policy, one which excludes expensive confrontation, including a new arms race.[13]

[12] Ibid., iii, 31.

[13] 'Russia: National Security Strategy to 2020', 12 May 2009, <http://www.isn.ethz.ch/Digital-Library/Publications/Detail/?id=154915> p. 13.

Finally, the Military Doctrine of the Russian Federation of 5 February 2010, approved by presidential edict, postulates that among the main external military dangers for the Russian Federation are 'the desire to endow the power projection potential of the North Atlantic Treaty Organization (NATO) with global functions carried out in violation of norms of international law', 'the violation of international accords by individual states, and also noncompliance with previously concluded international treaties in the field of arms limitation and reduction', and 'the use of military force on the territories of states contiguous with the Russian Federation in violation of the UN Charter and other norms of international law.'[14]

Foreign Minister Lavrov also often emphasizes 'international law' and Russia's particular and progressive commitment to the rule of law in international affairs.[15]

Apparently no P5 member of the UN SC has so intensely, repetitively, and protectively referred to 'international law' in its national security documents as Russia. Memorably, the National Security Strategy of President George W. Bush, issued on 20 September 2002 in the aftermath of the terrorist attacks of 11 September 2011,[16] did not emphasize international law much as a compass for US foreign policy. Even compared to the Treaty on European Union with its Article 3 para. 5 (consolidated version) which specifically emphasizes international law (although in a list of other compasses and values), Russia's official insistence on 'international law' has been more intense, righteous, and defensive.

International law scholarship in Russia refers to the country's foreign policy documents and positions favorably emphasizing the importance of international law as well.[17] For example, Anatoly Yakovlevich Kapustin, President of the Russian Association of International Law, has interpreted President Putin's 2007 Munich speech to mean that international law 'must be universal'.[18] Moreover, a recent leading Russian textbook of international law suggests that the message of the 2008 Foreign Policy concept was that international law must be 'universal ... both in the way it is understood and applied'.[19] Similarly, the recent textbook of the Diplomatic Academy of the Russian MFA claims that the Foreign Policy Concept of 2013 implies that generally recognized norms of international law must be fully universal 'from the point of view of their understanding and application'.[20] In these accounts, the US with its exceptionalism comes up as the hegemonic challenger of the universality of international law. In contrast, the trope of Russia

[14] <http://carnegieendowment.org/files/2010russia_military_doctrine.pdf>, 8, a, g, h. See also V. Mamontov, 'Menyaetsa Rossia, menyaetsya i ee voennaya doktrina', *Izvestia* 14.10.2010, <http://izvestia.ru/news/354178>.

[15] M. Barshtshevski, 'Diplomatichno govorya', *Rossiiskaya gazeta* 17.10.2013, <http://www.rg.ru/2013/10/17/lavrov.html>.

[16] <http://www.state.gov/documents/organization/63562.pdf>.

[17] See e.g. O. I. Tiunov, A. A. Kashirkina, A. N. Morozov, *Vypolnenie mezhdunarodnykh dogovorov Rossiiskoi Federatsii* (Moscow: Norma, 2012) 6–7 (referring to the Foreign Policy Concept of 2008 and its statements about the importance of international law).

[18] A. Kapustin (ed.) *Mezhdunarodnoe pravo* (Moscow: Gardariki, 2008) 10.

[19] G. V. Ignatenko, O. I. Tiunov (eds) *Mezhdunarodnoe pravo*, 6th edn (Moscow: Norma, 2013) 19.

[20] S. A. Egorov, 'Predislovie', in S. A. Egorov (ed.), *Mezhdunarodnoe pravo*, 5th edn (Moscow: Statut, 2014) 13–14.

being a pillar of international law has also been picked up by international law scholars at Kazan State University, who entitled their international law conference in 2012 'International Legal Order in the Contemporary World and Russia's Role in Strengthening It'.[21]

But here is where one needs to know first what Russians more specifically mean by 'international law'—in other words, all information and discussions that were contained in the previous part of this study dealing with international legal theory and doctrine in post-Soviet Russia. If there is a direct link, through the concept of legal consciousness in a country, between legal theory and state practice, then by defensively invoking 'international law', Russians are in fact defending their own statist vision of international law that is hostile to the West's anthropocentric ideas regarding international law. At the same time, there is a danger that some Westerners because of their inherent tendency to universalism would miss this comparative aspect—because international law in their eyes is 'universal', they would take Russian insistance on the significance of 'international law' at face value and miss the point that it is in some aspects a different idea of 'international law' that is used in the discourse.

But even if one is aware of the theoretical accents of Russia's narrow statist concept of international law, it is still necessary to examine whether Russia's rhetorical claim that it is a *katechon* or guardian of international law is backed up by deeds in state practice. Thus, what are the actual facts on the record? Has post-Soviet Russia indeed been a pillar of international law as the national strategic documents formulated in Moscow claim in a not too humble way?

2. An Outline of Russia's Post-Soviet Practice in International Law

In order to understand Russian approaches to international law today, one would first need to take a look back and see where Russia came from, i.e. the Soviet experience. In crucial aspects, the Soviet approach to international law was autarchic—official Moscow liked to talk about 'international law', like anybody else, but ultimately did not trust Western-dominated international law and kept a distance from its institutions.

For example, the USSR was not part of the capitalist Bretton Woods institutions or of the GATT. The main international organization that the USSR shared with the West in the context of international law was the UN where Moscow had a veto power in the SC, as the Russian Federation continues to have nowadays. In the context of the UN and its international legal order, Soviet 'sovereignty', or the

[21] I. A. Tarkhanov, A. I. Abdullin, G. I. Kurdyukov, R. S. Davletgil'deev (eds), *Materialy mezhdunarodnoi nauchno-prakticheskoi konferentsii 'Mezhdunarodnyi pravoporyadok v sovremennom mire i rol' Rossii v ego ukreplenii', posvyashennoi 90–letiu D.I. Fel'dmana* (Moscow: Statut, 2014).

'sovereignty' of any permanent member of the UN Security Council, was virtually untouched. Based on the underlying logic of the UN Charter, especially in the Soviet interpretation, the veto power meant that there could never legally be any use of military force against the will of any permanent member. This is what the 'Yalta formula' of the UN as the constitution of the international community was all about.

Nor did the USSR recognize the compulsory jurisdiction of the ICJ. Thus, the Eastern Block welcomed the famous *Nicaragua v. USA* case in the ICJ[22] as a judicial victory for international law, a case in which arguably a small progressive state won against an imperialistic superpower. At the same time, jurisdiction-wise, a similar case in the ICJ would not have been possible against the USSR because the Soviets did not recognize the ICJ's jurisdiction, even though after World War II, Moscow has continuously been able to count on sending a judge to the bench of the ICJ. In this sense, both superpowers were not on an equal footing in terms of international adjudication—even though this point does not justify US actions against Nicaragua at the time, and the ICJ's jurisdiction in the *Nicaragua v US* case was the main legally contested element in the ICJ case.

Moreover, only after the Helsinki Final Act of 1975 did Moscow very reluctantly and cautiously start to accept that human rights were beyond exclusive domestic jurisdiction in the meaning of the UN Charter.[23] In essence, however, fields such as international human rights law were from Moscow's perspective not a part of 'international law'. As previously indicated, the USSR had ratified a number of UN human rights treaties but this hardly changed its domestic practices regarding human rights for the better. International law in the Soviet mind was first of all about peace, security, and territorial control, and its key arrangements in the UN Charter reflected Moscow's power at the end of World War II.

Thus, when the last Soviet leader, Mr Gorbachev, started to publicly emphasize 'international law' in the mid-1980s, he connected it with the idea that the USSR had to open up and become less autarchic in its relationship with the outside world. The manifesto 'more international law' became a proxy slogan for opening up and reforming the stagnating USSR. One aspect of Mr Gorbachev's new thinking was that the USSR ratified a number of human rights and humanitarian law treaties, e.g. on 3 March 1987 it ratified the *Convention against Torture and Other Cruel, Inhuman or Degrading Treatment or Punishment*, on 29 September 1989 acceding to the two *Additional Protocols of the Geneva Conventions*, and on 16 August 1990 ratifying the *Convention on the Rights of the Child*.[24]

[22] See *Military and Paramilitary Activities in and against Nicaragua (Nicaragua v USA)*, Jurisdiction and admissibility, Judgment, 26 November 1984, ICJ Reports 1984, 392; Judgment on Merits, 27 June 1986, ICJ Reports 1986, 14.

[23] See D. C. Thomas, *The Helsinki Effect. International Norms, Human Rights, and the Demise of Communism* (Princeton: Princeton University Press, 2001).

[24] See 'Ratification of International Human Rights Treaties—the Russian Federation', *University of Minnesota Human Rights Library*, <http://www1.umn.edu/humanrts/research/ratification-russia.html>.

In February 1989, the USSR cancelled reservations that it had earlier made regarding the compulsory jurisdiction of the ICJ in the context of certain UN human rights treaties such as the *International Convention on the Elimination on All Forms of Racial Discrimination, Convention on the Prevention and Punishment of the Crime of Genocide*, and the *Convention against Torture and Other Cruel, Inhuman or Degrading Treatment or Punishment*.[25] Essentially, this created the first ever theoretical window of opportunity to make Moscow a party to an interstate lawsuit in front of the ICJ, an opportunity that Georgia was desperately trying to use in its case against the Russian Federation in 2008. The *Georgia v. Russia* case has remained Russia's first and only contentious case in the ICJ so far—although Russian commentators have admitted that this is not how they 'imagined Russia's first case in the ICJ'.[26] However, ultimately the ICJ had to establish that it did not have jurisdiction in the case brought by Georgia.[27]

The ICJ's jurisdiction drawn from these specific conventions is not to be confused with the optional clause declarations accepting the Court's jurisdiction under Article 36 (2) of the ICJ Statute. Of the UN SC's P5 members, only Great Britain currently accepts the compulsory jurisdiction of the ICJ, and its acceptance is restricted by significant reservations, particularly vis-à-vis the countries of the British Commonwealth. Nevertheless, it is fair to conclude that in comparison to the US, Russia (and historically, the USSR) has essentially avoided dispute settlement in the ICJ. Altogether, this means that the jurisdiction of the ICJ remains unlikely in the case of 'Great Powers', unless ad hoc agreement is reached in a specific dispute (always a matter for sovereign agreement). On that basis, major powers like Russia should be more humble when advertising themselves as pillars of international legal order; there are better factual grounds to argue that smaller states are 'better at' international law, of course also because their self-interest in international law is more genuine.

Russia's practice of not participating in judicial settlements could also be noticed in other areas of international law. For example, the USSR upon signature and the Russian Federation upon ratification of the UNCLOS made reservations regarding procedures entailing binding decisions provided for in section 2 of Part XV of the Convention.[28] On 22 November 2013, the ITLOS ordered the Russian government to release the *Arctic Sunrise*, a ship that belonged to Greenpeace and was registered in the Netherlands.[29] However, the Russian government argued

[25] See Ignatenko, O. I. Tiunov, *Mezhdunarodnoe pravo*, 408.

[26] I. A. Volodin, D. S. Taratukhina, 'Rossiisko-gruzin'skoe razbiratel'stvo v Mezhdunarodnom sude', *Rossiiskii ezhegodnik mezhdunarodnoga prava* 2008 (St Petersburg: 'Rossiya-Neva', 2009) 28–54 at 28.

[27] See ICJ, *Case concerning Application of the International Convention on the Elimination of All Forms of Racial Discrimination (Georgia v Russian Federation), Preliminary Objections, Judgment of 01.04.2011*, <http://www.icj-cij.org/docket/files/140/16398.pdf>. For further analysis, see P. Okowa, 'The International Court of Justice and the Georgia/Russia Dispute', 11 *Human Rights Law Review* 2011, 739–57.

[28] See *Declarations of States Parties relating to Settlement of Disputes in accordance with Article 298 (Optional Exceptions to the Applicability of Part XV, Section 2, of the Convention*, <https://www.itlos.org/fileadmin/itlos/documents/basic_texts/298_declarations_June_2011_english.pdf>.

[29] ITLOS, *The 'Arctic Sunrise' Case (Kingdom of the Netherlands v. Russian Federation)*, Order, 22 November 2013, <http://www.itlos.org/fileadmin/itlos/documents/cases/case_no.22/Order/C22_Ord_22_11_2013_orig_Eng.pdf>.

that the ITLOS lacked jurisdiction in the case, refused to comply with the judgment, and released the ship on its own terms and at its own sovereign decision in August 2014.

Altogether, it is much easier to think of one's state as a pillar of international law if inter-state dispute settlement has been made very rare and the country can almost never be held accountable for violations of international law.

Returning now to Soviet and Russian practice, on 1 October 1991, just a couple of months before its disintegration, the USSR also acceded to the *Optional Protocol to the International Covenant on Civil and Political Rights*, thus recognizing the competence of the UN Human Rights Committee to receive and consider communications from individuals.

During the post-Soviet period, the ideology of opening up Russia to international regimes was further pursued in key areas. Particularly important in this regard was European human rights law. The Russian political elites at that time sincerely thought that human rights were an area where Russia lagged behind Western Europe, and where it could learn from the anthropocentric West which had accumulated more experience with protection of individual rights. In turn, Russian willingness to join the Council of Europe was greeted by West European politicians who wanted to see that Russia now 'belonged to Europe', hoping to 'civilize' and re-socialize post-Soviet Russia *inter alia* with the help of the common discourse of human rights. To see Moscow coming under the ideological umbrella of Strasbourg—perhaps this was also part of the sweetness of the West's triumph in the Cold War.

Thus, in 1996 Russia became a member of the Council of Europe. On 5 May 1998, the Russian Federation became a party to the *European Convention for the Protection of Human Rights and Fundamental Freedoms* and a number of its Protocols. This made Russia subject to the jurisdiction of the European Court of Human Rights in Strasbourg, a step that for the first time in the history of international law significantly penetrated the veil of Russia's state sovereignty. Ratification essentially made the ECtHR the court of last instance in human rights matters for Russia. In this area of international law, if one were to compare the two superpowers of the Cold War era, the transformation in Russia has probably been the biggest. In contrast, it would currently be difficult to imagine the US accepting the jurisdiction of an international human rights court similar to the ECtHR. In 2009, Russia also ratified the revised European Social Charter.

Things went much more slowly with respect to Russia's accession to the international trade law regime. Russia's accession negotiations with the WTO (GATT) started in 1993 but it was only on 22 August 2012 that the WTO welcomed Russia as its 156th member. The length of WTO accession negotiations reflected, *inter alia*, the complexity of the subject matter but inevitably also Moscow's ambivalence about the underlying principles and norms of the WTO. By comparison, consider the fact that China became a WTO member on 11 December 2001.

In some other contexts, however, the Russian Federation has remained ambivalent or even reluctant about opening up to specific regimes created in international law. Consider the cases of the *Rome Statute of the International Criminal*

Court (ICC) and the *Kyoto Protocol to the United Nations Framework Convention on Climate Change*, both favourite global projects of EU states. On 13 September 2000, Moscow signed the *Rome Statute of the International Criminal Court* but has not ratified it. In May 2014, Russia and China vetoed a UN move to refer crimes committed in Syria to the ICC.[30] Of course, the US attitude to the Rome Statute has also remained negative although the degree of rejection has depended on the respective presidential administrations in Washington, DC. The US has not become a party to the ICC and is unlikely to do so in the foreseeable future.

Another example is the *Kyoto Protocol to the United Nations Framework Convention on Climate Change* which was signed on 11 December 1997 and became effective on 16 February 2005. The Russian Federation signed the Protocol on 11 March 1999 and ratified it on 18 November 2004—a step which satisfied the quantitative criteria related to the treaty and enabled it to be brought into force in 2005. However, apparently Russia saw the main value of the Kyoto Protocol in hoping to gain concessions from the EU, in particular in the context of WTO accession, and when these were not forthcoming, withdrew from active participation in the Convention.[31] Moscow announced that Russia would not join the second phase of the Kyoto Protocol which started on 1 January 2013.[32] In this context, it is also significant that the world's major producers of greenhouse gases—the US, China, and India—have not committed themselves internationally to reducing their greenhouse gas emissions.

In 2014, officials in Moscow made it public that the Russian Federation would not sign the *UN Arms Trade Treaty* adopted by the UN GA on 2 April 2013.[33] Earlier, the *United Nations Convention against Corruption* had been ratified with a number of significant reservations.[34]

Moscow has also remained ambivalent about the international legal regime covering international investments. On 16 June 1992, Russia signed the *Convention on the Settlement of Investment Disputes between States and Nationals of Other States* (the ICSID Convention) but it has not ratified the Convention. Without such ratification, however, foreign investors in Russia cannot always be sure of impartial international arbitration when investment disputes arise. Nevertheless, in some cases, ICSID arbitration is provided in specific bilateral investment treaties (BITs), such as in Russia's BIT with Romania of 1993.[35] Russia is currently party

[30] I. Black, 'Russia and China Veto UN Move to Refer Syria to International Criminal Court', 22.05.2014 *The Guardian*, <http://www.theguardian.com/world/2014/may/22/russia-china-veto-un-draft-resolution-refer-syria-international-criminal-court>.

[31] A. Bashkatova, 'Kiotskii protokol snova stal predmetom torga', *Nezavisimaya gazeta* 19.10.2012, <http://www.ng.ru/economics/2012-10-19/4_protokol.html>; A. Shapovalov, 'Nazad v Kioto', *Kommersant* 06.09.2012, <http://www.kommersant.ru/doc/2016205>.

[32] S. Kulikov, 'Rossiya ostaetsya v Kiotskom protokole s chistoi sovestyu', *Nezavisimaya gazeta*, 11.12.2012, <http://www.ng.ru/economics/2012-12-11/1_ecology.html>.

[33] I. Safronov, E. Chernenko, 'Rossiya budet torgovat' oruzhiem, kak umeet', *Kommersant* 17.05.2014, <http://kommersant.ru/doc/2473772>.

[34] D. Gorovtsov, 'Ogovorki ili blokirovki?' *Nezavisimaya gazeta* 28.03.2011, <http://www.ng.ru/politics/2011-03-28/3_kartblansh.html>.

[35] V. M. Shumilov, *Mezhdunarodnoe pravo*, 2nd edn (Moscow: 'Mezhdunarodnye otnoshenia', 2012) 506.

to approximately 60 BITs[36] but not all of them ensure equally strong protection for foreign investors.

Moreover, on 30 July 2009, President Putin issued a decree declaring Russia's rejection of the *Energy Charter Treaty* (ECT), an investment protection treaty in the area of energy. The ECT had been signed in December 1991 and came into force for the states that had ratified it in April 1998. Russia signed the ECT in 1994 but never ratified the treaty. Among practitioners and legal scholars, Moscow's decision triggered debates on the nature of Russia's continued legal obligations in the field of foreign investment protection in the energy sector.[37] On 30 November 2009 an Arbitral Tribunal that had been constituted under the Energy Charter Treaty and UNCITRAL arbitration ruled that the Russian Federation was bound by the Energy Charter Treaty notwithstanding that the treaty was never ratified by the Duma, by virtue of its provisional application of the Treaty.[38]

Farkhutdinov argues that Russia participates in the Energy Charter Treaty on a 'provisional basis'.[39] A political scientist, Andrei Belyi, argues that 'Russia stopped the provisional application of the Energy Charter, but never withdrew from the Treaty'.[40] The criticism that the Energy Charter Treaty represents first of all the interests of EU countries that are rich in capital but poorer than Russia in natural resources is often expressed in Russian scholarship.[41]

Thus, an initial overview of developments in different treaty areas raises the first question marks about the intensity of Russia's actual participation in international law. The Soviet tradition was to talk about international law 'from a distance' and at least in some contexts, post-Soviet Russia has continued with this tradition. Accessions to the Council of Europe and WTO have been celebrated as major breakthroughs for Russia. However, in the context of several other regimes the Russian government has put its sovereignty and national interests before international legal regulation.

Moreover, ongoing ambivalence stems from a number of important multilateral treaties that have been signed but not ratified. It seems that the thinking is that their signing at the end of the Soviet period or during the 1990s could have

[36] I. Z. Farkhutdinov, *Mezhdunarodnoe investitsionnoe pravo i protsess* (Moscow: Prospekt, 2013) 140.

[37] See S. Pritzkow, *Das völkerrechtliche Verhältnis zwischen der EU und Russland im Energiesektor. Eine Untersuchung unter Berücksichtigung der vorläufigen Anwendung des Energiecharta-Vertrages durch Russland* (Berlin: Springer, 2011); P. Roche, S. Petit, 'Russia's Withdrawal from the Energy Charter Treaty', Norton Rose Fulbright, August 2009, <http://www.nortonrosefulbright.com/knowledge/publications/22691/russias-withdrawal-from-the-energy-charter-treaty>; A. Marhold, 'In Too Deep—Russia, the Energy Charter Treaty and the Nord Stream Gas Pipeline', 12 *Baltic Yearbook of International Law* 2012 (Leiden: Martinus Nijhoff, 2013) 303–15.

[38] *Hulley Enterprises Limited v. The Russian Federation* (PCA Case No AA 227); *Veteran Petroleum Limited v. The Russian Federation* (PCA case No AA 228).

[39] Farkhutdinov, *Mezhdunarodnoe investitsionnoe pravo i protsess*, 368.

[40] A. Belyi, *Russia's Position on the Energy Charter*, Chatham House, 27 April 2012, <http://www.chathamhouse.org/sites/files/chathamhouse/public/Research/Russia%20and%20Eurasia/270412summary.pdf>, 3.

[41] See e.g. D. S. Boklan, *Mezhdunarodnoe ekologicheskoe pravo i mezhdunarodnye ekonomicheskie otnoshenia* (Moscow: Magistr; Infra-M, 2014) 69.

been a 'mistake' and reflected the weakness of the Russian state at the time. The same thinking extends to bilateral treaties. For example, on 14 June 2002, the State Duma adopted a declaration in which it stated that the 1990 US-Soviet treaty on maritime delimitation was against the national interests of Russia and would not be ratified.[42]

However, in order see more specifically what post-Soviet Russia's practice in international law has been like, we need to examine more closely crucial sub-fields of international law. For the purposes of the present overview, I have chosen three sub-fields: human rights law, international economic law, and *jus ad bellum*. In making this selection, I have consciously proceeded from the contemporary Western concept of international law which includes human rights law and international economic law as genuine parts of international law, on a par with issues of *jus ad bellum*.

i. Case study No 1: Russia in European and international human rights law

One example in which post-Soviet Russia can hardly be considered to have been a global leader or *katechon* in international law is European human rights law. The country joined the Council of Europe in 1996 and ratified the ECHR in 1998 but ever since the government of the Russian Federation has been almost constantly on record as a source of controversies, problems, tensions, and human rights backlashes in the CoE system.[43] Almost every year, the Parliamentary Assembly of the CoE and the European Parliament adopt resolutions condemning the situation with human rights and democratic institutions in Russia. Over recent years, the CoE member state with the biggest share among pending applications in Strasbourg has been the Russian Federation although it does not have the largest share of cases compared to the size of its population

In some ways, Russia's accession to the Council of Europe in the 1990s revived the old nineteenth-century debate between Westernizers and Slavophiles in Moscow and European capitals. Western Europe was again there for Russia in order to catch up with it and 'become more civilized/European', this time in the context of human rights. But what exactly was Russia supposed to catch up with? What was the standard, the legitimacy, and rationale behind it? Did Russia have to change its identity *because of* Europe and the West? Were human rights primarily a Western concept?

[42] See V. R. Avkhadeev, 'Vlianie norm mezhdunarodnoga prava na natsional'noe zakonodatel'stvo Rossiiskoi Federatsii v sfere razgranichenia morskikh prostranstv v Severnom ledovitom okeane', *Rossiiskii ezhegodnik mezhdunarodnoga prava* 2013 (St Petersburg: 'Rossiya-Neva', 2013) 169–80 at 173.

[43] See further on Russia's accession to the CoE in B. Bowring, *Law, Rights and Ideology in Russia. Landmarks in the Destiny of a Great Power* (London: Routledge, 2013) chs 8 and 9, and L. Mälksoo (ed.), *Russia and European Human Rights Law. The Rise of the Civilizational Argument* (Leiden: Brill, 2014).

Russia's membership in the CoE has been a project of Westernizers in Russia and those in Western Europe who saw Russia first of all as a European country, emphasizing that post-Soviet Russia must be re-socialized with European institutions, norms, and practices. In some ways, we can call this the ecumenical approach of hoping that ultimately, everything (and everyone) will again become 'one' in Europe.

Thus, in 1996 when Russia became a member of the CoE, an inclusive approach was consciously taken. The report prepared by CoE experts before Russia's accession came to the conclusion that the country's legal system did not correspond to the requirements of the CoE. Russia's Ministry of Justice came to a similar conclusion. Nevertheless, the country was optimistically admitted as a member—probably based on the thinking that:

> ...'identification' with the group—not banishment from the group—is perhaps more likely to propel the legal and political systems of illiberal states toward conformity with prevailing norms.[44]

Thus, the idea was that so-called 'acculturation' would help to fix the situation with human rights in Russia. However, the results of the project of 'civilizing/ Europeanizing' in the area of European human rights law since the 1990s, have been mixed in Russia. Russia's membership in the CoE has been a tumultuous one, especially in the political part of the CoE where deputies in the PACE have almost annually clashed over post-Soviet Russia's record on human rights and democracy. More than 15 years after Russia's accession it is not entirely clear who has transformed and 'civilized' whom more—the CoE Russia or Russia the CoE.

Inevitably, European human rights law will not be applied in an abstract vacuum but in concrete circumstances in each country. These circumstances are shaped by the legal consciousness of the judges, their notions of law, state sovereignty, and so on. For dealing with differences between European countries, the ECtHR has even developed a specific legal doctrine called the margin of appreciation. It is characteristic that only in 2013 did the Supreme Court of the Russian Federation explicitly instruct judges to take into account ECtHR practice in cases regarding other countries since these cases lay out the European human rights standard.[45]

The ECtHR cases that have been politically the easiest for the Russian government are human rights cases without strong political implications—unacceptable prison conditions, non-execution of court judgments, and other such unfortunate

[44] R. Goodman, D. Jinks, *Socializing States. Promoting Human Rights through International Law* (Oxford: OUP, 2013) 105.

[45] *Postanovlenie plenuma Verkhovnoga Suda Rossiiskoi Federatsii ot 27 iunya 2013.g No 21 'O primenenii sudami obshei iurisdiktsii Konventsii o zashite prav cheloveka i osnavnykh svobod ot 4 noiabrya 1950 goda i Protokolov k nei'*, <http://www.rg.ru/2013/07/05/konvencia-dok.html>. See also N. V. Timoshin, B. L. Zimnenko, 'O postanovlenii plenuma Verkhovnoga Suda Rossiiskoi Federatsii ot 27 iunya 2013.g No 21 "O primenenii sudami obshei iurisdiktsii Konventsii o zashite prav cheloveka i osnavnykh svobod ot 4 noiabrya 1950 goda i Protokolov k nei" ', *Rossiiskyi ezhegodnik mezhdunarodnoga prava* 2013 (St Petersburg: 'Rossiya-Neva', 2014) 80–115.

phenomena indicating the weakness of rule of law and human rights in Russia. There are indications that the Russian political class wants continued CoE support for reform of the country's deficient judicial system, criminal procedure, and so on in order to transform Russia into a 'civilized country' for its citizens.

However, being subject to the jurisdiction of the ECtHR has also brought along an unpleasant if not unexpected surprise for the Russian government—the ECtHR deals not only with overcrowded prison cells and personal misfortunes in the judicial system. Absent other international courts that could deal with similar subject matters, the ECtHR has ended up—through the lens of individual rights—resolving debates originating from conduct in World War II, territorial issues after the collapse of the USSR, the second Chechen military campaign in 1998–2000, the Georgian-Russian war and events leading to it, amongst others. In a number of instances, cases in the ECtHR have been proxy cases for wider political problems concerning international law, and almost always the outcomes have been negative for Russia. These outcomes have demonstrated that the Russian government has had wider problems with respect for international law, i.e. beyond specific individual violations of human rights.

The first wave of these human rights cases concerned the Russian military campaigns to reconquer rebellious Chechnya.[46] The Chechen cases in the ECtHR have demonstrated that the Russian Army at the time had a wider and systemic problem with following international humanitarian law in the Caucasus.[47] Concerning the Chechen cases, the Russian government at least did not file official protests in Strasbourg or argue that the Court had been 'politicized'. Perhaps Moscow considered the ECtHR's involvement a price that had to be paid while re-establishing Russia's control over Chechnya. Politically, having the Chechen cases dealt with in the ECtHR may even have been in the interests of Moscow because this enabled discussion about what had happened in Chechnya in a 'softer' language of human rights, although the actual issues at stake were serious violations of the laws of war in a non-international armed conflict.

Nevertheless, only recently in the case of *Abdulkhanov and Others v. Russia*, which concerned a Russian military strike on a village in Chechnya in February 2000, did Moscow for the first time acknowledge that there had been a violation of Article 2 of the ECHR in the context of the second Chechen war.

The reactions of official Moscow to the ECtHR grew more hostile when situations in other post-Soviet territories came into play and the classic elements of international law and geopolitical rivalry became intertwined. For example, in the case of *Ilaşcu v. Moldova and Russia*,[48] the ECtHR held Russia (and the Republic

[46] E. Gilligan, *Terror in Chechnya. Russia and the Tragedy of Civilians in War* (Princeton: Princeton University Press, 2010); P. Leach, 'The Chechen Conflict. Analysing the Oversight of the European Court of Human Rights', 6 *European Human Rights Law Review* 2008, 732–61.

[47] See e.g. *Isayeva v. Russia*, 24.02.2005; *Estamirov and Others v. Russia*, 12.10.2006; *Aslakhanova and Others v. Russia*, 18.12.2012; *Abdulkhanov and Others v. Russia*, 03.10.2013.

[48] *Case of Ilaşcu and Others v. Moldova and Russia* (Application No 48787/99), Judgment, 08.07.2004.

of Moldova) responsible for the torture of a group of pro-Romanian Moldovan politicians in Transdnistria.

However, contrary to what the ECtHR had found in this case, including during field trips to Chişinau and Tiraspol, Moscow had officially denied its control over or even explicit involvement in the situation in Transdnistria, which it had not officially recognized as an independent state. As a result, the Russian MFA issued a declaration condemning the ECtHR judgment and its 'double standards' used against Russia.[49] The statement of the MFA concluded in the following fashion:

> Russia has always fulfilled and will continue to fulfil its international obligations, including the rulings of the European Court. At the same time, this does not change our attitude to the ruling on the 'case of Ilascu,' which we regard as erroneous and obviously politicized.

Moscow's tactic in this case was denial, which may *inter alia* imply that it was not prepared to argue about a classic international law issue (sovereignty and de facto control over the territory of Transdnistria) in a case that was simultaneously a human rights case, i.e. a case of individual suffering and violation of rights. Russia's response to the *Ilaşcu* case reveals actual elements in the international legal consciousness of the Russian government's representatives Moscow's legal tactic was to deny the obvious—Russia had been and continued to be militarily, economically, and politically involved in Transdnistria.

Another case concerning Transdnistria was *Catan and Others v. Moldova and Russia*[50] which concerned the language rights of Moldovan (Romanian) language speakers in Transdnistria, which had prohibited using the Latin alphabet in schools and made other significant restrictions to education in the Moldovan (Romanian) language. In this case, too, the ECtHR found that the Transdnistrian separatist regime in Tiraspol could not survive without Russia's continued military, economic, and political support and that the closure of Moldovan/Romanian-language schools fell within Russia's jurisdiction under the Convention. The Court found a violation of Article 2 of Protocol 1 in respect of the Russian Federation. However, Russia's official representative in Strasbourg, Mr Georgy Matyushkin, criticized the judgment as 'politicized'.[51]

Relationships between Russia and Strasbourg worsened further when the Grand Chamber of the ECtHR issued its judgment in *Kononov v Latvia* in 2010.[52] This case[53] involved a war crime committed by a group of Soviet partisans at the end

[49] See Statement by the Russian MFA, 8 July 2004,<http://www.mid.ru/bdomp/brp_4.nsf/0/aedaea734e366074c3256ecb0054ed80!OpenDocument&Click=>.

[50] *Case of Catan and Others v. Moldova and Russia*, application Nos 43370/04; 8252/05; 18454/06, Judgment, 19.10.2012. See also B. Bowring, 'Delo Katan i drugie protiv Moldovy i Rossii: geopolitika i pravo na obrazovanie. I pochemu 'nekomu' fakticheski oznachaet rebenku', *Mezhdunarodnoe pravosudie* 2014 No 1 (9), 44–59.

[51] 'Putin: Rossiya mozhet vyiti iz yurisdiktsii ESPCh', *Grani*, 14.08.2014, <http://grani.ru/Politics/Russia/President/m.232059.html>.

[52] *Case of Kononov v. Latvia* (Application No. 36376/04), Judgment, 17.05.2010.

[53] See further B. Bowring, 'Postanovlenie Bol'shoi Palaty Evropeiskogo Suda po pravam cheloveka po delu "Kononov protiv Latvii" (17 maia 2010 goda). Prava li Rossiiskaya Federatsia

of World War II in a Latvian village where a group of villagers had been brutally killed, some of them burned alive. The Russian government participated in this case as a third party, supporting Mr Kononov who denied that his partisan group had committed a war crime. Although the final Grand Chamber verdict of the ECtHR came out clearly in favour of Latvia and against Mr Kononov, passions were initially stirred because the Chamber judgment had supported Mr Kononov with a narrow margin.[54]

The historical significance of the *Kononov* case was that this was the first case in which soldiers of a winning ally in World War II were convicted of a war crime in an international court. However, it also shed some light on Moscow's skeletons in the history closet regarding World War II, including the question whether in World War II the USSR may itself have committed crimes listed in the London Statute and condemned at the Nuremberg trials.

Moscow essentially did not recognize the *Kononov* judgment as legitimate and Mr Pavel Laptev, the then Russian representative at the CoE, even publicly argued that the rules of *jus in bello* did not apply in the same way to the winners of World War II as they applied to the aggressors and their individual supporters.[55] Again, Moscow made statements in the OSCE and elsewhere that called the *Kononov* case a 'very dangerous precedent'.[56] Judge Zorkin, Chairman of the Russian Constitutional Court, dedicated a whole critical analysis to the Kononov case although the case had never been in his court's docket.[57]

However, the idea that the rules of *jus in bello* protecting civilians, whatever their personal political sympathies, would apply in the same way to both sides of international armed conflict is the foundation of international humanitarian law. Mr Laptev's statements to the contrary essentially meant that Moscow did not consider international humanitarian law practically applicable to Soviet actions in World War II—because the USSR had fought a 'just war'. Again, this is a noteworthy aspect in the actual international legal consciousness of representatives of the Russian government. From the first part of this study, it comes to mind that Baron Taube suggested that during the Middle Ages, Byzantium had a self-serving understanding of the concept of *bellum justum* that differed from the prevailing concept in Latin lands.

Another case concerning the legacy of World War II was the Grand Chamber judgment in *Janowiec and Others v. Russia*[58] which concerned complaints by

v svoem ponimanii sootnoshenia politiki i mezhdunarodnoga prava', 2(3) *Mezhdunarodnoe pravosudie* 2012, 75–83; L. Mälksoo, 'Casenote on Kononov v Latvia', 105 *AJIL* 2011, 101–8.

[54] *Case of Kononov v. Latvia* (Application No 36376/04), Judgment, 24.07.2008.

[55] S. Batrul', 'Pavel Laptev. Srok zhizni Evropeiskogo suda mozhet byt' sokrashen', *Kommersant* 31.05.2010, <http://www.kommersant.ru/doc/1378599>.

[56] See Statement by Mr Anvar Azimov, Permanent Representative of the Russian Federation, at the meeting of the OSCE Permanent Council, regarding the *Kononov v. Latvia* judgment, 20 May 2010, <http://www.osce.org/pc/68227?download=true>; 'Russia Protests Strasbourg Court Decision against Soviet WWII Veteran', *Russia Today*, 24.10.2010, <http://rt.com/news/strasbourg-court-kononov-latvia/>.

[57] V. D. Zorkin, *Konstitutsionno-pravovoe razvitie Rossii* (Moscow: Norma, 2011) 427–32.

[58] *Case of Janowiec and Others v. Russia*, application Nos 55508/07 and 29520/09, Judgment, 21.10.2013.

relatives of victims of the 1940 Katyn massacre, i.e. the killing of thousands of Polish prisoners of war by the Soviet secret police during World War II. The ECtHR found that Russia had failed to comply with its obligations under Article 38, i.e. to furnish necessary facilities for examination of the case. The case highlighted once again that post-Soviet Russia had been far from exemplary at *Vergangenheitsaufarbeitung*, and that Soviet state crimes were not fully exposed or investigated although the matter has been discussed in the Russian media.[59] Perhaps the most disturbing part is that in the early 1990s conscious efforts at cleaning up the past were made but they were apparently stopped because the political elites concluded that full exposure was not in the interests of the Russian state.

Russia's own citizens have also tried to obtain justice from Strasbourg in cases regarding state crimes committed during the Stalinist period—for example deportees from Kalmykia filed a mass claim at the ECtHR asking for compensation for their mass deportation but failed because of lack of jurisdiction.[60]

Finally, the issue of Russia's sovereignty emerged in the context of the ECtHR in the *Markin v. Russia* case in 2010–12.[61] In this case, the visions of the Chairman of the Constitutional Court of the Russian Federation, Mr Zorkin, and the ECtHR clashed in an unlikely and seemingly trivial case involving gender equality in the Russian Army.[62] Russia's Constitutional Court, chaired by Judge Zorkin, had decided that Mr Markin's constitutional rights had not been violated when he received, as a man, a smaller child allowance than a female army service member would have received in similar circumstances.

Referring to gender equality, the ECtHR reversed this judgment and as a result, Judge Zorkin published a passionate article in the newspaper *Rossiiskaya gazeta* in which he argued that the ECtHR had gone far too far in restricting Russia's sovereignty.[63] What seems to have upset Judge Zorkin most was the 'mentor tone' of the ECtHR Chamber judgment, in particular the fact that it had suggested that Russia needed legislative amendments in order to fix the human rights violation and prevent future ones in similar situations. In his public response, Judge Zorkin essentially warned that Russia would not take any more humiliations and transgressions to its sovereignty from the ECtHR. When the *Markin* case returned to the Constitutional Court, it held that only Russia's Constitutional Court was authorized to suggest legislative amendments in order to comply with ECtHR rulings, not the ECtHR itself. At the same time, the final judgment of the Constitutional Court has also been characterized as pragmatic, ultimately

[59] A. Samarina, 'Katynski sindrom', *Nezavisimaya gazeta* 17.11.2009, <http://www.ng.ru/ng_politics/2009-11-17/14_katyn.html>.

[60] See A. Serenko, 'Kalmytskie pereselentsy doshli do Strasburga', *Nezavisimaya gazeta* 30.11.2012, http://www.ng.ru/regions/2012-11-30/6_kalmykia.html>.

[61] See ECtHR, Case of *Konstantin Markin v. Russia* (7 October 2010) No 30078/06; Case of *Konstantin Markin v. Russia* (22 March 2012) No 30078/06 (Grand Chamber).

[62] See also L. Mälksoo, 'Casenote on Markin v Russia', 106 *AJIL* 2012, 836–42.

[63] V. Zorkin, 'Predel ustupchivosti', *Rossiiskaia gazeta* (29 October 2010), <http://www.rg.ru/2010/10/29/zorkin.html>.

defusing—after warning shots had previously been fired by Judge Zorkin in a personal capacity—collusion with the ECtHR.

The Russian-Georgian war of August 2008 also had repercussions in the ECtHR because it, and events before it, became a source of interstate proceedings between Georgia and Russia in the ECtHR. Thus, on 3 July 2014, the Grand Chamber of the ECtHR found that Russia's policy in 2006 of arresting, detaining, and expelling large numbers of Georgian nationals violated the Convention.[64]

Finally, on 31 July 2014, in the *Yukos* case (of which more soon in another, related connection, i.e. investor-state arbitration), the ECtHR awarded significant compensation to the former shareholders of the company, €1,866 million.[65]

After this short survey of Russian state practice in the ECtHR, the government's claim that it has been a champion of international law and rule of law in world affairs strikes one as exaggerated, to put it euphemistically. The ECtHR cases have revealed systematic problems in the Russian government's attitude to international law beyond individual wrongdoing. Moreover, Russian human rights law scholar Anton Leonidovich Burkov in his seminal empirical study on the use of European human rights in Russia's courts has found that Russian judges tend to be reluctant to use law that is not explicitly native in Russia.[66] Considering the predominant dualist school of thought in legal theory, this is not too surprising. But again, this is not what a champion of international law among the states looks like.

To the contrary, there are reasons to argue that the membership of the Russian Federation has managed to transform the nature of the CoE. During the Cold War, the CoE was a club of ideologically like-minded states; during the post-Soviet period it has been turned into a forum for inter-civilizational dialogue and, to an important extent, tensions. The state that was initially supposed to get 'civilized' refuses to become so and has developed a partly critical and antagonistic approach to the ECtHR and the CoE blaming it for 'politicization' of human rights and anti-Russian bias.

Looking at recent Russian domestic initiatives on constitutional rights—on NGOs, sexual minorities, freedom of opinion, and freedom of assembly—we have not seen much European 'acculturation' of the Russian government but rather the opposite—official Moscow now partly holds the mainstream ideology of the CoE in contempt. The Venice Commission has *inter alia* criticized recent legislative amendments in Russia which have made the human rights situation worse.[67] Quite symbolically, the Chairman of the Constitutional Court Valery Zorkin has recently called liberalism 'one of the main problems of the world'.[68]

[64] *Georgia v. Russia (I)*, application No 13255/07, Grand Chamber judgment of 3 July 2014.

[65] *Case of OAO Neftyanaya Kompaniya YUKOS v. Russia* (Application No 14902/04), Judgment (just satisfaction), 31.07.2014.

[66] A. L. Burkov, *Konventsia o zashite prav cheloveka v sudakh Rossii* (Moscow: Wolters Kluwer, 2010) 304.

[67] A. Pushkarskaya, 'Venetsianskaya komissia ne soglasilas' s Konstitutsionnym sudom', *Kommersant* 30.06.2014, <http://kommersant.ru/doc/2502304>.

[68] I. Rodin, 'Zorkin vynes prigovor liberalizmu-gomoseksualizmu', *Nezavisimaya gazeta* 02.10.2014, <http://www.ng.ru/politics/2014-10-02/3_zorkin.html>.

Thus, it is not certain whether the inclusive approach to Russia's membership in the CoE has politically justified itself; retrospectively, a restrictive approach might have been more justified, at least initially.

For example, the Russian State *Duma* recently started to discuss critical surveys on the human rights situation in the US and the EU, prepared by the Commissioner of Human Rights at the Russian Ministry for Foreign Affairs, Mr Konstantin Dolgov.[69] Thus, instead of all CoE member states being in the same European boat regarding human rights protection, the current CoE has been turned into an antagonistic club where member states in a *quid pro quo* fashion publish critical reviews about each other's human rights records. With the 'European' legitimacy that membership in the CoE provides for post-Soviet Russia, it has been easier for the Kremlin to pedal backwards in terms of actual human rights protection—because whatever the Russian government decides, it is nevertheless a 'European' state, a CoE member.

Russia's leading politicians see the CoE in terms of power politics. The legitimacy that the organization gives to the Russian government became obvious when Mr Aleksei Pushkov, Chairman of the Foreign Affairs Committee in the State Duma, announced that there is 'zero' possibility that Russia would step out of the CoE even after its delegation's voting rights were suspended due to the annexation of Crimea in 2014. Pushkov emphasized that Russia is one of the five most important states in the CoE (along with Great Britain, Germany, Italy, and France) and would not want to leave the platform of the CoE to anti-Russian countries such as the Baltic States and Georgia.[70] However, President Putin has also said that Russia may step out from the CoE system of human rights should its national security interests dictate this; he particularly referred to the US practice of denouncing treaties as 'model'.[71]

In the context of international human rights law, too, Russia has taken a stance different from the EU countries and the US in the UN Human Rights Council where in 2009 it sponsored a resolution calling for a study on the contribution traditional values can make to human rights promotion. This initiative and outcome reflects the influential thought world of the Russian Orthodox Church and its Patriarch Kirill I. The European states and the US voted against the resolution but

[69] See Report on the Human Rights Situation in the EU, Russian MFA, 06.12.2012, <http://mid.ru/brp_4.nsf/0/F6501F42C40A25EE44257ACC004971FC>; E. Chernenko, 'Nekto ne mozhet byt' obraztsom demokratii' (interview with Mr Dolgov), *Kommersant* 29.10.2012, <http://www.kommersant.ru/doc/2055389>; S. Samokhina et al., 'MID zachital Amerike ee poprannye prava', *Kommersant* 23.10.2012, <http://www.kommersant.ru/doc/2050786>; Y. Paniev, 'MID RF vzyalsya za prava v Evrosoyuze', *Nezavisimaya gazeta* 06.12.2012, <http://www.ng.ru/world/2012-12-06/7_prava.html>.

[70] 'Aleksei Pushkov. Veroyatnost' vykhoda RF iz Soveta Evropy nulevaya', *Rossiiskaya gazeta* 26.06.2014, <http://www.rg.ru/2014/06/26/pushkov-anons.html>.

[71] 'Putin ne isklyuchil vozhmozhnosti vykhoda Rossii iz-pod yurisdiktsii ESPCh', Interfaks, 14.08.2014,<http://www.vedomosti.ru/politics/news/32131381/putin-ne-isklyuchil-vozmozhnosti-vyhoda-rossii-iz-pod>.

it was nevertheless passed by a narrow margin. Altogether, however, the outcome of this process hardly met the expectations of promoters of traditional values.[72]

It has become increasingly obvious that in its present form, Russia's membership in the CoE lacks ideological foundations; sufficient common values are absent. It cannot be ruled out that, as Peter the Great said in his time, the Russian government will 'use the CoE for twenty–thirty years' and then, having learned the necessary lessons from Western Europe, will build up its own human rights protection system in its own regional public order, *Großraum*, a normative space where other European states cannot pester Moscow for its stance on LGBT rights, the autonomy of NGOs, and so on.

ii. Case study No 2: international economic law

International economic law is a sub-field of international law in its own right although, as the previous, second, part of this study demonstrated, theoretical differences exist as to what extent it forms part of public international law. This is not the place to go into all relevant details of Russia's evolving practice in international economic law but to look at the implications of some prominent cases. Does the claim by the Russian government that it acts as a guardian of international law hold true in the practice of international economic law?

We can start by examining state practice in international investment law, which many authors consider an increasingly important part of international economic law.[73] One foundation for investor-state arbitrations has been the *Energy Charter Treaty* based on which the arbitral tribunals in The Hague on 18 July 2014 ordered the Russian government to pay to former shareholders of Yukos Oil Company the unprecedented sum of 50 billion USD for the expropriation of the company.[74] The Permanent Court of Arbitration served as a registry for this case. However, when the arbitral award was issued, it was commented on as part of Western sanctions against Russia and in this sense hopelessly 'politicized' again. Moscow has asked for revision of the arbitral award but Yukos shareholders are already preparing for filing lawsuits against Russia state property in Western countries in order to collect their compensation.[75]

Another basis of jurisdiction for investor-state arbitrations have been BITs. As already mentioned Russia is party to some 60 BITs but has not ratified the ICSID

[72] See *Study of the Human Rights Council Advisory Committee on promoting human rights and fundamental freedoms through a better understanding of traditional values of humankind*, 06.12.2012, <http://www.ohchr.org/Documents/HRBodies/HRCouncil/AdvisoryCom/Session10/A.HRC.22.71_en.pdf>.

[73] See e.g. K. Nadakavukaren Schefer, *International Investment Law. Text, Cases, Materials* (Cheltenham: Edward Elgar, 2013); R. Dolzer, C. Schreuer, *Principles of International Investment Law*, 2nd edn (Oxford: OUP, 2012).

[74] See *Hulley*, *Yukos* and *Veteran Petroleum* cases, Final awards of 18 July 2014, <http://www.pca-cpa.org/showpage.asp?pag_id=1599>.

[75] M. Sergeyev, 'Rossiu grozit arest imushtshestva po isku aktsionerov YUKOSa', *Nezavisimaya gazeta* 13.11.2014, <http://www.ng.ru/economics/2014-11-13/1_yukos.html>.

Convention. However, scholars also observe that under President Putin, Russia has taken a step back in terms of investor-state arbitration and failed to conclude further BITs.[76]

Based on some such BITs (e.g. with Germany, the UK, Denmark, Spain), the Russian government has recently participated in and faced legal defeats in a number of investor-state arbitrations before the Arbitration Institute of the Stockholm Chamber of Commerce. Some of the most visible investor-state arbitration cases have involved legal issues following from the destruction of the oil company chaired by Mr Khodorkovsky, Yukos.[77] For example, in *RosInvest*, the arbitrators found that Russia's measures constituted an unlawful expropriation.[78] In Russia, the awards were seen as a hit to Russia's image in the eyes of foreign investors.[79] Since Russia is not a party to ICSID, no arbitrations have taken place within its framework—possibly because Washington, DC, as a location is not 'neutral' enough for the Kremlin.

Moreover, in some cases beyond investor-state arbitration, the interests and rights of international investors have clashed with Russia's changing claims regarding the national interest. One such example was the Sakhalin-2 international investment project. Sakhalin-2 is the world's largest combined natural gas and oil development and a major international investment project. In December 2006, Gazprom, Russia's energy monopoly, which is owned by the government, seized control of the project. The share of Royal Dutch Shell, an Anglo-Dutch firm, was reduced in favour of Gazprom from 55 per cent to 27.5 per cent. Of the two Japanese investors, Mitsui's share declined from 25 per cent to 12.5 per cent and Mitsubishi's from 20 to 10 per cent. According to experts, the price Gazprom paid for the shares acquired was below the market rate.[80] The deal was preceded by threats from the Russian government and Gazprom to accept the changed circumstances or face the consequences for the investment project and business prospects in the future. Environmental concerns and accusations were also used in the process of reshuffling the investment deal.[81]

A similar case to Sakhalin-2 occurred in June 2007, when the Russian government went after the international oil company British Petroleum (BP) and

[76] See E. Glusker, 'Arbitration Hurdles Facing Foreign Investors in Russia. Analysis of Present Issues and Implications', 10 *Pepperdine Dispute Resolution Law Journal* 2010, 595–622 at 614–15.

[77] See *RosInvestCo UK Ltd v. the Russian Federation*, Final Award, 12 September 2010, <http://italaw.com/sites/default/files/case-documents/ita0720.pdf>; *Quasar de Valores SICAV S.A., et al. v. the Russian Federation*, Award, 20 July 2012, <http://cisarbitration.com/wp-content/uploads/2013/02/Quasar-de-Valores-SICAV-S.A.-et-al-vs-Russian_Federation.pdf>; *Renta 4 S.V.S.A. v. the Russian Federation*, Award on Preliminary Objections, 20 March 2009, <http://italaw.com/documents/Renta.pdf>.

[78] *RosInvest*, 633.

[79] A. Gorshkova, 'Delo Yukosa prineslo dividendy', *Kommersant* 27.07.2012, <http://www.kommersant.ru/doc/1988787>.

[80] A. E. Kramer, 'Shell Cedes Control of Sakhalin-2 to Gazprom', *NYTimes*, 21.12.2006, <http://www.nytimes.com/2006/12/21/business/worldbusiness/21iht-shell.3981718.html?_r=1&>; S. Bowers, 'Sakhalin Issues "Settled"—as Russia Takes 50% Stake', *The Guardian*, 22.12.2006, <http://www.theguardian.com/business/2006/dec/22/russia.oilandpetrol>.

[81] See D. S. Boklan, *Mezhdunarodnoe ekologicheskoe pravo i mezhdunarodnye ekonomicheskie otnoshenia* (Moscow: Magistr; Infra-M, 2014) 75.

threatened to revoke its development license. BP was forced to sell its 62.9 per cent stake in the largest natural gas field in Kovytka to Gazprom 'for pennies on the dollar'.[82]

What cases such as Sakhalin-2 and Kovytka demonstrate is that protection of international investments has its 'peculiarities' in Russia, at least in the economic sector of extracting natural resources. It has been impossible to speak of a strong rule of law in these cases in Russia. In the Sakhalin-2 case, when the Russian government felt confident enough to increase its shares in the deal, it essentially suggested to the foreign investors that there had been a change of circumstances and proposed a revision of the initial contract with the Anglo-Dutch and Japanese investors.

The highly complex and difficult nature of doing business in Russia's Far East also meant that for the investors there were not many alternatives to doing business with the Russian government. Therefore, the investors decided to accept the Russian argument of 'changed circumstances' although legally speaking they could also have insisted on the initial contract terms, if it had made economic sense in the long run and if legal protection of investments had favoured them.

The leading Russian scholar publishing on international investment law, Farkhutdinov, has justified the government's revisionist actions in the Sakhalin-2 case, arguing that in the early 1990s too many concessions had been made to foreign investors, the initial contract was not in Russia's interests, the natural gas price was much lower in the early 1990s, and generally that those had been troubled times (*smuta*) for Russia.[83] This may all be true in some sense but the revision of initial contract terms is not the best example of rule of law either.

Moreover, the problem with this interpretation of the early 1990s as *smuta* is a wider one—it can be extended to other questions too. Even the collapse of the USSR and Moscow's recognition of the independence of former Soviet republics could be said to have taken place in 'troubled times', and thus become subject to revisionist policies or further conditions. By analogy, the Kremlin has also used the *clausula rebus sic stantibus* argument domestically, in the context of constitutional law, while at the same leaving the Constitution as such untouched.

For example, the 1990s witnessed the 'parade of sovereignties' in a number of federal subjects in Russia. Yet when Mr Putin became President, many prerogatives and rights acquired by federal subjects were taken back by Moscow, with reference to changed circumstances in political life. The last federal subjects such as Tatarstan have yet to drop the name of 'President' in the title of their respective national leaders, as they are now legally required to do.[84]

Another aspect of state practice in international investment law is the question of state immunity when an arbitral award in favour of a foreign private

[82] See E. Glusker, 'Arbitration Hurdles Facing Foreign Investors in Russia. Analysis of Present Issues and Implications', 10 *Pepperdine Dispute Resolution Law Journal* 2010, 595–622 at 613.

[83] Farkhutdinov, *Mezhdunarodnoe investitsionnoe pravo i protsess*, 363, 373 et seq.

[84] A. Astaf'ev, 'Bashkiria menyaet nazvanie glavnoi dolzhnosti', *Kommersant* 26.12.2013, <http://kommersant.ru/doc/2377506>; A. Yunashev, 'Prezidentam respublik sdelali poslednee preduprezhdenie', *Izvestia* 16.12.2013, <http://izvestia.ru/news/562511>.

investor has been the issue at stake. A case in point is *Noga*, a Swiss company that in 1991–2 concluded contracts with the Russian government which, however, failed to deliver its part of the contract, oil for credit that the Swiss company had given. However, an interesting part of Noga's contract with the government of the Russian Federation had been that the latter gave up its 'sovereign immunity' in case of non-fulfilment of the contract. Noga sued the Russian government in the Arbitration Institute of the Stockholm Chamber of Commerce which in its awards in February and May 1997 and March 2001 awarded to Noga in excess of 23 million USD from the Russian government.[85]

However, what remained to be dealt with was enforcement of the arbitral award. Having received a favourable arbitral award, Noga went after Russian state property in France, Germany, Sweden, and Switzerland, referring to the waiver of jurisdiction in its contract with the Russian government.[86] Even a Russian ship, the *Sedov*, was temporarily seized while in foreign waters. However, the Russian government intervened diplomatically and its assets were freed again. Finally, the issue was solved so that the claims of Noga against the Russian government were bought by an unknown company behind which, in the opinion of experts, stood the Russian government.[87]

In this fashion, the Noga case demonstrates that the Russian government had a certain problem with the execution of investor-state arbitration awards as well as waiving its state immunity even in a deal of a purely commercial nature (*acta jure gestionis*). Western arbitration scholars and practitioners have been critical of the fact that in these cases the Russian government could escape financial responsibility too easily.[88] Leading Russian scholars, in turn, have concluded that Russia's legislation on foreign investment is not always compatible with the country's obligations under international treaties.[89] Even the very notion of 'foreign investment' differs to some extent in Russian legislation and international legal instruments.[90]

The government owned Gazprom has also been taken to the Arbitration Institute of the Stockholm Chamber of Commerce by Lithuania, which claimed that it had to pay too much for Russian gas.[91]

In the context of international trade law and the WTO, Russia's practice is still emerging. Some debates have already started to make it to the WTO dispute settlement system[92] but as yet there have been no judicially solved cases. The EU

[85] See Shumilov, *Mezhdunarodnoe pravo*, 128.

[86] See e.g. O. Pleshanova, 'Rossiu oblozhili shestietazhnym', *Kommersant* 26.10.2010, <http://www.kommersant.ru/pda/kommersant.html?id=1528888>.

[87] Shumilov, *Mezhdunarodnoe pravo*, 128.

[88] E. Gaillard, 'Effectiveness of Arbitral Awards, State Immunity from Execution and Autonomy of State Entities. Three Incompatible Principles', in E. Gaillard, J. Younan (eds), *State Entities in International Arbitration, IAI Series on International Arbitration No 4* (Huntington, NY: Juris Publishing, 2008) 179–93 at 185.

[89] Farkhutdinov, *Mezhdunarodnoe investitsionnoe pravo i protsess*, 37.

[90] Ibid., 169, 173.

[91] S. Kulikov, 'Litva tyanet "Gazprom" v sud', *Nezavisimaya gazeta* 04.10.2012, <http://www.kommersant.ru/doc/2382708>.

[92] I. Zubkov, 'Do kontsa goda Rossia podast isk v WTO protiv Ukrainy', *Rossiiskaya gazeta* 14.10.2014, <http://rg.ru/2014/10/14/isk-site-anons.html>.

has criticized Russia's practices in the context of WTO rules on a number of occasions.[93] Moreover, Christoph Schewe points out that during the post-Soviet period, the Russian government has had several politically motivated trade disputes with former Soviet republics and Warsaw Pact members.[94] For Moscow, trade with immediate European neighbours has traditionally not been 'just' trade; it has been part of international politics. Russia could hardly get used to being a member of the WTO when as a consequence of the annexation and war in Ukraine in 2014, the Western nations established economic sanctions against Russia, to which Moscow responded with its own economic sanctions. Currently under discussion is what outcomes would the WTO dispute settlement mechanism produce, while the Russian government has indicated changes in its attitude to its WTO commitments.[95] It remains to be seen how Moscow will apply the rule of law in international trade, and whether it will at some point discover, as it did in the case of the ECtHR, that too many legal restrictions are not so good from the viewpoint of state sovereignty.

Currently, in light of Western sanctions vis-à-vis Russia because of the war in Ukraine, Russia has started to respond by banning imported food from the West, mainly referring to 'health reasons'.[96] Moreover Russia's accession to the WTO has not changed the fact that in particular trade relations with nations once in the Soviet sphere of influence remain politicized. It remains to be seen whether affected states such as recently Ukraine, the Republic of Moldova or Poland (in the latter case, this involves the EU) will have the resources and energy to fight against discriminatory measures taken by Moscow.[97] Again, the main question is to what extent the WTO will socialize the Russian Federation, and in turn, to what extent the Russian Federation will manage to transform the WTO.

In conclusion, regarding international economic law it can be said that the Russian Federation has preserved some of the earlier Soviet autarchic approach. The contemporary attitude towards instruments and dispute settlement mechanisms in international economic law is no longer entirely autarchic but is nevertheless cautious. Characteristic and fully mirroring the theoretical views in

[93] A. Gorbachev, 'Chlenstvo v VTO nachalos' so skandalov', *Nezavisimaya Gazeta* 06.12.2012, <http://www.ng.ru/economics/2012-12-06/1_wto.html>; Yu. Paniev, 'Moskva i Brjussel' simmetrichno obsudyat prava cheloveka', *Nezavisimaya gazeta* 04.06.2013, <http://www.ng.ru/ideas/2013-06-04/6_rights.html>.

[94] C. Schewe, 'Russia in the WTO. The Bear on a Leash? Russia in International Trade Disputes and the Added Value of a WTO Membership', 47 *Journal of World Trade* 2013, 1171–201.

[95] D. A. Desierto, 'The EU/US v. Russia Trade Wars. Revisiting GATT Article XXI and the International Law on Unilateral Economic Sanctions', *EJIL: Talk!*, 22.09.2014, <http://www.ejiltalk.org/the-euus-v-russia-trade-wars-revisiting-gatt-article-xxi-and-the-international-law-on-unilateral-economic-sanctions-2/>; M. Lyutova, 'Rossiya gotova nachat' peregovory o peresmotre uslovii prisoedinenia k VTO', *Vedomosti* 26.09.2014, <http://www.vedomosti.ru/politics/news/33906261/zabor-ot-vto>.

[96] K. Demirjian, 'As the West steps up sanctions, Russia starts banning food', *Washington Post*, 02.08.2014, <http://www.washingtonpost.com/world/as-the-west-steps-up-sanctions-russia-starts-banning-food/2014/08/02/d7648ea9-af5b-461a-b312-ee6057918cc8_story.html?hpid=z11>.

[97] See e.g. V. Mironov, 'RF zapreshaet ukrainskie konservy i konfety', 28.07.2014, *Rossiiskaya gazeta*, <http://rg.ru/2014/07/28/konservi-site.html>.

Russian scholarship is the reaction of Mr Konstantin Dobrynin, a member of the constitutional affairs committee of the Federation Council, to the Yukos arbitration award. Dobrynin argues that the Russian government should not have recognized the jurisdiction of the arbiters in the first place because the issue at hand was of a 'public, not private law character'.[98] However, from the viewpoint of Russian theory of international law, the Russian government can always argue, as it does, that in the sphere of international economic relations Moscow does nothing more than protect its state sovereignty, which in turn continues to be the foundational principle of international law. Thus, from Moscow's viewpoint, less is more—less in the way of investors' rights and binding international mechanisms for dispute settlement means more sovereignty for Russia which, from the point of view of Russian thinking, equals more 'international law'.

iii. Case study No 3: Russia, post-Soviet wars, and *jus ad bellum*

Clearly, when the Russian government applauds itself for its progressive attitude towards international law in national strategy documents, it means in the first place the international law of peace and security, *jus ad bellum*, and much less so international human rights law or international economic law. As became clear from the legal theory analysis in this study, from the point of view of Russian theory and thinking these sub-fields are just not central enough in the constitution of international law. Thus, when the Russian government talks passionately about 'international law' and construes itself as its guardian, it does not really see or want to see the practice of the ECtHR or investor-state arbitration as significant parts of 'international law'.

Because of the importance of *jus ad bellum* in the Russian concept of international law, it is absolutely crucial to locate the Russian government's thinking on the territorial entitlement right. This is the key to the Russian government's thinking about international law generally; this *is* official Moscow's international law thinking. The roots of this thinking lie in a deeply realist worldview, and in order to understand this thinking one needs first to understand the ultimate vulnerability that Russia faced in 1991—the indeterminacy of Russia's borders after the collapse of the USSR. The Soviet Empire had been a version of the Russian Empire and having given up significant parts of the Empire in 1991 it was not crystal clear where the new, 'democratic' borders of Russia would lie after application of the principle of self-determination. The problem was twofold: separatism within the Russian Federation and the fate of ethnic Russians who remained living outside the borders of the Russian Federation.

The 1990s was Russia's period of weakness, with a real possibility that the disintegration of the USSR would be followed by the disintegration of the Russian Federation itself. Separatism in Chechnya but also, to a lesser extent, in Tatarstan

[98] M. Overchenko, A. Kornya, S. Titov, 'Pochemu Rossiya proigrala byvshim vladel'tsam YUKOSa $50 mlrd', *Vedomosti*, 04.08.2014, <http://www.vedomosti.ru/library/news/30942371/yukos-mog-obojtis-rossii-v-66-mlrd?full#cut>.

and Bashkiria constituted an existential headache for Moscow from the point of view of the territorial integrity of the Russian Federation. This is why the Russian government at that time firmly adhered to its interpretation of the UN Charter to the strict prohibition of use of military force in international law and resisted all Western attempts to legalize or legitimize humanitarian intervention.

The legal-political principle that was generally accepted when the USSR disintegrated in 1991 was *uti possidetis*, i.e. that former federal borders determined the borders of newly independent states. This meant that all former Soviet republics—from Armenia to Tajikistan—were entitled to independent statehood, unlike entities within former Soviet republics such as Chechnya (in Russia) or Abkhazia (in Georgia).

However, although the principle of *uti possidetis* was generally recognized by the international community and formally by Moscow as well, its first violations with Russia's involvement took place in the early 1990s—in Nagorno Karabakh, South Ossetia, Abkhazia, and Transdnistria. In all these cases, Russian military or paramilitary units as well as volunteers played a role in making sure that Nagorno Karabakh would not stay with Azerbaijan, South Ossetia and Abkhazia with Georgia, or Transdnistria with the Republic of Moldova. In these territories, frozen conflicts were born and the de facto situation on the ground differed from the situation *de jure*. At the same time, Moscow secured itself special extraterritorial rights in Crimea where Ukraine's sovereignty was recognized, based on the *uti possidetis* principle but Russia got to keep a sizeable Navy in Sebastopol.

The Russian government has construed the NATO military intervention in Kosovo in 1999 as the 'original sin' of post-Cold War international law. It has focused the debate on textual interpretation of the UN Charter while sticking to the argument that no military intervention could be legal without UN SC authorization or beyond self-defence against armed attack. Western scholars have gone along with this debate by agreeing that the military intervention in Yugoslavia may indeed have been 'illegal but legitimate' according to the UN Charter.

The real issue at stake in this debate was the contours and legitimacy of the veto power in post-Cold War conditions. Moscow's answer to the question 'What did the end of the Cold War and the disintegration of the USSR change in international law?' was: not much. Yes, after the end of the Cold War, countries in Central and Eastern moved out from Moscow's power orbit but, crucially from Moscow's point of view, this happened with the formal agreement of Moscow. Thus, the post-Cold War shrinking of the size of the Soviet/Russian Empire would not imply that the constitutional essence of international law had been changed. The text of the 'constitution' of the international community, the UN Charter, was still the same as was agreed upon in 1945.

In other words, the West has often seen revisionist impulses in post-Soviet Russian practice of international law, at least since President Putin.[99] However, the Kremlin has not seen itself at all this way because it has not seen the fall of

[99] R. Allisson, *Russia, the West, and Military Intervention* (Oxford: OUP, 2013) 170.

the Berlin Wall in 1989 and the collapse of the USSR in 1991 as normatively significant dates in international law. Typical of this thinking were President Putin's remarks at the Valdai Club meeting in October 2014:

> The Cold War ended, but it did not end with the signing of a peace treaty with clear and transparent agreements on respecting existing rules or creating new rules and standards. This created the impression that the so-called 'victors' in the Cold War had decided to pressure events and reshape the world to suit their own needs and interests. If the existing system of international relations, international law and the checks and balances in place got in the way of these aims, this system was declared worthless, outdated and in need of immediate demolition.[100]

In the same speech held just half a year after the annexation of Crimea, Mr Putin continued along the same lines:

> We have entered a period of differing interpretations and deliberate silences in world politics. International law has been forced to retreat over and over by the onslaught of legal nihilism. Objectivity and justice have been sacrificed on the altar of political expediency. Arbitrary interpretations and biased assessments have replaced legal norms.[101]

In official Russia's understanding the Charter restricts the use of military force to a minimum and favours the principle of state sovereignty. In particular, in Russia's interpretation, the international law of the UN Charter is a system of five powerful 'oligarchs', the winners of World War II (the P5 of the UN SC), against whose individual will no military intervention can be legally decided by any other power (the veto power of the P5). Arguments questioning the legitimacy of this oligarchic nature of the rights of the P5 have been pushed aside as concerning at best subjective claims regarding justice, not international law itself. Instead, criticism of the legitimacy of the oligarchic rights of the P5 is done away with as 'historical revisionism', as 'attempts to question the outcome of World War II'.

Regarding the NATO intervention in Kosovo in 1999, this was a scary precedent for Moscow because it invoked the possibility of foreign intervention *against Russia* if Moscow too needed to use military force against Russia's separatist minorities as it did in Chechnya. On the other hand, NATO's intervention was from official Moscow's point of view a violation of Russia's procedural rights under the UN Charter. To use military force against a sovereign nation without UN SC authorization and essentially notwithstanding the veto power meant rendering Russia's privileges and status in the post-1945 international community without substance.

In official Moscow's view, 'international law' primarily equals the global power arrangement of 1945, the deals of the conferences of Yalta and San Francisco. For Moscow, 'international law' is primarily what Stalin, Roosevelt, and Churchill agreed upon when setting a seal on the Allied victory. Thus, when Moscow

[100] President of Russia, Meeting of the Valdai International Discussion Club, 24 October 2014, <http://eng.kremlin.ru/news/23137>.

[101] Ibid.

rhetorically defends 'international law', it primarily defends its own power and special status enshrined in the UN Charter. Upon closer examination, criticisms regarding Western violations of international law reveal themselves as criticisms of the disbalance of power.[102] This is probably the most characteristic feature concerning the rhetoric regarding 'international law' in post-Soviet Russia's official foreign policy programmes and documents—that the discourse hides a hard core realist agenda behind a seemingly idealistic rhetoric about the importance of protecting 'international law'. In Russia, there has been much emphasis on legal formalism and textual interpretation of the UN Charter but little self-reflection regarding the legitimacy of specific arrangements in the international legal order, e.g. whether the right of the UN SC to block intervention aiming to stop imminent atrocities by a client state was absolute.

Part of official Moscow's thinking seems to have been that it does not matter so much what former constituents of the Russian Empire, formerly dependent peoples themselves, think or prefer in matters of geopolitics. Democracy and self-determination are fictions of sorts; smaller peoples are always subjects to competing outside influences, and to some extent 'brainwashed' by the predominant power(s). Their free will is by nature limited and their 'independence' essentially means merely that they can choose between two competing *Großräume* (e.g. moving from Moscow's sphere of influence to the EU's—i.e. essentially Germany's and France's—orbit). US diplomat George F. Kennan's (1904–2005) realist observation is perhaps revealing in this regard—'that the eye of the Kremlin can distinguish, in the end, only vassals and enemies'.[103]

However, this line of thinking also means that while Moscow emphatically emphasizes its own rights according to the international community's constitution of 1945 (the UN Charter), as *derzhava* it does not necessarily psychologically 'get' the part of this constitutional arrangement that in Article 2 para. 1 of the UN Charter is called the sovereign equality of states. The principle of sovereign equality of states means that even such small states have the right to make their own choices, to exercise self-determination. However, official Moscow is not too eager to talk about *that* part of the UN Charter and international law.

One illustration of this tendency has been Moscow's idea that it should have had a veto of sorts to the NATO enlargement in Eastern Europe. But what legal or moral principle exactly would have justified such a veto right if the nations of Central and Eastern Europe themselves eagerly wanted membership in NATO and its military protection? Moscow has criticized the fact that apparently during Soviet–Western negotiations about German reunification, Soviet leaders had been orally promised by US and NATO negotiators that NATO would not move further eastward (a claim which has been contested and certainly there is no

[102] See e.g. President of Russia, Meeting of the Valdai International Discussion Club, 24 October 2014, <http://eng.kremlin.ru/news/23137> (referring to the importance of 'balance of interests' and arguing that 'The crisis in Ukraine is itself a result of a misbalance in international relations').

[103] Quoted in: F. Zakaria, '"A Guest of My Time". The Kennan Diaries', *NYTimes* 21.02.2014, <http://www.nytimes.com/2014/02/23/books/review/the-kennan-diaries-by-george-f-kennan.html?_r=0.

such written agreement). But even if this was actually the case, the whole thinking behind this narrative ignores the possibility that Central and East European nations as subjects of international law could themselves make these choices; that no one else could give final and binding guarantees *for them*.

Moscow's conclusion has been that by expanding geopolitically while at the same time propagating human rights and anthropocentric values, *the West* has covered its realist motives behind idealist rhetoric. Putin's Russia is emphasizing 'international law' (the way it understands it) because the West in its rhetoric has abused protection of human rights and democratic legitimacy. Thus, Russian 'international law' has rhetorically been played against Western 'human rights and the right to democracy'. Russian authors emphasize that the UN Charter does not distinguish between democracies and non-democracies and to do otherwise, as the West has done, would go against the underlying logic of the UN Charter.[104]

The West did indeed have certain double standards when the cases of Kosovo and Chechnya are compared. The military crushing of separatists with heavy cost in civilian lives was allowed to happen in Chechnya (in the territory of the Russian Federation) whereas in Kosovo the state that tried to fight the separatists, Yugoslavia, was punished by military intervention and recognition of the secession of the disputed territory. The inevitable conclusion is that the main difference between these cases was that Russia had nuclear weapons and Yugoslavia did not, and that *quod licet Iovi non licet bovi*. However, this can also be a case of the resurrection of 'civilizational' international law against the universal paradigm—the West had less incentive to intervene in the name of international law in a chaotic region where Islamists were on the rise.

An example of subsequent Western international legal ideology has been the rise of the responsibility to protect (R2P) as an emerging legally relevant principle characteristic of the post-Cold War order. The principle was positively mentioned in the UN Secretary General's high-level Panel Report on Threats, Challenges and Change[105] in the making of which Yevgeny Maksimovich Primakov (b. 1929), Russia's Prime Minister during the Kosovo crisis, participated. However, leading legal minds in Russia have continued to treat the R2P principle with caution, as essentially old wine in new bottles, i.e. a Western attempt to sell the well-known and controversial idea of unilateral humanitarian intervention under a new label.[106] The NATO intervention in Libya in 2011 is often referred to, including by Primakov,[107] as a Western abuse of the responsibility to protect; arguing that the West went much further from the mandate of the UN SC.[108]

[104] N. Narochnitskaya, 'Rossia v novykh geopoliticheskikh real'nostyakh', in: '*. . . I vremya sobirat' kamni . . .' Evraziiskaya integratsia segodnya. 20 let posle raspada SSSR* (Moscow: Fond istoricheskoi perspecktivy, 2012) 3–14 at 5.

[105] See <http://www.unrol.org/doc.aspx?n=gaA.59.565_En.pdf>.

[106] Cf. V. S. Kotlyar, 'Teoria, praktika i perspektivy kontseptsii "otvetstvennost' po zashite" v svete printsipa verkhovenstva mezhdunarodnogo prava v mezhdunarodnykh otnosheniakh', *Rossiiskii ezhegodnik mezhdunarodnogo prava 2013* (St Petersburg: 'Rossiya-Neva', 2014), 52–65 at 65.

[107] Y. Primakov, 'Balkany i sovremennyi mir', *Nezavisimaya gazeta* 24.10.2011, <http://www.ng.ru/ideas/2011-10-24/9_balkany.html>.

[108] See further R. Allisson, *Russia, the West, and Military Intervention* (Oxford: OUP, 2013) 189 et seq.

Some Western legal scholars have influentially construed the UN Charter as the 'constitution' of the international community.[109] If so then it must be taken into account that since 1945 different regional-geopolitical views have existed as to the question which principles have priority in the UN Charter in case of collision. The West has increasingly emphasized the principles of human rights and democratic legitimacy, much more than has been the case in countries like Russia and China, which continue to emphasize state sovereignty and, in any case, the oligarchic veto rights of the P5 of the UN SC.

In essence, the global edifice of international law is stuck with the fact that there actually hardly ever was a genuine and deep-going agreement between Moscow and the West regarding the underlying values and principles of the post-World War II international legal order. During the Cold War, the UN SC was blocked almost all the time. The Gulf War, which was authorized by the UN SC in 1991, was thought of as a window of opportunity for making the P5 look in the same direction. At the same time, it must be remembered that the USSR was already economically and ideologically weak at that time. For example the diary of a key member in the entourage of the last Soviet leader, Mikhail Gorbachev, reveals that in 1990–1 when Moscow agreed in the UN SC with the US-led military use of force against Saddam Hussein's Iraq, it was not genuinely in favour of such military action but in the first place was power-wise not in a position to avoid it or turn it around.[110] Even in 1991, the Soviet view on Iraq was that the US had overstepped the authorization of the UN SC.[111]

Beyond non-recognized republics and frozen conflicts, the wider question was to what extent Russia wanted 'international law' to apply to former Soviet republics. Historically, Moscow was not used to taking into account 'international law' when it extended its former Empire. For example, the relationships between Moscow on the one hand and Ukraine, Georgia, or Moldova on the other had hardly ever been regulated by 'international law' and if they sporadically had, it was rather the Empire's arrangements for regulating vassal relationships, not stable international law between equal subjects.

Thus, when today's Moscow praises its commitment to international law, as it does in its foreign policy documents, it may even be sincere—except that it is not inclined to think of the full and unconditional applicability of international law vis-à-vis Georgia or the Republic of Moldova, for instance. In these countries, in Moscow's view instead of international law some sort of regional concrete order prevails. When Moscow emphasizes 'international law', it primarily keeps in mind its relations with the US, Britain, and China and the global edifice of international law, not so much its own historical-imperial 'Commonwealth', the lands of the former Russian and Soviet Empires. Trenin has put it aptly and yet

[109] B. Fassbender, *The United Nations Charter as the Constitution of the International Community* (Leiden: Brill, 2009).

[110] A. Tšernjajev, *1991. aasta. NSV Liidu presidendi abi päevik*, trans. U. Uibo (Tallinn: Vagabund, 2006) 103.

[111] R. Allisson, *Russia, the West, and Military Intervention* (Oxford: OUP, 2013) 38–40.

with all ambiguity with respect to the former Soviet republics: Russia perceives some of them 'as *separate* countries but not as *foreign* countries'.[112]

With respect to a number of post-Soviet republics that became nominally independent in 1991, the official Russian approach has been a mixture of international and Russia's unwritten post-imperial 'constitutional law'. Thus, two aspects have merged in practice: the newly emerged nations' nominal sovereignty on the one hand and Moscow's centuries-old imperial claim which in the post-Soviet period has been translated into sphere of influence (*Großraum*). Roy Allison also concluded in his recent study that Moscow does not seem to extend global international law fully to what he calls 'CIS regional order' or regional public order.[113] But again, one needs to re-emphasize that this logic is against the UN Charter.

In some ways, the Russian Empire changed shape after the collapse of the USSR. But this did not necessarily mean that the idea of the Empire fully disappeared. Even situations within the Russian Federation have certain 'international' elements. For example, Chechnya and Ingushetia within the Russian Federation have intensely argued about the course of their border as if they were nascent nation states within a *Großraum* rather than typical parts of a federal state.[114] The question whether Tatarstan had been 'occupied' by Muscovy has been discussed in Kazan, and so on.[115]

It is interesting that post-Soviet Russia let the lands with a Western Christian cultural heritage—Estonia, Latvia, and Lithuania—leave the Empire more easily than the historic lands of Byzantium where the Russian language was the lingua franca and Orthodox Christianity the main religion. Thus, resistance to the idea of Georgia or Ukraine joining NATO was apparently not just geopolitical; it was also 'civilizational'. The borders of the USSR were no red line for Moscow; but the historic territory of Eastern Christianity was. Quite tellingly, Patriarch Kirill I of Moscow has spoken in front of the Russian military that they should first of all be prepared to defend Russia's civilizational values.[116] When in 2014 the West responded with sanctions to Russian policies in Ukraine, the spokesperson of the ROC argued that this was a good thing because it gave a chance to develop 'Russian civilization'.[117]

The Russian–Georgian war of August 2008 broke out first of all because of Tbilisi's determination to become a member of NATO, i.e. the *Western* defence alliance.[118] In this war, President Saakashvili of Georgia made the first military

[112] Trenin, *Post-Imperium* (Moscow: Carnegie Endowment, 2012) 39.

[113] R. Allison, *Russia, the West, and Military Intervention* (Oxford: OUP, 2013) 18, 213.

[114] M. Muradov, 'Ramzan Kadyrov khochet vosstanovit'sya v granitsakh 1934 goda', *Kommersant* 05.09.2012, <http://www.kommersant.ru/doc/2015582>; V. Mukhin, 'Territorial'nye pretenzii silovoga kharaktera', *Nezavisimaya gazeta* 22.04.2013, <http://www.ng.ru/regions/2013-04-22/2_pretenzii.html>.

[115] G. Postnov, 'Ugolok mezhnatsional'nogo nesoglasia', *Nezavisimaya gazeta* 15.12.2011, <http://www.ng.ru/politics/2011-12-15/3_kartblansh.html>.

[116] A. Mel'nikov, 'Yadernyi shtshit protiv kul'ta pribyli', *Nezavisimaya gazeta* 24.08.2009, <http://www.ng.ru/regions/2009-08-24/2_patriarh.html>.

[117] V. Mal'tsev, 'RPTs stchitaet sanktsii pozitivnym shansom dlya strany', *Nezavisimaya gazeta*, 01.08.2014, <http://www.ng.ru/faith/2014-08-01/2_rpc.html>.

[118] See e.g. R. D. Asmus, *A Little War that Shook the World* (New York: Palgrave Macmillan, 2010).

move in South Ossetia, as the EU-sponsored report of Swiss diplomat Heidi Tagliavini suggests[119] and Saakashvili's competing Georgian politicians have retrospectively maintained.[120] However, the conditions for the clash between Georgia and Russia were prepared by Moscow which, rather than being a neutral 'peacekeeper', actively supported separatists in South Ossetia and Abkhazia, distributed Russian passports to the local population,[121] supported the local separatist forces with weapons, and thus also violated international law. Russian opposition politician and former economic adviser of President Putin, Andrei Nikolayevich Illarionov (b. 1961) has published an independent investigative report essentially arguing that official Moscow was responsible for the war.[122]

The Tagliavini report pointed a finger *inter alia* at President Saakashvili but retrospectively it can simply be seen as a strategy by some EU member states to diminish the problem and make it go away (at least from the European agenda). The main thesis that 'both sides were guilty' enabled Moscow to get away with its role in the outbreak of the war. For example, the Tagliavini report could also have emphasized that international legal mechanisms did not offer Georgia any credible options to regain the territories that belonged to it under international law. From the point of view of the Georgian government, the Moscow-sponsored concrete order trumped claims based on international law.

Quite similarly, Moscow continues to threaten the Republic of Moldova that should Chişinau join Romania or NATO, it would lose Transdnistria not only de facto but also *de jure*. It is first of all in this context that Transdnistria is kept and supported by Moscow as a bargaining chip.[123] The same was true vis-à-vis Ukraine, whose sovereignty over Crimea was recognized only at the time when Moscow thought that it could control the whole of Ukraine; that Ukraine as a country would also remain in its 'sphere of influence' in the post-Soviet period. Consequently, when the Maidan demonstrators pushed pro-Russian President Viktor Fedorovich Yanukovych (b. 1950) from power in early 2014, Moscow swiftly reacted by invading and annexing Crimea, without any regard to Ukraine's sovereign rights.

The evolution of Moscow's legal argumentation and views in these complex cases has been opportunistic and has not followed some overarching legal principle

[119] Report of the Independent Fact-Finding Mission on the Conflict in Georgia, September 2009, <http://www.ceiig.ch/Report.html>.

[120] See Yu. Roks, 'Voinu s Rossiei razvyazal Saakashvili', 25.10.2012 *Nezavisimaya gazeta*, <http://www.ng.ru/cis/2012-10-25/1_saakashvili.html>.

[121] See A. Peters, 'Extraterritorial Naturalizations. Between the Human Right to Nationality, State Sovereignty and Fair Principles of Jurisdiction', 53 *German Yearbook of International Law* 2010, 623–725 at 635 et seq.

[122] A. Illarionov, 'Kak gotovilas' voina', *Novaya gazeta* 24.06.2009, <http://www.novayagazeta.ru/politics/44604.html>; 'Kak gotovilas' voina. Posleslovie', *Novaya gazeta* 14.08.2009, <http://www.novayagazeta.ru/politics/43961.html>.

[123] See interview with D. Rogozin, 'Perspektiv uregulirovania ya na segodnya ne vizhu', *Kommersant* 20.11.2012, <http://kommersant.ru/doc/2070470>; V. Solov'ev, 'To, chem ya zanimayus', ne sovsem chinovnichya rabota', *Kommersant* 20.04.2012, <http://www.kommersant.ru/doc/1919430> ('if the politicians of Moldova decide that they will be Romanians then the borders will be different').

but reflected changing power politics. Until 2014, Russia claimed that sovereignty trumped self-determination but in 2014 partly destroyed its own earlier argumentation by its own actions in Ukraine. Russia was to some extent successfully able to construe the cases of South Ossetia and Abkhazia as a result of Georgia's violation of international law. However, in reality, South Ossetia and Abkhazia were Russia's response to Kosovo. Rather than pursuing a firm ideology of international law in its own right, Moscow first of all responded to Western claims and arguments in international law, i.e. symmetry with the West became part of its ideology of international law.

Sometimes, this search for symmetry with the West disregarded actual facts on a considerable scale. Since the 1990s, the West had talked much about genocide as the international 'crime of crimes'. Thus, Moscow did not shy away from blaming Georgia for acts of 'genocide' in South Ossetia although it was quickly clear that Moscow had massively exaggerated the number of civilian victims during the days of military conflict in South Ossetia.[124] Moscow initially claimed 1,500–2,000 civilian deaths in South Ossetia but less than a year later it was clear that the actual number of civilian victims had been 162 on the South Ossetian side and 188 on the Georgian side.[125]

Future historians will debate whether Russia's policy, which at least rhetorically favoured state sovereignty over self-determination, changed in 2014 or even in 2008. It is fascinating that just a few months before the Russian invasion and annexation of Crimea in March 2014, in his annual speech to Russian legislators President Putin publicly emphasized the importance of respecting 'international law'. Therefore, the annexation of Crimea constituted quite a U-turn in Russia's foreign policy and the government's rhetoric about international law. Regarding Crimea, the main argument was not that the annexation of Crimea was legal under international law but instead, *tu quoque*—Western nations had on earlier occasions violated the prohibition of use of military force, in particular in Kosovo. In its rhetoric concerning international law, Russia went from its previous trope of being a 'victim' of post-Cold War international law (e.g. because of Kosovo and Iraq) to the idea that international law had already been in deep crisis anyway.

On 18 March 2014, at the time when Russia annexed Crimea, in the Kremlin President Putin addressed State Duma deputies, Federation Council members, heads of Russian regions, and civil society representatives. In Putin's address, the question of the legality of Russia's actions in Crimea played the central role. In terms of style and logic of argumentation, it is instructive to examine President Putin's passages on international law at greater length here:

> ...what do we hear from our colleagues in Western Europe and North America? They say we are violating norms of international law. Firstly, it's a good thing that they at least remember that there exists such a thing as international law—better late than never.

[124] See R. Allisson, *Russia, the West, and Military Intervention* (Oxford: OUP, 2013) 157, 213.

[125] V. Trifonov, 'Obvinitel'nyi razgovor', *Kommersant* 04.07.2009, <http://www.kommersant.ru/doc/1199305>.

Secondly, and most importantly—what exactly are we violating? True, the President of the Russian Federation received permission from the Upper House of Parliament to use the Armed Forces in Ukraine. However, strictly speaking, nobody has acted on this permission yet. Russia's Armed Forces never entered Crimea; they were there already in line with an international agreement. True, we did enhance our forces there; however—this is something I would like everyone to hear and know—we did not exceed the personnel limit of our Armed Forces in Crimea, which is set at 25,000, because there was no need to do so.

Next. As it declared independence and decided to hold a referendum, the Supreme Council of Crimea referred to the United Nations Charter, which speaks of the right of nations to self-determination. Incidentally, I would like to remind you that when Ukraine seceded from the USSR it did exactly the same thing, almost word for word. Ukraine used this right, yet the residents of Crimea are denied it. Why is that?

Moreover, the Crimean authorities referred to the well known Kosovo precedent—a precedent our western colleagues created with their own hands in a very similar situation, when they agreed that the unilateral separation of Kosovo from Serbia, exactly what Crimea is doing now, was legitimate and did not require any permission from the country's central authorities. Pursuant to Article 2, Chapter 1 of the United Nations Charter, the UN International Court agreed with this approach and made the following comment in its ruling of July 22, 2010, and I quote: 'No general prohibition may be inferred from the practice of the Security Council with regard to declarations of independence,' and 'General international law contains no prohibition on declarations of independence.' Crystal clear, as they say.

I do not like to resort to quotes, but in this case, I cannot help it. Here is a quote from another official document: the Written Statement of the United States of America of April 17, 2009, submitted to the same UN International Court in connection with the hearings on Kosovo. Again, I quote: 'Declarations of independence may, and often do, violate domestic legislation. However, this does not make them violations of international law.' End of quote. They wrote this, disseminated it all over the world, had everyone agree and now they are outraged. Over what? The actions of the Crimean people completely fit in with these instructions, as it were. For some reason, things that Kosovo Albanians (and we have full respect for them) were permitted to do, Russians, Ukrainians and Crimean Tatars in Crimea are not allowed. Again, one wonders why.

We keep hearing from the United States and Western Europe that Kosovo is some special case. What makes it so special in the eyes of our colleagues? It turns out that it is the fact that the conflict in Kosovo resulted in so many human casualties. Is this a legal argument? The ruling of the International Court says nothing about this. This is not even double standards; this is amazing, primitive, blunt cynicism. One should not try so crudely to make everything suit their interests, calling the same thing white today and black tomorrow. According to this logic, we have to make sure every conflict leads to human losses.[126]

But just some years ago, in the ICJ's *Kosovo advisory opinion* case[127] proceedings, the Russian Federation had emphasized:

...the territorial integrity of States. [Conditions for secession] should be limited to truly extreme circumstances, such as an outright armed attack by the parent State, threatening

[126] 'Address by President of the Russian Federation', 18 March 2014, <http://eng.kremlin.ru/news/6889>.

[127] ICJ, *Accordance with International Law of the Unilateral Declaration of Independence in respect of Kosovo*, 22.07.2010, <http://www.icj-cij.org/docket/files/141/15987.pdf>.

> the very existence of the people in question. Otherwise, all efforts should be taken in order to settle the tension between the parent State and the ethnic community concerned within the framework of the existing State.[128]

In the Valdai speech of October 2014, Putin already emphasized that the right of peoples to self-determination was enshrined in Article 1 the UN Charter ('Read the article carefully') and consequently Russia's annexation of Crimea had been covered by international law.[129]

Thus, in a stunning turn in legal argumentation concerning the relationship between the principles of state sovereignty and the right of peoples to self-determination, President Putin suddenly started to refer to elements of the *US* legal argumentation in the Kosovo case, not Russia's own international legal position in the same case and generally before Crimea. This completely ignored the 'public demand for consistency in official commitments' that has been emphasized in Western discourse on international law.[130]

The Russian Federation had for years talked about the importance of the UN Charter but in the case of Crimea, suddenly there was no discussion of the implications of the UN Charter. The Constitutional Court of the Russian Federation approved of the accession of Crimea to the Russian Federation without hesitation and public discussions, since apparently no member of the Constitutional Court raised objections.[131] However, if international law is part of Russia's legal system, the Court should have elaborated on the compatibility of the annexation with the UN Charter, and the political argument of the restoration of 'historic rights' was of little value here.

It is because of fluctuating turns in argumentation, as from Kosovo to Crimea, in Moscow's normative rhetoric that in nations bordering Russia and in particular some former Soviet republics, the opposite image of the Russian government's attitude to international law is widespread among political and intellectual elites. In particular, Moscow is not seen as a guardian of international law but still a *derzhava* with imperialist reflexes that is inclined to use international law in a primarily instrumental way. Consequently, because for the Russian government, international law primarily equals Moscow's power according to the constitutional moment of 1945, it makes sense that it would want to promote 'international law'.

The real foundation of Russia's current concept of international law has become the idea of the 'Russian world', *russkyi mir*, a civilizational idea. A leading politician in the 'Republic of Donetsk' in Eastern Ukraine, Andrei Purgin, has argued in an interview that Russia is the inheritor of Byzantine civilization which also

128 Written Statement of the Russian Federation in the Kosovo Proceedings, 16.04.2009, point 88, <http://www.icj-cij.org/docket/files/141/15628.pdf>.

129 President of Russia, Meeting of the Valdai International Discussion Club, 24 October 2014, <http://eng.kremlin.ru/news/23137>.

130 R. Goodman, D. Jinks, *Socializing States. Promoting Human Rights through International Law* (Oxford: OUP, 2013) 150.

131 A. Pertsev, M. Gorokhova, 'Konstitutsionnyi sud oboshelsya bez slushanii po Krymu', *Kommersant* 19.03.2014, <http://kommersant.ru/doc/2433322>.

includes Armenia, Georgia, and further parts of Ukraine.[132] Moreover, Purgin claims:

We are rooted in the Byzantine tradition. Written laws are for us secondary and a sense of justice primary.[133]

This is exactly the same as conservative Russian intellectuals had argued in the nineteenth century, e.g. when Mikhail Nikiforovich Katkov (1818–87) wrote that 'the West relies on contract, the East on justice'.[134] However, without 'contract', not much would remain of international law the way we know it.

In order to understand what was actually going on in Crimea, one should thus not read official propagandistic justifications but for instance blunt statements by the likes of Dugin who commented on Russia's takeover of Crimea in 2014:

We restored our sovereignty and are firmly taking a course towards a multipolar world. We are building a different world order. And in our own world order the annexation of Crimea does not depend on Washington but on the very inhabitants of Crimea and the iron will of Moscow.[135]

In any case, the main tendency over recent years has been towards regionalization of international law, to create a parallel geopolitical and economic world to the EU and the West in Eurasia. On 29 May 2014, the Treaty establishing the Eurasian Economic Union was signed by the Presidents of Russia, Kazakhstan, and Belarus, it was ratified in October 2014 and the Union will become effective on 1 January 2015. It has been fascinating to see how Moscow has successfully learned from the EU's experience and translated the EU's idea of supranationality into the context of the Eurasian Economic Union.

However, one difference is that there is a sort of equilibrium between former Great Powers in the EU whereas the Eurasian Economic Union will always struggle with the imperial legacy of one major power (Moscow) considerably outweighing its satellites. In any case, a number of opinion leaders have seen in the Eurasian Economic Union first of all a civilizational project.[136] Moreover, over the spring of 2014 the Russian Ministry of Culture prepared a programmatic document 'Foundations of State Cultural Policy' which at least initially declared Russia a unique civilization, not part of Europe.[137]

In the meantime, the process of renewing the EU–Russia Partnership Treaty has come to a halt and little has remained of the idea of 'strategic' partnership.

[132] Yu. Smirnova, 'Der Mann, der die Republik Donezk erfand', *Die Welt* 16.05.2014, <http://www.welt.de/politik/ausland/article128065029/Der-Mann-der-die-Republik-Donezk-erfand.html>.

[133] Smirnova, 'Der Mann, der die Republik Donezk erfand'.

[134] M. Katz, *Mikhail N. Katkov. A Political Biography: 1818–1887* (The Hague: Mouton & Co., 1966) 179.

[135] A. Dugin, 'Realizm—mnimyi i podlinnyi', *Izvestia* 11.03.2014, <http://izvestia.ru/news/567249>.

[136] S. Roganov, 'Soyuz Sovetskikh Suverennykh Respublik?', *Izvestia* 30.12.2013, <http://izvestia.ru/news/563441>.

[137] Minkul'tury izlozhilo, 'Osnovy gosudarstvennoi kul'turnoi politiki', *Izvestia* 10.04.2014, <http://izvestia.ru/news/569016>.

The EU–Russia Partnership and Cooperation Agreement (PCA) was signed in 1994, entered into force in 1997 and had a duration of ten years, i.e. until 2007. Russia's accession to the WTO has not been able to solve all outstanding issues between the EU and the Russian Federation.[138] It is possible that rather than regulating relationships between a supranational block and a major sovereign state, the future legal arrangement will reflect the interrelationship between two neighbouring *Großräume*.

3. Conclusion on Post-Soviet Russia's State Practice in International Law

Let us attempt to summarize here, primarily based on the previous discussion of human rights law, international economic law, and *jus ad bellum* as well as Russia's record in international dispute settlement. The first conclusion reasserts what Roy Allison, a British international relations scholar, has recently pointed out. The English School of international relations distinguishes between pluralist and solidarist variants of international society, both having competing claims about the 'thickness' of the normative content of international society.[139] In this comparison, Russia comes across as a pluralist rather than as a solidarist country, perceiving a thinner set of common values.[140] This all reflects in post-Soviet Russia's practice in international law which for Russia remains more the international law of 'coexistence' and less of 'cooperation'. Already in 1946, the US diplomat George F. Kennan had postulated:

> Moscow has no abstract devotion to UNO ideals. Its attitude to that organization will remain essentially pragmatic and tactical.[141]

Today, it continues to be so that Moscow does not favour a very 'thick' international community but this mostly means that Moscow has a different understanding from the (mostly Western) globalists of what the UN ideals are—instead of global governance, the promotion of democracy, and human rights, Moscow sees balance of power between coexisting and competing greater spaces.

Allison also makes the point that in the most crucial field of international law in Russia's opinion, *jus ad bellum*, Russia has used a considerable amount of mimicking.[142] Similarly, Estonian philosopher and diplomat Kaupo Känd, with years of study and work experience in Russia and the Caucasus, has perceptively argued that Putin has made conscious efforts to create an alternative to the Western

[138] E. Chernenko, 'Soglashenie o beskonechnoi torgovle', *Kommersant* 02.04.2012, <http://www.kommersant.ru/doc/1906610>.

[139] R. Allisson, *Russia, the West, and Military Intervention* (Oxford: OUP, 2013) 15.

[140] Ibid., 209.

[141] 'Telegram, The Charge in the Soviet Union (Kennan) to the Secretary of State', Moscow, 22 February 1946, <http://www2.gwu.edu/~nsarchiv/coldwar/documents/episode-1/kennan.htm>.

[142] Allisson, *Russia, the West, and Military Intervention*, 213.

world, its simulacrum.[143] Indeed, Russia's official rhetoric regarding international law also reveals that notions like 'peacekeepers', 'genocide', and occasionally even 'international law' itself are used like in a simulacrum or concave mirror to Western uses. The words are the same but the meanings are different and, from the Western point of view, even distorted. For example, what the Kremlin called 'genocide' in South Ossetia was not genocide in the Western understanding. The West has also rejected the idea that what Roy Allisson has called 'Russian-style peace-keeping' in CIS countries would qualify as real peacekeeping.[144] Namely, in such cases Russian forces would first participate in the military conflict, create favourable facts on the ground and then transform its military presence into 'peacekeepers'.

At the same time, it is important to understand that the Russian parallel world or simulacrum of the West is an old phenomenon. It may be so that the Chairman of the Russian Constitutional Court does not really act like the nominal head of the judiciary branch in the US or Germany. Instead, Mr Zorkin may be influenced by the role of Konstantin Petrovich Pobedonostsev (1827–1907) as the Chief Procurator (Ober-Procurator) of the Holy Synod, a religious-political institution in Tsarist Russia.

Thus, behind the Russian simulacrum of Western international law is not just an individual politician such as President Putin or the government that he has appointed. Russian mistrust of the West is a collective phenomenon, has deep historical roots, and goes back to the period of Byzantine relations with the Latin world during the crusades. As a matter of principle, Constantinople just could not subjugate itself to the Latins, to become number two behind Rome; it had its own claim to truth and universality. Over recent centuries, different historical experiences have influenced the value systems in the respective regions. In some ways then, Russia, having left her Communist ideology behind, has nevertheless not returned to the elitist 'European Russia' of the Tsarist era but developed 'from Byzantium to Byzantium', as the Hungarian historian of ideas Géza Gecse has put it.[145] For lack of a better word but in order to emphasize differences from Western political culture, experts also tend to characterize aspects of Russia's political system as 'Byzantian' which, of course, serves primarily as metaphor.[146]

Today, too, public opinion surveys demonstrate that the Russian people continue to support political opinions that are not or are no longer the mainstream elsewhere in Europe. Thus, it is not certain whether it is entirely true what Daria Trenina and Mark Entin write:

[143] K. Känd, 'Venemaa telos—Lääne simulaakrum?', *Postimees*, 18.10.2008, <http://arvamus.postimees.ee/41763/kaupo-kand-venemaa-telos-laane-simulaakrum>.

[144] Allison, Allisson, *Russia, the West, and Military Intervention*, 19, 129.

[145] See G. Gecse, *Bütsantsist Bütsantsini. Suurvene mõttelaadi olemus* (Tallinn: Ajakirjade kirjastus, 2012).

[146] Yu. Smirnova, 'Der Westen misversteht das Machtsystem Putins', *Die Welt*, 27.07.2014, <http://www.welt.de/politik/ausland/article130594464/Der-Westen-missversteht-das-Machtsystem-Putin.html>.

> Russia fully shares the conviction that human rights are universal and must be protected in any society.... The values that are shared by others were never challenged or denied by Russia, they are common to Russia as well.[147]

However, what is the reality on the ground? For example, according to the Levada Centre the percentage of Russians who think that, for their state, order is more important than observing human rights is 55 per cent, and the number has increased over recent years.[148] An earlier poll comparing preferences for a 'strong hand' or democratic government came to similar conclusions, 55 per cent of Russians supporting the 'strong hand' model.[149]

Also different are perceptions regarding what went wrong in the European history of the twentieth century. In 2009, the majority of Russian respondents saw more positive than negative aspects in Stalin's historical role.[150] In 2013, 45 per cent of Russian respondents asked by VTSIOM supported restoration of the statue of Felix Dzherzhinsky, founder of the Cheka, in front of the FSB's main building in Moscow's Lubyanka whereas only 25 per cent were against.[151] When in 2009 the Parliamentary Assembly of OSCE in Vilnius adopted the resolution 'Divided Europe Reunited' which *inter alia* stated that 'European countries experienced two major totalitarian regimes, the Nazi and the Stalinist', 53 per cent of Russian respondents had a negative opinion about the resolution.[152]

Popular attitudes reflect the views of national leaders and vice versa. For example, it has been fascinating to compare European commemorations of the centennial of the beginning of World War I in 2014. In Western Europe, the prevailing tonality has been cautious and not self-righteous, often trying to analyse what went wrong altogether in the European state system during the fateful summer of 1914.[153] At the same time, in July 2014 when opening a new memorial commemorating World War I in Russia, President Putin *inter alia* claimed that victory in this war had been 'stolen' from Russia.[154]

Altogether, to sum up on this theme, as the Chairman of the Constitutional Court of the Russian Federation, Valery Zorkin, has somewhat worriedly pointed out: 71 per cent of Russian respondents did not consider themselves 'European'.[155]

[147] D. Trenina, M. Entin, 'Russia's Approach to the Universality of Human Rights', in R. Arnold (ed.), *The Universalism of Human Rights* (Dordrecht: Springer, 2013) 175–87 at 176, 184.

[148] 'Levada-Tsentr. Vse bol'she rossiyan schitaet, shto poryadok v strane vazhnee prav cheloveka', 25.09.2013, <http://grani.ru/Politics/Russia/m.219352.html>.

[149] I. Kriger, 'Instituty sil'nee reform', *Novaya gazeta* 27.01.2010, <http://old.novayagazeta.ru/data/2010/008/13.html>.

[150] V. Khamraev, 'Stalin poluchil bol'shinstvo k 130-letiu', *Kommersant* 19.12.2009, <http://www.kommersant.ru/doc/1296300>.

[151] ''Zheleznyi Feliks'. Pora vozhvrashat'sya na Lubyanku?' *VTSIOM*, 05.12.2013, <http://wciom.ru/index.php?id = 459&uid = 114632>.

[152] V. Khamraev, 'Rossiane vstupilis' za Stalina, kak za rodinu', *Kommersant* 03.08.2009, <http://www.kommersant.ru/doc/1215165>.

[153] See, in particular, the reception of C. Clark, *The Sleepwalkers. How Europe Went to War in 1914* (London: Penguin Books, 2013).

[154] Y. Klusova, 'Vladimir Putin. Pobeda v Pervoi mirovoi voine byla ukradena u Rossii', *Kommersant* 01.08.2014, <http://kommersant.ru/doc/2537963>.

[155] Zorkin, *Konstitutsionno-pravovoe razvitie Rossii*, 648.

Thus, from the Western viewpoint the challenge regarding post-Soviet Russia is not individual anti-Western politicians such as President Putin; the reality is that due to differences in history and culture, in certain aspects the Russian people differ in their values from the Western mainstream. In this sense, President Putin may well enjoy democratic legitimacy in Russia—because paradoxically, authoritarianism and the 'strong hand' style itself have surprisingly considerable popular backing in Russia. Moreover, unlike in post-World War II Germany, there has not been a serious *Vergangenheitsaufarbeitung* in post-Soviet Russia, and this fact has had an impact on international legal issues as well.

In a simulacrum of a concave mirror, things start to appear different and truth and falsehood become hard to distinguish. In this context, the Estonian politician and historian, Mart Nutt, Ph.D. (b. 1962), has critically observed, regarding the Russian government, that Moscow has a 'Byzantine' attitude towards international rules and precedents:

> The most visible activity by which one recognizes Byzantine diplomacy (and based on which one can predict future plans) is blaming others for what one is already doing or intends to do.[156]

For politicians critical of Moscow such as Nutt, the Russian government's insistence on its unwavering support of international law might rather cover for the fact that the Russian government sees in international law first of all an instrument in the arsenal of its foreign policy. In the conditions of anarchy prevailing in international relations, if a government is violating or going to violate international law, it may be in its interest to confuse its peers by rhetorically insisting on the importance of 'international law', and pointing out that it is others that violate it.

In this regard, there is a noteworthy connection with the question of international legal consciousness in Russia. Russia's leading legal minds both during the late Tsarist period and from perestroika onwards have lamented the historical predominance of 'legal nihilism' (*pravovoi nigilizm*) in the Russian people's and elite's consciousness.[157] The problem has sometimes also been depicted in Russian film, e.g. in the acclaimed movie *12*, by Nikita Sergeyevich Mikhalkov (b. 1945), one of the twelve jurors exclaims passionately that Russians will never want to live by strict legal rules because it would be too 'boring'.

The then President Medvedev, a St Petersburg-educated lawyer just like the current President, Mr Putin, even raised the problem of legal nihilism in his first annual address to the legislature in 2008.[158] The Chairman of the Constitutional Court, Valery Zorkin, has spoken of 'a thousand years of legal nihilism' in Russian

[156] M. Nutt, 'Bütsantsliku diplomaatia raudvara', Diplomaatia No 6/7 (130/131) 2014, <http://www.diplomaatia.ee/artikkel/butsantsliku-diplomaatia-raudvara/, 14>.

[157] See V. Tumanov, 'O pravovom nigilizme', 10 *Sotsialistichekoe gosudarstvo i pravo* 1989, 20–7.

[158] See e.g. 'Rossiya dolzhna preodolet' pravovoi nigilizm—Prezident Medvedev', *RIA Novosti*, 07.05.2008, <http://ria.ru/politics/20080507/106773965.html> and earlier, in the capacity of Vice Prime Minister, 'D. Medvedev. Rossiya—strana pravovoga nigilizma', *Prime-TASS*, 22.01.2008, <http://www.vedomosti.ru/newsline/news/2008/01/22/536208> ('Russia is a country of legal nihilism').

culture.[159] However, Zorkin probably does not even understand that when he himself accuses the Georgian government of acts of 'genocide' in South Ossetia[160] in a conflict where the Russian government was far from innocent, this rhetoric may also appear as an example of 'legal nihilism' to foreign observers. Moreover, when only 12 per cent of Russian respondents supported the Yukos arbitral award in July 2014 and the majority related to it negatively,[161]perhaps in this attitude was also a hint of 'legal nihilism', i.e. the idea that private property can be expropriated without proper compensation.

In retrospect then, the question is: if a country has a problem with legal nihilism domestically, how likely is it that it would simultaneously act as champion of the rule of law internationally? Theoretically, it could be that domestic law and international law are fields so distinct from each other that problems with 'legal nihilism' in the former would have no discernible impact on the country's conduct in foreign affairs. Adhering to Chernichenko's strictly dualist concept of international law and domestic law as two completely separate legal systems, this is at least theoretically possible. In principle, an autocrat can trample on the Constitution domestically but carefully honour treaties with other nations. But how likely is this? The monist concept and the idea of interconnectedness of all law suggest that 'legal nihilism' in domestic law would one way or another have an impact on the country's practice of international law as well.

Of course, some Russian scholars of international law have blamed *the US* for its 'legal nihilism' in the context of international law[162] and are generally convinced that it is the West that systematically cheats (as when promising Moscow not to extend NATO to Russia's borders but then still doing it). Through the mass media and their respective public discourses, different civilizational centres produce their own subjective truths which are virtually uncontested at home but may simultaneously appear entirely false or unproved abroad. Thus, each contested understanding of international law is in some ways regional and culturally shaped.

At the end of the day, Russia's concluding argument is not 'international law' which is at least historically a Western idea, after all. It is the civilizational critique of the West and particularly the critique that the West is unjust. For example, in a short science fiction novel *Without Sky* that was published precisely at the height of the Crimean crisis in March 2014, Natan Dubovitsky, who is widely believed to be Vladislav Yur'evitch Surkov[163] (b. 1964), a politician close to President Putin,

[159] Zorkin, *Konstitutsionno-pravovoe razvitie Rossii*, 9, 25, 31, 42, 646, 686 ('a thousand years of legal nihilism'), 509.

[160] V. D. Zorkin, *Konstitutsia i prava cheloveka v XXI veke. K 15-letiu Konstitutsii Rossiiskoi Federatsii i 60-letiu Vseobshei deklaratsii prav cheloveka* (Moscow: Norma, 2008) 11.

[161] M. Ivanov, 'Grazhdane ne khotyat platit' po schetam YUKOSa', *Kommersant*, 11.08.2014, <http://kommersant.ru/doc/2542807>.

[162] See State Duma deputy V. N. Likhachev, 'Rossia kak mezhdunarodno-pravovaya lichnost', in *Vestnik Diplomaticheskoi Akademii MID Rossii. Mezhdunarodnoe pravo* (Moscow: Diplomaticheskaya Akademia, 2013) 32–43 at 36; Shumilov, *Mezhdunarodnoe pravo*, 111–12, 135.

[163] See 'War by any other Name', *The Economist*, 05.07.2014, <http://www.economist.com/news/europe/21606290-russia-has-effect-already-invaded-eastern-ukraine-question-how-west-will>.

wrote about the first 'non-linear war' and his 'two-dimensional people' who were organically unable to lie and use words that 'hide the truth' unlike the dwellers of the City, which was 'the home of Satan' and where 'money and bombs were made'.[164] Indeed, who would need 'international law' in a world like this?

Final Conclusions of the Study

In 1438–9, just some years before the demise of the Byzantine Empire in 1453, the representatives of the Eastern and Western Christian churches met in Italy and through intense discussions tried to solve theological issues related to the Great Schism of 1054. The event became known as the Council of Florence and its aim was the restoration of the East–West Union. On 6 July 1439, an agreement was signed by the protagonists but when the Eastern bishops returned home, they found that their agreement with the West was broadly rejected by the monks and the conservative local population. Although the Byzantine Emperors remained committed to the agreement with the Latins until the conquest of Constantinople by the Turks, the Eastern Churches never 'ratified' the agreement reached at the Council of Florence.

The Metropolitan of Kiev, Moscow, and all Rus', Isidore (1385–1463), had led the Muscovite delegation to the Council, had signed the Union proclamation in Florence and forced the other Russian delegates also to sign it.[165] However, when Isidor returned to Moscow in March 1441, he tried to read the Bull of the Union at Moscow Kremlin's cathedral but was interrupted and arrested by Grand Duke Vasily II (1415–62) who subsequently tried Isidor as an apostate to the Orthodox faith.[166] However, quite interestingly, Isidor managed to flee to Kiev where he built up a Western-leaning school of theological thought.[167] Subsequently, the ideologues of Muscovy claimed that it was the new, third Rome and that Constantinople had been punished by God for giving in to the Latins in Florence.

Although this is not a story of international law *stricto sensu*, if there is one symbolic story conveying the essence of how Russian approaches to international law have come into being, this must be it. Almost 600 years later, Russian and Western representatives meet in the UN SC, PACE of the CoE, OSCE, and other settings, and have a number of continuous disagreements that go beyond rational geopolitical interests but touch upon the heart of political philosophy and ideology. Who gets to make the decisions? How should peoples be governed? What is the relationship between the individual and the government? What is understood

[164] N. Dubovski, 'Ilma taevata', trans. from Russian into Estonian by K. Pruul, 6 *Vikerkaar* 2014, 24–8.

[165] See N. Hamerman, 'The Council of Florence. The Religious Event that Shaped the Era of Discovery', *Schiller Institute*, <http://www.schillerinstitute.org/fid_91-96/922_council_of_florence.pdf>, 23–36 at 30.

[166] Ibid.

[167] See also D. W. Treadgold, *The West in Russia and China*, Vol. 1: *Russia 1472–1917* (Cambridge: CUP, 1973) 2–3.

as sacred?—Of course international and constitutional lawyers from different countries present different arguments about these fundamental questions. At the same time, one wonders in the context of Western–Russian normative relations to what extent, as Carl Schmitt once argued, concepts of public law have their roots, nowadays often unconsciously, in the long history of debates between different regional factions in Christian theology.

My main argument in this study has been that a crucial key to understanding the post-Soviet Russian approach to international law is the powerful idea of Russia's civilizational distinctness from the West. Sometimes this idea is explicit; sometimes implicit—but, more often than not, it is there. In this sense, it does not really matter whether one thinks of Russia as a 'European' country because to the extent that Europe is a geographical notion, the belongingness of Russia's Western part to Eastern Europe is undeniable. At the same time, it has also become clear that in significant contexts post-Soviet Russia continues to represent ideological opposition to the West. Altogether, we have witnessed another 'limit'[168] to international law and its universality.

In this study, the historic insights of three distinguished Russian international lawyers—Martens, Taube, and Hrabar—have proved particularly helpful for understanding the origins of the country's contemporary approaches to international law.

The main idea of Martens was that the government's approach to domestic law, order, and institutions shapes, influences, and to some extent even determines its approach to international law. I believe that in the present study, this hypothesis has proved to be true in the case of Russia. It makes sense that the same government that expropropriated Yukos and said that this had nothing to do with politics or Mikhail Khodorkovsky's person (while it did) would insist that it had sent no troops to Eastern Ukraine (while it had). The Kremlin's problematic approach to human rights law is equally reflected in international (European) and constitutional law, and one aspect can no longer meaningfully be distinguished from the other. In the same way that an authoritarian leader can liquidate already agreed rights and prerogatives of federal subjects without facing serious constitutional resistance, he can also invade and annex Crimea without too many legalistic questions being asked domestically.

When Foreign Minister Lavrov suggested on 27 September 2014 at the UN GA that the GA should in the future adopt a declaration committing to non-recognition of *coups d'état*,[169] it was not only an idiosyncratic interpretation of what had happened in Ukraine in February 2014 but a reflection of the existential fear of Russia's power elite that something similar to what happened to President Yanukovych in Kyiv might one day happen in Moscow as well. Again, domestic concerns of statehood and *raison d'état* were projected on Russia's concept of international law.

[168] See J. L. Goldsmith, E. A. Posner, *The Limits of International Law* (Oxford: OUP, 2005).

[169] O. Kirillova, 'Sergei Lavrov nazval Ukrainu zhertvoi politiki Zapada', *Kommersant* 27.09.2014, <http://kommersant.ru/doc/2577631>.

This observation does not have to mean that the behaviour of liberal states in the context of international law is always exemplary. A much discussed example would be the US- and UK-initiated war in Iraq in 2003 when the decision to invade the country without UN SC authorization was made by democratically elected liberal governments. However, when comparing the US and Russian style aggressions in the post-Cold War era, certain differences emerge. When formulating its policies, the Bush administration somewhat tuned down its rhetoric on international law which was up to a point honest in the sense that the administration must have known that they were going to violate norms of international law. At least they did not pretend that they were 'protectors' of international law while doing what they did. Furthermore, in cases like Guantanamo prisoners' rights and extraterritoriality, the US Supreme Court was there to some extent to balance and mitigate the initial approach taken by the White House and the Pentagon. However, in Russia, the non-democratic (in Western terms) political system does not have a mechanism for correction and renewal when clear violations of international law occur. In particular the judiciary has been the weak branch of power and no match to the executive in Russia.

Thus, in the case of US occupation of Afghanistan and Iraq, the main debate was about *which* law applies; in the case of Russian aggression against Ukraine the debate was absurdly held on the level of whether Russian military forces were in Ukraine at all in the first place. Precisely at the point in time when the Russian military 'on vacation' in Eastern Ukraine stopped the attempt by the Ukrainian army to reconquer Donetsk and Luhansk, in the sovereign territory of Ukraine, the Russian MFA declared that in Ukraine Moscow was in favour of a 'peaceful solution'.[170] In such instances, international law has been used as a 'foreign language' in Russia; a language in which it is possible to lie.

Another important international lawyer beside Martens was Baron Taube. Taube's ideas are important because he, more than any other scholar, has demonstrated how Russia has been historically and culturally with one foot in Europe and with another one outside it—and how this matters in the context of international law. Whether with *respublica Christiana* of the late Middle Ages or the Council of Europe of the early twenty-first century, Russia's tensions with *ius publicum europaeum* are historically grown and in this sense natural. Since 1917, Russia has constructed itself (again; after medieval Muscovy) as an anti-Western power, and the brief pro-Western thaw of the perestroika and early Yeltsin era did not last long. Perhaps, then, it is time to admit that the universalizing/Westernizing discourse vis-à-vis Russia has serious shortcomings and limitations.

Finally, with great sensitivity and often writing 'between the lines' as was typical of the totalitarian Soviet period, Hrabar has taught us what it has meant to be an international lawyer in Russia. International law as a discipline is close to the state government in any (Western) country as well—but in Russia, it has been even closer. In 2014, in striking contrast to the atmosphere in the US and UK

[170] A. Samozhnev, 'MID prizyvaet k mirnomu razresheniu krizisa na Ukraine', *Rossiiskaya gazeta*, 29.08.2014, <http://rg.ru/2014/08/29/mid-site.html>.

in the context of the Iraq war in 2003, no Russian international lawyer to my knowledge publicly declared the invasion and annexation of Crimea to be illegal under international law. More need not be said on this topic; it appears that international law as an academic discipline by and large continues to be subjugated to *raison d'état* in Russia.

If one had to capture the essence of Russian approaches to international law in one historically laden word, it would have to be—Byzantine. In the same way as Muscovy was ultimately unwilling to bow to Rome, today's Russia tends to eye ideological projects of the West (i.e. the US and primarily Protestant and Catholic Europe), including directions that they want to take international law in the twenty-first century, with suspicion. Geopolitics and the development of international law are interpreted in the light of Russia's opposition to the West that is bigger than Communism as an ideology ever was. In this sense, it is highly instructive to read late nineteenth-century/early twentieth-century international law scholars like Martens and Baron Taube because they explain where Russia has come from in terms of the history of international law.

Thus, while today Russian statesmen use the language of international law extensively, and claim that they are subjectively convinced that *Russia* is the defender of 'international law', this is not necessarily the same understanding of 'international law' as is predominant in the West. Russian politicians and often also scholars give to international law a specific meaning which is statist and ultimately reflects their idea of the Russian state as a strong *derzhava*, a unitary actor in international affairs that not only has a right to stay away from US-led globalist tendencies but is also entitled to a regional-historical 'greater space' (sphere of influence). Such sentiments, although not compatible with the UN Charter as far as the 'sphere of influence' is concerned, echo both in legal scholarship as well as in state practice. In the Russian mind, Russia is not ideologically constructed as just any other country, another sovereign state among the UN's 193 member states. In the Russian understanding, the country pursues a unique 'Russian idea' and, respectively, also has legitimacy to watch and guard its neighbourhood. The 'Byzantine' strain—in opposition to the Latin West—which the late Tsarist international law Russian-Baltic scholars such as Baron Taube explained and tried to ideologically distance themselves from, is also the ultimate foundation of the continuity between Soviet and post-Soviet approaches to international law in Russia.

This study has been extensively empirical and contains many facts and references about history, theory and post-Soviet state practice in Russia. In detail, these facts and interpretations have mostly spoken for themselves and there is no need to repeat them here, in the final conclusion. We have learned much about Russia but can this story, from the Byzantine-Kievan treaties of the eighth century to Russia's annexation of Crimea in 2014, also teach us anything about international law generally?

I would reiterate here that Russian thinking and conduct in the framework of international law cannot simply be explained by realist or liberal theories of international relations, i.e. that Russia is a historical Great Power and that it is authoritarian in that it tends to have a problem with liberal ideas. To be more precise, Russia currently of course has a problem with liberal ideas, as is also surely reflected in the country's practice and scholarly teachings of international law. However, the underlying issue is more fundamental than any Western political idea of 'regime change' or supporting Russia's liberal opposition might suggest. The problem is that liberals of the likes of Martens were always a minority in Russia, and their liberalism and commitment to 'Europe' did not necessarily reflect the genuine preferences of the majority of the population. After 1991 too, the liberal school of thought did not manage to gain power in Russia, either politically or intellectually.

The US and Russia are both historically Great Powers but, depending on their idea of their self and their mission in the world, their agendas in the framework of international law have occasionally been quite different. This difference has not just depended on which nation was in what position in the world order or American worship of the idea of individual freedom and Russia's historical tendency to authoritarianism. Each country's history and culture have supported their own outcomes and produced partly different thinking and ideas about what international law is for and about.

If this study has a concrete message then it concerns Western expectations about and projections of international law beyond the West, in major regional power centres such as Russia. Each time the argument of 'international law' arises there, especially in anti-Western claims, one needs to make sure with great care whether the words and concepts are actually understood and used in the same way or given a different meaning. In this study, I believe I have demonstrated that in Russia, such concepts have been partly filled with a different content. The same concept of international law once existed in Europe too but this was quite long time ago.

The Western idea of the universality of international law is of course also an idea with Messianic traits; probably the West has been the most Messianic power of them all. Thus, when Western scholars enthusiastically write about how international law will 'socialize' states, for example in the field of human rights or international trade law, what they implicitly seem to mean is that other states will eventually become more like the West. Surely, globalization has the potential of making different places more similar to each other but in reality the socialization between the West and the rest, including Russia, remains a two-way street. An equally important way of socialization would be that the West could learn more about other cultures and nations and not think that they have a monopoly over what 'international law' means. However, today Russians know incomparably more about Western thinking and debates on international law than Westerners know about how international law is constructed in Moscow, St Petersburg, and Kazan.

At the same time, the powerful Western idea of universality of international law has blurred our sense of the reality of international law on the ground outside the West. In the twenty-first century, there are no longer 'civilized' and 'uncivilized' peoples, but there nevertheless continue to be different legal cultures and if one accepts the term, different civilizations. Western liberal states may not necessarily behave 'better' in the context of international law[171] but nevertheless, non-Western states may in certain aspects behave differently in the context of law of nations. What is 'good' or 'bad' in such circumstances becomes a matter of value judgments, and values often tend to be different. For Western border countries like the Baltic States, that are militarily not very strong, treaties with Russia will also in the future have the potential to bring unexpected surprises and twists in interpretation. But Moscow has more generally the tendency to unilaterally 'revise' foreign treaties when power relations change in its favour.

In the end, however, it seems to me that the fact that international law is indeed partly 'different in different places' is a normalcy rather than an anomaly. Local cultures and civilizations beyond the West have been much more powerful and persistent than the Western (Hegelian) idea of universal progress has managed to be. A nation's sense of international law inevitably mirrors its practices and concepts of domestic law, for example the relationship between the state and the individual and of the value of contract. In the US, a very high opinion of the nation's achievements in the constitutional protection of civil rights has had a partly negative impact on the country's engagement with international human rights law.

In the light of the above, the future may well belong to regional public orders more than to universal international law which will inevitably remain thin compared to regional orders such as the EU and the nascent Eurasian Union. In the Russian interpretation, the UN SC is anyway nothing more than the directorium of the regional hegemons with a veto power. Perhaps the appropriate way to think of the UN SC is not that it is the World's Council but that it is the Council of the Worlds, including *russkyi mir*. In such a future, Russia can claim its regional 'Russian-style regional international law' together with Belarus and Kazakhstan in the way that the EU itself is also a specific advanced manifestation of regional international law. The crucial political question for the next decades will be which other—former Soviet but not necessarily only—nations beyond the three already mentioned will be included in the regional order of the Eurasian Union and the CSTO, the Russian equivalent of NATO. Another crucial question relates to how the two regional orders—the EU, which is strong economically but not unanimous militarily, and the Russian-led regional order, which is assertive militarily but less developed economically—will be able to shape their legal and political relationships with each other.

The question of the borders between the Russian-led regional order and the EU is a tricky one because on the official level the EU vehemently rejects the Huntingtonian idea of any civilizational *limes* between Western and Eastern Christianity in Eastern and Central Europe. At the same time, it is quite interesting that for example a study prepared by the European Council on Foreign Relations think-tank in 2007 came to the conclusion that Greece and Cyprus, i.e. heartlands of Orthodox Christianity, potentially acted as Russia's 'Trojan horses'

[171] J. E. Alvarez, 'Do Liberal States Behave Better? A Critique of Slaughter's Liberal Theory', 12 *EJIL* 2001, 183–246.

in the EU.[172] It will be interesting to see whether Serbia will become an EU member, and how it will relate to such normative debates between the West and Russia.

Nevertheless, it is clear that civilizational differences within Europe are not only and necessarily 'objective'; they are also ideologically constructed. Russia's increasing claim to the uniqueness of its 'civilization' can also be seen in this light. In the nineteenth century, Danilevsky wanted to include Poles, Czechs, and other Slavic peoples in a 'Slavic civilization' but the lesser brothers of Central Eastern Europe were not enthusiastic about the Russian thinker's grand pan-Slavic unification project. In a similar way, predominantly Orthodox nations in South Eastern Europe such as Romania and Bulgaria today prefer membership in the EU and NATO over the Russian-led regional order of the Cold War era. Thus, one needs to take Moscow's claim that it speaks in the name of Orthodox Christianity *cum grano salis*, as an overclaim. After all, Russia is a much younger Orthodox Christian country than Armenia and Georgia, for instance.

In international law that integrates 'greater spaces', regional public orders will be constitutionally different and reflect different cultures and value systems, even if methods of mimicking and 'simulacrum' are extensively used as in the case of Russia's simulacrum of the EU and Western vocabulary of international law. For example, in one regional public order, the individual has more rights vis-à-vis state power than in another. In some other regional orders, however, the individual gets to be part of more collective and patriotic projects which purport to give a higher meaning to the individual's life than the individualistic Western 'pursuit of happiness'. Of course, things are further complicated because at least so far Russia continues to participate in the public order of the CoE as well, although it has become partly a mystery why Moscow continues to support the game while feeling so visibly 'tortured' about the 'politicized' outcomes (in fact outcomes based on values that it does not fully share). In any case, Russia's 'civilizational' opposition to and scepticism regarding the West, even in the framework of their common membership in the CoE, is unlikely to go away any time soon. This aspect will continue to decisively shape the international law of the twenty-first century in Europe and Eurasia. In this evolving international law, the West can make realistic decisions if Russia is no longer treated as a 'flawed European' country that needs to make historical efforts to 'catch up' with the rest of Europe but as an independent non-Western actor with all normative consequences that follow from this characterization. Because its civilizational idea about itself partly differs from that of the West, Russia's participation in this area of international law and institutions, where Western political and legal ideas dominate, especially the regional *ius publicum europaeum*, could not genuinely help Russia (or the West) but instead, would create permanent problems of 'translation' and tensions regarding the values behind norms and, ultimately, compliance. In fact, the Petrine idea of 'civilizing'/'Europeanizing Russia may have been a dangerous delusion.

[172] M. Leonard, N. Popescu, *A Power Audit of EU-Russia Relations*, European Council on Foreign Relations, <http://www.ecfr.eu/page/-/ECFR-02_A_POWER_AUDIT_OF_EU-RUSSIA_RELATIONS.pdf>.

Bibliography

NATIONAL LAWS, INTERNATIONAL AND NATIONAL POLICY DOCUMENTS, SPEECHES OF NATIONAL LEADERS

'Address by President of the Russian Federation', 18 March 2014, <http://eng.kremlin.ru/news/6889>.

'Concept of the Foreign Policy of the Russian Federation', 12.02.2013, <http://www.mid.ru/bdomp/brp_4.nsf/e78a48070f128a7b43256999005bcbb3/76389fec168189ed44257b2e0039b16d!OpenDocument>.

Constitution of the Russian Federation, 12 December 1993.

Military Strategy of the Russian Federation, Presidential Decree of 5 February 2010 No 146, <http://carnegieendowment.org/files/2010russia_military_doctrine.pdf>.

'National Security Strategy to 2020', 12 May 2009, <http://www.isn.ethz.ch/Digital-Library/Publications/Detail/?id=154915>.

The National Security Strategy of the United States of America, September 2002, <http://www.state.gov/documents/organization/63562.pdf>.

Orthodox Declaration of Human Rights. Declaration on Human Rights and Dignity, 6 April 2006, <http://www.pravoslavieto.com/docs/human_rights/declaration_ru_en.htm>.

'Presidential Address to the Federal Assembly', 12.12.2013, <http://eng.kremlin.ru/transcripts/6402>.

President of Russia, Meeting of the Valdai International Discussion Club, 24 October 2014, <http://eng.kremlin.ru/news/23137>.

Report on the Human Rights Situation in the EU, Russian MFA, 06.12.2012, <http://mid.ru/brp_4.nsf/0/F6501F42C40A25EE44257ACC004971FC>.

Report of the Independent Fact-Finding Mission on the Conflict in Georgia, September 2009, <http://www.ceiig.ch/Report.html>.

Russia's 1995 Federal Law 'On International Treaties of the Russian Federation', State Duma, 15.07.1995, No 101-FZ.

The Secretary General's High-level Panel Report on Threats, Challenges and Change. A More Secure World: Our Shared Responsibility, 2004, <http://www.unrol.org/doc.aspx?n=gaA.59.565_En.pdf>.

Study of the Human Rights Council Advisory Committee on promoting human rights and fundamental freedoms through a better understanding of traditional values of humankind, 06.12. 2012, <http://www.ohchr.org/Documents/HRBodies/HRCouncil/AdvisoryCom/Session10/A.HRC.22.71_en.pdf>.

COURT CASES, RULINGS, STATE RESERVATIONS AND DECLARATIONS

Abdulakhanov and Others v. Russia, 03.10.2013, ECtHR.

Accordance with International Law of the Unilateral Declaration of Independence in respect of Kosovo, ICJ, 22.07.2010, <http://www.icj-cij.org/docket/files/141/15987.pdf>.

The 'Arctic Sunrise' Case (Kingdom of the Netherlands v Russian Federation), ITLOS, Order, 22 November 2013, <http://www.itlos.org/fileadmin/itlos/documents/cases/case_no.22/Order/C22_Ord_22_11_2013_orig_Eng.pdf>.

Aslakhanova and Others v. Russia, 18.12.2012, ECtHR.

Case concerning Application of the International Convention on the Elimination of All Forms of Racial Discrimination (Georgia v Russian Federation), Preliminary Objections, ICJ, Judgment of 01.04.2011, <http://www.icj-cij.org/docket/files/140/16398.pdf>.

Case of Catan and Others v. Moldova and Russia, application nos 43370/04; 8252/05; 18454/06, Judgment, 19.10.2012, ECtHR.

Declarations of States Parties relating to Settlement of Disputes in accordance with Article 298 (Optional Exceptions to the Applicability of Part XV, Section 2, of the Convention, <https://www.itlos.org/fileadmin/itlos/documents/basic_texts/298_declarations_June_2011_english.pdf>.

Estamirov and Others v. Russia, 12.10.2006, ECtHR.

Georgia v Russia (I), application no 13255/07, Grand Chamber judgment of 3 July 2014, ECtHR.

Hulley Enterprises Limited v. The Russian Federation (PCA Case No AA 226), <http://www.pca-cpa.org/showpage.asp?pag_id=1599>.

Case of Ilaşcu and Others v. Moldova and Russia (Application No 48787/99), Judgment, 08.07.2004, ECtHR.

Isayeva v. Russia, 24.02.2005, ECtHR.

Case of Janowiec and Others v. Russia, application Nos. 55508/07 and 29520/09, Judgment, 21.10.2013, ECtHR.

Case of Kononov v. Latvia (Application No. 36376/04), Judgment, 24.07.2008, ECtHR.

Case of Kononov v. Latvia (Application No. 36376/04), Judgment, 17.05.2010, ECtHR.

Case of *Konstantin Markin v. Russia* (7 October 2010) No 30078/06, ECtHR.

Case of *Konstantin Markin v. Russia* (22 March 2012) No 30078/06 (Grand Chamber).

Case of OAO Neftyanaya Kompaniya YUKOS v. Russia (Application No 14902/04), ECtHR, Judgment (just satisfaction), 31.07.2014.

Military and Paramilitary Activities in and against Nicaragua (Nicaragua v. USA), Jurisdiction and admissibility, Judgment, 26 November 1984, ICJ Reports 1984, 392; Judgment on Merits, 27 June 1986, ICJ Reports 1986, 14.

Plenum of the Supreme Court of the Russian Federation ruling 'On Application by Courts of General Jurisdiction of the Commonly Recognized Principles and Norms of International Law and the International Treaties of the Russian Federation', 10 October 2003, <http://www.supcourt.ru/catalog.php?c1=English&c2=Documents&c3=&id=6801>.

Plenum of the Supreme Court ruling 'On Application of the Convention for the Protection of Human Rights and Fundamental Freedoms of 4 November 1950 and Additional Protocols thereto by Courts of General Jurisdiction', 27 June 2013, <http://www.supcourt.ru/vscourt_detale.php?id=9155>.

Quasar de Valores SICAV S.A., et al. v. the Russian Federation, Award, 20 July 2012, <http://cisarbitration.com/wp-content/uploads/2013/02/Quasar-de-Valores-SICAV-S.A.-et-al-vs-Russian_Federation.pdf>.

Renta 4 S.V.S.A. v. the Russian Federation, Award on Preliminary Objections, 20 March 2009, <http://italaw.com/documents/Renta.pdf>.

RosInvestCo UK Ltd v. the Russian Federation, Final Award, 12 September 2010, <http://italaw.com/sites/default/files/case-documents/ita0720.pdf>.

Statement by the Russian MFA, 8 July 2004, <http://www.mid.ru/bdomp/brp_4.nsf/0/aedaea734e366074c3256ecb0054ed80!OpenDocument&Click=>.

Statement by Mr Anvar Azimov, Permanent Representative of the Russian Federation, at the meeting of the OSCE Permanent Council, regarding the *Kononov v. Latvia* judgment, 20 May 2010, <http://www.osce.org/pc/68227?download=true>.

Written Statement of the Russian Federation in the Kosovo Proceedings, 16.04.2009, ICJ, <http://www.icj-cij.org/docket/files/141/15628.pdf>.

Veteran Petroleum Limited v. The Russian Federation (PCA case No AA 228), <http://www.pca-cpa.org/showpage.asp?pag_id=1599>.

Yukos Universal Limited v. the Russian Federation (PCA Case No AA227), <http://www.pca-cpa.org/showpage.asp?pag_id=1599>.

MONOGRAPHS

A. H. Abashidze, A. M. Solntsev, K. V. Ageichenko, *Mirnoe razreshenie mezhdunarodnykh sporov. Sovremennye problemy* (Moscow: Rossiiskyi universitet druzhby narodov, 2011).

R. Allison, *Russia, the West, and Military Intervention* (Oxford: OUP, 2013).

J. E. Alvarez, *International Organizations as Law-makers* (Oxford: OUP, 2005).

J. E. Alvarez, *The Public International Law Regime Governing International Investment* (Leiden: Brill, 2011).

A. Anghie, *Imperialism, Sovereignty and the Making of International Law* (Cambridge: CUP, 2004).

L. P. Anufrieva, *Sootnoshenie mezhdunarodnogo publichnogo i mezhdunarodnogo chastnogo prava (sravnitel'noe issledovanie provovykh kategorii)* (Moscow; Rossiiskyi gosudarstvennyi torgovo-ekonomicheskii universitet, 2002).

D. Anzilotti, *Kurs mezhdunarodnoga prava* (Moscow: Pravovedenie, 1961).

R. D. Asmus, *A Little War that Shook the World* (New York: Palgrave Macmillan, 2010).

S. Baburin, *Krym naveki s Rossiyei. Istoriko-pravovoe obosnovanie vossoedinenia respubliki Krym i goroda Sevastopol s Rossiiakoi Federatsiei* (Moscow: Knizhnyi mir, 2014).

S. V. Bakhin (ed.), *Public and Private International Law. Problems and Prospects: Liber amicorum in honour of Ludmila N. Galenskaya* (St Petersburg: Publishing House of St Petersburg State University, 2007).

S. V. Bakhin (ed.), *Rossiiskaya Assotsiatsia Mezhdunarodnoga Prava 1957–2007. Biograficheskii slovar'* (St Petersburg: Publishing House of St Petersburg State University, 2007).

S. V. Bakhin (ed.), *International Relations and Law. A Look into the XXI Century. Materials of Conference in Honour of Professor Ludmila N. Galenskaya* (St Petersburg: Publishing House of St Petersburg State University, 2009).

Y. Ya. Baskin, D. I Feldman, *Istoria mezhdunarodnoga prava* (Moscow: Mezhdunarodnye otnoshenia, 1990).

V. A. Batyr', *Mezhdunarodnoe gumanitarnoe pravo*, 2nd edn (Moscow: Iustitsinform, 2011).

D. Bederman, *International Law in Antiquity* (Cambridge: CUP, 2007).

K. A. Bekyashev (ed.), *Mezhdunarodnoe publichnoe pravo*, 2nd edn (Moscow: Prospekt, 2003).

N. Berdyaev, *The Russian Idea* (New York: Macmillan, 1948).

N. Berdyaev, *The Origin of Russian Communism* (Ann Arbor: University of Michigan Press, 1962).

C. Bergbohm, *Staatsverträge und Gesetze als Quellen des Völkerrechts* (Dorpat: Mattiesen, 1877).

I. Berlin, *Russian Thinkers* (London: Penguin Books, 1994).

H. J. Berman, *Justice in the U.S.S.R. An Interpretation of Soviet Law* (Cambridge, MA: Harvard University Press, 1963).

N. A. Bezobrazov, *Issledovanie nachala vneshnego gosudarstvennogo prava* (St Petersburg, 1838).
P. N. Biryukov, *Mezhdunarodnoe pravo*, 5th edn (Moscow: Yurait, 2011).
D. S. Boklan, *Mezhdunarodnoe ekologicheskoe pravo i mezhdunarodnye eonomicheskie otnoshenia* (Moscow: Magistr Infra-M, 2014).
B. Bowring, *Law, Rights and Ideology in Russia. Landmarks in the Destiny of a Great Power* (London: Routledge, 2013).
A. B. Bozeman, *The Future of Law in a Multicultural World* (Princeton: Princeton University Press, 1971).
A. L. Bredikhin, *Suverenitet kak politiko-pravovoi fenomen* (Moscow: Infra-M, 2012).
E. G. von Bröcker (ed.), *Jahrbuch für Rechtsgelehrte in Russland*, 2 vols (Riga: Häcker, 1822 and 1824).
I. Brownlie, *Mezhdunarodnoe pravo (v dvukh knigakh)* (Moscow: "Progress", 1977).
R. Buchan, *International Law and the Construction of the Liberal Peace* (Oxford: Hart Publishing, 2013).
A. L. Burkov, *Konventsia o zashite prav cheloveka v sudakh Rossii* (Moscow: Wolters Kluwer, 2010).
O. V. Butkevich, *U istokov mezhdunarodnogo prava* (St Petersburg: Izdatel'stvo R. Aslanova 'Yuridicheskii tsentr Press', 2008).
W. E. Butler, *The Law of Soviet Territorial Waters. A Case Study of Maritime Legislation and Practice* (New York: Praeger, 1967).
W. E. Butler, *The Soviet Union and the Law of the Sea* (Baltimore: Johns Hopkins Press, 1971).
W. E. Butler, *Northeast Arctic Passage* (Alpen aan den Rijn: A.W. Sijthoff, 1978).
W. E. Butler (ed.), *International Law in Comparative Perspective* (Alphen aan den Rijn: Sijthoff, 1980).
W. E. Butler (ed.), *Perestroika and International Law* (Dordrecht: Martinus Nijhoff, 1990).
W. E. Butler, *Russian Law of Treaties* (London: Simmonds & Hill, 1997).
W. E. Butler, *The Law of Treaties in Russia and the Commonwealth of Independent States* (Cambridge: CUP, 2002).
W. E. Butler, *Russian Foreign Relations and Investment Law* (Oxford: OUP, 2006).
W. E. Butler, V. G. Tunkin (eds), *The Tunkin Diary and Lectures* (The Hague: Eleven International Publishing, 2012).
M. Byers, *Who Owns the Arctic? Understanding Sovereignty Disputes in the North* (Vancouver: Douglas & McIntyre, 2009).
J. Y. Calvez, *Droit international et souveraineté en U.S.S.R. L'Évolution de l'idéologie juridique soviétique depuis da la Révolution de l'Octobre* (Paris: A. Colin, 1953).
D. Carreau, P. Julliard, *Mezhdunarodnoe ekonomicheskoe pravo* (Moscow: 'Mezhdunarodnye otnoshenia', 2002)
A. Cassese, *International Law*, 2nd edn (OUP: Oxford, 2005).
S. V. Chernichenko, *Lichnost' i mezhdunarodnoe pravo* (Moscow: 'Mezhdunarodnye otnoshenia', 1974).
S. V. Chernichenko, *Teoria mezhdunarodnoga prava*, Vol. 1 and 2 (Moscow: NIMP, 1999).
S. V. Chernichenko, *Ocherki po filosofii i mezhdunarodnomu pravu* (Moscow: 'Nauchnaya kniga', 2009).
C. Clark, *The Sleepwalkers. How Europe Went to War in 1914* (London: Penguin Books, 2013).
J. Crawford, *Brownlie's Principles of International Law*, 8th edn (Oxford: OUP, 2012).
A. A. Danelyan, I. Z. Farkhutdinov, *Mezhdunarodnyi investitsionnyi arbitrazh. Uchebnoe posobie* (Moscow: Tsentr gumanitarnykh initsiativ, 2013).

G. M. Danilenko, *Law-Making in the International Community* (Leiden: Martinus Nijhoff Publishers, 1993).

N. Ya. Danilevsky, *Rossia i Evropa. Vzgljad na kul'turnye i politicheskie otnoshenia Slavjanskogo mira k Germano-Romanskomu*, 5th edn (St Petersburg: Panteleevs, 1895; first print in 1869), <http://www.runivers.ru/bookreader/book10067/#page/51/mode/1up>.

A. I. Dmitriev, W. E. Butler (eds), *Istoria mezhdunarodnoga prava* (Odessa: Feniks, 2013).

R. Dolzer, C. Schreuer, *Principles of International Investment Law*, 2nd edn (Oxford: OUP, 2012).

J. D. Douglass, Jr, *Why the Soviets Violate Arms Control Treaties* (Washington, DC: Pergamon-Brassey's, 1988).

A. F. Douhan, *Printsip nevmeshatel'stva vo vnutrennie dela gosudarstv. Sovremennye tendentsii* (Minsk: 'Pravo i ekonomika', 2009).

A. Dugin, *Proyekt Evrazia* (Moscow: Yauza EKSMO, 2004).

A. G. Dugin, *Geopolitika postmoderna* (St Petersburg: Amfora, 2007).

R. Dworkin, *Taking Rights Seriously* (Cambridge, MA: Harvard University Press, 1978).

S. A. Egorov (ed.), *Mezhdunarodnoe pravo*, 5th edn (Moscow: Statut, 2014).

O. O. Eichelmann, *Khrestomatia russkogo mezhdunarodnoga prava*, 2 vols (Kiev: Univ. Tip., 1887–9).

Yu. V. Emel'ianov, *Europa sudit Rossiu* (Moscow: Veche, 2007).

J. Engelmann, *Das Staatsrecht des Kaiserthums Rußland* (Freiburg: J. C. B. Mohr, 1889).

M. L. Entin, *V poiskakh partnerskikh otnoshenii. Rossia i Evropeiskii soyuz v 2004–2005 godakh* (St Petersburg: 'Rossiya-Neva', 2006).

M. L. Entin, *V poiskakh partnerskikh otnoshenii III. Rossia i Evropeiskii soyuz v 2008–2009 godakh* (Moscow: Zebra E, 2010).

J. P. G. Ewers, *Vom Ursprunge des russischen Staats. Ein Versuch, die Geschichte desselben aus den Quellen zu erforschen* (Riga: J. G. Hartmann's Buchhandlung, 1808).

J. P. G. Ewers, *Das älteste Recht der Russen in seiner geschichtlichen Entwickelung* (Dorpat: A. Sticinsky, 1826).

R. A. Falk (ed.), *The Vietnam War and International Law* (Princeton: Princeton University Press, 1970).

I. Z. Farkhutdinov, *Mezhdunarodnoe investitsionnoe pravo i protsess* (Moscow: Prospekt, 2013).

B. Fassbender, *The United Nations Charter as the Constitution of the International Community* (Leiden: Brill, 2009).

U. Fastenrath et al., *From Bilateralism to Community Interest. Essays in Honor of Judge Bruno Simma* (Oxford: OUP, 2011).

A. I. Filimonova (ed.), *Dvoinye standarty v zashite pravcheloveka. Kazus professor Sheshelya* (Moscow: 'Fond istoricheskoi perspektivy', 2009).

C. Focarelli, *International Law as Social Construct. The Struggle for Global Justice* (Oxford: OUP, 2012).

T. M. Franck, *The Empowered Self. Law and Society in the Age of Individualism* (Oxford: OUP, 1999).

R. Freedman, *The United Nations Human Rights Council. A Critique and Early Assessment* (London: Routledge, 2013).

W. Friedmann, *The Changing Structure of International Law* (New York: Columbia University Press, 1964).

F. Fukuyama, *The End of History and the Last Man* (New York: Avon Books, 1992).

K. S. Gadzhiev, *Geopoliticheskie gorizonty Rossii. Kontury novogo miroporyadka* (Moscow: Ekonomika, 2007).

L. N. Galenskaya, G. I. Kurdyukov, S. V. Bakhin (eds), *Mezhdunarodnoe pravo. Bibliographia. 1991–2005* (St Petersburg: 'Rossiya-Neva', 2010).

G. Gecse, *Bütsantsist Bütsantsini. Suurvene mõttelaadi olemus* (Tallinn: Ajakirjade kirjastus, 2012).

I. Get'man-Pavlova, *Mezhdunarodnoe pravo*, 2nd edn (Moscow: Yurait, 2013).

G. Gidel, *Le Droit international public de la mer*, Vol. 3 (Paris: Recueil Sirey, 1934).

E. Gilligan, *Terror in Chechnya. Russia and the Tragedy of Civilians in War* (Princeton: Princeton University Press, 2010).

T. Ginsburg and A. Simpser (eds), *Constitutions in Authoritarian Regimes* (Cambridge: CUP, 2014).

G. Ginsburgs, *From Soviet to Russian International Law. Studies in Continuity and Change* (Leiden: Martinus Nijhoff, 1998).

J. L. Goldsmith, E. A. Posner, *The Limits of International Law* (Oxford: OUP, 2005).

G. W. Gong, *The Standard of Civilization in International Society* (Oxford: OUP, 1984).

R. Goodman, D. Jinks, *Socializing States. Promoting Human Rights through International Law* (Oxford: OUP, 2013).

M. V. Gorbachev, *Tsivilizatsionnaya metodologia v politicheskoi komparativistike* (Saratov: Saratovskaya Gosudarstvennaya Akademia Prava, 2011).

V. E. Grabar, *The History of International Law in Russia, 1647–1917. A Bio-Bibliographical Study*, trans. and ed. W. E. Butler (Oxford: Clarendon Press, 1990).

N. I. Grachev, *Proiskhozhdenie suvereniteta. Verkhovnaya vlast' v mirovozzrenii i praktike gosudarstvennogo stroitel'stva traditsionnogo obshetva* (Moscow: Zertsalo-M, 2009).

W. Grewe, *Die Epochen der Völkerrechtsgeschichte* (Baden-Baden: Nomos, 1984).

K. Grzybowsky, *Soviet Public International Law. Doctrines and Diplomatic Practice* (Alpen aan den Rijn: A.W. Sijthoff, 1970).

W. E. Hall, *A Treatise on International Law*, 3rd edn (Oxford: Clarendon Press, 1890).

F. de Hartingh, *Les Conceptions soviétiques du droit de la mer* (Paris: R. Pichon, 1960).

Harvard University Catalogue (Cambridge, MA: Harvard University, 1927).

M. Head, *Evgeny Pashukanis. A Critical Reappraisal* (New York: Routledge, 2008).

J. Henderson, *The Constitution of the Russian Federation. A Contextual Analysis* (Oxford: Hart Publishing, 2011).

L. Henkin, *How Nations Behave*, 2nd edn (New York: Praeger, 1979).

J. L. Hildebrand, *Soviet International Law: An Exemplar for Optimal Decision Theory Analysis* (Cleveland: Case Western Reserve University, 1968).

S. Hopgood, *The Endtimes of Human Rights* (Ithaca, NY: Cornell University Press, 2013).

S. P. Huntington, *The Clash of Civilizations and the Remaking of World Order* (New York: Simon & Schuster, 1996).

M. Hussner, *Die Übernahme international Rechts in die russische und deutsche Rechtsordnung* (Stuttgart: ibidem Verlag, 2005).

C. C. Hyde, *Mezhdunarodnoe pravo, ego ponimanie i primenenie Soedinennymi Shtatami* (Moscow: 'Mezhdunarodnye otnoshenia', 1985).

G. V. Ignatenko, *Mezhdunarodnoe pravo i vnutrigosudarstvennoe pravo. Problemy sopryazhennosti i vzaimodeistvia* (Moscow: Norma, 2012).

G. V. Ignatenko, O. I. Tiunov (eds), *Mezhdunarodnoe pravo* (Moscow: Norma, 2013).

V. Illyashevitch, *Pribaltiitsy na rossiiskoi diplomaticheskoi sluzhbe* (Tallinn: Tarbeinfo, 2005).

T. Iuzefovich, *Dogovory Rossii s Vostokom, politicheskie i torgovye* (St Peterburg: Tip. O. I. Bakst, 1869).

V. S. Ivanenko (ed.), *100-letiye initsiativy Rossii. Ot Pervoi konferentsii mira 1899 g. k Tret'ei konferentsii mira 1999.g. Sbornik materialov* (St Petersburg: St Petersburg State University, 1999).

V. S. Ivanenko (ed.), *The International Scientifically Practical Conference 'The World, Safety and International Law: A Sight in the Future, St Petersburg, 12 April 2003* (St Petersburg: St Petersburg University Publishing House, 2004).

I. A. Ivannikov, *Istoria politiko-pravovoi mysli o forme rossiiskogo gosudarstvo* (Moscow: Yurlitinform, 2012).

M. W. Janis, *The American Tradition of International Law. Great Expectations 1789–1914* (Oxford: OUP, 2004).

M. W. Janis, *America and the Law of Nations 1776–1939* (Oxford: OUP, 2010).

E. Jimenez de Arechaga, *Sovremennoe mezhdunarodnoe pravo* (Moscow: 'Progress', 1983).

B. Yu. Kagarlitski, *Periferiinaya imperia. Rossia i mirosistema* (Moscow: Librokom, 2011).

R. Kalamkaryan, Y. Migachev (eds), *Mezhdunarodnoe pravo: Uchebnik*, 2nd edn (Moscow: EKSMO, 2006).

P. A. Kalininchenko, *Evropeiskyi Soyuz. Pravo i otnoshenia s Rossiei* (Moscow: Norma Infra-M, 2012).

M. A. Kaplan, N. de Katzenbach, G. Tunkin, *Modernes Völkerrecht. Form oder Mittel der Aussenpolitik* (Berlin: Berlin Verlag, 1965).

A. Ya. Kapustin (ed.), *Mezhdunarodnoe pravo* (Moscow: Gardariki, 2008).

V. A. Kartashkin, *Prava cheloveka v mezhdunarodnom i vnutrigosudarstvennom prave* (Moscow: Institut gosudarstva i prava RAN, 1995).

M. Katz, *Mikhail N. Katkov. A Political Biography: 1818–1887* (The Hague: Mouton & Co, 1966).

D. Kennedy, *The Dark Sides of Virtue. Reassessing International Humanitarianism* (Princeton: Princeton University Press, 2004).

I. O. Khlestova, *Yuridiktsionnyi immunitet gosudarstva* (Moscow: Yurisprudentsia, 2007).

J. von Kirchmann, *Die Werthlosigkeit der Jurisprudenz als Wissenschaft. Ein Vortrag, gehalten in der juristischen Gesellschaft zu Berlin*, 3rd edn (Berlin: Springer, 1848).

J. L. Klüber, *Noveishee evropeiskoe mezhdunarodnoe pravo*, trans. from French (Moscow: August Semen, 1828).

D. Kochenov, F. Amtenbink (eds), *The European Union's Shaping of the International Legal Order* (Cambridge: CUP, 2014).

Y. M. Kolosov, E. S. Krivchikova (eds), *Mezhdunarodnoe pravo*, 2nd edn (Moscow: 'Mezhdnarodnye otnoshenia', 2005).

Yu. M. Kolosov, E. S. Krivchikova, P. V. Savas'kov (eds), *Evropeiskoe mezhdunarodnoe pravo* (Moscow: 'Mezhdunarodnye otnoshenia', 2005).

A. V. Kornev, A. B. Borisov, *Pravovaya mysl' v dorevolutsionnoi Rossii* (Moscow: EKSMO, 2005).

E. A. Korowin, *Das Völkerrecht der Übergangszeit. Grundlagen der völkerrechtlichen Beziehungen der Union der Sowjetrepubliken* (Berlin: Stilke, 1929).

M. Koskenniemi, *The Gentle Civilizer of Nations. The Rise and Fall of International Law 1870–1960* (Cambridge: CUP, 2002).

M. Koskenniemi, *Report of the Study Group of the ILC, 'Fragmentation of International Law. Difficulties arising from the Diversification and Expansion of International Law'*, 13 April 2006, <http://untreaty.un.org/ilc/documentation/english/a_cn4_l682.pdf>.

N. I. Kostenko, *Mezhdunarodnoe ugolovnoe pravo. Sovremennye teoreticheskie problemy* (Moscow: Yurlitinform, 2004).

V. S. Kotlyar, *Mezhdunarodnoe pravo i sovremennye strategicheskie kontseptsii SShA i NATO*, 2nd edn (Kazan: Tsentr innovatsionnykh tekhnologii, 2008).

A. A. Kovalev, S. V. Chernichenko, *Mezhdunarodnoe pravo*, 3rd edn (Moscow: Prospekt, 2008).

F. I. Kozhevnikov, *Russkoe gosudarstvo i mezhdunarodnoe pravo* (Moscow: Iurizdat, 1947).

F. I. Kozhevnikov, *Sovetskoe gosudarstvo i mezhdunarodnoe pravo. 1917–1947 gg. (Opyt istoriko-pravovoga issledovania)* (Moscow: Yuridicheskoe izdatel'stvo, 1948).

F. I. Kozhevnikov, *Russkoe gosudarstvo i mezhdunarodnoe pravo (do XX veka)* (Moscow: Zertsalo, 2006).

P. P. Kremnev, *Raspad SSSR. Mezhdunarodno-pravovye problemy* (Moscow: Zertsalo-M, 2005).

V. Kudryavtsev, V. Chkhikvadze, E. Lukasheva (eds), *International Covenants on Human Rights and Soviet Legislation* (Moscow: Novosty Press Agency, 1986).

V. I. Kuznetsov, B. R. Tuzmukhamedov (eds), *Mezhdunarodnoe pravo*, 2nd edn (Moscow: Norma, 2007).

G. de Lacharrière, *La Politique juridique extérieure* (Paris: IFRI Economica, 1983).

T. Långström, *Transformation in Russia and International Law* (Leiden: Martinus Nijhoff, 2003).

I. Lapenna, *Conceptions soviétiques de droit international public* (Paris: A. Pedone, 1954).

D. B. Levin, *Nauka mezhdunarodnogo prava v Rossii v kontse XIX i nachale XX v. Obshie voprosy teorii mezhdunarodnogo prava* (Moscow: Nauka, 1982).

D. Lieven. *Empire. The Russian Empire and Its Rivals* (Yale: Nota Bene, 2002).

A.-K. Lindblom, *Non-governmental Organisations in International Law* (Cambridge: CUP, 2005).

F. von Liszt, *Mezhdunarodnoe pravo v sistematicheskom izlozhenii*, trans. V. E. Hrabar (Yur'ev: Mattiesen, 1909).

Y. M. Lotman, *Universe of the Mind. A Semiotic Theory of Culture, with a foreword by U. Eco* (London: Tauris, 1990).

Y. M. Lotman, *Vnutri myslyashikh mirov. Chelovek—tekst—semiosfera—istoria* (Moscow: 'Yazyki russkoi kul'tury', 1996).

Y. M. Lotman, *Semiosfera* (St Petersburg: Iskusstvo, 2000).

E. A. Lukasheva, *Chelovek, pravo, tsivilizatsia: normativno-tsennostnoe izmerenie* (Moscow: Norma, 2009).

I. I. Lukashuk, *Mezhdunarodnoe pravo. Obshaya chast'*, 2nd edn (Moscow: Beck, 2001).

I. I. Lukashuk, *Mezhdunarodnoe pravo. Osobennaya chast'*, 2nd edn (Moscow: Beck, 2001).

I. I. Lukashuk, *Sovremennoe pravo mezhdunarodnykh dogovorov*, Vol. 1 (Moscow: Wolters Kluwer, 2004).

I. I. Lukashuk, *Pravo mezhdunarodnoi otvetstvennosti* (Moscow: Wolters Kluwer, 2004).

E. McWhinney, *Peaceful Coexistence and Soviet-Western International Law* (Alpen aan den Rijn: A.W. Sijthoff, 1964).

M. Malia, *Russia under Western Eyes. From the Bronze Horseman to the Lenin Mausoleum* (Cambridge, MA: Belknam Press, 1999).

L. Mälksoo, *Illegal Annexation and State Continuity. The Case of the Incorporation of the Baltic States by the USSR* (Leiden: Martinus Nijhoff, 2003).

L. Mälksoo (ed.), *Russia and European Human Rights Law. The Rise of the Civilizational Argument* (Leiden: Brill, 2014).

S. Yu. Marochkin, *Deistvie i realizatsia norm mezhdunarodnoga prava v pravovoi sisteme Rossiiskoi Federatsii* (Moscow: Norma, 2011).

F. F. Martens, *Sobranie traktatov i konventsii zaklyuchennykh Rossieyu s inostrannymi derzhavami*,Vol. 2 (St Petersburg: A. Böhnke, 1875).

F. F. Martens, *Le Conflit entre la Russie et la Chine. Ses origines, son développement et sa portée universalle: étude politique* (Bruxelles: C. Muquardt, 1880).

F. De Martens, *Traité de droit international, traduit par A. Léo, Tome 1* (Paris: Librairie A. Maresco Ainé, 1883).

F. F. Martens, *Sobranie traktatov i konventsii zaklyuchennykh Rossieyu s inostrannymi derzhavami*, Vol. 8 (St Petersburg: A. Böhnke, 1888).

F. F. Martens, *Sobranie traktatov i konventsii zaklyuchennykh Rossieyu s inostrannymi derzhavami*, Vol. 9 (St Petersburg: A. Böhnke, 1892).

F. F. Martens, *Sovremennoe mezhdunarodnoe pravo tsivilizovannykh narodov*, Vol. 1 (Moscow: Yuridischeskii Kolledzh MGU, 1996).

K. F. von Martens, *Diplomatiia, ili rukovodstvo k poznaniiu vneshnikh gosudarstvennykh snoshenii dlia posviashaiushikh sebia diplomaticheskoi sluzhbe Barona K. Martensa* (Moscow: Selivanovskii, 1828).

B. Maurach and B. Meissner (eds), *Völkerrecht in Ost und West* (Stuttgart: Kohlhammer, 1967).

B. Meissner, *Sowjetunion und Völkerrecht. Eine bibliographische Dokumentation* (Köln: Verlag Wissenschaft und Politik, 1963).

G. M. Melkov (ed.), *Mezhdunarodnoe pravo* (Moscow: RIOR, 2009).

A. B. Mezyaev, *Pravo obvinyaemogo v mezhdunarodnom ugolovnom prave* (Kazan: 'TISBI', 2010).

C. Miéville, *Between Equal Rights. A Marxist Theory of International Law* (Leiden: Brill, 2004).

A. A. Moiseev, *Suverenitet gosudarstva v mezhdunarodnom prave* (Moscow: Vostok Zapad, 2009).

H. Münkler, *Imperien. Die Logik der Weltherrschaft—vom Alten Rom bis zu den Vereinigten Staaten* (Berlin: Rowohlt, 2005).

K. Nadakavukaren Schefer, *International Investment Law. Text, Cases, Materials* (Cheltenham: Edward Elgar, 2013).

A. V. Naumov, A. G. Kibal'nik, V. N. Orlov, P. V. Volosyuk (eds), *Mezhdunarodnoe ugolovnoe pravo* (Moscow: Yurait, 2013)

I. B. Neumann, *Russia and the Idea of Europe. A Study in Identity and International Relations* (London: Routledge, 1996).

J. E. Nijman, *The Concept of International Legal Personality. An Inquiry into the History and Theory of International Law* (The Hague: TMC Asser, 2004).

A. Nollkaemper, J. E. Nijman (eds), *New Perspectives on the Divide between National and International Law* (Oxford: OUP, 2007).

A. Nollkaemper, *National Courts and the International Rule of Law* (Oxford: OUP, 2012).

I. Nossova, *Russia's International Legal Claims in Its Adjacent Seas. The Realm of Sea as Extension of Sovereignty*, Ph.D. thesis, University of Tartu (2013), <http://dspace.utlib.ee/dspace/bitstream/handle/10062/31198/nossova_irina.pdf?sequence=1>.

A. Nussbaum, *A Concise History of the Law of Nations* (New York: Macmillan, 1954).

Y. Onuma, *A Transcivilizational Perspective on International Law* (Leiden: Martinus Nijhoff, 2010).

C. Osakwe, *The Participation of the Soviet Union in Universal International Organizations. A Political and Legal Analysis of Soviet Strategies and Aspirations inside ILO, UNESCO and WHO* (Leiden: A.W. Sijthoff, 1972).

B. I. Osminin, *Zaklyuchenie i implementatsia mezhdunarodnykh dogovorov i vnutrigosudarstvennoe pravo* (Moscow: Infotropic, 2010).

K. Parlett, *The Individual in the International Legal System. Continuity and Change in International Law* (Cambridge: CUP, 2011).

Patriarch Kirill of Moscow, *Freedom and Responsibility. A Search for Harmony—Human Rights and Personal Dignity* (London: Darton, Longman and Todd, 2011).

R. Pipes, *Russia under the Old Regime*, 2nd edn (London: Penguin Books, 1993).

R. Pipes, *Vixi. Memoirs of a Non-belonger* (New Haven: Yale University Press, 2003).

R. Portmann, *Legal Personality in International Law* (Cambridge: CUP, 2010).

E. A. Posner, *The Perils of Global Legalism* (Chicago: University of Chicago Press, 2009).

S. Prakash Sinha, *Legal Polycentricity and International Law* (Durham: Carolina Academic Press, 1996).

S. Pritzkow, *Das völkerrechtliche Verhältnis zwischen der EU und Russland im Energiesektor. Eine Untersuchung unter Berücksichtigung der vorläufigen Anwendung des Energiecharta-Vertrages durch Russland* (Berlin: Springer, 2011).

V. V. Pustogarov, *Our Martens. F. F. Martens, International Lawyer and Architect of Peace*, ed. and trans. from the Russian by W. E. Butler (The Hague: Kluwer Law International, 2000).

J. Quigley, *Soviet Legal Innovation and the Law of the Western World* (Cambridge: CUP, 2012).

B. Ramundo, *Peaceful Coexistence. International Law in the Building of Communism* (Baltimore: Johns Hopkins Press, 1967).

E. Rauch, *Die Sowjetunion und die Entwicklung des Seevölkerrechts* (Berlin: WAV, 1982).

G. v. Rauch, *Die Universität Dorpat und das Aufdringen der frühen Aufklärung in Livland. 1690–1710* (Essen: Essener Verlagsanstalt, 1943).

D. Rauschning, V. N. Rusinova (eds), *Rossiiskaya Federatsia v Evrope. Pravovye aspekty sotrudnichestva Rossii s evropeiskimi organizatsiami* (Moscow: 'Mezhdunarodnye otnoshenia', 2008).

J. Rawls, *The Law of Peoples* (Cambridge, MA: Harvard University Press, 1999).

A. Roberts, *Is International Law International?* (Oxford: OUP, forthcoming).

A. Roberts, P. Stephan, P.-H. Verdier, M. Versteeg (eds), *Comparative International Law* (Oxford: OUP, forthcoming).

W. Rückert, *Das Völkerrecht in der Rechtsprechung des russischen Verfassungsgerichts* (Berlin: Berliner Wissenschaftsverlag, 2005).

J. Saar, *XXI sajandi väljakutse. Tsivilisatsioonid, kultuurid, väärtused* (Tallinn: Hea raamat, 2014).

E. V. Safronova, *Mezhdunarodnoe publichnoe pravo. Teoreticheskie problemy* (Moscow: RIOR, 2013).

P. Sands, *Lawless World. Making and Breaking Global Rules* (London: Penguin Books, 2006).

M. Sarkisyants, *Russland und der Messianismus des Orients* (Tübingen: J. C. B. Mohr, 1955).

Sbornik dogovorov Rossii s Kitaem, 1689–1881 g. (St Petersburg: Izdatel'stvo MID, 1889).

W. A. Schabas, *Genocide in International Law* (Cambridge: CUP, 2000).

H. Scheu, *Das Völkerrecht in den Beziehungen Chinas zu den europäischen Seemächten und zu Russland. Ein Beitrag zur Geschichte des Völkerrechts* (Frankfurt a. M.: difo-druck schmacht, 1971).

C. Schirren, *Zur Geschichte des Nordischen Krieges* (Kiel: Walter G. Mühlau, 1913).

C. Schmitt, *Über die drei Arten rechtswissenschaftlichen Denkens* (Hamburg: Hanseatische Verlagsanstalt, 1934).

C. Schmitt, *Völkerrechtliche Großraumordnung mit Interventionsverbot für raumfremde Mächte. Ein Beitrag zum Reichsbegriff* (Berlin: Rechtsverlag, 1941).

C. Schmitt, *Der Nomos der Erde im Völkerrecht des jus publicum europaeum* (Köln: Greven Verlag, 1950).
C. Schmitt, *Politische Theologie. Vier Kapitel zur Lehre von der Souveränität*, 7th edn (Berlin: Duncker & Humblot, 1996).
M. Schmöckel, *Die Großraumtheorie. Ein Beitrag zur Geschichte der Völkerrechts -wissenschaft im Dritten Reich, insbesondere der Kriegszeit* (Berlin: Duncker & Humblot, 1994).
T. Schweisfurth, *Der internationale Vertrag in der modernen sowjetischen Völkerrechtstheorie* (Köln: Verlag Wissenschaft und Politik,1968).
T. Schweisfurth, *Sozialistisches Völkerrecht? Darstellung—Analyse—Wertung der sowjet-marxistischen Theorie vom Völkerrecht 'neuen Typs'* (Berlin: Springer, 1979).
A. P. Sereni, *The Italian Conception of International Law* (New York: Columbia University Press, 1943).
P. P. Shafirov, *Rassuzhdenie, kakie zakonnye prichiny Petr I, tsar i povelitel' vserossiiskii, k nachatiu voiny protiv Karla XII, korolya shvedskogo, v 1700 godu imel* (A Discourse Concerning the Just Causes of the War between Sweden and Russia: 1700–21) (Moscow: Zertsalo-M, 2008).
R. A. Shepenko, *Vvedenie v pravo VTO. Kurs antidempingovogo regulirovania* (Moscow: Prospekt, 2014).
V. M. Shumilov, *Mezhdunarodnoe ekonomicheskoe pravo* (Rostov: Feniks, 2003).
V. M. Shumilov, *Mezhdunarodnoe finansovoe pravo* (Moscow: 'Mezhdunarodnye otnoshenia', 2005).
V. M. Shumilov, *Mezhdunarodnoe pravo*, 2nd edn (Moscow: 'Mezhdunarodnye otnoshenia', 2012).
V. M. Shurshalov, *Mezhdunarodnye pravootnoshenia* (Moscow: 'Mezhdunarodnye otnoshenia', 1971).
E. K. Simson, *Sistema mezhdunarodnoga prava*, Vol. 1 (St Petersburg, 1900).
A. Yu. Skuratova, *Mezhdunarodnye prestuplenia. Sovremennye probemy kvalifikatsii* (Moscow: Norma, 2012).
G. S. Starodubtsev, *Mezhdunarodno-pravovaya nauka Rossiiskoi emigratsii* (Moscow: Kniga i biznes, 2000).
Y. E. Svechinskaya, *Imperskaya ideologia v rossiiskoi gosudarstvenno-pravovoi mysli* (Moscow: Yurlitinform, 2011).
A. N. Talalaev, *Pravo mezhdunarodnykh dogovorov*, 2 vols (Moscow: Garant, 2011).
T. Taracouzio, *The Soviet Union and International Law. A Study Based on the Legislation, Treaties and Foreign Relations of the Union of Socialist Soviet Republics* (New York: Macmillan, 1935).
A. Tarkhanov, A. I. Abdullin, G. I. Kurdyukov, R. S. Davletgil'deev (eds), *Materialy mezhdunarodnoi nauchno-prakticheskoi konferentsii 'Mezhdunarodnyi pravoporyadok v sovremennom mire i rol' Rossii v ego ukreplenii', posvyashennoi 90-letiu D.I. Fel'dmana* (Moscow: Statut, 2014).
M. A. Taube, *Istoria zarozhdenia sovremennogo mezhdunarodnoga prava (Srednie veka)*, Vol. 1 (St Petersburg: I. I. Schmidt, 1894) and Vol. 2 (Kharkov: Zil'berberg, 1899).
M. Freiherr von Taube, *Russland und Westeuropa. (Russlands historische Sonderentwicklung in der europäischen Völkergemeinschaft)* (Berlin: Stilke, 1928).
M. A. Taube, *'Zarnitsy'. Vospominania o tragicheskoi sud'be predrevolyutsionnoi Rossii (1900–1917)* (Moscow: ROSSPEN, 2007).
N. Taylor Saito, *Meeting the Enemy. American Exceptionalism and International Law* (New York: NYU Press, 2010).

R. G. Teitel, *Humanity's Law* (Oxford: OUP, 2011).
D. C. Thomas, *The Helsinki Effect. International Norms, Human Rights, and the Demise of Communism* (Princeton: Princeton University Press, 2001).
O. I. Tiunov, A. A. Kashirkina, A. N. Morozov, *Vypolnenie mezhdunarodnykh dogovorov Rossiiskoi Federatsii* (Moscow: Norma, 2012).
A. de Tocqueville, *Democracy in America*, ed. J. P. Meyer, trans. by G. Lawrence, Vol. 1, part 2 (New York: Harper, 1969).
J. Toman, *L'Union soviétique et le droit des conflits armés*, Ph.D. thesis (Geneva, 1997).
E. Tomson, *Kriegsbegriff und Kriegsrecht der Sowjetunion* (Berlin: Berlin-Verlag, 1979).
J. P. Trachtman, *The Future of International Law: Global Government* (Cambridge, CUP, 2013).
D. W. Treadgold, *The West in Russia and China. Religious and Secular Thought in Modern Times*, Vol. 1 *Russia 1472–1917* and Vol. 2 *China 1582–1949* (Cambridge: CUP, 1973).
A. Tsygankov, *Russia and the West from Alexander to Putin. Honor in International Relations* (Cambridge: CUP, 2012).
A. P. Tsygankov, *Russia's Foreign Policy. Change and Continuity in National Identity*, 3rd edn (Lanham: Rowman & Little, 2013).
D. Trenin, *Post-Imperium. Evraziiskaya istoria* (Moscow: ROSSPEN, 2012).
J. F. Triska and R. M. Slusser, *The Theory, Law and Policy of Soviet Treaties* (Stanford, CA: Stanford University Press, 1962).
A. Tšernjajev, *1991. aasta. NSV Liidu presidendi abi päevik*, trans. U. Uibo (Tallinn: Vagabund, 2006).
A. S. Tumanova, R. V. Kiselev, *Prava cheloveka v pravovoi mysli i zakonotvorchestve Rossiiskoi imperii vtoroi poloviny XIX-nachala XX veka* (Moscow: NIU VShE, 2011).
G. I. Tunkin, *Theory of International Law*, trans. W. E. Butler (Cambridge, MA: Harvard University Press, 1974).
G. I. Tunkin, *Teoria mezhdunarodnoga prava*, original in 1970 (Moscow: Zertsalo-M, 2009).
H.-J. Uibopuu, *Die Völkerrechtssubjektivität der Unionsrespubliken der UdSSR* (Berlin: Springer, 1975).
I. A. Umnova, *Pravo mira. Kurs lektsii* (Moscow: Eksmo, 2011).
E. T. Usenko, G. G. Shinkaretskaya, *Mezhdunarodnoe pravo* (Moscow: Yurist, 2005).
E. T. Usenko, *Ocherki teorii mezhdunarodnoga prava* (Moscow: Norma, 2008).
B. Utin, *Über die Ehrenverletzung nach russischem Recht seit dem 17. Jahrhundert* (Dorpat: Laakmann, 1857).
R. M. Valeev, *Mezhdunarodnoe ekologicheskoe pravo* (Moscow: Statut, 2012).
R. Valeev, G. Kurdyukov (eds), *Mezdhunarodnoe pravo. Osobennaya chast'* (Moscow: Statut, 2010).
R. M. Valeev, G. I. Kurdyukov (eds), *Mezhdunarodnoe pravo. Obshaya chast'* (Moscow: Statut, 2011).
G. M. Vel'iaminov, *Mehdunarodnoe ekonomicheskoe pravo i protsess* (Moscow: Wolters Kluwer, 2004).
A. Verdross, *Mezhdunarodnoe pravo* (Moscow: Inostrannaya literatura, 1959).
N. I. Veselovskii (ed.), *Pamiatniki diplomaticheskikh i torgovykh snoshenii Moskovskoi Rusi s Persiei*, 3 vols (St Petersburg: Iablonskii i Perott, 1890–8).
A. N. Vylegzhanin, *Reshenia mezhdunarodnoga suda OON po sporam o razgranichenii morskikh prostranstv* (Moscow: Yuridicheskaya literatuura, 2004).
A. N. Vylegzhanin (ed.), *Mezhdunarodnoe pravo* (Moscow: Yurait, 2009).

A. N. Vylegzhanin (ed.), *Mezhdunarodnoe ekonomicheskoe pravo* (Moscow: 'Knorus', 2012).
A. N. Vylegzhanin et al. (eds), *Rossiya i mezhdunarodnoe pravo. Materialy mezhdunarodnoi konferentsii, posvyashennoi 100-letiyu F. I. Kozhevnikova (Moskva, 15.10.2004.g.)* (Mos cow: 'MGIMO-Universitet', 2006).
A. Ya.Vyshinski, *Voprosy mezhdunarodnoga prava i mezhdunarodnoi politiki* (Moscow: Gosiurizdat, 1951).
R. P. Ward, *An Enquiry into the Foundation and History of the Law of Nations in Europe from the Time of the Greeks and Romans to the Age of Grotius* (London: Strahan and Woodfall, 1795).
T. Ware, *The Orthodox Church* (London: Penguin Books, 1997).
S. Weill, *The Role of National Courts in Applying International Humanitarian Law* (Oxford: OUP, 2014).
H. Wheaton, *Elements of International Law*, 6th edn (Boston: Little, Brown & Co., 1855).
F. Witte, *Ein Blick auf die geschichtliche Entwickelung des älteren russischen Erbrechts, bis zum Gesetzbuche des Zaren Alexei Michailowitch (1649)* (Dorpat: Schünemann's Witwe, 1848).
X. Yang, *State Immunity in International Law* (Cambridge: CUP, 2012).
A. Yanov, *Patriotizm i natsionalizm v Rossii 1825–1921*, 2nd edn (Moscow: Akademkniga, 2002).
B. L. Zimnenko, *Mezhdunarodnoe pravo i pravovaya sistema Rossiiskoi Federatsii* (Moscow: Statut, 2010).
A. Zinov'ev, *Zapad* (Moscow: Algoritm, 2007).
V. D. Zorkin, *Rossia i Konstitutsia v XXI veke*, 2nd edn (Moscow: Norma, 2008).
V. D. Zorkin, *Konstitutsia i prava cheloveka v XXI veke. K 15-letiu Konstitutsii Rossiiskoi Federatsii i 60-letiu Vseobshei deklaratsii prav cheloveka* (Moscow: Norma, 2008).
V. D. Zorkin, *Konstitutsionno-pravovoe razvitie Rossii* (Moscow: Norma, 2011).
A. B. Zubov (ed.), *Istoria Rossii. XX vek: 1939–2007* (Astrel' AST, Moscow, 2009).

ARTICLES AND CHAPTERS IN BOOKS

A. Kh. Abashidze, 'Kontseptsia "gegemonii" v sovremennom mezhdunarodnom prave', in *Vestnik Diplomaticheskoi Akademii MID Rossii. Mezhdunarodnoe pravo* (Moscow: Diplomaticheskaya Akademia, 2013) 166–79.
'Aleksei Pushkov. Veroyatnost' vykhoda RF iz Soveta Evropy nulevaya', *Rossiiskaya gazeta* 26.06.2014, <http://www.rg.ru/2014/06/26/pushkov-anons.html>.
J. E. Alvarez, 'Are Corporations "Subjects" of International Law?', in 9 *Santa Clara J. Int'l L.* 1 (2011), available at: <http://digitalcommons.law.scu.edu/scujil/vol9/iss1/1>.
J. E. Alvarez, 'State Sovereignty is Not Withering Away. A Few Lessons for the Future' in A. Cassese (ed.), *Realizing Utopia. The Future of International Law* (Oxford: OUP, 2012) 26–37.
A. Astaf'ev, 'Bashkiria menyaet nazvanie glavnoi dolzhnosti', *Kommersant* 26.12.2013, <http://kommersant.ru/doc/2377506>.
V. R. Avkhadeev, 'Vlianie norm mezhdunarodnoga prava na natsional'noe zakonodatel'stvo Rossiiskoi Federatsii v sfere razgranichenia morskikh prostranstv v Severnom ledovitom okeane', *Rossiiskii ezhegodnik mezhdunarodnoga prava* 2013 (St Petersburg: 'Rossiya-Neva', 2013) 169–80.

G. M. Badr, 'A Survey of Islamic International Law', in M. W. Janis, C. Evans (eds), *Religion and International Law* (Leiden: Martinus Nijhoff, 2004) 95–101.

P. Baker, '3 Presidents and a Riddle Named Putin', *New York Times* 23.03.2014, <http://www.nytimes.com/2014/03/24/world/europe/3-presidents-and-a-riddle-named-putin.html?_r=0#/#time315_8525>.

S. V. Bakhin, 'Pravo integratsionnykh obrazovanii. Voprosy konkurentsii system prava', in V. S. Bakhin (ed.), *Mezhdunarodnye otnoshenia i pravo. Vzglyad v XXI vek* (St Petersburg: St Petersburg State University, 2009) 90–145.

S. V. Bakhin, 'Paradoksy professora Martensa', *Rossiiskii ezhegodnik mezhdunarodnoga prava* 2009 (St Petersburg: 'Rossia-Neva', 2010) 35–53.

S. V. Bakhin, 'Razmyshlenia o nauchnom nasledii professora R. L. Bobrova (k 100-letiu so dnia rozhdenia)', in *Materialy nauchno-prakticheskoi konferentsii 'Mezhdunarodnoe pravo: vchera, segodnia, zavtra', 8–9 oktyabria 2010.g. K 100-letiu so dnia rozhdenia professora Romana L'vovicha Bobrova* (St Petersburg: 'Rossiya Neva', 2011) 28–40.

M. Barshtshevski, 'Diplomatichno govorya', *Rossiiskaya Gazeta* 17.10.2013, <http://www.rg.ru/2013/10/17/lavrov.html>.

A. Bashkatova, 'Kiotskii protokol snova stal predmetom torga', *Nezavisimaya gazeta* 19.10.2012, <http://www.ng.ru/economics/2012-10-19/4_protokol.html>.

S. Batrul', 'Pavel Laptev. Srok zhizni Evropeiskogo suda mozhet byt' sokrashen', *Kommersant* 31.05.2010, <http://www.kommersant.ru/doc/1378599>.

T. Bekbulatova, "My zhivem v khishnem lesu", *Kommersant* 08.06.2013, <http://www.kommersant.ru/doc/2207919>.

A. Belyi, *Russia's Position on the Energy Charter*, Chatham House, 27 April 2012, <http://www.chathamhouse.org/sites/files/chathamhouse/public/Research/Russia%20and%20Eurasia/270412summary.pdf>.

E. Benvenisti, A. Cohen, 'War is Governance. Explaining the Logic of the Laws of War from a Principal-Agent Perspective', 112 *Michigan Law Review* 2013, 1363–416.

M. R. Berandze, 'K voprosu o pravosub'ektnosti transnatsionalnykh korporatsii v mezhdunarodnom prave', in I. A. Tarkhanov et al. (eds), *Materialy mezhdunarodnoi nauchno-prakticheskoi konferentsii 'Mezhdunarodnyi pravoporyadok v sovremennom mire i rol' Rossii v ego ukreplenii', posvyashennoi 90-letiu professora Fel'dmana Davida Isaakovicha* (Moscow: Statut, 2014) 268–74.

H. J. Berman, 'The Weightier Matters of the Law', in R. Berman (ed.), *Solzhenitsyn at Harvard. The Address, Twelve Early Responses, and Six Later Reflections* (Washington, DC: Ethics and Public Policy Center, 1980) 99–113.

N. Bhuta, 'The Role International Actors Other than States can Play in the New World Order', in A. Cassese (ed.), *Realizing Utopia. The Future of International Law* (OUP: Oxford, 2012) 61–75.

I. Black, 'Russia and China Veto UN Move to Refer Syria to International Criminal Court', 22.05.2014 *The Guardian*, <http://www.theguardian.com/world/2014/may/22/russia-china-veto-un-draft-resolution-refer-syria-international-criminal-court>.

S. Bowers, 'Sakhalin Issues "Settled"—as Russia Takes 50% Stake', *The Guardian*, 22.12.2006, <http://www.theguardian.com/business/2006/dec/22/russia.oilandpetrol>.

B. Bowring, 'Postanovlenie Bol'shoi Palaty Evropeiskogo Suda po pravam cheloveka po delu "Kononov protiv Latvii" (17 maia 2010 goda). Prava li Rossiiskaya Federatsia v svoem ponimanii sootnoshenia politiki i mezhdunarodnoga prava', 2(3) *Mezhdunarodnoe pravosudie* 2012, 75–83.

B. Bowring, 'Delo Katan i drugie protiv Moldovy i Rossii. Geopolitika i pravo na obrazovanie. I pochemu "nekomu" fakticheski oznachaet rebenku', 1(9) *Mezhdunarodnoe pravosudie* 2014, 44–59.

A. Bradford, E. Posner, 'Universal Exceptionalism in International Law', 52 *Harvard ILJ* 2011, 3–54.

W. E. Butler, 'International Law and the Comparative Method', in W. E. Butler (ed.), *International Law in Comparative Perspective* (Alpen aan den Rijn: Sijthoff, 1980) 25–40.

W. E. Butler, 'Anglo-American Research on Soviet Approaches to Public International Law', in W. E. Butler (ed.), *International Law in Comparative Perspective* (Alpen aan den Rijn: A. W. Sijthoff, 1980), 169–90.

W. E. Butler, 'Teoretiko-metodologischeskie osnovy issledovania istorii mezhdunarodnoga prava', in A. I. Dmitriev (ed.), *Istoria mezhdunarodnoga prava* (Odessa: Feniks, 2013) 7–69.

A. Cassese, 'A Plea for a Global Community Grounded in a Core of Human Rights', in A. Cassese (ed.), *Realizing Utopia. The Future of International Law* (Oxford: OUP, 2012) 136–43.

A. Cassese, 'Towards a Moderate Monism. Could International Rules Eventually Acquire the Force to Invalidate Inconsistent National Laws?', in A. Cassese (ed.), *Realizing Utopia. The Future of International Law* (Oxford: OUP, 2012) 187–99.

I. A. Chebotareva, 'Ponyatie spetsial'nykh printsipov mezhdunarodnoga prava', in V. S. Bakhin (ed.), *Mezhdunarodnye otnoshenia i pravo. Vzglyad v XXI vek* (St Petersburg: St Petersburg State University, 2009) 254–70.

E. Chernenko, 'Soglashenie o beskonechnoi torgovle', *Kommersant* 02.04.2012, <http://www.kommersant.ru/doc/1906610>.

E. Chernenko, 'Nekto ne mozhet byt' obraztsom demokratii' (interview with Mr Dolgov), *Kommersant* 29.10.2012, <http://www.kommersant.ru/doc/2055389>.

S. V. Chernichenko, 'Eshe raz o mezhdunarodnoi pravosub'ektnosti individov', 4 *Moskovski zhurnal mezhdunarodnoga prava* 2005, 11–26.

S. V. Chernichenko, 'O bor'be s terroristami na inostrannoi territorii', in A. G. Lisitsyn-Svetlanov (ed.), *Novye vyzovy i mezhdunarodnoe pravo* (Moscow: Institut gosudarstva i prava RAN, 2010) 99–103.

S. V. Chernichenko, 'Vopros o sootnoshenii mezhdunarodnoga i vnutrigosudarstvennogo prava kak pravovykh sistem (razmyshlenia po povodu nekotorykh knig kolleg)', in S. V. Bakhin (ed.), *Mezhdunarodnye otnoshenia i pravo. Vzglyad v XXI vek* (St Petersburg: St Petersburg State University, 2009) 52–89.

V. Chernichenko, 'Vzglyad na opredelennye polozhenia konstitutsii Rossiiskoi Federatsii s mezhdunarodno-pravovykh pozitsii', in *Vestnik Diplomaticheskoi Akademii MID Rossii. Mezhdunarodnoe pravo* (Moscow: Diplomaticheskaya Akademia, 2013) 44–63.

N. Christof, 'Professors, We Need You!', *NY Times* 15.02.2014, <http://www.nytimes.com/2014/02/16/opinion/sunday/kristof-professors-we-need-you.html>.

A. A. Danelyan, 'Mezhdunarodnyi investitsionnyi arbitrazh—institut mezhdunarodnogo investitsionnogo prava', in *Vestnik Diplomaticheskoi Akademii MID Rossii. Mezhdunarodnoe pravo* (Moscow: Diplomaticheskaya Akademia, 2013) 201–21.

M. Davletbaev, M. Isayeva, 'Arkhaichnyi iazyk rossiiskoi diplomatii', *Vedomosti*, 13.08.2014, <http://www.vedomosti.ru/opinion/news/32059251/arhaichnyj-yazyk-rossijskoj-diplomatii>.

K. Demirjian, 'As the West steps up sanctions, Russia starts banning food', *Washington Post*, 02.08.2014, <http://www.washingtonpost.com/world/as-the-west-steps-up-sanctions-russia-starts-banning-food/2014/08/02/d7648ea9-af5b-461a-b312-ee6057918cc8_story.html?hpid=z11>.

D. A. Desierto, 'The EU/US v. Russia Trade Wars. Revisiting GATT Article XXI and the International Law on Unilateral Economic Sanctions', *EJIL: Talk!*, 22.09.2014, <http://www.ejiltalk.org/the-euus-v-russia-trade-wars-revisiting-gatt-article-xxi-and-the-international-law-on-unilateral-economic-sanctions-2/>.

N. G. Doronina, 'Istoria pravovoga regulirovania investitsii v mezhdunarodnom chastnom prave', in V. S. Bakhin (ed.), *Mezhdunarodnoe publichnoe i chastnoe pravo. Problemy i perspektivy* (St Petersburg: St Petersburg State University, 2007) 272–92.

N. Dubovski, 'Ilma taevata', translated from Russian into Estonian by K. Pruul, 6 *Vikerkaar* 2014, 24–8.

A. Dugin, 'Realizm—mnimyi i podlinnyi', *Izvestia* 11.03.2014, <http://izvestia.ru/news/567249>.

M. L. Entin, 'Vyzovy vremeni i novoe videnie mezhdunarodnoga, nadnatsional'nogo i vnutrigosudarstvennogo prava', in A. G. Lisitsyn-Svetlanov (ed.), *Novye vyzovy i mezhdunarodnoe pravo* (Moscow: Institut gosudarstva i prava RAN, 2010), 27–44.

I. Z. Farkhutdinov, 'Mezhdunarodnaja pravosubyektnost' v XXI veke. Problemy i tendentsii', in S. Bakhin (ed.), *Mezhdunarodnye otnoshenia i pravo. Vzglyad v XXI vek* (St Petersburg: St Petersburg State University, 2009) 198–214.

I. Z. Farkhutdinov, 'Suverenitet gosudarstva i mezhdunarodnoe pravo. Vyzovy globalizatsii', in A. G. Lisitsyn-Svetlanov (ed.), *Novye vyzovy i mezhdunarodnoe pravo* (Moscow: Institut gosudarstva i prava RAN, 2010) 53–66.

B. Fassbender, ' "Völkerrecht und Landesrecht". Zur Genese und heutigen Bedeutung der Konfrontation zweier Rechtsordnungen', 4 *AJP/PJA* 2014, 437–50.

A. Filippov, 'Suverenitet kak politicheskii vybor', in N. Garadzha (ed.), *Suverenitet. Sbornik* (Moscow: 'Evropa', 2006) 173–200.

T. M. Franck, 'The Emerging Right to Democratic Governance', 86 *AJIL* 1992, 46–91.

E. Gaillard, 'Effectiveness of Arbitral Awards, State Immunity from Execution and Autonomy of State Entities. Three Incompatible Principles', in E. Gaillard, J. Younan (eds), *State Entities in International Arbitration, IAI Series on International Arbitration No 4* (Huntington, NY: Juris Publishing, 2008) 179–93.

L. N. Galenskaya, 'O poniatii mezhdunarodnoga ugolovnoga prava', *Sovetskii ezhegodnik mezhdunarodnoga prava* 1969 (Moscow: Academy of Sciences of the USSR, 1970) 247.

L. N. Galenskaya, 'Tendentsia razvitia pravovoga regulirovania mezhdunarodnykh otnohenii v XXI veke', in S. V. Bakhin, *Mezhdunarodnye otnoshenia i pravo. Vzglyad v XXI vek* (St Petersburg: St Petersburg State University Publishing, 2009) 28–41.

L. N. Galenskaya, 'Kategoria printsipov kak pravovykh regulyatorov mezhdunarodnykh otnoshenii', *Materialy nauchno-prakticheskoi konferentsii 'Mezhdunarodnoe pravo: vchera, segodnya, zavtra', 8-9 oktyabrya 2010.g. K 100-letiu so dnya rozhdenia professora Romana L'vovicha Bobrova* (St Petersburg: 'Rossia-Neva', 2011) 58–79.

V. V. Gavrilov, 'Mesto i rol' mezhdunarodnogo prava v pravovoi sisteme Velikobritanii', 4(279) *Pravovedenie* 2008, 209–17.

O. Gerasimenko, 'Mestnykh stavit' nel'zya—oni dogovoryatsya i ustroyat respubliku', 02.07.2012 *Kommersant Vlast'*, <http://www.kommersant.ru/doc/1966881>.

E. Glusker, 'Arbitration Hurdles Facing Foreign Investors in Russia. Analysis of Present Issues and Implications', 10 *Pepperdine Dispute Resolution Law Journal* 2010, 595–622.

A. Gorbachev, 'Chlenstvo v VTO nachalos' so skandalov', *Nezavisimaya Gazeta* 06.12.2012, <http://www.ng.ru/economics/2012-12-06/1_wto.html>.

D. Gorovtsov, 'Ogovorki ili blokirovki?' *Nezavisimaya gazeta* 28.03.2011, <http://www.ng.ru/politics/2011-03-28/3_kartblansh.html>.

A. Gorshkova, 'Delo Yukosa prineslo dividendy', *Kommersant* 27.07.2012, <http://www.kommersant.ru/doc/1988787>.

J. Habermas, 'Does the Constitutionalization of International Law Still Have a Chance?' in *The Divided West* (London: Polity Press, 2006) 115 et seq.

N. Hamerman, 'The Council of Florence. The Religious Event that Shaped the Era of Discovery', *Schiller Institute*, <http://www.schillerinstitute.org/fid_91-96/922_council_of_florence.pdf>, 23–36.

J. N. Hazard, 'Cleansing Soviet International Law of Anti-Marxist Theories', 32 *AJIL* 1938, 244–52.

M. Heidegger, 'Brief über den "Humanismus"', in M. Heidegger, *Gesamtausgabe I, Abteilung. Veröffentlichte Schriften 1914–1970, Band 9: Wegmarken* (Frankfurt a. M.: Vittorio Klostermann, 1976).

V. Hrabar, 'Foreword', in F. v. Liszt, *Mezhdunarodnoe pravo v sistematicheskom izlozhenii*, 4th Russian edn (Yur'ev: K. Mattiesen, 1917).

G. V. Ignatenko, 'Roman L'vovich Bobrov—uchenyi, myslitel', nastavnik, kollega', in *Materialy nauchno-prakticheskoi konferentsii 'Mezhdunarodnoe pravo: vchera, segodnya, zavtra', 8–9 oktyabrya 2010.g. K 100-letiu so dnya rozhdenia professora Romana L'vovicha Bobrova* (St Petersburg: 'Rossia-Neva', 2011) 5–10.

M. V. Il'in, 'Suverenitet. Razvitie ponyatinoi kategorii', in M.V. Il'in, I. V. Kudryashova (eds), *Suverenitet. Transformatsia poniatii i praktik* (Moscow: 'MGIMO-Universitet', 2008) 14–42.

A. Illarionov, 'Kak gotovilas' voina', *Novaya gazeta* 24.06.2009, <http://www.novayagazeta.ru/politics/44604.html>.

A. Illarionov, 'Kak gotovilas' voina. Posleslovie', *Novaya gazeta* 14.08.2009, <http://www.novayagazeta.ru/politics/43961.html>.

M. Iovane, 'Domestic Courts Should Embrace Sound Interpretative Strategies in the Development of Human Rights-Oriented International Law', in A. Cassese (ed.), *Realizing Utopia. The Future of International Law* (Oxford: OUP, 2012) 607–25.

A. S. Ispolinov, 'Rol' investitsionnykh arbitrazhei v razvitii sovremennogo investitsionnogo prava', in *Vestnik Diplomaticheskoi Akademii MID Rossii. Mezhdunarodnoe pravo* (Moscow: Diplomaticheskaya Akademia, 2013) 180–93.

V. S. Ivanenko, 'Mezhdunarodnye dogovory i konstitutsia v pravovoi sisteme Rossii. 'Voina verkhovenstv' ili mirnoe vzaimodeistvie?', in 3(290) *Pravovedenie* 2010, 135–61.

M. Ivanov, 'Grazhdane ne khotyat platit' po schetam YUKOSa', *Kommersant*, 11.08.2014, <http://kommersant.ru/doc/2542807>.

K. Känd, 'Venemaa telos—Lääne simulaakrum?', Postimees, 18.10.2008, <http://arvamus.postimees.ee/41763/kaupo-kand-venemaa-telos-laane-simulaakrum>.

A. Ya. Kapustin, 'Kontseptsia mezhdunarodnoi organizatsii. Sovremennye tendentsii i protivorechivye tolkovania', in V. S. Bakhin (ed.), *Mezhdunarodnoe publichnoe i chastnoe pravo. Problemy i perspektivy* (St Petersburg: St Petersburg State University 2007) 85–113.

A. Ya. Kapustin, 'Mezhdunarodnoe gumanitarnoe pravo i novye vyzovy', in A. G. Lisitsyn-Svetlanov (ed.), *Novye vyzovy i mezhdunarodnoe pravo* (Moscow: Institut gosudarstva i prava RAN, 2010) 44–53.

I. I. Karandashov, 'Printsip *pacta sunt servanda* i chast' 4 stat'i 15 Konstitutsii Rossiiskoi Federatsii. Predely ikh tolkovania i primenenia v Rossiiskoi Federatsii', *Rossiiskii ezhegodnik mezhdunarodnoga prava* 2012 (St Petersburg: 'Rossiya-Neva', 2013) 174–89.

D. Kennedy, 'The Disciplines of International Law and Policy', 12 *Leiden JIL* 2008, 9.

U. Khaliq, 'The International Court of Justice and its Use of Islam. Between a Rock and a Hard Place?' in 2 *Oxford Journal of Law and Religion* 2013, 98–118.

V. Khamraev, 'Stalin poluchil bol'shinstvo k 130-letiu', *Kommersant* 19.12.2009, <http://www.kommersant.ru/doc/1296300>.

V. Khamraev, 'Rossiane vstupilis' za Stalina, kak za rodinu', *Kommersant* 03.08.2009, <http://www.kommersant.ru/doc/1215165>.

O. N. Khlestov, 'OON i aktual'nye problemy zastshity prav cheloveka', in *Vestnik Diplomaticheskoi Akademii MID Rossii. Mezhdunarodnoe pravo* (Moscow: Diplomaticheskaya Akademia, 2013) 15–31.

O. N. Khlestov, 'Rossiiskaya doktrina mezhdunarodnoga prava', 3(58) *Evraziiskii juridicheskii zhurnal* 2013, 19–22.

Y. Kholmogorov, 'Organizatsia pobezhdennykh natsii', 27.10.2014.*Izvestia*, http://izvestia.ru/news/578574.

O. Kirillova, 'Sergei Lavrov nazval Ukrainu zhertvoi politiki Zapada', *Kommersant* 27.09.2014, <http://kommersant.ru/doc/2577631>.

P. Klein, 'Jean Salmon et l'école de Reims' in *Droit de pouvoir, pouvoir du droit. Mélanges offerts à Jean Salmon* (Brussels: Bruylant, 2007) 19–38.

Y. Klusova, 'Vladimir Putin. Pobeda v Pervoi mirovoi voine byla ukradena u Rossii', *Kommersant* 01.08.2014, <http://kommersant.ru/doc/2537963>.

L. V. Korbut, 'Analiticheskii obzor raboty 56-go Ezhegodnogo Sobrania Rossiiskoi Assotsiatsii mezhdunarodnoga prava 26–28 iunya 2013.g', in *Rossiiskyi ezhegodnik mezhdunarodnoga prava 2013* (St Petersburg: 'Rossiya-Neva', 2014), 407–35.

A. Kornya, 'Konstitutsionnyi sud ne nashel politiki v stat'yakh svoego predsedatelya', *Kommersant*, 04.08.2014, <http://www.vedomosti.ru/politics/news/30942521/politpro svet-ot-zorkina>.

M. Koskenniemi, 'The Case for Comparative International Law', 20 *Finnish Yearbook of International Law* 2009, 1–8.

V. S. Kotlyar, 'Teoria, praktika i perspektivy kontseptsii "otvetstvennost' po zashite" v svete printsipa verkhovenstva mezhdunarodnogo prava v mezhdunarodnykh otnosheniakh', *Rossiiskii ezhegodnik mezhdunarodnogo prava 2013* (St Petersburg: 'Rossiya-Neva', 2014), 52–65.

A. Kovler, O. Chernishova, 'The June 2013 Resolution No. 21 of the Russian Supreme Court. A Move Towards Implementation of the Judgments of the European Court of Human Rights', 33 *Human Rights Law Journal* 2013, 263–6.

Ko Kwan Sik, 'The Establishment of Diplomatic Relations and the Scope of Diplomatic Immunity. The Dutch Experience with China', in J. A. Cohen (ed.), *China's Practice of International Law. Some Case Studies* (Cambridge, MA: Harvard University Press, 1972), 57–85.

A. E. Kramer, 'Shell Cedes Control of Sakhalin-2 to Gazprom', *NYTimes*, 21.12.2006, <http://www.nytimes.com/2006/12/21/business/worldbusiness/21iht-shell.3981718.html?_r=1&>.

I. Kriger, 'Instituty sil'nee reform', *Novaya gazeta* 27.01.2010, <http://old.novayagazeta.ru/data/2010/008/13.html>.

S. Kulikov, 'Litva tyanet "Gazprom" v sud', *Nezavisimaya gazeta* 04.10.2012, <http://www.kommersant.ru/doc/2382708>.

S. Kulikov, 'Rossiya ostaetsya v Kiotskom protokole s chistoi sovestyu', *Nezavisimaya gazeta*, 11.12.2012, <http://www.ng.ru/economics/2012-12-11/1_ecology.html>.

C. Landauer, 'Regionalisms, Geography, and the International Legal Imagination', 11 *Chicago JIL* 2010–11, 557–95.

P. Leach, 'The Chechen Conflict. Analysing the Oversight of the European Court of Human Rights', 6 *European Human Rights Law Review* 2008, 732–61.

M. Leonard, N. Popescu, *A Power Audit of EU-Russia Relations*, European Council on Foreign Relations, <http://www.ecfr.eu/page/-/ECFR-02_A_POWER_AUDIT_OF_EU-RUSSIA_RELATIONS.pdf>.

'Levada-Tsentr. Vse bol'she rossiyan schitaet, shto poryadok v strane vazhnee prav cheloveka', 25.09.2013, <http://grani.ru/Politics/Russia/m.219352.html>.

V. N. Likhachev, 'Rossia kak mezhdunarodno-pravovaya lichnost', in *Vestnik Diplomaticheskoi Akademii MID Rossii. Mezhdunarodnoe pravo* (Moscow: Diplomaticheskaya Akademia, 2013) 32–43.

E. Limonov, 'Bitva za Ukrainu', *Izvestia*, 28.11.2013, <http://izvestia.ru/news/561521>.

A. Lowenfeld, 'Public Law in the International Arena. Conflict of Laws, International Law, and Some Suggestions for their Interaction', 163 *RCADI* 1979-II (Leiden: Martinus Nijhoff) 311.

I. I. Lukashuk, 'Foreword', in S. Bakhin (ed.), *Bibliograficheskii slovar' Rossiiskoi Akademii Mezhdunarodnoga Prava 1957–1997* (St Petersburg: Izdatel'stvo yuridicheskogo fakul'teta St Petersburg State University, 2008) 4–5.

M. Lyutova, 'Rossiya gotova nachat' peregovory o peresmotre uslovii prisoedinenia k VTO', *Vedomosti* 26.09.2014, <http://www.vedomosti.ru/politics/news/33906261/zabor-ot-vto>.

A. Makarychev and V. Morozov, 'Is "Non-Western Theory" Possible? The Idea of Multipolarity and the Trap of Epistemological Relativism in Russian IR', 15 *International Studies Review* 2013, 328–50.

Y. N. Maleev, 'Primenenie sily v mezhdunarodnyh otnosheniakh v sovremennom ponimanii', in A. G. Lisitsyn-Svetlanov (ed.), *Novye vyzovy i mezhdunarodnoe pravo* (Moscow Institut gosudarstva i prava RAN, 2010) 75–91.

L. Mälksoo, 'Soviet Genocide? Soviet Mass Deportations in the Baltic States and International Law', 14 *Leiden Journal of International Law* 2001, 757–87.

L. Mälksoo, 'The Science of International Law and the Concept of Politics. The Arguments and Lives of the International Law Professors at the University of Dorpat//Yur'ev/Tartu 1855–1985', 76 *British Year Book of International Law* 2005 (Oxford: OUP 2006) 383–501.

L. Mälksoo, 'Casenote on Kononov v Latvia', 105 *AJIL* 2011, 101–8.

L. Mälksoo, 'Casenote on Markin v Russia', 106 *AJIL* 2012, 836–42.

L. Mälksoo, 'Russia-Europe', in B. Fassbender, A. Peters (eds), *The Oxford Handbook of the History of International Law* (Oxford: OUP, 2012) 764–86.

L. Mälksoo, 'F. F. Martens and His Time. When Russia Was an Integral Part of the European Tradition of International Law', 25(3) *EJIL* 2014, 811–29.

L. Mälksoo, 'International Legal Theory in Russia—A Civilizational Perspective, or: Can Individuals be Subjects of International Law?', in F. Hoffmann, A. Orford (eds), *The Oxford Handbook on the Theory of International Law* (Oxford: OUP, forthcoming in 2015).

V. Mal'tsev, 'RPTs stchitaet sanktsii pozitivnym shansom dlya strany', *Nezavisimaya gazeta*, 01.08.2014, <http://www.ng.ru/faith/2014-08-01/2_rpc.html>.

B. N. Mamlyuk, U. Mattei, 'Comparative International Law', 36 *Brooklyn Journal of International Law* 2011, 385–452.

V. Mamontov, 'Menyaetsa Rossia, menyaetsya i ee voennaya doktrina', *Izvestia* 14.10.2010, <http://izvestia.ru/news/354178>.

A. Marhold, 'In Too Deep—Russia, the Energy Charter Treaty and the Nord Stream Gas Pipeline', 12 *Baltic Yearbook of International Law* 2012 (Leiden: Martinus Nijhoff, 2013) 303–15.

S. Markov, 'Predislovie', in V. Krashennikova, *Amerika-Rossia. Kholodnaya voina kul'tur. Kak amerikanskie tsennosti prelomlyayut videnie Rossii* (Moscow: Evropa, 2007).

I. S. Marusin, 'Mezhdunarodnyi ugolovnyi tribunal po byvshei Yugoslavii', in V. S. Bakhin (ed.), *Mezhdunarodnoe publichnoe i chastnoe pravo. Problemy i perspektivy* (St Petersburg: St Petersburg State University, 2007) 262–71.

T. D. Matveeva, 'Chelovek i mezhdunarodnoe pravo (k voprosu o mezhdunarodnoi pravosub'ektnosti individa)', *Rossiiskiy ezhegodnik mezhdunarodnoga prava* 2010 (St Petersburg: 'Rossiya-Neva', 2011) 52–67.

T. D. Matveeva, 'Evolyutsia doktriny mezhdunarodnoi pravosub'ektnosti', *Rossiiskiy ezhegodnik mezhdunarodnoga prava* 2012 (St Petersburg: 'Rossiya-Neva', 2013) 27–42.

'D. Medvedev: Rossiya—strana pravovoga nigilizma', *Prime-TASS*, 22.01.2008, <http://www.vedomosti.ru/newsline/news/2008/01/22/536208>.

A. Mel'nikov, 'Yadernyi shtshit portiv kul'ta pribyli', *Nezavisimaya gazeta* 24.08.2009, <http://www.ng.ru/regions/2009-08-24/2_patriarh.html>.

A. B. Mezyaev, 'Mezhdunarodnyi ugolovnyi tribunal po byvshei Yugoslavii—nezakonnyi, zavisimyi i pristrastnyi sud', in A. I. Filomonova (ed.), *Dvoinye standarty v zashite prav cheloveka: kazus professor Sheshelya* (Moscow: 'Fond istoricheskoi perspektivy', 2009) 50–98.

B. A. Mezyaev, *Ubiistvo Slobodana Milosevica v Gaagskom tribunale. Nekotorye fakty i voprosy mezhdunarodnoga prava*, <http://www.trinitas.ru/rus/doc/0215/003a/0215 1012.htm>.

'Minkul'tury izlozhilo "Osnovy gosudarstvennoi kul'turnoi politiki" ', *Izvestia* 10.04.2014, <http://izvestia.ru/news/569016>.

V. Mironov, 'RF zapreshaet ukrainskie konservy i konfety', 28.07.2014, *Rossiiskaya gazeta*, <http://rg.ru/2014/07/28/konservi-site.html>.

V. Mukhin, 'Territorial'nye pretenzii silovoga kharaktera', *Nezavisimaya gazeta* 22.04.2013, <http://www.ng.ru/regions/2013-04-22/2_pretenzii.html>.

R. A. Müllerson, in R. A.Müllerson, G. I. Tunkin (eds), *Kurs mezhdunarodnoga prava v 7 tomakh*, Vol. 1 (Moscow: Nauka, 1989) 161.

M. Muradov, 'Ramzan Kadyrov khochet vosstanovit'sya v granitsakh 1934 goda', *Kommersant* 05.09.2012, <http://www.kommersant.ru/doc/2015582>.

N. Narotchnitskaya, 'Rossiya v novykh geopoliticheskikh real'nostiakh', in: *'... I vremya sobirat' kamni ...' Evraziiskaya integratsia segodnya. 20 let posle raspada SSSR* (Moscow: Fond istoriechskoi perspektivy, 2012) 4 et seq.

A. Nussbaum, 'Frederic de Martens. Representative Tsarist Writer on International Law', 22 *Nordisk Tidsskrift International Ret og Jus Gentium* 1952, 51–66.

A. Nußberger, 'The Reception Process in Russia and Ukraine', in H. Keller, A. Stone Sweet (eds), *A Europe of Rights. The Impact of the ECHR on National Legal Systems* (Oxford: OUP, 2008) 603–74.

M. Nutt, 'Bütsantsliku diplomaatia raudvara', 6/7(130/131) *Diplomaatia* 2014, <http://www.diplomaatia.ee/artikkel/butsantsliku-diplomaatia-raudvara/>.

P. Okowa, 'The International Court of Justice and the Georgia/Russia Dispute', 11 *Human Rights Law Review* 2011, 739–57.

Y. Onuma, 'When was the Law of International Society Born? An Inquiry of the History of International Law from an Intercivilizational Perspective', 2 *Journal of the History of International Law* 2000, 1–66.

M. Overchenko, A. Kornya, S. Titov, 'Pochemu Rossiya proigrala byvshim vladel'tsam YUKOSa $50 mlrd', *Vedomosti*, 04.08.2014, <http://www.vedomosti.ru/library/news/30942371/yukos-mog-obojtis-rossii-v-66-mlrd?full#cut>.

Y. Paniev, 'MID RF vzyalsya za prava v Evrosoyuze', *Nezavisimaya gazeta* 06.12.2012, <http://www.ng.ru/world/2012-12-06/7_prava.html>.

Yu. Paniev, 'Moskva i Brjussel' simmetrichno obsudyat prava cheloveka', *Nezavisimaya gazeta* 04.06.2013, <http://www.ng.ru/ideas/2013-06-04/6_rights.html>.

A. Parfenova, 'Posle reshenia Gaagskogo suda izmenenia v Konstitutsii neobkhodimy', 05.08.2014, *Kommersant*, <http://www.kommersant.ru/doc/2539335>.

A. Pertsev, M. Gorokhova, 'Konstitutsionnyi sud oboshelsya bez slushanii po Krymu', *Kommersant* 19.03.2014, <http://kommersant.ru/doc/2433322>.

A. Peters, 'Extraterritorial Naturalizations. Between the Human Right to Nationality, State Sovereignty and Fair Principles of Jurisdiction', 53 *German Yearbook of International Law* 2010, 623–725.

A. Peters, 'Are we Moving towards Constitutionalization of the World Community?', in A. Cassese (ed.), *Realizing Utopia. The Future of International Law* (Oxford: OUP, 2012) 118–35.

O. Pleshanova, 'Rossiu oblozhili shestietazhnym', *Kommersant* 26.10.2010, <http://www.kommersant.ru/pda/kommersant.html?id=1528888>.

G. Postnov, 'Ugolok mezhnatsional'nogo nesoglasia', *Nezavisimaya gazeta* 15.12.2011, <http://www.ng.ru/politics/2011-12-15/3_kartblansh.html>.

Y. Primakov, 'Balkany i sovremennyi mir', *Nezavisimaya gazeta* 24.10.2011, <http://www.ng.ru/ideas/2011-10-24/9_balkany.html>.

S. Pritzkow, 'Kontinuität und Diskontinuität. Sowjetisches und modernes russisches Völkerrechtsdenken im Vergleich', 6 *Osteuropa Recht* 2008, 397–406.

A. Pushkarskaya, 'Venetsianskaya komissia ne soglasilas' s Konstitutsionnym sudom', *Kommersant* 30.06.2014, <http://kommersant.ru/doc/2502304>.

V. V. Putin, 'A Plea for Caution from Russia', *New York Times*, 11.09.2013, <http://www.nytimes.com/2013/09/12/opinion/putin-plea-for-caution-from-russia-on-syria.html?hp&_r=0>.

'Putin ne isklyuchil vozhmozhnosti vykhoda Rossii iz-pod yurisdiktsii ESPCh', *Interfaks*, 14.08.2014, <http://www.vedomosti.ru/politics/news/32131381/putin-ne-isklyuchil-vozmozhnosti-vyhoda-rossii-iz-pod>.

'Putin. Rossiya mozhet vyiti iz yurisdiktsii ESPCh', *Grani*, 14.08.2014, <http://grani.ru/Politics/Russia/President/m.232059.html>.

Putin, 'Rossia zanimaet printsipial'nuyu pozitsiu po kosovskomu voprosu',*Rossiiskaya gazeta* 16.10.2014, <http://rg.ru/2014/10/16/poziciya-anons.html>.

'Putin's Prepared Remarks at 43rd Munich Conference on Security Policy', 12.02.2007, <http://www.washingtonpost.com/wp-dyn/content/article/2007/02/12/AR2007021200555.html>.

I. de la Rasilla del Moral, 'The Case for Comparative International Law in Question—A Response to Martti Koskenniemi's The Case for Comparative International Law', 23 *Finnish Yearbook of International Law* 2012.

M. W. Reisman, 'Sovereignty and Human Rights in Contemporary International Law', 84 *AJIL* 1990, 866.

C. Reus-Smit, 'The Politics of International Law', in C. Reus-Smit (ed.), *The Politics of International Law* (Cambridge: CUP, 2004) 14–44.

P. Roche, S. Petit, 'Russia's Withdrawal from the Energy Charter Treaty', Norton Rose Fulbright, August 2009, <http://www.nortonrosefulbright.com/knowledge/publications/22691/russias-withdrawal-from-the-energy-charter-treaty>.

I. Rodin, 'Vlast' menyaet taktiku v otnoshenii Konstitutsii', *Nezavisimaya Gazeta* 28.11.2013, <http://www.ng.ru/politics/2013-11-28/1_konstitutsia.html>.

I. Rodin, 'Zorkin vynes prigovor liberalizmu-gomoseksualizmu', *Nezavisimaya gazeta* 02.10.2014, <http://www.ng.ru/politics/2014-10-02/3_zorkin.html>.

K. S. Rodionov, 'Iz istorii ekstraditsii v Rossii', *Rossiiskii ezhegodnik mezhdunarodnoga prava* 2012 (St Petersburg: 'Rossiya-Neva', 2013) 108–33.

S. Roganov, 'Soyuz Sovetskikh Suverennykh Respublik?', *Izvestia* 30.12.2013, <http://izvestia.ru/news/563441>.

'D. Rogozin. Perspektiv uregulirovania ya na segodnya ne vizhu', *Kommersant* 20.11.2012, <http://kommersant.ru/doc/2070470>.

Yu. Roks, 'Voinu s Rossiei razvyazal Saakashvili', 25.10.2012 *Nezavisimaya gazeta*, <http://www.ng.ru/cis/2012-10-25/1_saakashvili.html>.

S. Rosenne, 'The Influence of Judaism on the Development of International Law. An Assessment', in M. W. Janis, C. Evans (eds), *Religion and International Law* (Leiden: Martinus Nijhoff, 2004) 63–94.

E. N. Ros'hin, 'Suverenitet. Osobennosti formirovania poniatia v Rossii', in M. V. Il'in, I. V. Kudryashova (eds), *Suverenitet. Transformatsia ponyatii i praktik* (Moscow: 'MGIMO-Universitet', 2008) 58–91.

Rossiiskii iuridicheskii zhurnal No 3 2013, 8–71, roundtable on the fragmentation of international law.

'Rossiya dolzhna preodolet' pravovoi nigilizm—Prezident Medvedev', *RIA Novosti*, 07.05.2008, <http://ria.ru/politics/20080507/106773965.html>.

'Rossiyane o Konstitutsii', *Levada Tsentr*, 10.12.2013, <http://www.levada.ru/10-12-2013/rossiyane-o-konstitutsii>.

'Russia Protests Strasbourg Court Decision against Soviet WWII Veteran', *Russia Today*, 24.10.2010, <http://rt.com/news/strasbourg-court-kononov-latvia/>.

E. L. Sadykova, 'Mezhtsivilizatsionnyi dialog kak institut sistemy mezhdunarodnykh otnoshenii', in *Vestnik Diplomaticheskoi Akademii MID Rossii. Mezhdunarodnoe pravo* (Moscow: Diplomaticheskaya Akademia, 2013) 248–57.

I. Safronov, E. Chernenko, 'Rossiya budet torgovat' oruzhiem, kak umeet', *Kommersant* 17.05.2014, <http://kommersant.ru/doc/2473772>.

A. Samarina, 'Katynski sindrom', *Nezavisimaya gazeta* 17.11.2009, <http://www.ng.ru/ng_politics/2009-11-17/14_katyn.html>.

S. Samokhina et al., 'MID zachital Amerike ee poprannye prava', *Kommersant* 23.10.2012, <http://www.kommersant.ru/doc/2050786>.

A. Samozhnev, 'MID prizyvaet k mirnomu razresheniu krizisa na Ukraine', *Rossiiskaya gazeta*, 29.08.2014, <http://rg.ru/2014/08/29/mid-site.html>.

O. Schachter, 'The Invisible College of International Lawyers', 72 *Northwestern University Law Review* 1977, 217.

C. Schewe, 'Russia in the WTO. The Bear on a Leash? Russia in International Trade Disputes and the Added Value of a WTO Membership', 47 *Journal of World Trade* 2013, 1171–201.

A. Semakov, 'Sootnoshenie mezhdunarodnoga i rossiiskogo prava kasatel'no korennykh narodov', *Gumilev Center*, 20.04.2011, <http://www.gumilev-center.ru/soootnoshenie-mezhdunarodnogo-i-rossijjskogo-prava-kasatelno-korennykh-narodov/>.

A. Serenko, 'Kalmytskie pereselentsy doshli do Strasburga', *Nezavisimaya gazeta* 30.11.2012, <http://www.ng.ru/regions/2012-11-30/6_kalmykia.html>.

M. Sergeyev, 'Rossiu grozit arest imushtshestva po isku aktsionerov YUKOSa', *Nezavisimaya gazeta* 13.11.2014, <http://www.ng.ru/economics/2014-11-13/1_yukos.html>.

Y. Shany, 'Should the Implementation of International Rules by Domestic Courts be Bolstered?', in A. Cassese (ed.), *Realizing Utopia. The Future of International Law* (Oxford: OUP, 2012) 200–9.

O. S. Shaposhnikova, 'Mezhdunarodnyi investitsionnyi arbitrazh. Istoria i aktual'nye problemy', *Rossiiskii ezhegodnik mezhdunarodnoga prava* 2012 (St Petersburg: 'Rossiya-Neva', 2013) 207–19.

A. Shapovalov, 'Nazad v Kioto', *Kommersant* 06.09.2012, <http://www.kommersant.ru/doc/2016205>.

L. N. Shestakov, 'Vstupitel'noe slovo', in F. I. Kozhevnikov, *Russkoe gosudarstvo i mezhdunarodnoe pravo* (do XX veka) (Moscow: Zertsalo, 2006) v–viii.

G. G. Shinkaretskaya, 'Polozhenie fakticheski sushestvuyushikh rezhimov (nepriznannykh gosudarstv)', in AG. Lisitsyn-Svetlanov (ed.), *Novye vyzovy i mezhdunarodnoe pravo* (Moscow: Institut gosudarstva i prava RAN, 2010) 158–75.

D. Simes, 'Glavenstvo rossiiskoi konstitutsii', *Izvestia* 14.11.2013, <http://izvestia.ru/news/560625>.

B. Simma, 'From Bilateralism to Community Interest in International Law', 250 *RCADI* 1994, at 217 et seq.

A.-M. Slaughter, 'International Law in a World of Liberal States', 6 *EJIL* 1995, 503–38.

A.-M. Slaughter, W. Burke-White, 'The Future of International Law is Domestic (or, the European Way of Law)', 47 *Harvard International Law Journal* 2006, 327–52.

Yu. Smirnova, 'Der Mann, der die Republik Donezk erfand', *Die Welt* 16.05.2014, <http://www.welt.de/politik/ausland/article128065029/Der-Mann-der-die-Republik-Donezk-erfand.html>.

Yu. Smirnova, 'Der Westen misversteht das Machtsystem Putins', *Die Welt,* 27.07.2014, <http://www.welt.de/politik/ausland/article130594464/Der-Westen-missversteht-das-Machtsystem-Putin.html>.

V. Solov'ev, 'To, chem ya zanimayus', ne sovsem chinovnichya rabota', *Kommersant* 20.04.2012, <http://www.kommersant.ru/doc/1919430>.

A. Taska, 'Enesemääramisõigusest rahvusmõrvani.—Nõukogude Liidu sõnad ja teod Eesti Vabariigi ja rahva suhtes', 2 *Looming* 1989, 235–46.

Baron M. de Taube, 'Études sur le développement historique du droit international dans l'Europe Orientale', 1926 *RCADI,* 345–533.

Y. Tavrovskii, 'Ideologia imperatorov i gensekov', 5.12.2012 *Nezavisimaya Gazeta,* <http://www.ng.ru/ideas/2012-12-05/5_ideology.html?insidedoc>.

'Telegram, The Charge in the Soviet Union (Kennan) to the Secretary of State', Moscow, 22 February 1946, <http://www2.gwu.edu/~nsarchiv/coldwar/documents/episode-1/kennan.htm>.

E. Teslova, 'Reshenia ESPCh perestanut' byt' obyazatel'nymi dlya rossiiskikh sudov', 24.12.2013 *Izvestia,* <http://izvestia.ru/news/563034>.

N. V. Timoshin, B. L. Zimnenko, 'O postanovlenii plenuma Verkhovnoga Suda Rossiiskoi Federatsii ot 27 iunya 2013.g No 21 "O primenenii sudami obshei iurisdiktsii Konventsii o zashite prav cheloveka i osnavnykh svobod ot 4 noiabrya 1950 goda i Protokolov k nei"', *Rossiiskyi ezhegodnik mezhdunarodnoga prava* 2013 (St Petersburg: 'Rossiya-Neva', 2014) 80–115.

V. L. Tolstykh, 'Iazyk i mezhdunarodnoe pravo', 2 *Rossiiskii yuridicheskii zhurnal* 2013, 44–62.

D. Trenina, M. Entin, 'Russia's Approach to the Universality of Human Rights', in R. Arnold (ed.), *The Universalism of Human Rights* (Dordrecht: Springer, 2013) 175–87.

V. Trifonov, 'Obvinitel'nyi razgovor', *Kommersant* 04.07.2009, <http://www.kommersant.ru/doc/1199305>.

V. Tumanov, 'O pravovom nigilizme', 10 *Sotsialistichekoe gosudarstvo i pravo* 1989, 20–7.

B. Tuzmkukhamedov, 'Kak voevat' po pravilam?', *Nezavisimaya Gazeta* 15.02.2010, <http://www.ng.ru/courier/2010-02-15/11_wars.html>.

B. Tuzmukhamedov, 'Yuridicheskie spory v Kampale', *Nezavisimaya gazeta* 07.06.2010, <http://www.ng.ru/dipkurer/2010-06-07/9_kampala.html>.

B. Uspenski, 'Kirikulõhe ja XVII sajandi kultuurikonflikt', in *Vene kultuuri jõujooni. Valik artikleid*, trans. from Russian to Estonian by P. Lepik (Tartu: Ilmamaa, 2013) 295–349.

Ya. I. Vaslavskyi, 'Nositeli suvereniteta. Analiz konstitutsionnykh dokumentov', in M. V. Il'in, I. V. Kudryashova (eds), *Suverenitet. Transformatsia ponyatii i praktik* (Moscow: 'MGIMO-Universitet', 2008) 92–102.

G. Verdirame, '"The Divided West". International Lawyers in Europe and America', 18 *EJIL* 2007, 553–80.

V. S. Vereshtshetin, 'O nekotorykh kontseptsiakh v sovremennoi doktrine mezhdunarodnoga publichnoga prava', in V. S. Bakhin (ed.), *Mezhdunarodnye otnoshenia i pravo. Vzglyad v XXI vek* (St Petersburg: St Petersburg State University Publishing House, 2009) 43–51.

E. Vlasenko, 'Andrei Zubov. Menya uvolili na prikazu sverkhu', *Grani*, <http://grani.ru/Society/Law/m.227066.html>.

I. A. Volodin, D. S. Taratukhina, 'Rossiisko-gruzin'skoe razbiratel'stvo v Mezhdunarodnom sude', *Rossiiskii ezhegodnik mezhdunarodnoga prava* 2008 (St Petersburg: 'Rossiya-Neva', 2009) 28–54.

'War by any other Name', *The Economist*, 05.07.2014, <http://www.economist. com/news/europe/21606290-russia-has-effect-already-invaded-eastern-ukraine-question-how-west-will>.

S. Yegorov, 'Vklad Rossii v razvitie mezhdunarodnogo gumanitarnogo prava', in *Vestnik Diplomaticheskoi Akademii MID Rossii. Mezhdunarodnoe pravo* (Moscow: Diplomaticheskaya Akademia, 2013) 69–85.

A. Yunashev, 'Prezidentam respublik sdelali poslednee preduprezhdenie', *Izvestia* 16.12.2013, <http://izvestia.ru/news/562511>.

F. Zakaria, '"A Guest of My Time". The Kennan Diaries, *NYTimes* 21.02.2014, <http://www.nytimes.com/2014/02/23/books/review/the-kennan-diaries-by-george-f-kennan.html?_r=0>.

N. D. Zakharova, 'Individ—sub'ekt mezhdunarodnoga prava', 11 *Sovetskoe gosudarstvo i pravo* 1989, 112–18.

O. Zakharova, 'Na raznykh yazykakh. Evropa apelliruet k pravovym tsennostiam, Rossia—k moral'no-nravstevennym', 25.03.2013 *Nezavisimaya gazeta*, <http://www.ng.ru/ideas/2013-03-25/9_values.html>.

V. Zastrow, 'Intermezzo. Der Westen und Russland', *Frankfurter Allgemeine Zeitung*, 14.09.2014,<http://www.faz.net/aktuell/politik/ausland/europa/25-jahre-nach-dem-mauerfall-will-russland-eine-weltmacht-werden-13151867.html>.

'"Zheleznyi Feliks". Pora vozhvrashat'sya na Lubyanku?' *VTSIOM*, 05.12.2013, <http://wciom.ru/index.php?id = 459&uid=114632>.

V. Zorkin, 'Predel ustupchivosti', *Rossiiskaia gazeta* (29 October 2010), <http://www.rg.ru/2010/10/29/zorkin.html>.

V. Zorkin, 'Krizis mezhdunarodnoga prava. Sovremennyi kontekst', *Rossiiskaya gazeta*, 20.06.2014, <http://www.rg.ru/2014/06/19/zorkin-poln.html>.

I. Zubkov, 'Do kontsa goda Rossia podast isk v WTO protiv Ukrainy', *Rossiiskaya gazeta* 14.10.2014, <http://rg.ru/2014/10/14/isk-site-anons.html>.

FILMS, MULTIMEDIA RESOURCES, WEBSITES

Audiovisual Library of International Law, United Nations, <http://www.un.org/law/avl/>.

Brat 2, <https://www.youtube.com/watch?v=K9TRaGNnjEU>.

Evraziiskii yuridicheskii zhurnal, <http://www.eurasialaw.ru/>.

O. N. Khlestov, interview given to A. A. Moiseev' on Crimea and international law, <https://www.youtube.com/watch?v=ovVJqGtEBG8&list=UUAYiTNgrhlJ0yQXdhW7ZVLg>.

Mezhdunarodnoe pravosudie, <http://ilpp.ru/journal/mp/>.

Moscow Journal of International Law, <http://www.mjil.ru/index_eng.htm>.

'Ratification of International Human Rights Treaties—the Russian Federation', *University of Minnesota Human Rights Library*, <http://www1.umn.edu/humanrts/research/ratification-russia.html>.

Rossiiskii yuridicheskii zhurnal, <http://www.ruzh.org/>.

Index

Printed and bound by CPI Group (UK) Ltd, Croydon, CR0 4YY